GRAMMATICAL RELATIONS:
A FUNCTIONALIST PERSPECTIVE

TYPOLOGICAL STUDIES IN LANGUAGE (TSL)

A companion series to the journal "STUDIES IN LANGUAGE"

Honorary Editor: Joseph H. Greenberg

General Editor: Michael Noonan

Assistant Editors: Spike Gildea, Suzanne Kemmer

Volumes in this series will be functionally and typologically oriented, covering specific topics in language by collecting together data from a wide variety of languages and language typologies. The orientation of the volumes will be substantive rather than formal, with the aim of investigating universals of human language via as broadly defined a data base as possible, leaning toward cross-linguistic, diachronic, developmental and live-discourse data. The series is, in spirit as well as in fact, a continuation of the tradition initiated by C. Li (*Word Order and Word Order Change, Subject and Topic, Mechanisms for Syntactic Change*) and continued by T. Givón (*Discourse and Syntax*) and P. Hopper (*Tense-Aspect: Between Semantics and Pragmatics*).

Volume 35

T. Givón (ed.)

Grammatical Relations: A Functionalist Perspective

GRAMMATICAL
RELATIONS
A FUNCTIONALIST PERSPECTIVE

Edited by

T. GIVÓN
University of Oregon

JOHN BENJAMINS PUBLISHING COMPANY
AMSTERDAM/PHILADELPHIA

™ The paper used in this publication meets the minimum requirements of American National Standard for Information Sciences — Permanence of Paper for Printed Library Materials, ANSI Z39.48-1984.

Library of Congress Cataloging-in-Publication Data

Grammatical relations : a functionalist perspective / edited by T. Givón.
   p.   cm. -- (Typological studies in language, ISSN 0167-7373; v. 35)
   Includes bibliographical references and index.
   Contents: Ergativity and grammatical relations in Karao / Sherri Brainard -- Evolution of grammatical relations in Cariban / Spike Gildea -- Grammaticalization. clause union, and grammatical relations in Ecuadorian Highland Spanish / Marleen Haboud -- The direct object in bi-transitive clauses in Indonesian / Bambang Kaswanti Purwo -- Serial verbs and grammatical relations in Akan / E.K. Osam -- Zero anaphora and grammatical relations in Mandarin / Ming-Ming Pu -- Dative shifting and double objects in Sahaptin / Noel Rude.
   1. Grammar, Comparative and general--Grammatical categories. 2. Grammar, Comparative and general--Grammaticalization. 3. Functionalism (Linguistics) I. Givón, Talmy, 1936- . II. Series.
P240.5.G73   1997
415--dc21   97-23075
ISBN 90 272 2931 7 (hb.) / 90 272 2932 5 (pb.) (European; alk. paper)   CIP
ISBN 1-55619-645-8 (hb.) / 1-55619-646-6 (pb.) (U.S.; alk. paper)

John Benjamins Publishing Co. • P.O.Box 75577 • 1070 AN Amsterdam • The Netherlands
John Benjamins North America • P.O.Box 27519 • Philadelphia PA 19118-0519 • USA

Contents

Editor's Preface   vii

Grammatical Relations: An Introduction   1
    T. Givón

Ergativity and Grammatical Relations in Karao   85
    Sherri Brainard

Evolution of Grammatical Relations in Cariban: How Functional
    Motivation Precedes Syntactic Change   155
    Spike Gildea

Grammaticalization, Clause Union and Grammatical Relations
    in Ecuadorian Highland Spanish   199
    Marleen Haboud

The Direct Object in Bi-transitive Clauses in Indonesian   233
    Bambang Kaswanti Purwo

Serial Verbs and Grammatical Relations in Akan   253
    E.K. Osam

Zero Anaphora and Grammatical Relations in Mandarin   281
    Ming-Ming Pu

Dative Shifting and Double Objects in Sahaptin   323
    Noel Rude

Editor's Preface

Ever since the 1970s, the discussion of grammatical relations by function-ally-oriented grammarians has focused primarily the functional correlates of GRs, such as cognitive accessibility or discourse topicality. Functionalists have thus, with some interesting exceptions, ceded the discussion of the structural aspects of GRs to the various formal schools, such as Relational Grammar, Lexical Functional Grammar, Role Reference Grammar or GB. While certainly divergent in many interesting ways, the formal approaches to GRs share one comon assumption — the discreteness and non-graduality of categories, and thus of grammatical relations.

As elsewhere in the study of natural categories, however, discretenes can only be achieved by selecting few — usually one — necessary-and-sufficient feature(s) out of all properties of subjects or objects, and then making binary, either/or decisions on subjecthood and objecthood based on such feature(s). The resulting description invariably ignores the evidence that points toward gradation of subjecthood and objecthood and degree of grammaticalization, both within the same language and cross-linguistically.

Ever since Edward Keenan's seminal work (1975, 1976), it has been ap-parent that subjecthood and objecthood can only be characterized adequately by a basket of properties, some functional (reference, topicality), others overt (word order, verb agreement, nominal case-marking), others involving the control of grammatical processes (rule-governed behavior). Keenan's work, it turns out, is fully consonant with a prototype approach to categories, whereby natural types, including grammatical categories, can be firm and distinct in the main without losing residual gradation and flexibility.

This volume presents a functionalist perspective on grammatical relations without neglecting their structural correlates. Building on Keenan's pioneer-ing work, we try to apply this double-barrel, commonsensical approach to a number of typological phenomena that have frustrated relational analysis over the years: serial verbs, ergativity, promotion and demotion, clause union, diachronic change, and degree of grammaticalization. In addition to the theoretical introduction by the editor, the volume includes papers on Karao (Philippine), Carib languages, Ecuadorian Highlands Spanish, Indonesian, Akan (Niger-Congo), Mandarin Chinese and Sahaptin (Macro-Penutian).

GRAMMATICAL RELATIONS:
An Introduction

T. Givón

Linguistics Department
University of Oregon

1. Preamble

Grammatical roles occupy a privileged position at the very hub of clausal syntax. They form the matrix not only of the grammar of simple clauses, but also of the major grammatical processes[1] associated with syntactic complexity — promotion to direct object, de-transitivization, complementation and causativization, nominalization, relativization, raising, and various types of anaphoric reference and agreement. The bulk of functionalist work on grammatical relations proper has tended to center on documenting and explaining the functional correlates of subjecthood and direct objecthood (see eg. Zubin 1972, 1979; Hawkinson and Hyman 1974; Givón 1976, 1983, 1984a, 1984b, 1992; Cooreman 1982, 1985, 1988; Rude 1985, 1987; *inter alia*). One important early functionalist volume, Li (ed. 1976), contained a number of papers dealing with more formal aspects of subjecthood. But since then, functionalists have contended themselves for the most part with the comforting observation that:

a. There was a strong ('iconic') correlation between being the subject and being the main clausal topic.
b. There was likewise a strong ('iconic') correlation between being the direct object and being the secondary topic.
c. One could thus safely ignore grammatical relations, since they mapped so reliably onto pragmatic function(s).

The study of grammatical relation was thus ceded to various formal schools, such as Relational Grammar (RG), Lexical-Functional Grammar (LFG) or Government and Binding (henceforth GB). In some of those, the empirical integrity of the observed facts has become enmeshed in formal, theory-internal considerations.

This seeming division of labor, with functionalists ceding the study of formal properties of grammar to formalists, is indeed curious. If one believes, as functionalist profess to, that communicative functions map ('correlate') in a non-arbitrary way onto grammatical structures, then the independent definition of grammatical structure is a requisite step in demonstrating such mapping; otherwise *correlation* slides into *tautology*. For this reason, the study of strictly formal properties of grammatical relations — nominal case-marking, verbal agreement, word order, and behavioral constraints — is a necessary component of a functionalist approach to the subject.

This is not to say that the study of formal properties needs to be undertaken in a functional vacuum. As is often the case, a more comprehensive understanding of the formal properties of grammatical relations turns out to suggest a functional interpretation.

What is more, a comprehensive treatment of the subject requires placing the rule-governed behavior of subjects and objects in the wider context of a general, cognitively-based theory of human categorization. I will attempt to suggest here how such a theory of categorization accommodates the more conspicuous off-prototype instances of grammatical relations, such as those found in verb-serializing and ergative languages.

2. Semantic vs. grammatical case: The dissociation test

Within Generative Grammar, the resurgence of interest in case-roles may be dated back to Gruber (1965) and Fillmore (1968). However, both of those concerned themselves primarily with the grammatical consequences of **semantic roles** (agent, patient, dative, benefactive, associative, location, instrument, etc.).

To demonstrate, even in the most superficial way, that a case-role is grammatical rather than semantic, one must demonstrate its dissociation from semantic roles. That is, one must show that it admits more than one semantic case-role. For a nominative language such as English, with unmarked subject and direct object, such a demonstration is relatively easy. Consider:

(1) **Multiple semantic roles of the grammatical subject:**
     a. **Patient of state:**
         She is tall
     b. **Patient of change:**
         She is falling asleep
     c. **Dative:**
         She is dreaming
     d. **Agent:**
         She is writing a letter

(2) **Multiple semantic roles of the grammatical object:**
     a. **Patient of state:**
         He saw her
     b. **Patient of change:**
         He pushed her
     c. **Ablative:**
         He approached her
     d. **Allative:**
         He left her
     e. **Ingressive:**
         He entered the house
     f. **Dative:**
         He gave her a book
     g. **Benefactive:**
         He built her a house

There are, of course, languages where the grammatical role of either subject or direct object is not marked by a unifying morphology. In the most extreme case, that of active-stative languages (Lakota, Choctaw), the nominal morphology of what would pass for subject in English is split according to semantic roles (agent, patient, dative). Nominal arguments in such a language retain their semantically-sensitive case morphology regardless of whether they are subjects or objects. A less extreme situation of this type may be seen in ergative languages, where subject case-marking is split according to transitivity (see section 6. below). In both types, however,

other criteria for subjecthood — word order, behavior-and-control properties — may still reveal a formal basis for grammatical subject or object.

Likewise, in many — perhaps most — languages the nominal morphology of what passes for direct-object in English is confined mostly to
the patient semantic role. No morphological provisions are made in such
languages for promoting non-patient objects into this case-role.[2] But again,
other criteria for direct objecthood, such as word order and behavioral constraints, often reveal the formal unity of the category direct object even
when it is not morphologically unified.

3. Empirical criteria for grammatical relations

3.1. *The prototype clustering approach to categories*

Formal accounts of grammatical case within the generative paradigm, such
as those given by RG or GB, have most often backed themselves into a
corner by having to define subjecthood and objecthood in fully discrete
terms. Such an approach to categories requires the linguist to make painful
and sometime arbitrary choices among the various grammatical properties
(membership criteria) that *tend* to cluster around the subject and the object.
When two criteria clash, as is often the case, one must be adjudicated as
counting more than the other. And NPs with intermediate — borderline —
properties are then forced into either one or another discrete category.

The universal validity of ranking our multiple criteria for subjecthood
or objecthood relative to each other is a notoriously thorny issue in the cross-
linguistic study of grammatical relations. In typological comparisons, the
discrete single-criterion approach to categorization leads to considerable
mischief. The subject in languages that abide by the designated single criterion is counted as subject. The subject in languages that lack that single
criterion is counted as non-subject, in spite of the fact that it still abide by
many other criteria for subjecthood.[3]

The approach I pursue here owes its cognitive foundations to an alternative theory of human categorization elaborated by Eleanor Rosch.[4] Within
this approach, the membership in a natural category need not be determined by a single feature, but rather by a **cluster** of characteristic features.
The most typical members of a category are those that display the greatest
number of those features, and may be thus considered the category's **proto-**

type. The majority of members display a great number of the clustered features; they thus closely resemble the prototype. In statistical terms, such members distribute within close proximity of the population's **mean**. But a minority of the membership may display fewer of the characteristic features; they are less like the prototype, and are further away from the population's mean.

The prototype approach to categorization allows the cognitive psychologist, the linguist, and presumably the information-processing organism to reconcile two conflicting aspects of natural categories:

a. The bulk of the members of a population are easily and unambiguously assigned to distinct categories.
b. A certain residual fluidity, flexibility, and context-dependent discrimination is retained, allowing for change, variation, and learning.[5]

In such a pragmatic compromise, the ambiguous categorial status of a small minority of a population does not impinge on the unambiguous status — and rapid processing — of the bulk.

3.2. *The clustering approach to grammatical relations*

Something resembling a prototype clustering approach to grammatical relations was first suggested in two pioneering papers by Edward L. Keenan. In the first, Keenan (1975) notes that three overt coding properties tend to be associated with grammatical subjects:

a. word order
b. verb agreement
c. nominal case morphology

He further notes that the cross-linguistic study of passive-clause subjects reveals a biased distribution of these three properties: Languages that have (c) tend to also have (b); those that have (b) tend to also have (a); but not vice versa. An implicational hierarchy thus characterizes the cross-linguistic distribution of the three coding properties of passive subjects:

(3) **Implicational hierarchy of coding properties of passive subjects** (Keenan 1975):

nominal case-marking > verb agreement > word order

In his second paper, Keenan (1976) extends this approach to a larger cluster of properties. In addition to the overt coding properties (3), two groups of properties are suggested:

a. Functional properties: semantic, referential, pragmatic.
b. Formal properties: rule-governed behavior in relevant syntactic environments.

The functional properties considered by Keenan (1976) may be summarized as:

(4) **Functional properties of grammatical subjects** (Keenan 1976):
a. independent existence
b. indispensability
c. absolute, presupposed or persistent reference
d. definiteness
e. topicality
f. agentivity

With the exception of agentivity (4f), which is probably misplaced on the list,[6] Keenan's functional properties are all reference-related, and can be reduced to (or derived from) a single property — **topicality**. That is, they are all predictable reflections of the fact that the clause's grammatical subject tends to code the current discourse topic at the time when the clause is being processed. This is not to suggest that more formal properties are completely divorced from topicality, but only to note that the mapping between the formal and the functional properties of a grammatical category is not always obvious, and that even in the best cases such mapping depends on an elaborate chain of theoretical reasoning.[7]

In discussing the advantages of his clustering approach to grammatical subjecthood, Keenan (1976: 323-331) notes that such an approach accommodates the well-documented observation that the subjects of complex ("non-basic") clauses tend to display fewer subject properties than the subjects of the simple ("basic") clause. In other words, in the same language the subjects of simple clauses tend to be more **prototypical** than the subject of the complex clauses.[8] This observation harkens back to Keenan's earlier paper (1975). Indeed, it is only in the limited context of passive clauses that Keenan (1976) notes the cross-linguistic implications of his clustering approach — that the subject in some languages displays more subject properties than the subject in other languages. Or put another way, that the **grammaticalization** of the pragmatic function "main clausal topic" is a matter of degree and maybe thus exhibit typological variation.

Two other papers in the Li (ed. 1976) volume skate near the clustering approach to subjecthood. In the first, Li and Thompson (1976) argue for a typology of topic-prominent vs. subject-prominent languages. On further inspection, their suggestion boils down to the fact that topic-prominent languages tend to lack two of the overt morphological coding properties on Keenan list — case marking and verb agreement. Lacking an explicit clustering framework, Li and Thompson use the term "topic-prominent" as a stand-in for "morphologically less-marked", "less grammaticalized" or "less prototypical" subject.[9]

In a somewhat similar vein, Anderson (1976) notes that in "deep" ergative languages both overt-morphological and formal-behavioral properties reveal the same ergative-absolutive split. In "shallow" ergative languages, on the other hand, only the morphology reveals this split, while behavior-and-control properties follow a nominative-accusative pattern. Within a clustering approach, this again boils down to observing that relational categories such as ergative, absolutive, nominative and accusative grammaticalize in different languages to different degrees.

4. Formal properties of subjects and objects

4.1. *Preamble*

Keenan (1976: 324) divides the formal properties of grammatical subjects into two separate clusters — **overt coding properties** (3) and **behavior-and-control properties**. His analysis can be easily extended to grammatical relations in general. This extension is not only possible but may be unavoidable, because most often it is the *contrast* between subject and object or between direct and indirect object — rather than the single relation itself — that is marked by formal properties (Wierzbicka 1981).

A more-or-less exhaustive list of Keenan's behavior-and-control properties should include:

(6)   **Behavior-and-control properties:**
    a.   promotion to direct object
    b.   demotion from direct object (antipassive)
    c.   passivization
    d.   reflexivization
    e.   causativization
    f.   equi-NP reference in complementation
    g.   raising
    h.   possessor promotion
    h.   anaphoric co-reference in chained clauses
    i.   co-reference in relativization, WH-question, cleft constructions
      and participial clauses

The applicability — or relevance — of formal properties in (3) and (6) to a particular grammatical relation is then determined by answering the question:

> Does one need to mention a particular grammatical relation in the definition of a particular grammatical process?

When the answer is yes, the property is relevant; when the answer is no, it is irrelevant. But the relevance of particular properties to particular grammatical relations is highly selective, both within the same language and cross-linguistically. In the following sections we will illustrate this briefly.

4.2. *Overt coding properties*

Overt coding properties (3) have always figured prominently in determining the grammatical roles of clausal participants. But an exclusive reliance on these properties is not without problems. To begin with, as Keenan (1976) has pointed out, overt coding properties cluster most reliably around the subject of simple ("basic") clauses, but much less so around the subject of complex ("non-basic") clauses. Further, the applicability of overt coding properties to grammatical relations even in simple clauses varies from one language to another, or within the same language from one case-role to the other. For example, Modern Hebrew has rigid SVO order, a morphologically-unmarked subject, morphologically-marked definite/direct object and indirect objects, and obligatory subject agreement. In such a language, all three overt coding properties are relevant to grammatical relations. But they are not relevant to the same degree. Word order is relevant to all grammatical relations. Case marking is relevant to objects, and only by contrast to subjects. And grammatical agreement is relevant only to subjects.

In languages with flexible (pragmatically controlled) word order, word order is not relevant to grammatical relations. Thus in Spanish and Biblical Hebrew (rigid VO, flexible S), word order is relevant to the object but not to the subject. And in languages like Papago, Ute, Walbiri or Nez Perce (flexible S,O), word order is not relevant to any grammatical relation.

In languages with no verb agreement, such as Mandarin, verb agreement is obviously irrelevant to grammatical relations. On the other hand, in languages with both subject and object agreement, such as Swahili or Spanish, verb agreement is relevant to both grammatical relations.

Similarly, in languages with partial or altogether absent nominal case morphology, nominal case-marking is obviously irrelevant to grammatical relations. English partially resembles such a language, in that both the subject and direct object are morphologically unmarked, but indirect objects are morphologically marked. Other languages may go further along this typological dimension, in having little or no nominal case morphology. In the following section I will describe briefly a more radical example of such a language, in which the bulk of case-marking morphology is loaded on the verb.

4.3. *Verb-coding of grammatical roles*

A milder case of verb-coding of both the subject and object roles' has been described in various Philippine languages, whether interpreted as nominative (Schachter 1976; Givón 1979a) or ergative (Brainard 1994b). Similar situations involving only the object role have been described in KinyaRwanda (Kimenyi 1976) and Nez Perce (Rude 1985). In these two languages, direct objects are marked uniformly regardless of their semantic role. For patient direct-objects, this nominal marking suffices. When a non-patient is promoted to direct object status, an added verbal affix marks its semantic role.

Perhaps the most radical example of verb-coding of case-roles is found in the Campa Arawak languages of Peru.[10] In these languages, there is virtually no nominal case-marking of NPs, with the exception of one semantically-bleached locative prefix. Subject pronominal agreement by verb prefix is near obligatory. Direct-object pronominal agreement by verb suffix is optional, and is controlled by pragmatic considerations of topicality.

Somewhat reminiscent of KinyaRwanda and Nez Perce, the semantic role of many non-patient objects is marked by a verb affix. Thus (from Machiguenga):[11]

(7) **Intransitive clause:**
     impogini i-kam-ana-i   o-ime
     then   3m-die-DIR-REAL 3f-husband
     '. . . then her husband died . . .'

(8) **Transitive clause, DO = topical patient:**
     no-nevent-av-aka-ri   no-tineri
     1-see/DIST-RECIP-PERF-**3m** 1-son-in-law
     '. . . I saw my son in law in the distance . . .'

(9) **Transitive, DO = anaphoric topical patient:**
     i-kisa-vintsa-vaget-ake-ro-tyo
     3m-mistreat-DES-DUR-PERF-**3f**-EMPH
     '. . . he was very mean to her . . .'

(10) **Transitive, DO = non-topical patient:**
     a. *o-g-unte-ta   onko-shi*
         3f-eat-DUR-MOM uncucha-leaf
         '. . . she ate *uncucha* leaves . . .'

     b. *i-aga-vaget-i-ra   o-tineri   i-vatsa*
         3m-get-DUR-REAL-SUB 3f-son-in-law 3m/CL-meat
         '. . . when her son-in-law got meat . . .'

(11) a. **Less-topical ASSOC object:**
         o-mag-imo-ig-a-i   o-ishinto
         3f-sleep-ASSOC-PL-HAB-REAL 3f-daughter
         '. . . she lived with her daughters . . .'

     b. **More topical ASSOC object:**
         o-mag-imo-ta-i-ri-ra   o-tineri
         3f-sleep-ASSOC-HAB-REAL-**3m**-SUB 3f-son-in-law
         '. . . living with her son-in-law . . .'

Dative objects are obligatorily promoted to DO, but the verb is not obligatorily coded for their semantic case-role:

(12) a. **Verb unmarked for semantic case-role:**
  ga-ra   pi-p-aig-i-ro   p-iniro
  NEG-SUB 2-give-PL-REAL-**3f** 2-mother
  '. . . (he said:) Don't give your mother (any) . . .'

  b. **Verb marked for trans-locative case-role:**
  o-m-p-u-te-na   no-shinto   kamona
  3f-IRR-give-TRSL-IRR-**1** 1-daughter chonta-palm
  '. . . my daughters may give me chonta-palm . . .'

Among overt coding properties, word order is obviously important for defining grammatical relations in Machiguenga. But the locus of nominal case-marking has shifted away from the more common location — the noun or NP — to the verb, where pronominal agreement and case-role affixes have become integrated into a complex inflectional system.

4.4. *Behavior-and-control properties*

4.4.1. *The problem of applicability*

Much like overt coding properties, behavior-and-control correlates of grammatical roles are not always applicable across the board. Within the same language, some rules-governed syntactic processes may be relevant only to the subject or only to the object. In nominative languages, for example, promotion to direct-object (6a) or demotion from direct-object (antipassive; (6b)) are relevant only to the direct-object, but not to the subject. In ergative languages, on the other hand, grammatical processes that create or destroy direct-objects directly affect transitivity — and thus automatically also the case-role of the agent (ergative vs. absolutive).

In the same vein, morphological causativization tends to leave the embedded-clause *object* relatively unaffected, so that it most often retains the same grammatical role it had in the corresponding simple clause. In contrast, causativization is much more likely to affect the grammatical role of the *causee* (embedded-clause subject). And further, a considerable range of cross-language variation exists as to the grammatical role assigned to the causee (Comrie 1976; Cole 1976/1984).

Across languages, some rules may be relevant to a particular grammatical relation in one language but not in another. For example, in Turkish,

Ute and KinyaRwanda, separate patterns exist for subject vs. object relativization. In other words, relativization is sensitive to both grammatical relations in such languages. At the other extreme, in Japanese and Mandarin Chinese, relativization takes the same pattern in all case-roles, and is thus altogether oblivious to grammatical relations.

In the same vein, in languages with a promotional passive, passivization is often relevant to both the subject and direct object roles, as in English, KinyaRwanda or Nez Perce. On the other hand, in languages with a non-promotional impersonal passive, passivization is often relevant to only the subject (demoted agent) role, but not to the object, as in Spanish or Ute. The applicability of a particular behavior-and-control property to a particular grammatical role must be determined on a case-by-case and language-by-language basis.

4.4.2. *Conflicts with overt coding properties*

The prototype clustering approach to grammatical relations gives rise to one predicament that is not acknowledged in more discrete, either/or approaches to grammatical relations. This has to do with the fact that on occasion an overt coding property of a grammatical relation — say subject — conflicts with one or more behavior-and-control properties. A simple example will illustrate this.

In general, it seems, the word order criterion for direct objecthood conforms much better to the behavior-and-control criteria than does nominal case-marking. In English, the direct object in simple transitive clauses is morphologically unmarked, and directly follows the verb. In dative-shifted clauses, both objects appear morphologically unmarked. But only the first of the two unmarked objects — the semantic dative directly following the verb — is accessible to passivization. The second, the semantic patient, is not:

(13) a. **DAT-shifted clause:**
          She showed him a book
      b. **Dative-DO passive:**
          He was shown a book
      c. **Patient-DO passive:**
          *The/A book was shown him

In the corresponding non-shifted clause, on the other hand, word order and case-marking coincide. The patient is both post-verbal and morphologically marked as DO, and only the patient is accessible to passivization:

(14) a. **Non-shifted clause:**
She showed the book to two prospective buyers
 b. **Patient-SUBJ passive:**
The book was shown to two prospective buyers
 c. **Dative-SUBJ passive:**
*They were shown the/a book to

The same discrimination, this time in both passivization and relativization, is revealed in another "double direct-object" construction in English. Again, the unmarked object adjacent to the verb is accessible, the other one is not. Thus compare:

(15) a. **Underlying double-object clause:**
They elected him president
 b. **First-OBJ relativization:**
The man they elected president . . .
 c. **Second-OBJ relativization:**
*The president they elected him . . .
 d. **First-OBJ passivization:**
He was elected president
 e. **Second-OBJ passivization:**
*The president was elected him

In the same vein, Keenan's (1975, 1976) cross-language comparisons clearly show that of all overt coding-properties of subjects, word order is the more universal one — it is more likely to persist in "non-basic" clause types such as the passive. That is, the topic of the de-transitive (passive or inverse) clause can occupy the typical subject position without necessarily displaying either the typical case-marking or control of verb agreement. Thus (Nepali):[12]

(16) a. **Active:**
Ava-le   Maya-lay   hirka-y-in
Ava-ERG Maya-DAT hit-PAST-**3sf**
'Ava hit Maya'

 b. **De-transitive:**
Maya-lay   Ava-dwara hirka-i-y-o
Maya-DAT Ava-OBL   hit-DETRANS-PAST-**1sm**

In the de-transitive clause (16b), the patient gains neither subject case-marking nor control of verb agreement. But being now the topical participant, the patient can assume the characteristic clause-initial subject position.

A ranking similar to Keenan's (1975) is implicit in Li and Thompson's (1976) typology of "subject prominent" vs. "topic-prominent" languages. The latter turn out to lack subject-related morphology, but not of subject-related word order. A similar ranking — this time of behavior-and-control criteria over morphological criteria — is also evident in Anderson's (1976) treatment of "deep" vs. "shallow" ergative languages. In the latter, the ergative-absolutive split affects only the morphology, while behavior-and-control properties follow a nominative-accusative split. Under their surface morphological glaze, "shallow" ergative languages are thus really — behaviorally — nominative-absolutive. In "deep" ergative languages, on the other hand, all subject properties are said to follow the ergative-absolutive split. These languages thus exhibit an ergative organization of grammatical relations in a 'deeper' sense.

A succint demonstration of the dissociation between behavior-and-control ("deep") and overt coding ("shallow") properties has been shown in Japanese, a nominative language (Shibatani 1977). We will return to this issue further below, after surveying a representative sample of behavior-and-control properties of grammatical relations.

4.4.3. *Relativization and grammatical relations*

In some languages, relativization is irrelevant to grammatical relations, since all case-roles are relativized by the very same strategy. This is true in Japanese, where the same **gap strategy** is used (zero anaphora) for all case-roles. Thus:[13]

> (17) a. **Simple clause:**
>   *otoka-ga onna-ni   tegami-o kaita*
>   man-SUBJ woman-DAT letter-ACC sent
>   'The man sent a letter to the woman'
>
>   b. **Subject REL-clause:**
>   [0] *onna-ni tegami-o kaita otoka-wa . . .*
>   woman-DAT letter-ACC sent man-TOP
>   'The man who sent a letter to the woman . . .'

    c. **Accusative REL-clause:**
       otoka-ga onna-ni **[0]** *kaita tegami-wa* . . .
       man-SUBJ woman-DAT   sent letter-TOP
       'The letter that the man sent to the woman . . .'

    d. **Dative REL-clause:**
       otoka-ga **[0]** *tegami-o kaita onna-wa* . . .
       man-SUBJ   letter-ACC sent woman-TOP
       'The woman to whom the man sent a letter . . .'

In other languages, relativization strategy differentiates, to various degrees and by varying means, between case-roles. This may be seen in Hebrew, where the general relativization strategy is that of anaphoric pronouns.

Since verb agreement is obligatory in Hebrew, subject relativization requires only pronominal agreement on the verb:

(18) a. **Simple clause (anaphoric subject):**
       hi *ba-a*   *hena etmol*
       she came-**she** here yesterday
       'She came here yesterday'

     b. **Subject REL-clause:**
       ha-isha   **she-***ba-a*   *hena etmol* . . .
       the-woman REL-came-**she** here yesterday
       'the woman who came here yesterday . . .'

For direct-object relativization, a post-verbal anaphoric pronoun is used — optionally in one-level embedding. That is, the strategy alternates with the Japanese gap strategy and the English word order strategy:

(19) a. **Simple clause (anaphoric DO):**
       Yoav ohev ot-a
       Yoav loves DO-**her**
       'Yoav loves her'

     b. **REL-clause (NP-NP-V order):**
       ha-isha   **she-***Yoav ohev (ot-a)* . . .
       the-woman REL-Yoav loves (DO-**her**)
       'the woman that Yoav loves . . .'

The anaphoric-pronoun relativization strategy becomes obligatory for indirect objects:

(20) a. **Simple clause (anaphoric DAT object):**
          Yoav   natan   l-a   et-ha-sefer
          Yoav gave-he to-**her** DO-the-book
          'Yoav gave her the book'

      b. **REL-clause (anaphoric DAT object):**
          ha-isha   she-Yoav   natan   l-a   et-ha-sefer . . .
          the-woman REL-Yoav gave-he to-**her** DO-the-book
          'The woman to whom Yoav gave the book . . .'

In KinyaRwanda, relativization discriminates more explicitly among all three grammatical relations. One strategy is used for subjects, essentially the same one as in Hebrew (18).[14] Another one is used for the most common direct object — the patient. It is the same word order cum gap (zero anaphora) strategy as in English. Thus compare:

(21) a. **Main clause:**
          umugabo y-a-kubis-e   abagore
          man   he-PAST-hit-ASP women
          'the man hit the women'

      b. **Subject REL-clause:**
          umugabo u-a-kubis-e   abagore . . .
          man   he/REL-PAST-hit-ASP women
          'the man who hit the women . . .'

      c. **DO REL-clause (patient-DO):**
          abagore umugabo y-a-kubis-e . . .
          women   man   he-PAST-hit-ASP
          'the women that the man hit . . .'

When the object to be relativized is not a patient, it must be first promoted to DO, a process through which it gains verb-marking of its semantic role. Only then can it be relativized. The promotion to DO system in KinyaRwanda is illustrated in:

(22) a. **DO = patient:**
          umugore y-ooher-eje   umubooyi ku-isoko
          woman   she-send-ASP cook   LOC-market
          'The woman sent the cook to the market'

b. **DO = locative:**
*umugore y-ooher-eke-**ho**   isoko   umubooyi*
woman   she-send-ASP-LOC market cook
'The woman sent to the market the cook'

(23) a. **DO = patient:**
*umugabo ya-tem-eje igiti **n**-umupaanga*
man   he-cut-ASP tree INSTR-saw
'The man cut the tree with a saw'

b. **DO = instrument:**
*umugabo ya-tem-ej-**eesha**   umupaanga igiti*
man   he-cut-ASP-INSTR saw   tree
'The man used the saw to cut the tree'

(24) a. **DO = patient:**
*Maria ya-tets-e   inkoko   **n**-agahiinda*
Mary   she-cook-ASP chicken MANN-sorrow
'Mary cooked the chicken regretfully'

b. **DO = manner:**
*Maria ya-tek-**an**-ye   agahiinda inkoko*
Mary   she-cook-MANN-ASP sorrow   chicken
'Mary regretfully cooked the chicken'

(25) a. **DO = patient:**
*umuhuungu ya-riimb-jye ururiimbi **na**-umugore*
boy   he-sing-ASP song   ASSOC-woman
'The boy sang the song with the woman'

b. **DO = associative:**
*umuhuungu ya-riimb-**an**-ye   umugore ururiimbi*
boy   he-sing-ASSOC-ASP woman   song
'The boy sang with the woman a song'

(26) a. ***DO = patient (obligatory promotion):**
Yohani y-ooher-eje ibaruwa **ku-Maria*
John   he-send-ASP letter   DAT-Mary

b. **DO = dative-benefactive:**
*Yohani y-ooher-**er**-eje   Maria ibaruwa*
John   he-send-BEN-ASP Mary letter
'John sent Mary a letter'

With its extensive promotion-to-DO system, KinyaRwanda exhibits a strong relational constraint on relativization:

(27) **Relational constraints on relativization (KinyaRwanda):**
   a. Only subjects and direct objects are accessible to relativization.
   b. Non-patient objects must be promoted to DO before they can be relativized.

Thus compare:

(28) a. **Locative REL-clause:**
   *isoko   umugore y-ooher-eke-**ho**   umubooyi . . .*
   market woman   she-send-ASP-**LOC** cook
   'The market the woman sent the cook to . . .'

   b. **Instrument REL-clause:**
   *umupaanga umugabo ya-tem-ej-**eesha**   igiti . . .*
   saw   man   he-cut-ASP-**INSTR** tree
   'The saw the man cut the tree with . . .'

   c. **Manner REL-clause:**
   *agahiinda Maria ya-tek-**an**-ye   inkoko*
   sorrow   Mary   she-cook-**MANN**-ASP chicken
   'the regret with which Mary cooked the chicken . . .'

   d. **Associative REL-clause:**
   *umugore umuhuungu ya-riimb-**an**-ye   ururiimbi . . .*
   woman   boy   he-sing-**ASSOC**-ASP song
   'The woman with whom the boy sang the song . . .'

   e. **Dative-benefactive REL-clause:**
   *umugore Yohani y-ooher-**er**-eje   ibaruwa . . .*
   woman   John   he-send-**BEN**-ASP letter
   'the woman that John sent the letter to . . .'

Another relativization pattern involving strong relational constraints is found in Philippine languages, such as Bikol. Interpreted as a nominative language,[15] Bikol has a voice system in which all non-agents can be promoted to subject/topic of the passive/inverse. In the passive/inverse clause, the promoted subject loses its normal active-clause semantic-role affix, but the semantic role of the subject/topic is coded on the verb. Thus consider:

(29) a. **Agent-topic ('active voice'):**
          nag-ta'o 'ang-lalake ning-libro sa-babaye
          AGT-give TOP-man   PAT-book DAT-woman
          'The man gave a book to the woman'

      b. **Patient-topic ('passive-voice' #1):**
          na-ta'o   kang-lalake 'ang-libro sa-babaye
          PAT-give AGT-man   TOP-book DAT-woman
          'The book was given to the woman by the man'

      c. **Dative-topic ('passive-voice' #2):**
          na-ta'o-an   kang-lalake ning-libro 'ang-babaye
          DAT-give-DAT AGT-man   PAT-book TOP-woman
          'The woman was given a book by the man'

(30) a. **Agent-topic ('active voice'):**
          *nag-putul 'ang-lalake ning-tubu **gamit**(-'ang)-lanseta*
          AGT-cut   TOP-man   PAT-cane INSTR-knife
          'The man cut sugar-cane with a knife'

      b. **Instrument-topic ('passive-voice' #3):**
          pinag-putul kang-lalake ning-tubu 'ang-lanseta
          INSTR-cut   AGT-man   PAT-cane TOP-knife
          'The knife was used by the man to cut sugarcane'

(31) a. **Agent-topic ('active voice'):**
          *nag-bakal 'ang-lalake ning-kanding **para**-sa-babaye*
          AGT-buy TOP-man   PAT-goat   BEN-DAT-woman
          'The man bought a goat for the woman'

      b. **Benefactive-topic ('passive-voice' #4):**
          pinag-bakal-an kang-lalake ning-kanding 'ang-babaye
          BEN-buy-DAT   AGT-man   PAT-goat   TOP-woman
          'The woman was bought a goat by the man'

This voice system is coupled to relativization by imposing the following relational constraint:

(32) **Relational constraints on relativization (Bikol)** (Givón 1979a:
      ch. 4):
      a. Only a subject is accessible to relativization, (i.e. can be
          the coreferentially-deleted argument in the REL-clause).

b. In order for a non-subject/agent of the active to be
relativized, it must be first promoted to subject via
inversion/passivization.

Examples of how the various semantic roles are relativized as subjects
of the passive/inverse are given below:

(33) a. **Agent REL-clause:**
marai 'ang-lalake
good   TOP-man
    ***na nag**-ta'o ning-libro sa-babaye*
    REL AGT-give PAT-book DAT-woman
'The man who gave a book to the woman is good'

b. **Patient REL-clause:**
marai 'ang-libro
good   TOP-book
    ***na na**-ta'o kang-lalake sa-babaye*
    REL PAT-give AGT-man   DAT-woman
'The book that was given to the woman by the man is good'

c. **Dative REL-clause:**
marai 'ang-babaye
good   TOP-woman
    ***na na**-ta'o-**an**   kang-lalake ning-libro*
    REL DAT-give-DAT AGT-man   PAT-book
'The woman that was given a book by the man is good'

d. **Instrument REL-CLAUSE:**
marai 'ang-lanseta
good   TOP-knife
    ***na pinag**-putul kang-lalake ning-tubu*
    REL INSTR-cut   AGT-man   PAT-cane
'The knife the man to cut sugar-cane with is good'

e. **Benefactive REL-clause:**
marai 'ang-babaye
good   TOP-woman
    ***na pinag**-bakal-**an** kang-lalake ning-kanding*
    REL BEN-buy-DAT   AGT-man   PAT-goat
'The woman that was bought a goat for by the man is good'

4.4.4. *Passivization and grammatical relations*

In principle, passivization can be relevant to all three grammatical relations, in languages where non-subjects of the active can become *bona fide* grammatical subjects of the passive. In some languages, however, passivization is opaque to grammatical relations. These are languages with a **non-promotional passive**, where all non-subject NPs retain in the passive clause their active-clause case-marking. Most commonly, non-promotional passives impose no relational restrictions on the type of non-agent object that can become topic-of-passive — all non-agent semantic roles, direct and indirect object alike, can become topic-of-passive. As illustration, consider Ute (Uto-Aztecan), where in the passive clause only the non-agent topic can control pronominal agreement on the verb:[16]

(34) **Patient (DO):**
    a. **Active:** *ta'wá-ci̱ sivą́ą̱tu-ci pa̱x̂á-qa*
            man-SUBJ goat-OBJ kill-ANT
            'The man killed the goat'

    b. **Passive:** *sivą́ą̱tu-ci pa̱x̂á-ta-pu̱ga*
            goat-OBJ kill-PASS-REM
            'Someone killed the goat'
            'The goat was killed' (by someone)

(35) **Instrumental:**
    a. **Active:** *ta'waá-ci̱ wií-ci-m tu̱ká-qa-'u*
            man-SUBJ knife-OBJ-INSTR eat-ANT-he
            'The man ate with a knife'

    b. **Passive:** *wií-ci-m tu̱ká-ta-qa-ax̂*
            knife-OBJ-INSTR eat-PASS-ANT-it
            'Someone ate with a knife'

(36) **Locative:**
    a. **Active:** *mamá-ci̱ tu̱vú̱pu̱-vwan 'aví-kya-'u*
            woman-SUBJ ground-OBJ-on lie-ANT-she
            'The woman lay on the ground'

    b. **Passive:** *tu̱vú̱-pu̱-vwan 'aví-ta-qa-ax̂*
            ground-OBJ-on lie-PASS-ANT-it
            'Someone lay on the ground'

(37) **Associative:**

    a. **Active:**   *máama̲-ci-u*   *'áapa-ci-wa*   *wų́ų̲ka-qa-qa-amų̲*
              women-SUBJ-PL boy-OBJ-**with** work-PL-ANT-**they**
              'The women worked with the boy'

    b. **Passive:** *'áapa-ci-wa* *wų́ų̲ka-qa-ta-qa-'u*
              boy-OBJ-***with*** work-PL-PASS-ANT-**he**
              'Some persons worked with the boy'

(38) **Manner:**

    a. **Active:**   *mamá-ci̲*   *pų̲ká-wų́ų̲ka-qa-'u*
              woman-SUBJ **hard**-work-ANT-**she**
              'The woman worked hard'

    b. **Passive:** *pų̲ká-wų́ų̲ka-ta-qa*
              hard-work-PASS-ANT
              'Someone worked hard'

Philippine languages such as Bikol (see above),[17] where passivization discriminates between the subject an all object types lumped together (see (29), (30), (31) above), represent an intermediate typological situation. Passivization indeed furnishes evidence for the distinction subject vs. non-subject, so that the grammatical relation 'subject' is indeed supported by this syntactic rule. But the rule is silent on the distinction between direct and indirect object. In other words, it does not support the grammatical relation 'direct object'.

In KinyaRwanda, finally, the very same promotion-to-DO mechanism used in relativization is also used in passivization. And this mechanism licenses a similar relational constraint on passivization as on relativization (see (27), (28) above):

(39) a. Only direct objects can be made subjects of the passive.

      b. Before a non-patient object can be promoted to subject
          of the passive, it must be first promoted to DO.

In other words, promotion to DO in KinyaRwanda is an obligatory feeder to passivization. Thus compare:

(40) a. **Patient subject-of-passive:**
         umubooyi y-ooher-ej-we   *ku-isoko*
         cook/SUBJ he-send-ASP-**PASS** LOC-market
         'The cook was sent to the market'

b. **Locative subject-of-passive:**
   *isoko   ry-ooher-ej-**we-ho**   umubooyi*
   market/SUBJ it-send-ASP-PASS-LOC cook
   '*The market was sent the cook to'
   'Someone sent the cook to the market'

c. **Instrument subject-of-passive:**
   *umupaanga wa-tem-**eesh**-ej-**we**   igiti*
   saw/SUBJ   it-cut-INSTR-ASP-PASS tree/OBJ
   'The saw was used to cut the tree'

d. **Manner subject-of-passive:**
   *agahiinda   ga-tek-**an-w**-e   inkoko*
   sorrow/SUBJ it-cook-MANN-PASS-ASP chicken
   '*Regret was cooked the chicken with'
   'Someone cooked the chicken regretfully'

e. **Associative subject-of-passive:**
   *umugore   ya-riimb-**an-w**-e   ururiimbi*
   woman/SUBJ she-sing-ASSOC-PASS-ASP song/OBJ
   '*The woman was sung a song with'
   'Someone sang a song with the woman'

f. **Dative-benefactive subject-of-passive:**
   *Maria   y-ooher-**er**-ej-**we**   ibaruwa*
   Mary/SUBJ she-send-BEN-ASP-PASS letter/OBJ
   'Mary was sent a letter'

4.4.5. *Equi-NP deletion and grammatical relations*

On a graded scale, the control of coreference in embedded complement clauses — equi-NP deletion (henceforth Equi) — comes as close as any syntactic rule to being uniformly applied cross-linguistically as any relationally-governed syntactic process. But even this process is not immune to some typological variability.

Within the same language, Equi applies differentially to grammatical relations in different types of complement-taking verb. In modality verbs ('want', 'start', 'try' etc.), Equi is relevant to the subject of both clauses:

(41) **She** wanted **[0]** to leave

In manipulation verbs ('force', 'tell', 'make'), on the other hand, Equi is relevant to the subject of the complement and the object of the main clause:

(42) She told **him** [0] to leave

In English and many other languages, the human object of manipulative verbs (42) is unmistakably a direct object, so that Equi can be formulated in terms of the subject of the complement and the direct object of the main clause. Equi is here relevant to both grammatical relations. In other languages, however, Equi in manipulative-verb complements is more problematic.

In Hebrew, for example, the manipulee takes different case-roles following different manipulation verbs:

(43) a. *hixrax-nu*   **ot-a**   *la-avor   dira*
         force/PAST-we **DO-**her INF-move apartment
         'We forced her to switch apartments'

      b. *amar-nu   l-a   la-avor   dira*
         tell/PAST-we **DAT-**her INF-move apartment
         'We told her to switch apartments'

      c. *azar-nu   l-a   la-avor   dira*
         help/PAST-we **DAT-**her INF-move apartment
         'We helped her switch apartments'

      d. *mana-nu   **mi-***mena la-avor   dira*
         prevent/PAST-we **from-**her INF-move appartment
         'We prevented her from switching apartments'

However, the *et*-marked object in Hebrew is not quite a direct object, but rather still a semantically — albeit grammatically restricted — role, that of **definite patient**. Equi in manipulative verb complements in Hebrew thus applies to a certain class of object *semantic* roles, rather than to the grammatical direct-object role.

4.4.6. *Reflexives and grammatical relations*

Another behavior-and-control property that is widely applicable to one grammatical relation — the subject — is reflexivization. The 'true' reflexive invariably is controlled by the subject, although the coreferentially-deleted argument may be either direct or indirect object:

(44) a. **Direct-object reflexive:**
      She hurt **herself**
   b. **Indirect-object reflexive:**
      She was thinking about **herself**

Equally applicable to grammatical subjecthood is possessive reflexivization, as in:

(45) a. **Direct-object reflexive:**
      He shunned **his own** mother
   b. **Indirect-object reflexive:**
      She didn't go to **her own** mother, but rather . . .

5. Gradations and indeterminacy of grammatical relations

5.1. *Preamble*

The ambiguous status of the Hebrew direct object — neither a purely semantic patient case nor a purely pragmatic/grammatical direct-object case (see section 6.3.4.5. above) — is indicative of a broad range of facts that a prototype clustering approach to grammatical relations cannot ignore. In various formal approaches to subjecthood and objecthood, this problem is dispatched with single-trait definitions that produces unambiguous discrete classes. But a responsible empirical account of grammatical relations has no recourse to this taxonomic luxury. It must not only own up to indeterminancy and gradation, but also strive to explain them in a principled way.

5.2. *Gradation of direct objecthood*

There is a well-documented semantic and pragmatic overlap between the categories definite patient (Hebrew), dative and human patient (Spanish), dative and pronominal patient (Provencal), dative and topical patient (Newari, Nepali). The pragmatic common denominator is transparent — **topicality**. The semantic common thread is equally transparent — an **affected human** participant.[18] A truly grammatical direct-object role, fully independent of semantic roles so as to pass the dissociation test (see section 2.),

most commonly arises diachronically from the reanalysis of an erstwhile
dative or associative case. Both semantic roles are typically human and thus
inherently topical. But different languages are synchronically at different
stages along this grammaticalization — de-semanticization — continuum.
Table (46) below scales some languages along this diachronic continuum.

(46) **Continuum of grammaticalization toward a
      de-semanticized DO:**

language	type of object role	freedom of promotion to direct object
	most semantic	
a. Japanese	patient	no promotion
b. Hebrew	definite patient	no promotion
c. Spanish	dative, human patient	no promotion
Provencal	dative, pronoun patient	no promotion
Newari	dative, topical patients	no promotion
d. Ute	patient, dative, benefac.	no promotion[19]
e. Tzotzil	patient, dative, benefac. possessor of object	obligatory prom.
f. English	direct object	some prom.[20]
g. Nez Perce, KinyaRwanda	direct object	fully promotional
	most grammatical	

5.3. Gradation of subjecthood

The universality of formal subject properties (cf. Keenan 1976) is always
complicated by the fact that many behavior-and-control syntactic processes
are not equally distributed across languages. For example, few languages
display much if any **raising**, so conspicuous in English. Many languages exhibit no morphological promotion to direct object (Sherpa, Japanese, Hebrew,
Ute). Many have a non-promotional passive (Uto-Aztecan, Tibeto-Burman),
or a non-promotional inverse (Plains Cree, Modern Greek, Maasai). Many
serial-verb languages have no embedded complements, and thus no syn-

tactic difference between Equi and zero anaphora (Supyire, Akan, Miskitu). Keenan's (1976) behavior-and-control properties are not evenly distributed cross-linguistically, so that the subject of one language may display one subset while that of another language another. This variability does not automatically mean that the subject of language A is less subject-like than that of language B. But Keenan's large basket of subject properties now appears to be not quite as easy to apply — uniformly — across languages. And the apparent variation raises two important issues of interpretation:

a.   degree of grammaticalization
b.   relative ranking of subject properties.

As a brief illustration of the potential magnitude of cross-language variability, consider the following table of the availability of various formal subject properties in a number of nominative languages.

(47)   **Distribution of formal subject properties in a sample of nominative languages**

properties

	overt coding			behavior-and-control		
	word order	**verb agreement**	**case marking**	**Equi**	**reflexive**	**zero anaph.**
English	+	+/–	–	+	+	+
Mandarin	+	–	–	+	+	–
Japanese	+	–	+	+	+	–
Spanish	–	+	–	+	+	+
Bibl. Hebrew	–	+	–	+	+	+
Ute	–	+/–[21]	–	+	+	–
Early Latin	+	+	+	+	+	+
Late Latin	–	+	+	+	+	+
Krio	+	–	–	+	+	+

The only language in our sample (47) that exhibits all six subject properties on the list is Early Latin. Other languages miss between one and three. A simple-minded approach to prototype clustering would be to invoke **degree of grammaticalization** at this juncture: languages with fewer subject properties have a less prototypical — less grammaticalized — subject. Such an approach was implicit in Li and Thompson's (1976) typology, which took into account only overt morphological features. But the problem is a bit more complex.

The only properties on the list that are unambiguously present in all languages are two behavior-and-control properties — *Equi* and *reflexivization*. The third behavioral property, *zero anaphora* in clause-chaining, is subject-controlled in six of the languages, but not in Mandarin, Japanese and Ute. In these three, zero anaphora does not discriminate, at least in principle, between the subject and the object.[22] Is there a principled **relative ranking** by which some formal subject properties can be shown to count more than others?

5.4. *A functional account of cross-language variability:*
The ranking of formal subject and object properties

Full documentation of formal subject and object properties in all languages is not yet available. Most conspicuously missing is fuller documentation of behavior-and-control properties. The vast majority of these formal properties of grammatical relations are transparently linked to topicality and referential continuity.[23] Of the entire list, only three — reflexivization, causativization and Equi — have some semantic components. But referential continuity remains an important ingredient in these three as well. The more-or-less full list includes:

(48) **Behavior-and-control properties:**
  a. promotion to direct object
  b. demotion from direct object (antipassive)
  c. passivization
  d. inversion
  e. reflexivization
  f. causativization
  g. equi-NP in complementation
  h. raising
  i. possessor acention
  j. anaphoric co-reference in chained clauses
  k. co-reference in relativization, WH-question and cleft constructions.

Can these formal properties be ranked, in a principled way, relative to Keenan's (1975) ranking of overt coding properties?

My strong suspicion is that Keenan's (1975) intuition was essentially sound, and that his ranking — case marking least universal, pronominal agreement more universal, word order most universal — can be easily and naturally extended. This can be done my observing that of those three overt coding properties, word order correlates most closely to topicality (Givón 1988), to subjecthood (Keenan 1976), and to direct objecthood (Givón 1984a). Pronominal agreement is heavily associated with topicality (Givón 1976). And morphological case is the least associated with topicality. A principled relative ranking of the formal properties of grammatical relations thus arises out of a transparent functional principle:

(49) **Correlation between universality and functional transparency of subject and object properties:**
"The more closely a formal property of subjects and objects is associated with their pragmatic function of topicality, the more universal it is likely to be in its cross-language distribution."

The relative ranking is then:

(50) **Ranking of all properties of grammatical roles according to universality and functional transparency:**

most universal
a. Functional reference-and-topicality properties
b. Behavior-and-control properties
c. Word order
d. Grammatical agreement
e. Nominal case-marking
least universal

This ranking, if valid, suggests an underlying general principle: Morphology, and in particular nominal case morphology, is the least universal trait of grammatical relations. Being the most grammaticalized, ritualized or automated feature in grammar,[24] morphology has a higher potential for dissociation from semantic or pragmatic function, in this case the topicality function of subjects and objects. Syntactic behavior-and-control properties of grammatical relations, at the other extreme, are more universal precisely because they are more transparently motivated by the pragmatic function of subjects and objects. The most universal properties of grammatical relations are their functional properties, i.e. those listed by Keenan (1976) as reference properties.

Whether principle (49) can serve as a basis for *weighting* various subject properties to decide cases when different principles come in conflict remains to be seen. One highly conspicuous case of such conflict, 'surface' ergative languages (Anderson 1976), will be discussed in section 6. below. But the effect of diachronic change in introducing functional opacity into both morphology and syntax is universal and well documented.[25]

6. Grammatical relations in ergative languages

6.1. *Overt coding properties in ergative languages*

6.1.1. *Nominal morphology: Split subject marking*

The nominal case-marking morphology of nominative-accusative languages is maximally aligned with the discourse-pragmatic function of subjects and objects, i.e. their relative topicality. Regardless of transitivity, the clause's main topic is marked morphologically in a unified way — as *nominative*. What stands out immediately about ergative languages is the split morphological marking of the clause main topic. The subject/agent of the transitive clause is marked as *ergative*, the subject of the intransitive clause as *absolutive*. And in many ergative languages the object/patient of the transitive clause is also marked as *absolutive* case. As illustration of this nominal case-marking pattern, consider first the pattern of Nepali:[26]

(51)   a.   **Intransitive:**
           kita:b   *tebul-ma thi-y-o*
           book/ABS table-LOC be-PAST-1sm
           'The book is on the table'

       b.   **Transitive (non-human patient):**
           Raj-le   *kukhura*   *poka-y-o*
           Raj-ERG chicken/ABS cook-PAST-1sm
           'Raj cooked the/a chicken'

A human patient/object, however, is marked as *dative* rather than absolutive in Nepali:

(52) **Transitive (human patient):**
Omi-le Raj-lay hirka-y-in
Omi-ERG Raj-DAT hit-PAST-1sf
'Omi hit Raj'

In Nepali, the split in marking the absolutive NP is only partial. In Nez Perce this split is complete, with absolutive subjects being unmarked and absolutive direct objects being marked (Rude 1985):

(53) a. **Intransitive:**
hi-páayna háama
3/ABS-arrived man/ABS
'The man arrived'

   b. **Transitive:**
yu's-ne pu-ut'eye piyée-pim
poor-DO 3/ERG-whipped brother-ERG
'The older brother whipped the poor one'

6.1.2. *Control of verb agreement*

In both Nepali and Nez Perce above, pronominal agreement on the verb is controlled by the subject — regardless of whether it is absolutive or ergative. However, in Nepali the same set of pronominal verb-suffixes is used with either absolutive and ergative subjects. Verb agreement is thus fully controlled by the nominative NP. Such an agreement pattern is also reported in Walbiri (Hale 1973), and is probably the most common pattern in ergative languages (Anderson 1976; Comrie 1977).

The situation in Nez Perce is actually more complex. Verb agreement is indeed controlled by the subject in both transitive and intransitive clauses. But the actual pronominal form used is selected according to transitivity: One set of verb-prefixed pronouns is controlled by absolutive subjects (53a), the other by ergative subjects (53b).

A third type of agreement in an ergative language is reported in many Mayan languages, where in the intransitive clause the verb agrees only with the absolutive subject. In the transitive clause, the verb agrees with *both* the absolutive object and the ergative subject. Thus, from Jacaltec (Craig 1977):

(54) a. **Intransitive clause (ABS agreement):**
      ch-in   *axni*
      AUX-ABS/1 bathe
      'I bathed'

   b. **Transitive clause (ABS and ERG agreement):**
      ch-in   *haw-ila*
      AUX-ABS/1 ERG/2-see
      'You saw me'

A similar agreement pattern is also reported in Inuit Eskimo (Kalmár 1980) and in Basque (Mejías-Bikandi 1991). And likewise in Kapampangan, when interpreted as an ergative language.[27] Thus (Keenan 1976):

(55) a. **Antipassive intransitive (ABS agreement):**
      s-um-ulat-ya   *ing-lalaki ng-poesia*
      AGT/IRR-write-**he** ABS-boy   OBL-poetry
      'The boy will write poetry/a poem'

   b. **Ergative-transitive (ABS and ERG agreement):**
      i-sulat-na-ya   *ning-lalaki ing-poesia*
      PAT-write-**it-he** ERG-boy   ABS-poetry
      'The boy wrote the poem'

One way of interpreting the naturalness of the double-agreement pattern in these ergative languages could be to suggest that the ergative clause arose via re-analysis of an erswhile *inverse*, where a double agreement — with both the subject and topicalized object — is indeed natural.[28]

Only rarely does verb-agreement in an ergative language display clear absolutive control, i.e. a clear non-nominative pattern. This pattern is reported in Khinalug, a N.E. Caucasian language, where the verb agrees with the class/gender of the absolutive NP. Thus (Comrie 1977):

(56) **Intransitive subject agreement:**
   a. *l-ig-ild   sacax-0/-q'iqoma"*
      man/ABS silent-M
      'The man is silent'

   b. *xním̓k'ir   sacax-z-q'iqoma"*
      woman/ABS silent-F
      'The woman is silent'

(57) **Transitive object agreement:**
   a. *b-ij-i   shi   t-i-0/-k'í*
      father-**ERG** son/**ABS** awaken-**M**
      'The father awakened the son'
   b. *b-ij-i   rishi   t-i-z-k'í*
      father-**ERG** daughter/**ABS** awaken-**F**
      'The father awakened the daughter'

The control of verb agreement in ergative languages can follow a nominative pattern, a nominative pattern with some modifications, or — apparently much more rarely — a purely ergative-absolutive pattern, as in Khinalug. Verb agreement thus seems to be more universally predictable than case-marking, in that it tends to follow more closely a nominative control pattern, i.e. abide by the pragmatic function of the subject as the main topical argument in the clause.

One must note, finally, that the verb agreement pattern in both nominative and ergative languages is to quite an extent the product of the particular grammaticalization pathway through which particular constructions — nominative or ergative — arose. This is a rather involved subject that will not be pursued further here.[29]

6.1.3. *Word order in ergative languages*

As is to be expected following the preceding discussion and hierarchy (50), word order is rather insensitive to the difference between nominative and ergative grammatical organization. Thus, in SOV-ordered ergative languages such as Basque, Eskimo or Nepali, both the ergative subject of the transitive and the absolutive subject of the intransitive occupy the same clause-initial position. Similarly, in VSO-ordered ergative languages such as Jacaltec, Chamorro, Bikol or Maori, both ergative and absolutive subjects claim the post-verbal position. Likewise in pragmatically-controlled ('free-order') ergative languages such as Nez Perce, Walbiri or Dyirbal, word order is equally irrelevant to the absolutive or ergative status of agents and patients. Put another way, word order — whether grammaticalized or not — tends to follow the pragmatics of topicality rather than the semantics of transitivity.[30] In an ergative language, the absolutive subject of an intransitive clause and the ergative subject of an transitive clause are both topical. And they are just as topical as, respectively, nominative subject of an intransitive and transitive clause in a nominative language, respectively. In the same vein, the absolutive patient in an ergative language is much less topical than the ergative agent, much like the accusative patient in a nominative language is less topical than the nominative agent.[31]

6.2. *Behavior-and-control properties in ergative languages*

6.2.1. *Preamble*

As both Anderson (1976) and Comrie (1977) note, in most ergative languages, behavior-and-control properties are controlled by the same nominative-accusative split that governs them in nominative languages. The ergativity of such languages is thus purely morphological or "shallow". In a few languages, the ergative-absolutive contrast goes beyond case-marking morphology, affecting rule-governed syntactic behavior. Implicit in the distinction between "shallow" and "deep" ergative languages is the very same **weighting** of relation-related properties seen in (50) above, by which behavior-and-control properties are ranked higher — i.e. more universal — than surface morphology. "Shallow" ergative languages are thus, deep down, nominative languages with misleading surface morphology (Anderson 1976).

As noted above (50), the privileged status of behavior-and-control properties, as somehow reflecting grammatical relations more faithfully, has considerable factual support even apart from ergativity. The feasibility of this idea is further supported the cross-linguistic distribution of the four logically-possible types of association between case-marking morphology and behavior-and-control properties:

(58) **Types of association between morphological and behavior-and-control features:**

	morphology	behavior/control	languages
a.	nominative	nominative	(English, Hebrew, Ute)
b.	nominative	ergative	/////
c.	ergative	nominative	(Basque, Jacaltec, Nepali)
d.	ergative	ergative	(Dyirbal, Eskimo, Karao)

There is a clear gap in the attested distribution of the four logically-possible types — type (58b) is unattested. In addition, there is also an equal

if less visible gap in frequencies: The number of languages of type (58d) —
"deep" ergative languages — is extremely small.[32] The biased distribution
of the four possible types in (58) suggests a strong tendency for syntax
to follow nominative-accusative control. Only a small sub-set of ergative
languages ever violates this tendency. In the following sections we will
survey some of the most conspicuous examples of ergative-absolutive control of syntactic behavior.

6.2.2. *Control of Equi*

The control of Equi-NP deletion (or coreference) in complement clauses is
one of the least likely behavior-and-control feature to show ergative-absolutive control. But occasionally one finds such cases, as in Khinalug (Comrie
1977). In complements of manipulative verbs in Khinalug, the manipulee
is coded as absolutive if the complement is intransitive, but as ergative if
the complement is transitive:

(59)   a.   **Intransitive complement:**
            as-ir   gada   tochkwi   jukwathma"
            I-DAT boy/ABS get.up/INF want
            'I want the boy to get up'

       b.   *as   jukwathma" hin-i   phsha"   q'izi*
            I/ABS want   she-ERG bread/ABS bake/INF
            'I want her to bake bread'

This is limited in Khinalug, so that Equi in the complements of modality
verbs reveals no trace of ergative-absolutive control (Comrie 1977):

(60)   a.   **Intransitive complement:**
            hin-u   lik'úvri   muxwizhma"
            she-DAT sing/INF   can
            'She can sing'

       b.   **Transitive complement:**
            hin-u   phsha"   q'izi   muxwizhma"
            she-DAT bread   bake/INF   can
            'She can bake bread'

One must point out, however, that there is another way of interpreting
the data in (59): The complement of 'want' may not be an infinitive but

rather a *subjunctive* complement. The absolutive (59a) and ergative (59b) manipulee is thus not the object of the main verb, but rather the undeleted *subject* of the complement. Indeed, an ergative-marked manipulee is just as bizarre and unprecedented in ergative languages as would a nominative-marked manipulee in a nominative language (see Comrie 1976, Cole 1984, or Givón 1990: ch. 13). But marking the manipulee as *subject* would be natural in subjunctive complements, as in Spanish:

> (61) a. **Intransitive complement:**
>   *Quiere   que Juan   se-vaya*
>   wants/she SUB Juan/NOM REF-go/SUBJUN
>   'She wishes that John would leave'
>
> b. **Transitive complement:**
>   *Quiere   que Juan coma   su bocadillo*
>   wants/she SUB Juan eat/SUBJUN his sandwich
>   'She wishes that John would eat his sandwich'

As we shall see further below, even the most extreme "deep" ergative language retains nominative control of Equi.

6.2.3. *Control of reflexivization*

Reflexivization is another syntactic process that in even the most syntactically-ergative languages display nominative control. That is, the non-subject NP becomes the reflexive pronoun regardless of transitivity:

> (62) **Intransitive clause:**
>   a. Mary talks **to herself**
>   b. *****Herself** talks to Mary
>
> (63) **Transitive clause:**
>   a. Mary shot **herself**
>   b. *****Herself** shot Mary

An absolutive-controlled pattern of reflexivization would be:

> (64) a. **Intransitive clause:**
>   **Herself** talked to Mary
>   b. **Transitive clause:**
>   Mary shot **herself**

To my knowledge no language, ergative or nominative, displays this pattern. As an illustration of nominative control of reflexivization in an ergative language, consider Tagalog (Philippine):[33]

(65) a. **Intransitive clause (ABS subject):**
          nag-trabajo ang-lalaki para sa-babae
          AGT-work   ABS-man   for   OBL-woman
          'The man worked for the woman'

      b. **Reflexive (ABS subject control):**
          *nag-trabajo ang-lalaki para sa-sarili **niya***
          AGT-work   ABS-man   for   OBL-SELF **his**
          'The man worked for himself'

      c. **Transitive clause (ERG subject):**
          *p-**in**-atay **ng**-lalaki **ang**-aso*
          PAT-kill   ERG-man   ABS-dog
          'The man killed the dog'

      d. **Reflexive (ERG subject control):**
          *p-**in**-atay **ng**-lalaki **ang**-sarili **niya***
          PAT-kill   ERG-man   ABS-self   **his**
          'The man killed himself'

There is, however, a variant of (65d) where, seemingly, the controlling agent reverts to absolutive, thus appearing in an intransitive **antipassive** construction. In that construction, the reflexive morpheme incorporates into the verb:[34]

(66) a. **Antipassive clause (ABS subject/agent):**
          nag-patay ang-lalaki (ng-aso)
          AGT-kill   ABS-man   OBL-dog
          'The man killed (a dog)'

      b. **Reflexive (ABS subject control):**
          *nag-p-**akam**-atay ang-lalaki*
          AGT-REFL-kill   ABS-man
          'The man self-killed'

However, antipassivization is not obligatory for reflexivizing a transitive clause, most commonly antipassive clauses are objectless, and are thus syntactically *intransitive*. One can thus interpret the reflexive in (66b) the same way as the reflexive in (65b) — control by the absolutive subject of an intransitive clause.

6.2.4. *Control of zero anaphora in chained clauses*

Probably the most startling example of ergative-absolutive control of a syntactic process was Dixon's (1972) report of the control of zero anaphora in Dyirbal. In nominative languages, the nominative (subject) tends to exert control of zero anaphora in clause-chaining. That is:

(67) a. **Nominative INT to nominative TR:**
          The woman came and [0] hit the man
      b. **Nominative TR to nominative INT:**
          The woman hit the man and [0] left

In Dyirbal, Dixon (1972) reported an *absolutive* control of zero-anaphora. To be translated this pattern into English meaningfully would require passivization of the transitive clause:

(68) a. **Absolutive INT to absolutive TR:**
          The man came and the woman hit [0]
          (**The man** came and [0] was hit by the woman)
      b. **Absolutive TR to absolutive INT:**
          The woman hit **the man** and [0] left
          (**The man** was hit by the woman and [0] left)

Since Dyirbal exhibited both patterns, it was of interest to see which one predominates. A text-frequency study by Cooreman (1988) revealed that the nominative pattern (67) predominated in Dyirbal discourse. A similar result was reported for Tagalog by Cooreman et al. (1984). But at least in one Philippine language, Karao (Brainard 1994a), the absolutive control of zero anaphora — pattern (68) — predominates in text.

6.2.5. *Control of relativization*

If one interprets Philippine languages as nominative (Schachter 1976; Givón 1979a), then relativization is controlled by the nominative (subject) relation, as was noted earlier (32):

(32) **Relational constraints on relativization (Bikol)**
(Givón 1979a: ch. 4):
  a. Only a subject is accessible to relativization, (i.e. can be the coreferentially-deleted argument in the REL-clause).
  b. In order for a non-subject/agent of the active to be relativized, it must be first promoted to subject via inversion/passivization.

If a Philippine language is interpreted as an ergative language, however,[35] relativization automatically turns out to be controlled by the absolutive argument. Thus, in re-interpreting Bikol as an ergative language, the absolutive subject of the intransitive clause is directly accessible to relativization:

(69) a. **Simple intransitive clause:**
       nag-turog 'ang-babaye
       AGT-sleep ABS-woman
       'The woman slept'

      b. **Absolutive subject relativization:**
       marai 'ang-babaye na nag-turog
       good ABS-woman REL AGT-sleep
       'The woman who slept is good'

A semantically-transitive event may appear either as a direct-active (ergative) clause, where the agent is ERG-marked and the patient ABS-marked; or as an antipassive clause, where the agent is ABS-marked and the patient takes an oblique-patient case:

(70) a. **Ergative clause:**
       na-akul kang-lalake 'ang-kanding
       PAT-hit ERG-man ABS-goat
       'The man hit the goat'

      b. **Antipassive clause:**
       nag-pakul 'ang-lalake ning-kanding
       AGT-hit ABS-man PAT-goat
       'The man hit a/some goat'

The agent cannot be relativized from the ergative pattern (70a), only from the antipassive pattern (70b). That, the must be demoted to *absolutive* before it is accessible to relativization. The patient, on the other hand, is accessible to relativization from the ergative pattern (70a), in which it is the *absolutive* argument:

(71) a. **Agent relativization (antipassive pattern):**
marai 'ang-lalake na nag-pakul ning-kanding
good ABS-man REL AGT-hit PAT-goat
'The man who hit the goat is good'

b. **Patient relativization (ergative pattern):**
marai 'ang-kanding na na-akul kang-lalake
good ABS-goat REL PAT-hit ERG-man
'The goat that the man hit is good'

Finally, all oblique arguments must be promoted to absolutive — thus to *direct object* — as pre-condition for access to relativization. The re-interpretation of a Philippine language as an ergative language thus converts the promotion-to-subject system into a promotion to direct-object system reminiscent of the one seen in KinyaRwanda. As in KinyaRwanda, the semantic role of the absolutive non-patient DO is morphologically coded on the verb. Thus compare:

(72) a. **Patient ABS/DO:**
na-ka'ag kang-lalake 'ang-libro sa-lamesa
PAT-put ERG-man ABS-book LOC-table
'The man put the book on the table'

b. **Locative ABS/DO:**
pinag-ka'ag-an kang-lalake 'ang-lamesa ning-libro
LOC-put ERG-man ABS-table PAT-book
'The man put on the table a book'

The patient is accessible to relativization only via pattern (72a), where it is the absolutive DO. The locative is accessible to relativization only via pattern (72b), where it has been promoted to absolutive DO:

(73) a. **Relativization of ABS/DO patient:**
marai 'ang-libro na k-in-a'ag kang-lalake sa-lamesa
good ABS-book REL PAT-put ERG-man LOC-table
'The book that the man put on the table is good'

b. **Relativization of ABS/DO locative:**

marai 'ang-lamesa **na** *pinag-ka'ag-an kang-lalake*
good ABS-table   REL LOC-put   ERG-man

ning-libro
PAT-book

'The table that the man put a book on is good'

Other obliques must likewise be promoted to absolutive DO before they are accessible to relativization.

The relational constraints on Bikol relativization can be thus given in terms of the absolutive grammatical relation:

(74) **Relational constraints on relativization in Bikol interpreted as an ergative language:**
  a. Only an absolutive NP can be the coreferentially-deleted argument in the REL-clause.
  b. The subject of a transitive clause must be **demoted** to absolutive status — via antipassivization — in order to become accessible to relativization.
  c. An oblique non-patient argument of the active must be **promoted** to absolutive — to direct-object — in order to become accessible to relativization.

6.2.6. *Raising to object*

Raising is a rare phenomenon outside English and relatively few like-minded languages. In the few nominative languages that tolerate raising, raising-to-object applies only to the subject — nominative — of the complement clause.[36] But in at least in one ergative language, Karao (Philippine), raising an absolutive direct object is possible.[37] Raising in Karao is attested for only one verb, and is a sub-pattern of Equi in modality-verb complementation. Thus (Brainard 1994a, in this volume):[38]

(75) a. **Simple intransitive clause:**
    man-pasiyal 'i-bi'i
    AGT-visit   ABS-woman
    'The woman will go visiting'

b. **Equi with intransitive complement:**

*piyan **na**-bi'i '**a**   **man**-pasiyal*
want ERG- SUB AGT-visit
'The woman wants to go visiting'

This pattern is probably rather marginal.

6.2.7. *Overview: Mixed control of syntactic processes and gradation in grammatical relations*

In her summary of the control of relational properties in Karao, Brainard (1994a, in this volume) presents the following distribution:

(76) **Relational control of subject properties in Karao** (Brainard 1994a):

property	type of control		
	nominative		absolutive
case morphology			ERG/ABS
word order	NOM		
verb agreement		(irrelevant)	
equi	NOM		
relativization	NOM/ACC		
pseudo-cleft			ABS
zero anaphora			ABS
raising	ACC	?	ABS
passivization	ACC		
promotion to DO	ACC		
antipassive	ACC		
reflexivization	NOM		

The summary suggests that even in a language as syntactically — "deeply" — ergative as Karao, the majority of syntactic behavior-and-control properties are controlled by either the nominative or by the accusative. Only two syntactic processes — zero anaphora and pseudo-cleft — show clear absolutive control.[39]

In the diachronic shift from nominative to ergative in Philippine languages, the correspondence of clause-types is:

(77) **Diachronic correspondence of clause-types along the NOM-to-ERG shift in Philippine languages:**

construction   **nominative** ⟶ **ergative**

	construction	nominative	ergative
a.	AGT-focus	direct-active	antipassive
b.	PAT-focus	inverse/passive	ergative/patient-DO
c.	OBL-focus	inverse/passive	ergative/oblique-DO

That this correspondence is diachronically valid is supported by the suggestion of similar correspondences in Indonesian languages (Rafferty 1982; Verhaar 1985). It is also mirrored by similar correspondence in Sahaptian between the nominative organization of Sahaptin and the ergative organization of Nez Perce (Rude 1991).

Brainard's results also support the validity our extension of Keenan's (1975, 1976) hierarchic prediction. First, relational properties can be ranked in terms of the degree of their association with the pragmatic function grammatical relation (50). And second, properties that are more transparently associated with the pragmatic function of grammatical relations distribute more uniformly — thus more universally — across languages (principle (49)).

A more general conclusion concerns the validity of a discrete approach to grammatical relations. Such approach is intrinsically incapable of capturing either the typological generalizations *or* the typological variability seen in ergative languages. The tendency of for case-marking to be controlled by one set of grammatical relations (ERG/ABS), while the rest of the grammar marches to the drum of another set (NOM/ACC), is impenetrable to a discrete approach. Nor is fact that even in "deep" ergative languages, the degree and manner to which some syntactic processes are controlled by the ERG/ABS relations may vary considerably. A theoretical frame-work that does not recognize **degree of grammaticalization** of what are essentially universal functional domains ('parameters'), in this case universals of discourse-pragmatic notions such as primary and secondary topic — will gloss over these typological differences as 'superficial' or 'uninteresting'.[40]

A final consideration here concerns the relationship between grammatical and cognitive universals. Our survey thus far has tended to support

Anderson's (1976) suggestion that behavior-and-control properties of subjects and objects are more universal, and that morphology — or at least nominal case-marking — is a more superficial property of grammatical relations.

But three facts about behavior-and-control syntactic properties must be remembered:

a.   Some relationally controlled syntactic processes — relativization, raising, passive — pertain to low-frequency **complex clauses**. Others, on the other hand — zero anaphora, dative shift, reflexive — are high-frequency simple clauses.

b.   Complex clauses are **infrequent** in human discourse, appearing roughly at a ratio of 1:10 as compared to simple (main, declarative, affirmative, active) clauses Givón 1995, ch. 2).

c.   Complex syntax is acquired much later by children.

In both language acquisition and everyday language use, the overt coding properties of subjects and objects are much more frequently encountered than at least some of the "deeper" behavior-and-control properties. Since child acquisition of grammar is heavily driven by input frequencies, one would thus suspect that when children acquire a "shallow" ergative language, they confront from the very start two conflicting principles of relational organization — an ergative-absolutive control of the morphology, and a nominative control of zero anaphora, equi and reflexivization. The later acquisition of other nominatively-controlled complex structures then presumably reinforces the nominative control principle. A cognitively-based, empirical investigation of this issue remains to be undertaken.

7.   Grammatical relations in serial-verb languages

7.1. *Syntactic configuration and grammatical relations*

Various accounts have suggested the likelihood that serial-verb clauses involve multiple verb phrases under a single clausal node. Some formal accounts also insist that the various VP nodes are all subordinated to a single ('highest') VP node. With or without a 'higher' VP node, several configurations of the hierarchic organization of the serial clause VP may be envisioned:[41]

(79)   a.   b.

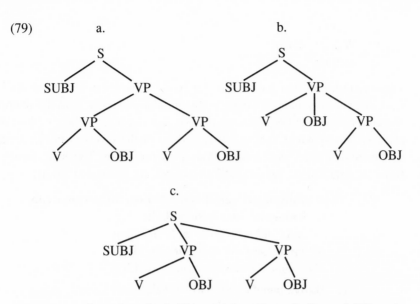

Accepting a formal multiple-VP model, with each 'lower' VP node dominating a verb and a (possible) object, amounts to a tacit concession that a single clause need not have a unified set of grammatical relations, at least as far as the object is concerned.

In this section I will re-examine the status of grammatical relations in serial-verb languages more closely, beginning with the grammatical object. I will then turn to the seemingly less controversial relation, that of the grammatical subject, surveying constructions in which subjecthood too turns out to be problematic. The predicament of subjecthood in serial-verb languages, however, is a predicament only within the confines of a certain formal approach. The predicament thus turns out to be, in a large measure, self-inflicted.

7.2. *Multiple objects in serial clauses*

The most extensive analysis of objecthood in serial-verb languages can be found in Byrne's (1987) exhaustive syntactic description of Saramaccan, *Grammatical relations in a Radical Creole*. In addition to overt coding properties of objects and verbs, Byrne examines several behavior-and-control properties to assess the grammatical status of clauses with multiple verbs and objects; in particular:

a. relativization
b. WH-movement
c. clefting

These tests reveal that the multiple verbs in Saramaccan serial clauses behave syntactically like the single verbs of simple clauses. And the multiple objects is serial clauses likewise behave like the single objects of simple clauses. This syntactic fact stands regardless of the diversity of the semantic function of the serial constructions in Saramaccan. The main semantic types of serialization Byrne (1987) examines are illustrated below:

(80) **Main multi-object serial constructions in Saramaccan**
   a. **Instrumental case with 'take':**
      di mii tei di pau naki di dagu
      the child **take** the stick *hit*   the dog
      'The child hit the dog with a stick'

   b. **Dative/benefactive with 'give':**
      a sei di wosu da   di womi
      he *sell* the house **give** the man
      'He sold the house **to/for** the man'

   c. **Directional-deictic with 'go'/'come':**
      a tsa   di meliki go/ko   a   di konde
      he **carry** the milk   **go/come** LOC the village
      'He took/brought the milk **to** the village'

   d. **Directional-deictic with 'go'/'come':**
      a waka go/ko   a   di opolani
      he *walk* **go/come** LOC the airplane
      'He walked **to/from** the airplane'

   e. **Directional-deictic complementizers 'go'/'come':**
      de ke go/ko   wasi di   wagi
      they want **go/come** *wash* the   car
      'They want to **go/come** (and) wash the car'

   f. **Perfective aspect with 'finish':**
      Kofi bi-fefi   di wosu kaba
      Kofi PERF-paint the house **finish**
      'Kofi **had** painted the house'

g. **The comparative 'pass':**
a ***bigi pasa*** *di mii*
he ***big*** pass the child
'He is bigg**er than** the child'

h. **The comparative 'more':**
a bigi ***moon*** *di mii*
he big **more** the child
'He is bigg**er than** the child'

Byrne's (1987) conclusions are well worth citing:

> "... in most serial types a particular serial string is best looked at as **a series of finite subordinate clauses** ... That is, because of ... [overt coding and behavior-and-control properties; TG] ... most of the serial verbs in this chapter are finite Ss ..." (1987: 242; emphases added)

While reaching this conclusion, Byrne does not ignore the problem of gradual grammaticalization:

> "... if the analysis of *moon* 'more' is correct, then it represents the most radical change of the serials studied in this chapter; while all the serials analyzed show at least some minimal indications of change towards non-finite status for some speakers, only *moon* 'more' has categorically achieved this result for all speakers ..." (1987: 242)

It is important to emphasize that the finite syntactic properties of Saramaccan serial verbs observed by Byrne (1987) reveals once again the strong dissociation between semantic and syntactic components of grammaticalization. While semantically grammaticalized, most serial verbs in (80) retain their syntactic verbal properties. Consequently, their objects retain their direct-objecthood relation vis-a-vis the verb.[42] Byrne's conclusion — that serial-verb clauses are best looked at "as a series of finite subordinate clause" — is forced upon him by the pre-empirical — Aristotelian — demands of the formalism:

One verb = one clause.

When combined with an extreme configurational approach to grammatical relation, this account demands that only a VP dominated by S can harbor a grammatical object.[43]

Essentially the same general conclusions — multiple VPs with multiple DOs — were reached by Osam (1993, in this volume) in his study of grammatical objecthood in Akan. The bi-transitive 'give' in Akan can take two syntactic frames, one non-serial, the other serial:

(81) a. **Non-serial variant (dative more topical):**
   Kofi ma-a   papa-no sika
   Kofi give-PAST man-the money
   'Kofi gave the man money'

   b. **Serial variant (patient more topical):**
   Kofi de   sika-no   ma-a   papa-no
   Kofi **take** money-the give-PAST man-the
   'Kofi gave the money to the man'

The patient object is naturally definite when topicalized in (81b), but naturally indefinite in (81a). When testing for object pronominalization, only the topicalized dative can be pronominalized in the non-serial (81a):[44]

(82) a. *Kofi ma-a   **no**   sika*
   Kofi give-PAST **him** money
   'Kofi gave him money'

   b. **Kofi ma-a   papa-no [0]*
   Kofi give-PAST man-the **it**
   '*Kofi gave the man it'

In the serial construction (81b), on the other hand, both objects can be pronominalized:

(83) a. *Kofi **de** [0] ma-a   papa-no*
   Kofi **take it** give-PAST man-the
   'Kofi gave it to the man'

   b. *Kofi **de** sika-no   ma-a   **no***
   Kofi **take** money-the give-PAST **him**
   'Kofi gave the money to him'

The same discrimination occurs in relativization. Only the dative object can be relativized out of the non-serial (81a):

(84) a.   *papa-no a   Kofi ma-a   **no** sika   no*[45] . . .
               man-the REL Kofi give-PAST **him** money the . . .
               'The man Kofi gave money to . . .'

      b.   **sika-no   a   Kofi ma-a   papa-no* . . .
               money-the REL Kofi give-PAST man-the

But both objects can be relativized out of the serial variant (81b):

(85) a.   *papa-no a   Kofi **de** sika-no   ma-a   **no** no* . . .
               man-the REL Kofi **take** money-the give-PAST **him** the
               'The man to whom Kofi gave the money . . .'

      b.   *sika-no   a   Kofi **de** [0] ma-a   papa-no* . . .
               money-the REL Kofi **take it**   give-past man-the
               'The money that Kofi gave (to) the man'

Osam (1993) concludes that by all three criteria for direct objecthood — word order, control of object pronominalization, and control of object relativization — the two-verb serial clause (81b) has **two grammatical objects**, one per verb. This is true in spite of the fact that the serial verb *de* 'take' is morphologically the most grammaticalized in Akan, never taking any finite inflections; and in spite of the fact that *de* is semantically grammaticalized and does not mean 'take' in these serial constructions.

Other bi-transitive verbs in the 'give' class may vary in their syntactic behavior. Thus, 'teach' has no corresponding serial variant and allows no word order variation, and its patient object cannot be pronominalized. But 'teach' allows the patient to be definitized (within the fixed DAT-PAT order) and relativized:

(86) a. **Indefinite patient:**
           Kofi kyerɛ-ɛ   mbofra-no ndwom
           Kofi teach-PAST children-the song
           'Kofi taught the children a song'

      b. **Definite patient:**
           Kofi kyerɛ-ɛ   mbofra-no ndom-no
           Kofi teach-PAST children-the song-the
           'Kofi taught the song to the children'

c. ***Fronted patient:**
   *Kofi kyerę-ę   ndom-no mbofra-no
   Kofi teach-PAST song-the children-the

d. **Pronominalized dative:**
   *Kofi kyerę-ę   **họn**   ndwon*
   Kofi teach-PAST **them** song
   'Kofi taught them a song'

e. ***Pronominalized patient:**
   *Kofi kyerę-ę   mbofa-no   [0]
   Kofi teach-PAST children-the **it**
   ('Kofi taught it to the children')

f. **Relativized dative:**
   *mbofa-no   **a**   Kofi kyerę-ę   **họn**   ndwom . . .*
   children-the REL Kofi teach-PAST **them** song
   'the children that Kofi taught a song (to) . . .'

g. **Relativized patient:**
   *ndwon-no **a**   Kofi kyerę-ę   mbofa-no   [0]*
   song-the   REL Kofi teach-PAST children-the **it**
   'the song that Kofi taught (to) the children . . .'

The patient object of 'teach' thus passes two objecthood tests — definitization and relativization. It fails two others — post-verbal position and pronominalization.

Finally, Akan bi-transitive verbs with non-human indirect objects ('put
on', 'take off', 'put in', 'take out', 'cover with', 'spread on') also require
the use of serial verbs. While the two VPs appear in a fixed order, both
objects are accessible to definitization, pronominalization and relativization.
And the semantically grammaticalized verb may be either the first or the
second in the clause:

(87) a. *Esi **de**   ekutu-no   to-o   famu*
        Esi **take** orange-the put-PAST floor
        'Esi put the orange on the floor'

     b. *Esi yi-i   tam-no   fi-i   pon-no-don . . .*
        Esi take-PAST cloth-the **leave**-PAST table-the-on
        'Esi took the cloth off the table'

c. *Esi hue-e   nsu   **gu**-u   ankora-no-mu*
   Esi pour-PAST water **put**-PAST barrel-the-in
   'Esi poured the water into the barrel'

(88) a. **Pronominalized patient:**
   *Esi yi-i   [0] **fi**-i   pon-no-don . . .*
   Esi take-PAST it   **leave**-PAST table-the-on
   'Esi took it off the table'

b. **Pronominalized locative:**
   *Esi yi-i   tam-no   **fi**-i   [0]-don . . .*
   Esi take-PAST cloth-the **leave**-PAST it-on
   'Esi took the cloth off it'

c. **Relativized patient:**
   *tam-no   a   Esi yi-i   [0] **fi**-i   pon-no-don . . .*
   cloth-the REL Esi take-PAST it   **leave**-PAST table-the-on
   'the cloth that Esi took off the table . . .'

d. **Relativized locative:**
   *pon-no   a   Esi yi-i   tam-no   **fi**-i   [0]-don . . .*
   table-the REL Esi take-PAST cloth-the **leave**-PAST it-on
   'the table off of which Esi took the cloth . . .'

By the four test for direct objecthood that apply in simple one-verb clauses in Akan — post-verbal position, word order, pronominalization and relativization — both objects in these serial clauses are bona fide direct objects.

7.3. *The grammatical subject in serial clauses*

Most serial-verb clauses arise diachronically from equi-subject (SS) clause chains, so that the problems they create for grammatical relations tend to involve the multiple objects in the condensed, grammaticalized clause. The single subject NP of the clause is semantically the subject of *both* verbs, thus formally of *both* lower-level VPs. Some serial clauses, however, arise diachronically from the condensation of switch-subject (DS) clause chains. This type of clause-chaining is well recognized, at least semantically, even in a language with no switch-reference morphology. Compare the following serial clauses in Akan, one SS-serial, the other DS-serial (Osam 1993):

(89) a. **Equi-subject (SS) serial clause:**
          *Kofi tur   abofra-no **ma**-a   Esi*
          Kofi carry/PAST children-the **give**-PAST Esi
          'Kofi carried the children for Esi'
          (*Hist.*: 'Kofi carried the children
                    and (*he*) gave them to Esi')

      b. **Switch-subject (DS) serial clause:**
          Esi yi-i   tam-no fi-i   pon-no-don
          Esi take-PAST cloth-the **leave**-PAST table-the-on
          'Esi took the cloth off the table'
          (*Hist.*: 'Esi took the cloth and *it* left the table')

As a chain-medial clause prior to condensation, the second clause in (89a) was an equi-subject (SS) clause; while the second clause in (89b) was a switch-subject (DS) clause. This phenomenon is rather common in serializing languages. But is there any indication in Akan that 'cloth' in (89b) bears a *subject* grammatical relation to the serial verb 'leave'? By Osam's (1993) syntactic criteria — word order, pronominalization, relativization — 'cloth' bears only an *object* relation — to 'take' — but no relation whatever — subject or object — to 'leave'.

The same resultative-causative DS-serial clauses are found in most serializing languages. Thus, consider the contrast between SS and DS serial clauses in Miskitu, where the SS/DS morphology of clause chaining is retained in serial clauses (Hale 1991):

(90) a. **SS serial clause:**
          Baha usus-ka   pali-i   wa-n
          that buzzard-CSN fly-PAR/SS go-PAST/3
          'The buzzard flew away'
          (*Historically*: 'The buzzard flew and (*he*) went')

b. **DS serial clause:**
   *Yang truk-kum atk-**ri***   *wa-**n***
   I   truck-a   sell-DS/1 go-PAST/3
   'I sold the truck away'
   (*Historically*: 'I sold the truck and *it* went')

Byrne (1987, 1992) proposes an **embedded clause** analysis of all serial clauses in Saramaccan. He posits the — syntactically embedded but semantically chained — 'deep structure' (91b) as the underlying syntactic structure of the serial clause (91a). That is (Byrne 1992: 203):

(91) a. *a bi fefi di wosu **kaba***
   he TNS paint the house **finish**
   'He **had** painted the house'

    b.

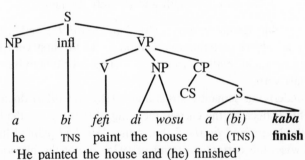

        'He painted the house and (he) finished'

Since (91a) arose from an equi-subject (SS) chained construction, (91b) is only deceptively an adequate account of its semantic and syntactic properties.[46] For a switch-subject (DS) serial constructions, Byrne's account would be even more problematic. Thus consider such an account of the Akan clause (89b):

(92) a. **Switch-subject (DS) serial clause:**
   Esi yi-i   *tam-no **fi**-i*   *pon-no-don*
   Esi take-PAST cloth-the **leave**-PAST table-the-on
   'Esi took the cloth **off** the table'

b.

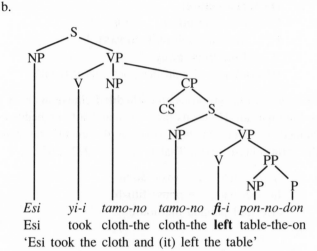

Esi	yi-i	tamo-no	tamo-no	fi-i	pon-no-don
Esi	took	cloth-the	cloth-the	**left**	table-the-on

'Esi took the cloth and (it) left the table'

By all available formal criteria, 'cloth' in (89b)/(92) and 'truck' in (90b) bear only an *object* grammatical relation — to the first verb in the clause, but no grammatical relation whatever — subject or otherwise — to the second (serial) verb.

As underlying semantic structures, (91b) and (92b) do not fare much better. This is because the current meaning of (91a) is not the historical 'He painted the house and *finished*', but rather 'He *had* painted the house'.

Likewise, the current meaning of (92a) is not the historical "Esi took the cloth and it *left* the table" but rather "Esi took the cloth *off* the table". Byrne's (1987, 1992) proposal thus glosses over the fact that both **grammaticalization** and **clause union** have taken place. Both processes are diachronic mappings from older to newer structures — and meanings, rather than synchronic mappings from deep to surface structure. This topic will be explored in more detail in the next section.

8.   Grammatical relations and clause union

8.1. *Preamble*

The problem of both syntactic and semantic representation of serial-verb clauses is rooted in our notion of **clause union**. In both embedding and serializing languages, what started historically as two verbal clauses, each with its own verb and set of relation-bearing grammatical arguments, can condense over time into a single event clause with a unified set of grammatical arguments. Clause union, viewed diachronically, may be thus defined as:

(93)   "The process by which two clauses with two sets of arguments, with each set bearing grammatical relations in its proper clause, are merge into a single clause, within which all arguments now bear grammatical relations as a single set".

The two major venues for obtaining syntactic complexity — embedding and serialization — involve starkly different diachronic strategies to create complex multi-verb structures, i.e. clause union. Embedding languages arrive at clause union via the route of **verb complementation**. Serializing languages arrive at clause union, often with the very same semantic value, via the route of **clause chaining**. In this section we will review the ramifications of this major typological constrast for grammatical relations.

8.2. *Syntactic constraints on clause union*

In both embedding and serializing languages, two major types of relational configurations can partake in clause union — equi-subject (SS) and switch-subject (DS). The two types have somewhat different consequences in clause union, so that we will consider them separately.

8.2.1. *Clause union in equi-subject (SS) configurations*

8.2.1.1. *Equi-subject (SS) clause union in embedding languages*

Clause union of equi-subject (SS) configurations is the main diachronic source of grammaticalized auxiliaries and eventually of tense-aspect-modal and directional markers in language (Givón 1971, 1973, 1984b; Heine 1993). In embedding languages, the initial syntactic configuration for SS clause union is equi-subject (SS) **complementation**. The V-plus-COMP verb phrase in an embedding language is constructed by analogy to the V-plus-OBJ verb phrase of the simple clause. The main verb retains all finite inflections, such as tense-aspect-modality and pronominal affixes. The complement verb is either partially or fully nominalized, exhibiting a less-finite form.

In both VO and OV languages, SS-complementation places the complement verb directly adjacent to the main verb (Givón 1971). Thus compare the VO complementation pattern of English (94a) with the OV pattern of Ute (94b):

(94) **Equi-subject (SS) in embedding languages:**
    a. **English (VO):**

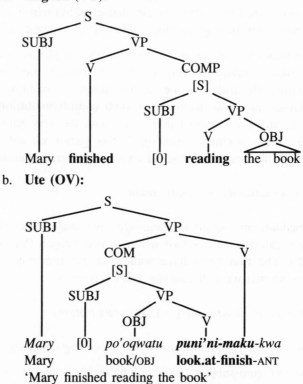

    b. **Ute (OV):**

                         Mary   [0]   *po'oqwatu*   ***puni'ni-maku**-kwa*
                         Mary   book/OBJ   **look.at-finish**-ANT
                         'Mary finished reading the book'

When the main verb ('finish') grammaticalizes into a perfect(ive) aspect, it becomes — at least initially — a finite **auxiliary verb** that remains, morpho-syntactically, the main verb of the complex two-verb clause. This is the case with the English example (94a). When that auxiliary cliticizes, it becomes a prefix (VO) or a suffix (OV) on the complement verb, which is now the main verb. With cliticization, the erstwhile auxiliary now brings all its finite morphology to the new main verb, as is the case in the Ute example (94b).

8.2.1.2. *Equi-subject (SS) clause union in serializing languages*

In serial-verb languages, two independent factors conspire against complete clause union. First, the chained structure most commonly prevents verb adjacency, by scattering the verbs on opposite sides of object NPs. One of the verbs in the clause may have grammaticalized semantically, but the two non-adjacent verbs cannot co-lexicalize. As an illustration of this, compare the SS-complementation of the embedding languages in (94) above with the verb-serializing Saramaccan (VO) and Supyire (OV) in (95) below:

(95) **Equi-subject (SS) in a serializing language:**

    a. **Saramaccan (VO)** (Byrne 1987):

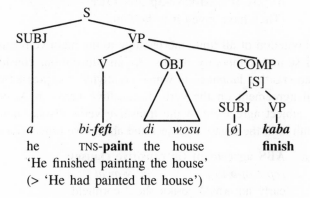

        'He finished painting the house'
        (> 'He had painted the house')

    b. **Supyire (OV)** (Carlson 1989):

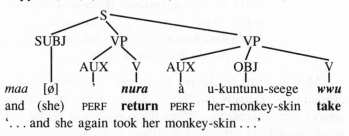

        '. . . and she again took her monkey-skin . . .'

When 'finish' in (95a) and 'return' in (95b) grammaticalize as aspect markers, they have no adjacent main verb to criticize on.[47]

    The second factor is tangentially related to the first. As noted above, the complementation structure that eventually gives rise to clause union in an embedded language is structured by analogy with a verb-object configuration. In such a configuration, the main verb retains all finite verbal features, while the complement verb is nominalized, non-finite or less-finite. When clause union occurs under such a configuration, the grammaticalized main verb — now co-lexicalized with the complement verb — contributes all its finite inflections to the combined single lexical verb. As an illustration of this, consider the Spanish auxiliaries:

(96) a. *se-lo-est-amos*   *explicando*
      DAT/3s-ACC/3sm-be-**1p** explain/PART
      'We are explaining it to him/her'

    c. *se-la-h-an*   *dado*
      DAT/3s-ACC/3sf-have-**3p** give/PART
      'They have given it to her/him'

The gravitation of all finite morphology to the main verb can, on occasion, yield strange temporary results. As an illustration, consider Acatec (Mayan), an ergative language in which ergativity is expressed only in the pronominal agreement on the verb. Intransitive verbs in Acatec display absolutive subject agreement, while transitive verbs display double agreement — with both the ergative subject and absolutive object (Zavala 1993):

(97) a. **ABS agreement (intransitive clause):**
      sep   oj-ø-to-j   *'ix y-awal*
      early IRR-ABS/**3**-go-IRR she 3-cornfield
      '... She'll go to her cornfield...'

    b. **ERG & ABS agreement (transitive clause):**
      ø-y-i'-on-ab'   *pax-aa-tej jun sq'an   juun*
      ABS/**3**-ERG/**3**-take-AGTV-EVID DIR-DIR-DIR one yellow paper
      '... that one also took a cigarette...'

Motion verbs in Acatec have been grammaticalizing as directional auxiliaries (eventually directional clitics), along the familiar route of equi-subject complementation. When the complement clause is intransitive, the absolutive subject agreement gravitates to the auxiliary alone, with the complement verb now marked only by a non-finite *irrealis* marker (Zavala 1993):

(98) *x-**ach**-jul*   *wey-oj*
COM-ABS/s2-come sleep-IRR
'You're coming to sleep'

When the complement clause is transitive, several agreement patterns are possible. In one type, when the main verb 'go' is not yet semantically grammaticalized, the intransitive auxiliary retains agreement with its absolutive logical subject, and the transitive complement agrees with both its ergative subject and absolutive object. Both verbs thus retain the agreement pattern they would have in a simple-clause (Zavala 1993):

(99) *ch-**in**-b'et-ey*   *ø-**in**-tx'a-on*   *'el ko-pichil ti'*
INC-ABS/1-go-DIR ABS/3-ERG/1s-wash-AGTV DIR 1p-clothes PROX
'. . . I went to wash our clothes . . .'

But another, more grammaticalized, pattern also exists, in case when 'go' is semantically grammaticalized as a 'future' marker. In this pattern, the agreement splits in a way that defies the logic of simple-clause grammatical relations. The auxiliary now agrees with the absolutive *object* of the embedded transitive verb, while the embedded verb agrees only with its ergative subject (Zavala 1993):

(100) *oj-**ach**-to-j*   *w-il*   *an*
IRR-ABS/2s-go-IRR ERG/1-see 1s
'I'm going to see you'

Modal verbs display another grammaticalization pattern yet, whereby the grammaticalized modal auxiliary loses its absolutive agreement altogether, while the embedded verb retains its simple-clause agreement pattern (ABS agreement for intransitives, ERG-ABS agreement for transitives) (Zavala 1993):

(101) a. **Intransitive complement (ABS agreement):**
*chi-ske' **in**-b'ey   an*
INC-can ABS/1s-walk 1s
'I can walk'

     b. **Transitive complement (ERG-ABS agreement):**
*chi-ske' **ach**-**w**-il-on   an*
INC-can ABS/2s-ERG/1s-see-AGTV 1s
'I can see you'

This modal pattern is also found when 'go' is fully grammaticalized as *future* marker, as in (Zavala 1993):

(102) a. **Intransitive complement (ABS agreement):**
to-j   *in-jul-oj*
go-IRR ABS/1s-come-IRR
'I'm going to come (here)'

b. **Transitive complement (ERG-ABS agreement):**
to-j   *ø-w-a'*   lo-w   naj an
go-IRR ABS/3-ERG/1s-give eat-INT 3s   1s
'I'm going to let him eat'

In all clause union patterns in Acatec, the auxiliary and complement verbs are adjacent. When they finally co-lexicalize, the combined new main verb carries all the finite verbal inflections of the clause. But the inflectional pattern is often morphotactically scrambled, thus at odds with the pattern of the simple clause.

In serializing languages, as noted above, the diachronic precursor of clause union — clause chaining — tends to disperse the verbs among the object NPs. Further, in many serial-verb language (Akan, Saramaccan, Ijo), the verbs in the precursor chained structure are all equally finite (or equally non-finite). Thus when an erstwhile chain condenses into a single serial clause, the verbs in it do not diverge in finite marking.

A serial verb may have grammaticalized semantically, but it continues to carry its verbal morphology long after losing verbal meaning. What is more, even in languages where finite verbal morphology had consolidated on a single verb in the precursor chain — and thus on single verb in the resulting serial clause, that verb could just as easily be the semantically-bleached grammaticalized verb. Thus, in Miskitu (OV) the grammaticalized chain-final 'go' in (103) displays all finite marking, while the semantic main-verb 'fly' is non-finite (Hale 1991):

(103) *Baha usus-ka   pali-i wa-n*
that   buzzard-CNS fly-INF go-PAST/3
'That buzzard flew away'

Similarly in Saramaccan (VO) the grammaticalized chain-final 'give' in (104) carries the finite inflection, while the semantic main-verb 'buy' goes unmarked (Byrne 1992):

(104) *Kofi bai di buku **bi**-da   di muyee*
      Kofi buy the book **TNS**-give the woman
      'Kofi bought the book for the woman'

The conflation of both factors — verb dispersal and lack of consolidated single locus for finite verbal morphology — renders clause union in serializing languages a radically different syntactic affair than in an embedding language. Even in equi-subject clauses, serializing languages tend to preserve much of the original morpho-syntax of the chained structure, retaining multi-VP structures and multi-object relations.

8.2.2. *Clause union in switch-subject (DS) configurations*

8.2.2.1. *Switch-subject (DS) clause union in embedding languages*

Switch-subject (DS) clause unions involve a family of broadly **causative** or **resultative** constructions. These structures are broadly patterned on DS-complementation of manipulative verbs ('make', 'cause', 'force', 'let' etc.)[48] In embedding languages, this pattern concentrates all finite marking on the main manipulative verb, leaving the complement verb nominalized, non-finite or less-finite. Semantically, the co-reference constraint on such structures is that the *agent* of the complement is the *manipulee* of the main verb.

Syntactically, the manipulee bears an *object* relation to the main verb. But there is no syntactic evidence to support the contention that the manipulee retains subject relation to the complement verb:[49]

(105) a.   She **told** Marvin **to wash** the dishes
      b.   He **made** Susan **quit** her job

In SOV languages, the main causative verb in DS complementation always winds up adjacent to the complement verb. As an illustration of this, consider the following from Ute (Givón 1980):

(106)

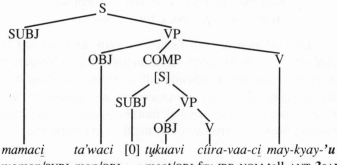

*mamaci_*   *ta'waci* [0] *ty_kuavi* *ciira-vaa-ci_ may-kyay-'u*
woman/SUBJ man/OBJ   meat/OBJ fry-IRR-NOM tell-ANT-**3sAN**
'The woman told the man to fry the meat'

The adjacency of the main and complement verbs makes co-lexicalization, and thus clause union, only a matter of time — provided the main verb grammaticalizes semantically.[50] This has in fact occurred in the morphological causative in Ute:

(107)

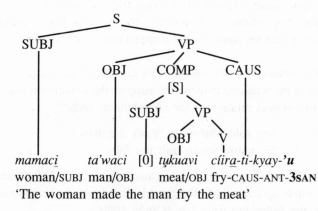

*mamaci_*   *ta'waci* [0] *ty_kuavi* *ciira_-ti-kyay-'u*
woman/SUBJ man/OBJ   meat/OBJ fry-CAUS-ANT-**3sAN**
'The woman made the man fry the meat'

The syntactic structure given in (107) is actually too abstract, since clause union leaves us a complex bi-transitive verb with two objects — one the causee, the other the patient of 'fry':

(108)

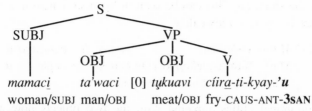

> *mamaci* *ta'waci* [0] *tykuavi* *ciira-ti-kyay-'u*
> woman/SUBJ man/OBJ meat/OBJ fry-CAUS-ANT-**3SAN**
> 'The woman made the man fry the meat'

Neither overt coding nor behavior-and-control tests can show that the two objects bear their respective object relations to anything but the same unified causative verb.

By several syntactic criteria, the two surface objects in Ute are not on a par, neither in causative constructions nor in other double-object constructions. First, their order is rigid, with the more topical human causee preceding the inanimate patient. Second, the more topical, fronted causee lays claim to object agreement. Thus compare:

(109) *mamaci *tykuavi* *ta'waci* *ciira-ti-kyay-ax*
  woman/SUBJ meat/OBJ man/OBJ fry-CAUS-ANT-**3SINAN**

The same constraint is seen in other two-object constructions in Ute, as with the obligatorily-promoted benefactive NP. That NP must be the direct object, must command object agreement, and must precede the patient object:

(110) a. **Simple transitive clause:**
  mamaci *tykuavi* *ciira-qa-ax*
  woman/SUBJ meat/OBJ fry-ANT-**3SINAN**
  'The woman fried the meat'

  b. *mamaci* *ta'waci* *tykuavi* *ciira-ku-qay-'u*
  woman/SUBJ man/OBJ meat/OBJ fry-**BEN**-ANT-**3SAN**
  'The woman fried the meat for the man'

  c. *mamaci *tykuavi* *ta'waci* *ciira-ku-qay-ax*
  woman/SUBJ meat/OBJ man/OBJ fry-**BEN**-ANT-**3SINAN**

In embedding SVO languages, the situation is compounded a bit by the fact that there is no automatic adjacency in DS-complementation (see (105b) above). But over time, a VO languages can affect **predicate raising** to remedy the situation. This can be seen in Spanish, where in a sense the two verbs are ready to co-lexicalize:

> (111) *María **se-la**-hizo*   *comer la manzana **a**   Juan*
> Mary   **him-it**-make/PRET/3s eat/INF the apple   DAT John
> 'Mary made John eat the apple'

The pronominal clitics agreeing with the two objects now appear at the beginning of the verbal complex, regardless of the fact that 'apple' is the patient of 'eat'. And there is no morpho-syntactic evidence that the two objects bear their respective grammatical relations to two different verbs, or partake in two different VPs.

Clause-union in embedding languages is often a matter of degree. In general, the syntactic integration of the complement clause into the main clause involves four structural features (Givón 1990a: ch. 13):

> (112) **Structural features of clause integration:**
>   a. co-lexicalization of the two verbs
>   b. the relation integration of the agent-of-complement (causee) into the main clause
>   c. the morphology — finite/non-finite — of the complement verb
>   d. separation between the clauses by a subordinator or pause

These sub-components tend to exhibit strong association, so that creating a clear grammatical case-role for the causee — agent of the complement clause — inside the main clause is but one facet of clause union. In general, implicative verbs of manipulation ('make', 'cause', 'force'), whose complement event is co-temporal with the main event, are more likely to be co-lexicalized with their complements; while non-implicative verbs ('tell', 'order', 'ask') are less likely. On the scale of event-and-clause integration, causative and resultative constructions are ranked at the very top. And **morphological causatives** arise as the natural clause union consequence of the complementation of causative verbs.

While the causee in morphological causatives indeed bears a grammatical object relation to the combined causative verb, its exact case marking is open to considerable cross-language variation. Comrie (1976) has suggested a universal syntactic **bumping hierarchy** by which the causee occupies the highest available object relation that is not yet occupied by semantic objects of the complement verb:

(113) DO > IO > OBL

Thus in French, if the complement is intransitive, the causee is marked as DO. If the complement is transitive, the causee is marked as dative. And if the complement is bi-transitive, the causee is marked as an oblique agent-of-passive (Comrie 1976):

(114) a. *Je ferai   courir **Henriette***
        I make/FUT run/INF **Henriette/DO**
        'I'll make H. run'

     b. *Je ferai   manger les gateaux **à**   Henriette*
        I make/FUT eat/INF the cakes   DAT Henriette
        'I'll make H. eat the cookies'

     c. *Je ferai   écrir une lettre   au   directeur **par** Jean*
        I make/FUT write a   letter/DO DAT/the director **by** John
        'I'll make Jean write a letter to the director'

But as both Comrie (1976) and Cole (1976/1984) point out, many other variants of causee case-marking are possible, including doubling on the direct-object case, doubling on the dative case, and more. A well known case in Japanese illustrates semantic control over the choice of case-role: Accusative when the causee has less control, dative when it retains more control:[51]

(115) a. *Oji-ga   Odette-o   odor-**ase**-ta*
        Prince-SUBJ Odette-ACC dance-CAUS-PAST
        'The prince made Odette dance'

     b. *Oji-ga   Odette-**ni**   odor-**ase**-ta*
        Prince-SUBJ Odette-ACC dance-CAUS-PAST
        'The prince let Odette dance'

Less acknowledged perhaps is the fact that when case-doubling occurs, the behavior-and-control properties of the like-coded objects are rather different. As noted throughout, surface morphology does not disclose the entire story of grammatical relations. We have already seen one such a case in Ute (examples (108), (109), (110) above). A more extensive example may be seen in the double-object bi-transitive clauses in Bantu. In such clauses, only one of the objects — the more topical human dative/benefactive — can occupy the post-verbal DO position, and only that object controls object agreement. Thus, in Swahili:

(116) a. *Watoto wa-li-m-p-ia*   *Juma kitabu*
children they-PAST-**him**-give-BEN Juma book
'The children gave Juma a book'

    b. **watoto wa-li-m/ki-p-ia*   *kitabu Juma*
children they-PAST-**him/it**-give-BEN book   Juma

    c. **watoto wa-li-ki-p-ia*   *Juma kitabu*
children they-PAST-**it**-give-BEN Juma book

Further, only the dative/benefactive object is accessible to passivization, which is promotional in Bantu. And once the dative/benefactive becomes the subject, the patient DO controls object agreement, and the agent is demoted to *chômeur*:

(117) a. *Juma a-li-ki-p-i-wa*   *kitabu (kwa watoto)*
Juma he-PAST-**it**-give-BEN-PASS book   (by   children)
'Juma was given the book (by the children)'

    b. **kitabu ki-li-m-p-i-wa*   *Juma (kwa watoto)*
book   **it**-PAST-**him**-five-BEN-PASS Juma (by   children)

    c. **Juma a-li-wa-p-i-wa*   *kitabu (kwa watoto)*
Juma he-PAST-**them**-give-BEN-PASS book   (by   children)

When a double-object construction arises in Swahili via morphological causativization, exactly the same discrimination between the two objects is observed, with the human causee claiming both the post-verbal position and control of object agreement:

(118) a. *Juma a-li-ki-soma*   *kitabu*
Juma he-PAST-it-read book
'Juma read the book'

    b. *wa-li-m-som-esha*   *Juma kitabu*
they-PAST-**him**-read-CAUS Juma book
'They made Juma read a/the book'

c. *wa-li-**ki**-som-esha*   *Juma kitabu*
   they-PAST-**it**-read-CAUS Juma book

d. *wa-li-**ki**/**m**-som-esha*   *kitabu Juma*
   they-PAST-**it**/**him**-read-CAUS book   Juma

And again, only the causee is now accessible to passivization:

(119) a. *Juma a-li-**ki**-som-esh-wa*   *kitabu (kwa watoto)*
         Juma he-PAST-**it**-read-CAUS-PASS book   (by   children)'
         'Juma was made to read a book (by the children)'

   b. **Kitabu ki-li-**m**-som-esh-wa*   *Juma (kwa watoto)*
      book   he-PAST-**it**-read-CAUS-PASS Juma (by   children)

   b. **Juma a-li-**wa**-som-esh-wa*   *kitabu (kwa watoto)*
      Juma he-PAST-**them**-read-CAUS-PASS book   (by   children)

Clause union in an embedding language thus forces the same kind of hierarchized grammatical relations as one finds in such languages in multi-object main clauses. Having a single co-lexicalized verb and having an integrated set of grammatical relations thus seem to go hand in hand.

Note, finally, that clause union is fundamentally a diachronic process. As elsewhere in grammaticalization, the semantic component of clause union — grammaticalized verb and cognitive event integration — come on line first and rapidly, outpacing the much slower and gradual syntactic realignment (Givón 1975, 1991; Heine et al. 1990). During this gradual process, intermediate stages can display considerable sensitivity to various semantic factors. An example from Spanish causative clause union may illustrate this. When the underlying patient of the complement verb is non-human, predicate raising and thus full clause union proceed seemingly to full co-lexicalization of the two verbs:

(120) *se-**la**-hizieron   comer la manzana a   Juan*
      him-it-made/3p eat/INF the apple   DAT Juan
      'They made John eat the apple'

When the underlying patient is human, the potential for case-role confusion is apparently real enough to block full clause union. The causee is now placed between the two verbs, thus effectively nullifying predicate raising. In the resulting construction, each object follows its semantically-proper verb, with object agreement likewise dispersing:[52]

(121) a. *le-hizieron   a   María pegar-le   a   Juan*
          her-made/3p DAT Maríahit/INF-**him** DAT Juan
          'They made Maria hit Juan'

     b. ***se-le**-hizieron   pegar a   María a   Juan*
          her-him-made/3p hit/INF DAT María DAT Juan

8.2.2.2. Switch-subject (DS) clause union in serializing languages

In a rather obvious way, serializing languages again fail here to create true clause union. Of the four syntactic devices universally used to code clause-integration (112), serializing languages skip three:

a.   They tend to keep the multi-verbs in the serial clause apart, so that they do not co-lexicalize (112a)

b.   They tend to keep the objects apart with their respective verbs or even VPs, so that several object may bear the same grammatical relation within the clause — each to its own verb or VP (112b)

c.   They often do not concentrate all finite morphology on one verb and mark the rest as non-finite (112c).

The only structural device serializing languages use consistently to indicate clause integration is the lack of subordinator or pause (112d).

With respect to the subject relation, serializing languages stand on a par with embedding languages, facing the same problem in the analysis of switch-subject (DS) marged clauses. Thus, consider again the resultative DS-serial construction:

(122) a. **Akan** (Osam 1993, This volume):
          Esi yi-i   tam-no fi-i   pon-no-don
          Esi take-PAST cloth-the **leave**-PAST table-the-on
          'Esi took the cloth **off** the table'
          (*Hist.*: 'Esi took the clause and *it* left the table')

     b. **Miskitu** (Hale 1991):
          *Yang truk-kum atk-**ri**   wa-**n***
          I   truck-a   sell-**DS/1** go-**PAST/3**
          'I sold the truck away'
          (*Hist.*: 'I sold the truck and *it* went')

   c. **Tok Pisin** (Givón 1991):

      . . . em layt nau paya i-kamap . . .

         she light now fire PRED-come.up

      '. . . She lights the fire . . .'

      (*lit.*: 'She lights the fire and *it* comes up')

   d. **Tok Pisin** (Givón 1991):

      . . . em tromwey sospan i-go . . .

         she threw.away saucepan PRED-go

      'She threw the saucepan away'

      (*lit.*: 'She threw the saucepan and *it* went')

   e. **Kalam** (Givón 1991):

      *. . . mon d-angiy-**ek**   yin-**ip** . . .*

         wood take-light-PAST/SEQ/DS/3s burn-PERF/3s

      '. . . She lights the wood . . .'

      (*lit.*: 'She takes and lights the wood and *it* burns')

In all of these examples, the object of the first verb is semantically the subject of the second. But no syntactic test, aside from SR morphology, can show that the object NP is anything but a grammatical object in the serial clause.

The same also applies to causative constructions in serializing languages:

(123) a. **Supyire** (Carlson 1990):

      *mii à   u   **karima** à   ngukuu **lyi***

      I   PERF him **force** PERF chicken **eat**

      'I forced him to eat the chicken'

      (*lit.*: 'I forced him and *he* ate the chicken')

   b. **Ijo** (Williamson 1965):

      *woni u   mie-**ni**   indi die-**mi***

      we   him make-ASP fish share-ASP

      'We made him share the fish'

      (*lit.*: 'We made him and *he* shared the fish')

   c. **Ijo** (Williamson 1965):

      *ari u   mie mu-**mi***

      I   him make go-ASP

      'I chased him away'

      (*lit.*: 'I chased him and *he* went')

And likewise with the limited serial-resultative pattern in English:

(124) a. They shot him dead
          ('They shot him and *he* is dead')
      b. They struck him dumb
          ('They struck him and *he* became dumb')
      c. She broke the box open
          ('She broke it so that *it* opened')
      d. He packed/stuffed it full of rocks
          ('He packed/stuffed it and *it* is full of rocks')
      e. She wiped/rubbed it dry/clean
          ('She wiped/rubbed it and *it* is dry/clean')
      f. They pried the door open
          ('They pried the door and *it* is open')

A 'deep' syntactic representation of such DS-serial clauses as embedded subordinate structures, along the lines proposed by Byrne (1987, 1992), would be:

(125) a. **Switch-subject (DS) serial clause:**
          Esi yi-i   tam-no   fi-i   pon-no-don
          Esi take-PAST cloth-the **leave-PAST** table-the-on
          'Esi took the cloth **off** the table'
      b. **'Deep' syntactic representation:**

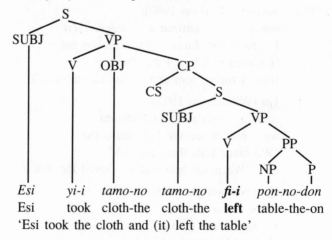

          Esi   yi-i   tamo-no   tamo-no   fi-i   pon-no-don
          Esi   took   cloth-the cloth-the **left** table-the-on
          'Esi took the cloth and (it) left the table'

But what exactly does structure (125b) represent? Surely it could not represent the synchronic *syntactic* structure, since synchronically (125a) is a single clause with a single subject. Neither could it represent the synchronic *semantic* structure, since — with the exception of true causative constructions like (123) — the second verb in our DS-serial clauses of the type (125) is semantically grammaticalized. It has no verbal meaning but rather prepositional meaning. And there is not sense in which any NP in the clause is its semantic subject. Finally, structure (125b) cannot represent the *diachronic* precursor — syntactic *or* semantic — of the DS-serial clause (125a) because that precursor was a chained (coordinate) structure rather than embedded (subordinate) one.

One must conclude then, however reluctantly, that grammatical relations in serial clauses cannot be squeezed into the syntactic mould of embedding languages. The two types exhibit genuine differences in their syntactic structure. Complete clause union, with co-lexicalized verbs and total re-alignment of grammatical relations, often does not occur in serializing languages, or at least not to the same extent as it does in embedding languages. At the very least, multiple object relations survive the condensation into a single clause. By all available syntactic tests, serial clauses tend to display multiple verbs, multiple direct-objects, and thus multiple VPs (Sebba 1987) long after one or more of the verbs have grammaticalized, semantically or even morphology.

As for the subject relation, clause union in serializing languages does indeed occur. So that by all available syntactic tests serial clauses have a single grammatical subject. In the case of DS-serial clauses, this single grammatical subject is the 'underlying' semantic subject of only the *first* verb. It bears its grammatical relation — and the pragmatic function of main clausal topic — not to individual verbs or VPs in the complex clause, but rather to the entire merged clause. Which makes a considerable amount of sense in light of the strong parsimonious tendency in human discourse to have only one topical referent per clause.[53]

8.2.3. *Degree of grammaticalization and re-analysis of grammatical relations*

There is a certain correlation, albeit not a perfect one, between the degree of semantic grammaticalization of the main verb and the re-alignment of

grammatical relations in clause union. Consider first the contrast between
the non-grammaticalized verb 'want' and the grammaticalized modal 'will'
in English:

(126) a. I **want to** eat the apple
      b. *The apple **wants to** be eaten
      c. I **will** eat the apple
      d. The apple **will** be eaten

Historically, 'will' meant 'want' and selected a *dative* subject. It also had
the same syntactic properties as 'want', so that (126b) would have been
equally implausible then. Only when 'will' became semantically bleached
and lost its earlier selectional restrictions could the patient/object of the
complement verb be promoted to the subject of the passive clause (126d).
But now it is not a selected subject of the modal 'will', but rather a selected
patient-subject of the passive 'be eaten'.

In the same vein, compare the behavior of the grammaticalized modal
'can' with its non-grammaticalized semantic equivalent 'be able to':

(127) a. She **was able** to eat the apple
      b. *The apple **was able** to be eaten
      c. She **can** eat the apple
      d. The apple **can** be eaten

Similarly, compare the long-grammaticalized progressive auxiliary 'be' with
the more recently grammaticalizing 'keep', 'finish', 'stop' and 'resume':

(128) a. He **was** fixing the roof
      b. The roof **was** being fixed
      c. He **kept** fixing the roof
      d. ??The roof **kept** being fixed
      e. He **finished** washing the dishes
      f. ??The dishes **finished** being washed
      g. She **stopped** writing her memoirs
      h. ??Her memoirs **stopped** being written
      i. She **resumed** writing her memoirs
      j. ??Her memoirs **resumed** being written

Likewise, consider the slightly less clear contrast between the long-
grammaticalized modal 'should' and its close semantic equivalent 'need to':

(129) a. They **should** build the house there
b. The house **should** be built there
c. They **need** to build the house there
d. ?The house **needs** to be built there

The fact that early grammaticalization of 'need' is in progress is evident from seeming acceptability of passive expressions such as:

(130) a. It **needs** to be done
b. This paper **needs** to be careful edited
c. His room **needs** to be cleaned

What we observe here is a correlation between the degree of grammaticalization of an erstwhile main verb and the completion of clause union. When a main verb is not fully grammaticalized, it continues to exert strong semantic — in this case animacy — restrictions on its subject. The lower-clause patient is semantically inadmissible as subject of the main verb. Nor is the complement-clause patient admissible as patient of the main verb, because the main verb does not take that type of a patient. Being inadmissible as a patient, the lower-clause object is also inadmissible as a main-clause *object*. It thus cannot be promoted to subject-of-passive in the *main* clause for two related reasons, one semantic, the other syntactic:

a. The main verb will not tolerate it semantically, neither as its agent nor as its patient.
b. As grammatical object of an embedded clause, it cannot be promoted to subject-of-passive in another clause.

When the erstwhile main-verb reaches full (semantic) grammaticalization, so that it exerts no selectional restrictions of its own, the erstwhile complement verb becomes — semantically — the main (and only) verb. Only then can the lower-verb patient bear an object relation within the unified clause — and thus become accessible to passivization.

9. Recapitulation

9.1. *The clustering approach to grammatical relations*

In spite of the immense cross-language diversity in the treatment of grammatical relations, a coherent set of general principles can be discerned. Those principles seem paradoxical until one adopts a **prototype** approach to grammatical categories. This approach recognizes the **clustering** of many features to determine subjecthood and objecthood, even when none of the features is by itself necessary or sufficient. Some of these features involve concrete (overt) coding properties; others involve more abstract behavior-and-control properties. In spite of the considerable potential for incoherent results inherent in this approach, the cross-language clustering of subject and object properties in fact yields strong generalizations:

  i.   The degree of overt coding of subject and object may vary, and this variation may be described as **degree of grammaticalization**.

  ii. Subject or object features that are more directly associated with underlying *pragmatic* function (topicality) are more likely to be universal, with an implicational hierarchy that extends Keenan's (1975, 1976) predictions:

> nominal case-marking
> grammatical agreement
> word order
> behavior-and-control features

  iii. A configurational account of grammatical relations, especially of grammatical subjecthood, is a woefully inadequate formal means of accounting for the actual syntactic facts.

9.2. *Ergativity and grammatical relations*

In most ergative languages, the discrepancy between universal predictions and language-specific facts is confined to nominal case-marking, the least universal feature of our cluster of relational properties. Even in the small number of "deep" ergative languages, where some behavior-and-control features deviate from the nominative organization principle, the deviations are partial, and the majority of syntactic rules still display nominative-accusative control. This reinforces our observation concerning the more universal nature of relational properties that are associated with the pragmatic function of subjects and objects.

9.3. *Serial verbs and grammatical relations*

There is no skirting the fact that verb-serializing languages retain, for a long time after clause-chains have condensed into single serial clauses, multi-object relational structure. In this sense, the multi-VP analysis of Sebba (1987) and Larson (1991) is indeed correct — with one glaring exception: The syntactic facts do not support a single VP-node analysis. A more abstract syntactic analysis, the one that attempts to view serialization as clausal embedding (Byrne 1987, 1992), turns out to account well for neither meaning nor syntax nor diachrony.

9.4. *Clause union and grammatical relations*

The difference between clause embedding vs. clause chaining represents a profound typological dichotomy in the diachronic pathways languages can take toward clause union. In embedding languages, clause union is achieved much more completely, with a single, integrated set of grammatical relations and a single lexical verb that bears all finite verbal inflections. In serializing languages, clause union remains weaker and partial, allowing for the retention — often for a long time — of multi-verb, multi-object, and thus multi-VP structures. This **syntactic scattering**, however, does not affect the grammatical subject, for a reason that is partially diachronic: Clause-chains are overwhelmingly **equi-topic**, even when interlaced with an occasional switch-topic (DS) clause. The condensation process in clause union thus tends to yield a single-topic clause, and therefore also a single-subject clause.

Notes

*   I am indebted to Marlene Haboud for comments on the Spanish data; to Jiffi Arboleda for the Tagalog data; to John Haiman for a critical reading of an earlier draft of this work; and most of all to the various participants in this volume for access to their data. An earlier version of this paper appeared as ch. 5 of my "Functionalism and Grammar" (1995).

1. I use the term "processes" in a lame attempt to circumvent the naive cognitive interpretation of complex structures as "derived" — by various "transformations" — from underlying simple structures. Chomsky's distinction between performance and competence makes it relatively easy to view the derivational metaphor as a formal convenience, an entity in the realm of competence with no implied consequences in the realm of performance. Still, the tendency to extend the reach of the derivational metaphor beyond the realm of the formal model persists. This is, one suspects, a natural outcome of taking theoretical models seriously, i.e. assuming that they have real empirical consequences.

2. See Givón (1984a).

3. The mischief is by no means limited to formal grammarians. Thus, Li and Thompson's (1976) much cited typology of "topic prominent" vs. "subject prominent" languages is founded on the selection of morphology — nominal case-marking and grammatical agreement — as the criteria for subjecthood, relegating all other criteria to irrelevance.

4. Most immediately relevant are Rosch (1973, 1975), Rosch and Mervis (1975), Rosch and Lloyd (1978). But see also Posner and Keele (1968), Tversky (1969, 1975), Hyman and Frost (1975), Posner (1986), or Givón (1986), _inter alia_.

5. This predicament has plagued the study of categories at least since Aristotle, who attempted a less-than-elegant solution to the problem by assigning categorial rigidity to the synchronic medium of "forms", while relegating inter-categorial diachronic flux to another medium, the _synolon_ (Tweedale 1986). Another reflection of this problem is seen in the distribution of attended vs. automated processing (Givón 1989: ch. 7, 1995: ch. 8). Automated processing is more heavily dependent on rigid categories, and is in general faster, less error-prone, and less context sensitive.

6. The fact that the majority of verbs in a language may require an agentive subject is not a good argument for suggesting that agentivity is a diagnostic subject-property, and the opposite is in fact expected if one is to adopt our criterion of dissociation (cf. (1), (2) above). The subjects of non-agentive verbs in either nominative or ergative languages do not display fewer of subject properties — either functional or formal — than the subjects of transitive verbs. If anything, in some ergative language the absolutive subjects of intransitive clauses display _more_ subject properties than the ergative subjects of transitive clauses (see section 6. below).

7. See Hawkinson and Hyman (1974); Givón (1976a, 1979a: ch. 4, 1992); _inter alia_. This more elaborate chain of theoretical arguments resembles an **explanation** more than it does a **reduction**, although the difference between the two is often a matter of degree.

8. See discussion of markedness of clause-types in Givón (1995: ch. 2). Obviously not all "non-basic" clauses have reduced subject properties. Most typical in this respects are passives (Keenan 1975), inverses (Givón 1995: ch. 3), and existential-presentatives (Hetzron 1971; Bresnan and Kanerva 1988; Bresnan 1993).

9. The substantive claim that the subject in any language is somehow less "topic prominent" has never been defended, nor is it likely to stand, given the mountain of data suggesting that the functional correlates of grammatical subjecthood — Keenan's "reference properties" — are the most universal of all subject properties; see Givón (1983), Cooreman (1988), as well as Givón (1995: ch. 3).

10. For the classification of Machiguenga and Arawak see David Payne (1991).

11. The Machiguenga examples below are all taken from texts collected and analyzed by Betty Snell (in personal communication).

12. Raj Shresta (in personal communication).

13. For a comprehensive discussion of the typology of REL-clauses see Givón (1990a: ch. 15), where sources for all the data in this section are cited.

14. The slight difference involves the fact that in KinyaRwanda the subject pronominal agreement on the verb for 3rd-person singular human takes one form in main clauses (*y*-) and another form in subject REL-clauses (*u*-). For other genders, the difference is only in tone. In Hebrew, on the other hand, the same pronominal form is used on the verb in both main and relative clauses.

15. One can assume that the nominative interpretation of Philippine grammar, as in Schachter (1976) or Givón (1979a: ch. 4), represents an earlier diachronic stage. An ergative interpretation (cf. Brainard, in this volume) converts the Philippine promotional system from promotion to subject (i.e. inversion) to promotion to DO; in which case the interaction between promotion and relativization now resembles that of KinyaRwanda.

16. For further discussion of Ute relativization see Givón (1990: ch. 14), where the sources for all the data in this section are cited.

17. Again interpreted as a nominative language.

18. See Givón (1976a).

19. One may argue that datives and benefactives in Ute are "obligatorily promoted" to direct object, a situation reminiscent of that in Bantu and Mayan.

20. In English, promotion to DO is optional and applicable primarily to dative and benefactive objects. In terms of text frequency, however, the vast majority of datives and benefactives appear as direct objects (Givón 1984a).

21. Pronominal agreement in active clauses in Ute can be controlled by either the subject or the object, so that it is irrelevant to grammatical relations. But plural agreement on the verb is controlled by the subject, and is thus relevant.

22. The story is a bit more complicated, since in all three the frequency of zero subjects is no doubt much higher than that of zero objects, due to the much higher probability of subject continuity (Givón 1983; Pu, in this volume).

23. See Keenan (1976) and, more explicitly, Givón (1979a: ch. 4, 1984b, 1990).

24. For identifying the 'ritualization' and 'emancipation' of grammar with grammatical-

ization see Haiman (1991). For the connection between grammaticalization and automaticity, see Givón (1979a: ch. 5, 1989: ch. 7). Haiman tends to over-estimate the degree to which grammar can become emancipated from function.

25.   See e.g. Givón (1979a: chapter 6: "Where does crazy syntax come from?").

26.   From Raj Shresta (in personal communication).

27.   When interpreted as a nominative pattern, this Philippine language then exhibits subject agreement in the active and double agreement in the passive/inverse (Keenan 1976: 330).

28.   See discussion of Kimbundo in Givón (1995: ch. 3).

29.   For the rise of verb-agreement from independent pronouns see Givón (1976a). Many ergative clauses arise diachronically from erstwhile inverse constructions, as was probably the case in Kapampangan and Nez Perce (see above). Their verb-agreement pattern thus often reflects the morphology of the source inverse clause (see again Givón 1995: ch. 3).

30.   For the pragmatics of word order see Givón (1988, 1992).

31.   This was for a while challenged for "deep" ergative languages such as Dyirbal, where Dixon (1972) claimed that the absolutive object is the clausal topic. However, a text-based measure of the topicality of the agents and patients in Dyirbal transitive clauses (Cooreman 1988) settled the issue, as it was settled for another Australian ergative language (Tsunoda 1985, 1987), as well as for several Philippine languages such as Tagalog (Cooreman et al. 1984), Cebuano (T. Payne 1994) or Karao (Brainard 1994b).

32.   This cannot be supported by a hard count, but the most common examples mentioned are Dyirbal, Eskimo and Philippine languages. One could probably add to this at least some Indonesian languages, such as Indonesian and Balinese. My own impression is that the common denominator here is a relatively recent shift to ergativity, whereby the absolutive-controlled behavior-and-control properties of ergative clauses are really a leftover of a *nominative*-control in an inverse/passive clause, i.e. a patient-topicalizing clause. The absolutive control of grammatical properties in a "deep" ergative clause makes perfect sense as an instance of nominative pattern in a passive/inverse clause.

33.   Jiffy Arboleda (in personal communication).

34.   *Ibid.*

35.   For ergativity in Philippine languages see T. Payne (1983, 1994), Cooreman et al. (1984), Brainard (1994a, 1994b, in this volume) *inter alia*.

36.   The lone exception to that has been reported in ChiChewa (Trithart 1977), where an L-dislocated — topicalized — object of the complement can be raised to object of the main clause.

37.   Brainard (1994a, in this volume) reports no raising of a subject of any kind — erga-

tive or absolutive. But this may be an accidental gap, given that all her examples are text-derived.

38. The Karao data are somewhat simplified below in terms of morphophonemics and criticization. All verbs are in the imperfective (irrealis) mode.

39. Since pseudo-cleft is a relative-clause pattern, one could surmise that relativization in Karao may have also been absolutive-controlled till recently. In Bikol this is still the case. If Bikol turns turns out to behave like Karao in zero anaphora control, that would make it a "deeper" ergative by one more syntactic property (relativization). In Tagalog, on the other hand, zero-anaphora can be controlled by either the absolutive or the nominative, with nominative control predominating in discourse (Cooreman et al. 1984).

40. These two epithets are the ones most frequently used for dismissing recalcitrant facts in current GB and in the early 1960's GG, respectively.

41. See discussion in Givón (1995: ch. 4). For some of the formal accounts, see Larson (1991), Sebba (1987), Byrne (1987, 1992).

42. In a subsequent paper, Byrne (1992) recognizes this discrepancy formally by proposing two separate tree-diagrams for some serial constructions, one to account for the syntax, the other for the semantics. In both diagrams, however, each verb must be dominated by a clausal (S) node.

43. Larson (1991) dropped the necessity for a clause node for each serial phrase, retaining a lower VP node for it, along the lines suggested in (79a,b) above.

44. Inanimate pronouns are *zero* in Akan, with minor exceptions.

45. The scope of the final *no* 'the', which must bracket the REL-clause, is the entire relative clause rather than the indefinite 'money'.

46. This semantic account captures only the diachronically-prior meaning of the grammaticalized 'finish', but not the diachronically-prior chained (coordinate) structure. Both the meaning of the verb (verb to aspect) and the structural configuration (chained to single clause) have been modified by grammaticalization. Byrne's account is neither semantically not syntactically adequate (see further below).

47. These are of course not the only possible configurations in serializing language, so that in some cases verb-adjacency can occur — when a single-verb serial phrase precedes the semantic main verb in a VO language, or follows it in an OV language. Thus compare for Saramaccan (VO) (Byrne 1987):

> de ke **go wasi** di wagi
> they want **go wash** the car
> 'They want to go (and) wash the car'

And for Supyire (OV) (Carlson 1989):

> fyinga à pyi à mpii **jo** à **kwo,**
> python PERF be PERF those **swallow** PERF **finish**
> 'The python had finished swallowing those ...'

48.   See Givón (1990: ch. 13).

49.   The seeming exceptions turn out to be non-reduced subjunctive complements, where
       no clause union is involved, as in Spanish:

       María dijo a Juan que se-fuera
       Maria said to Juan SUB REFL-go/SUBJUN/3s
       'Mary told John that he should leave'

       Or Hebrew:

       Hi amra lo   she-hu ye-lex   lo
       she told   DAT/3sm SUB-he 3sm-go/IRR DAT/3sm
       'She told him that he should leave'

50.   In Yaqui, another Uto-Aztecan language, all complement-taking main verb co-lexical-
       ize with their complement verbs (Givón 1990: ch. 13).

51.   Atsuko Hayashi (in personal communication); see general discussion in Cole (1976/1984).

52.   Marleen Haboud (in personal communication).

53.   See Givón (1992, 1995: ch. 8).

54.   See Givón (1990b).

References

Anderson, S. 1976. "On the notion of subject in ergative languages." In *Subject and
    Topic*, C.N. Li (ed.). New York: Academic Press.
Brainard, S. 1994a. "Ergativity and grammatical relations in Karao." In *Karao Gram-
    mar*, S. Brainard. PhD dissertation, University of Oregon, Eugene (ms).
Brainard, S. 1994b "Voice and ergativity in Karao." In *Voice and Inversion*, T. Givón
    (ed.). Amsterdam: John Benjamins [Typological Studies in Language 28].
Bresnan, J. 1993. "Locative inversion and the architecture of UG." Stanford University
    (ms).
Bresnan, J. and J.M. Kanerva. 1988. "Locative inversion in ChiChewa: A case study of
    factorization in grammar." Stanford University (ms).
Byrne, F. 1987. *Grammatical Relations in a Radical Creole*. Amsterdam: John Ben-
    jamins [Creole Language Library 3].
Byrne, F. 1992. "Tense, scope and spreading in Saramaccan." *Journal of Pidgin and
    Creole Languages* 7.2.
Carlson, R. 1989. *A Grammar of Supyire: Kampwo Dialect*. PhD dissertation, University
    of Oregon, Eugene (ms).
Cole, P. 1976/1984. "The treatment of the causee in universal grammar." *I.J.A.L.*
Comrie, B. 1973. "The ergative: Variations on a theme." *Lingua* 32.
Comrie, B. 1976. "The syntax of causative constructions: Cross language similarities

and divergences." In *The Grammar of Causative Constructions, Syntax and Semantics* 6, M. Shibatani (ed.). New York: Academic Press.

Comrie, B. 1977. "Ergativity." University of So. California (ms).

Cooreman, A. 1982. "Topicality, ergativity and transitivity in narrative discourse: Evidence from Chamorro." *Studies in Language* 6.3.

Cooreman, A. 1985. *Transitivity and Discourse Continuity in Chamorro Narrative*. PhD dissertation, University of Oregon, Eugene (ms).

Cooreman, A. 1988. "Ergativity in Dyirbal discourse." *Lingua* 26.

Cooreman, A., B. Fox and T. Givón. 1984. "The discourse definition of ergativity." *Studies in Language* 8:1.

Craig, C. 1977. *The Structure of Jacaltec*. Austin: University of Texas Press.

Craig, C. (ed.) 1986. *Categorization and Noun Classification*. Amsterdam: John Benjamins [Typological Studies in Language 7].

Dahlstrom, A. 1986. *Plains Cree Morphosyntax*, PhD dissertation, UC Berkeley (ms).

Dixon, R.M.W. 1972. *The Dyirbal Language of North Queensland*, Cambridge: Cambridge University Press.

Fillmore, C. 1968. "The case for the case." In *Universals of Linguistic Theory*, E. Bach and R.T. Harms (eds). New York: Holt, Rinehart and Winston.

Givón, T. 1971. "Historical syntax and synchronic morphology: An archaeologist's field trip." *CLS* 7, University of Chicago: Chicago Linguistics Society.

Givón, T. 1973. "The time-axis phenomenon." *Language* 49.4.

Givón, T. 1975. "Serial verbs and syntactic change: Niger-Congo." In *Word Order and Word Order Change*, C. Li (ed.). Austin: University of Texas Press.

Givón, T. 1976a. "Topic, pronoun and grammatical agreement." In C.N. Li (ed.). 1976.

Givón, T. 1976b. "Some constraints on Bantu causativization." In *The Grammar of Causative Constructions, Syntax and Semantics* 6, M. Shibatani (ed.). New York: Academic Press.

Givón, T. 1979a. *On understanding Grammar*. New York: Academic Press.

Givón, T. (ed.) 1979b. *Discourse and Syntax, Syntax and Semantics* 12. New York: Academic Press.

Givón, T. (1980a) *Ute Reference Grammar*, Ignacio, CO: Ute Press.

Givón, T. (ed.) 1983. *Topic Continuity in Discourse: Quantified Cross-Language Studies*. Amsterdam: John Benjamins [Typological Studies in Language 3].

Givón, T. 1984a. "Direct object and dative shifting: The semantics and pragmatics of case." In *Objects*, F. Plank (ed.). New York/London: Academic Press.

Givón, T. 1984b. *Syntax: A Functional-Typological Introduction*, vol. I. Amsterdam: John Benjamins.

Givón, T. 1986. "Categories and prototypes: Between Plato and Wittgenstein." In *Categorization and Noun Classification*, C. Craig (ed.). Amsterdam: John Benjamins [Typological Studies in Language 7].

Givón, T. 1988. "The pragmatics of word order flexibility." In *Typology and Language Universals*, E. Moravcsik et al. (eds). Amsterdam: John Benjamins [Typological Studies in Language 17].

Givón, T. 1989. *Mind, Code and Context: Essays in Pragmatics*, Hillsdale, NJ: Erlbaum.

Givón, T. 1990a. *Syntax: A Functional-Typological Introduction*, vol. II. Amsterdam: John Benjamins.

Givón, T. 1990b. "Ute reflexives, complementation and clause integration." In *Development and Diversity: Linguistic Variation Across Time and Space*, J.A. Edmonson, C. Fagin and P. Mühlhäusler (eds). (C.J. Bailey Festschrift), Dallas: UT Arlington.

Givón, T. 1991. "Some substantive issues concerning verb serialization: Grammatical vs. cognitive packaging." In C. Lefebvre (ed.) 1991.

Givón, T. 1992. "The grammar of referential coherence as mental processing instructions." *Linguistics* 30.1.

Givón, T. (ed.) 1994. *Voice and Inversion*. Amsterdam: John Benjamins [Typological Studies in Language 28].

Givón, T. 1995. *Functionalism and Grammar*. Amsterdam: John Benjamins.

Gruber, J. 1965. *Studies in Lexical Relations*. PhD dissertation, MIT, Cambridge, Mass. (ms).

Haiman, J. 1991. "The bureaucratization of language." In *Linguistic Studies Presented to John L. Finlay*, H.C. Wolfart (ed.). Winnipeg: Algonquian and Iroquoian Linguistics [Memoir 8].

Hale, K. 1973. "Person marking in Walbiri." In *A Festschrift for Morris Halle*, New York: Holy, Rinehart and Winston.

Hale, K. 1991. "Misumalpan verb-sequencing constructions." In *Serial Verbs: Grammatical, Comparative and Cognitive Approaches*, C. Lefebvre (ed.). Amsterdam: John Benjamins [SSLS 8].

Hawkinson, A. and L. Hyman. 1974. "Natural topic hierarchies in Shona." *Studies in African Linguistics*.

Heine, B. 1993. *Auxiliaries: Cognitive Forces and Grammaticalization*. Oxford: Oxford University Press.

Heine, B., U. Claudi and F. Hünnemeyer. 1990. *Grammaticalization: A Conceptual Framework*, Chicago: University of Chicago Press.

Hetzron, R. 1971. "Presentative function and presentative movement." *Studies in African Linguistics*, supplement 2.

Hyman, R. and N.A.H. Frost. 1975. "Gradients and schema in pattern recognition." *Attention and Performance, V*, New York: Academic Press.

Kalmár, I. 1980. "The antipassive and grammatical relations in Eskimo." In *Ergativity: Toward a Theory of Grammatical Relations*, F. Plank (ed.). New York/London: Academic Press.

Keenan, E. 1975. "Some universals of passive in relational grammar." *CLS 11*. University of Chicago: Chicago Linguistics Society.

Keenan, E. 1976. "Toward a universal definition of 'subject'." In C.N. Li (ed.) 1976.

Kimenyi, A. 1976. *A Relational Grammar of KinyaRwanda*, PhD dissertation, UCLA.

Larson, R.K. 1991. "Some issues in verb serialization." In *Serial Verbs: Grammatical, Comparative and Cognitive Approaches*, C. Lefebvre (ed.). Amsterdam: John Benjamins [SSLS 8].

Lefebvre, C. (ed.). 1991. *Serial Verbs: Grammatical, Comparative and Cognitive. Approaches*. Amsterdam: John Benjamins [SSLS 8].

Li, C. (ed.). 1975. *Word Order and Word Order Change*. Austin: University of Texas Press.

Li, C.N. (ed.). 1976. *Subject and Topic*. New York: Academic Press.

Li, C.N. and S. Thompson. 1976. "Subject and topic: A new typology of language." In *Subject and Topic*, C.N. Li (ed.). New York: Academic Press.

Mejías-Bikandi, R. 1991. "Case marking in Basque." *International Journal of Basque Linguistics and Philology (ASJU)* XXV.2.

Osam, E.K. 1993. "Grammatical relations in Akan." University of Oregon, Eugene (ms).

Payne, David. 1991. "The classification of Maipuran (Arawakan) languages based on shared lexical retentions." *Handbook of Amazonian Languages*, vol. 3. The Hague: Mouton de Gruyter.

Payne, T. 1983. "Role and reference related subject properties and ergativity in Yúpik Eskimo and Tagalog." *Studies in Language* 6.1.

Payne, T. 1994. "The pragmatics of voice in a Philippine language: Actor-focus and goal-focus in Cebuano." In *Voice and Inversion*, T. Givón (ed.). Amsterdam: John Benjamins [Typological Studies in Language 28].

Posner, M. 1969. "Abstraction and the process of recognition." In *The Psychology of Learning and Motivation*, vol. 3, G.H. Bowers and J.T. Spence (eds). New York: Academic Press.

Posner, M. 1986. "Empirical studies of prototypes." In *Categorization and Noun Classification*, C. Craig (ed.). Amsterdam: John Benjamins [Typological Studies of Language 7].

Posner, M. and S. Keele. 1968. "On the genesis of abstract ideas." *Journal of Experimental Psychology* 77.

Rafferty, E. 1982. *Discourse Structure of the Chinese Indonesian of Malang*. Jakarta: Atma Jaya University [Linguistic Studies in Indonesian and Languages of Indonesia 12].

Rhodes, R. 1991. "The Algonquian inverse and grammatical relations." unpublished communication, UC Berkeley (ms).

Rosch, E. 1973. "Natural categories." *Cognitive Psychology* 4.

Rosch, E. 1975. "Human categorization." In *Advances in Cross-Cultural Psychology*, N. Warren (ed.). London: Academic Press.

Rosch, E. and C.B. Mervis. 1975. "Family resemblance: Studies in the internal structures of categories." *Cognitive Psychology* 7.

Rosch, E. and B. Lloyd (eds) 1978. *Cognition and Categorization*. Hillsdale, NJ: Erlbaum.

Rude, N. 1985. *Studies in Nez Perce Grammar and Discourse*, PhD dissertation, University of Oregon.

Rude, N. 1987. "Topicality, transitivity and the direct object in Nez Perce." *I.J.A.L.* 52.2.

Rude, N. 1991. "Origin of the Nez Perce ergative NP suffix." *I.J.A.L.* 57.1.

Rude, N. 1992. "Voice in Nez Perce and Sahaptin: Some functional differences." University of Oregon, Eugene (ms).

Schachter, P. 1976. "The subject in Philippine languages: Topic, actor, actor-topic or none of the above." In *Subject and Topic*, C.N. Li (ed.). New York: Academic Press.

Sebba, M. 1987. *The Syntax of Serial Verbs.* Amsterdam: John Benjamins [Creole Language Library 2].

Shibatani, M. (ed.) 1976. *The Grammar of Causative Constructions, Syntax and Semantics,* New York: Academic Press.

Shibatani, M. 1977. "Grammatical relations and surface case." *Language* 53.4.

Thompson, S. 1973. "Resultative verb compounds in Mandarin Chinese: A case for lexical rules." *Language* 49.2.

Trithart, L. 1977. *Relational Grammar and Chichewa Subjectivization Rules.* MA Thesis, Los Angeles: UCLA.

Tsunoda, T. 1985. "Ergativity and coreference in Warrungu discourse." *Nagoya University Working Papers in Linguistics* 1.

Tsunoda, T. 1987. "Ergativity, accusativity and topicality." *Nagoya University Working Papers in Linguistics* 2.

Tversky, B. 1969. "Pictorial and verbal encoding in a short-term memory task." *Perception and Psychophysics* 6.

Tversky, B. 1975. "Pictorial encoding of sentences in sentence-picture comparisons." *Quarterly Journal of Experimental Psychology* 27.

Tweedale, M. 1986. "How to handle problems about forms and universals in Aristotle's work." University of Auckland, NZ (ms).

Verhaar, J. 1985. "On iconicity and hierarchy." *Studies in Language* 9.1.

Wierzbicka, A. 1981. "Case marking and human nature." *Australian Journal of Linguistics* 1.

Williamson, K. 1965. *A Grammar of the Kolokuma Dialect of Ijo.* Cambridge: Cambridge University Press [West African Language Monograph 2].

Zavala, R. 1993. "Se les esta moviendo el tapete: Gramaticalización de verbos de movimiento en Akateko." 2do Encuentro de Linguistica en el Noroeste, Universidad de Sonora, Hermosillo (ms).

Zubin, D. 1972. *The German Case System: Exploitation of the Dative-Accusative Opposition Comment,* MA Thesis, Columbia University (ms).

Zubin, D. 1979. "Discourse function of morphology: The focus system in German." In *Discourse and Syntax, Syntax and Semantics* 12, T. Givón (ed.). New York: Academic Press.

Ergativity and Grammatical Relations in Karao

Sherri Brainard
Summer Institute of Linguistics

1. Introduction

This paper is an investigation of ergativity and grammatical relations in Karao, a language of the Northern Philippines.[1] In a previous study (Brainard 1994b), I have analyzed various clause types that encode semantically transitive verbs in Karao and have identified three voice constructions: active, passive and antipassive. I have also shown that Karao is unmistakably a morphologically ergative language. An important question for ergative languages is, what are the grammatical relations of the language?[2] This question is often coupled with a second one: What pattern of control do syntactic processes follow in these languages? For most morphologically ergative languages, syntactic processes follow a nominative pattern of control; that is, the most agentive argument of a transitive clause and the required argument of a single-argument clause control the majority of these processes (Anderson 1976; Comrie 1978; Dixon 1979).[3] This suggests that ergativity is a surface phenomenon that has no consequences for syntactic control. For a smaller number of morphologically ergative languages, syntactic processes follow a 'mixed' pattern of syntactic control (Van Valin 1981). That is, for some syntactic processes, the most agentive argument of a transitive clause and the required argument of a single-argument clause control the process; for other processes, the least agentive argument of a transitive clause and the required argument of a single-argument clause control the process. In a 'mixed' pattern then, each required argument of the transitive clause controls several syntactic processes, with neither argument controlling a significant

majority. For an exceptional few morphologically ergative languages, claims
have been made that syntactic processes follow an ergative pattern of control; that is, the least agentive argument of a transitive clause and the
required argument of a single-argument clause control the majority of the
syntactic processes. Syntactic processes in Dyirbal (Dixon 1972), in particular, have been presented as evidence that ergativity is not just a surface phenomenon, but a phenomenon that extends to syntactic control as well. The
question then is, what happens in Karao?

   To answer these questions, we will investigate the major coding properties and syntactic processes in Karao. In doing so, we will see that Karao
has two grammatical relations, a subject and an object, and displays a
'mixed' pattern of syntactic control.

2. Morphosyntax of the Karao voice system

Karao is a verb-initial language, and has a typical Philippine-type verbal
clause structure which has traditionally been called a 'voice system' or a
'focus system'. In a basic verbal clause, each NP is preceded by a case
marker: *'i* (*-y*), an absolutive marker; *na*, an ergative marker or an oblique
marker; or *cha* (*-d*), an oblique marker.[4,5] Every verbal clause has one
required NP that is preceded by the absolutive marker *'i*; the semantic role
of the absolutive NP is identified by an affix on the verb. Within Philippine
linguistics, the absolutive NP has been referred to as the 'nominative NP'
or the 'focused NP' or the 'topic'.

   It is important to note that in Philippine languages, verb affixes and
semantic roles do not have a one-to-one correspondence, and this is also
true for Karao. Consequently, one cannot assume that when the same affix
occurs on two different verbs, it identifies the same semantic role for the
absolutive NP.[6] For this study, I have identified semantic roles using labels
associated with a restricted version of localist case grammar developed by
DeLancey (1984, 1985, 1991), since this model provides a consistent and
revealing analysis of the semantic roles of Karao verbs.[7] Within DeLancey's version of localist case grammar, semantic roles are limited to Agent,
Theme, and Location. Agent is defined as the cause of the state or event
encoded in the verb; Theme is an entity that changes physical location or
state; Location is a physical site or a state.[8] The localist model also includes

'nonnuclear' arguments that are analyzed as core arguments of nonnuclear clauses that have been integrated into the nuclear clause; in Karao, the verb of such nonnuclear clauses is absent. Thus, Instrument and Associative are Nonnuclear Themes; Source and Beneficiary are Nonnuclear Locations. Fillmore-type semantic roles are also included here as a convenience for those unfamiliar with localist case grammar. The findings for grammatical relations and syntactic control in Karao are the same regardless of whether localist or Fillmore-type labels are used for semantic roles.

Verbs in Karao are usually marked for perfective or imperfective aspect.[9] Perfective aspect represents an event as a whole and is usually associated with completed events; imperfective aspect represents the internal structure of an event and is usually associated with events that have not been completed, including those that have not been initiated, and those that have been initiated but have not yet been completed. Verbs can also signal other aspects, such as continuous and habitual, and moods, such as intentional and abilitative. (See Brainard 1994b for details.)

An example of a basic intransitive clause in Karao is given in (1), and a basic transitive clause in (2).[10]

(1) *ʿonjoʿkow*   *ʿi*   *ngaʿnga*
   ʿon   *-joʿkow* *ʿi*   *ngaʿnga*
   ACT/TH/IMPFT-sleep   ABS child
   'The child will sleep'.

In (1), *joʿkow* 'to sleep' is a semantically intransitive verb that takes one argument: a Theme (Experiencer). The argument *ngaʿnga* 'child' is preceded by the absolutive marker *ʿi*; the verb affix *ʿon-* signals that the semantic role of the absolutive argument is Theme (Experiencer).

(2) *kapkafen*   *na toʿoy*   *mangka*
   kapkap -en   *na toʿo -ʿi*   *mangka*
   chop   -ACT/TH/IMPFT ERG person-ABS mango
   'The person will chop the mangoes'.

In (2), *kapkap* 'to chop' is a semantically transitive verb that takes two arguments: an Agent and a Theme (Patient). The argument *mangka* 'mango' is preceded by *-y*, an allomorph of the absolutive marker *ʿi*; the verb affix *-en* signals that the semantic role of the absolutive argument is Theme (Patient).

A comparison of the case markers in (1) and (2) shows that Karao has a typical ergative case-marking pattern: the single required argument in the intransitive clause in (1) and the least agentive argument in the transitive clause in (2) are preceded by the same marker, *ʿi* (or its allomorph *-y*), while the most agentive argument in the transitive clause is preceded by a different marker, *na*.

The clause in (2) is an example of the active voice construction in Karao. In Philippine linguistics, this clause type has been referred to as the 'goal-focus' or the 'goal-topic' construction. An example of the antipassive construction is given in (3), and the passive construction in (4).

(3) *mengapkap*   *ʿi*   *toʿo*   *na*   *mangka*
     meN   *-kapkap* *ʿi*   *toʿo*   *na*   *mangka*
     ACT/AG/IMPFT-chop   ABS person OBL mango
     'The person will chop some mangoes'.

In the antipassive construction, the most agentive argument, *toʿo* 'person', is preceded by the absolutive marker *ʿi*, and is cross-referenced by *meN-*, indicating that the absolutive NP is an Agent; the least agentive argument, *mangka* 'mango', has been demoted and is preceded by the oblique marker *na*.

(4) *mekapkap*   *ʿi*   *mangka*
     me   *-kapkap* *ʿi*   *mangka*
     PASS/IMPFT-chop   ABS mango
     'The mangoes will be chopped'.

In the passive construction, the least agentive argument, *mangka* 'mango', is preceded by the absolutive marker *ʿi*; the verb affix *me-* signals that the event is a state. Strictly speaking, *me-* does not have a semantic role morpheme as do most other verb affixes, and so does not identify the semantic role of the absolutive NP; however, *me-* occurs only with an absolutive NP that is a Theme (Patient). The most agentive argument, *toʿo* 'person', in its transitive counterpart in (2) has been deleted.[11]

3. Definition of grammatical relation

For this study, an argument is identified as a grammatical relation if it satisfies four criteria. The first criterion is unique coding. Coding refers to structural, or formal, coding; that is, morphology and word order. In order to distinguish between arguments of a clause, languages usually encode different arguments in different ways. Cross-linguistically, arguments are most commonly distinguished by three types of coding properties: case marking, verb agreement, and word order (Keenan 1975, 1976). Coding properties usually distinguish those arguments that are required by the verb, such as Agents and Themes (Patients), from those that are not, such as nonnuclear arguments (Instrument, Beneficiary Associative, etc.). They also distinguish required arguments from each other. It follows, then, that if a language has grammatical relations, each grammatical relation should be encoded differently in the clause structure in order to distinguish it from other grammatical relations and from oblique arguments. We would also expect these grammatical relations to be distinguished by at least one of the three coding properties that commonly differentiate grammatical relations, namely case marking, verb agreement, and word order; however, this expectation does not rule out the possibility that arguments in a given language might be distinguished by other language-specific coding properties, or by only language-specific coding properties. The coding criterion, then, provides a structural means of identifying grammatical relations.

The second criterion is syntactic control.[12,13] Traditionally, a grammatical relation is defined as an argument that bears a relation to the verb. In operational terms, an argument may be said to bear a relation to a verb if it plays a central role in the operation of a syntactic process, in which case it is the syntactic control for the process. Syntactic processes can be grouped into two kinds: (1) those that change the relation of an argument to the verb (e.g. promotion to direct object, passivization, and antipassivization), and (2) those that control coreferential deletion (e.g. equi-NP deletion, relativization, clefting, and zero anaphora in chained clauses) (Keenan 1975, 1976). The syntactic control criterion provides a behavioral means of identifying grammatical relations.

The third criterion for grammatical relations is exclusion. If a certain argument consistently functions as the syntactic control of a process to the exclusion of other arguments in a clause, this demonstrates that syntactic processes differentiate between arguments. Thus, the exclusion criterion provides a second behavioral means of identifying grammatical relations. More importantly, it provides a means of distinguishing between grammatical relations and demonstrates that not all grammatical relations bear the same relation to the verb.

The fourth criterion for grammatical relations is multiple semantic roles. If an argument encodes different semantic roles, yet consistently controls a syntactic process regardless of its semantic role, then the one-to-many relation between the argument and the semantic roles confirms that semantic roles do not map directly onto the syntactic structure of a clause in a one-to-one manner. This criterion provides evidence for the presence of a level of syntactic relations that is independent of semantic role.

For Karao, we will specify that an argument is a grammatical relation if: it is uniquely identified by at least one coding property, it controls at least one syntactic process to the exclusion of all other arguments, and as a syntactic control, it encodes different semantic roles. If the ergative and the absolutive NP of a transitive clause satisfy these criteria, verifying that they are grammatical relations, then assignment of the labels 'subject' and 'object' will be made following associations commonly found in languages between syntactic control, semantic roles, and topicality in transitive clauses.[14] Specifically, the more agentive and more topical argument, which would be the ergative NP, will be identified as the subject, and the less agentive and less topical argument, which would be the absolutive NP, will be identified as the object. This identification will be further verified by noting the kinds of syntactic processes that each argument controls. In general, relation-changing processes are a means of establishing the particular identity of a grammatical relation (i.e. subject or object); thus, there is generally no disagreement that the object controls promotion to direct object and passivization. On the other hand, coreferential deletion processes are usually not a means of establishing the identity of a grammatical relation since syntactic control of these processes varies from language to language. Once the subject and object of a transitive clause are identified, it then remains to be seen which of these arguments controls the majority of the coreferential deletion processes.

4. Patterns of syntactic control

Cross-linguistically, control of syntactic processes is organized along one of three patterns: (1) a nominative pattern in which the required argument of a single-argument clause and the subject of a transitive clause control most of the processes, (2) an ergative pattern in which the required argument of a single-argument clause and the object of a transitive clause control most of the processes, and (3) a 'mixed' pattern in which the required argument of a single-argument clause combines with the subject of a transitive clause to control some syntactic processes (following a nominative pattern), and with the object to control other syntactic processes (following an ergative pattern).

Patterns of syntactic control are defined here in terms of 'subject' and 'object', and 'required argument of a single-argument clause' for several reasons. The first reason is to underline the notion that the crucial question for identifying patterns of syntactic control is, which required argument of a transitive clause controls the majority of the syntactic processes in a language? We know that for most languages, the subject (i.e. the most agentive argument) of a transitive clause controls the majority of these processes, regardless of whether a language is morphologically nominative or ergative. What we don't know is whether it is also possible for the object (i.e. the least agentive argument) of a transitive clause to control the majority of these processes in, at least, some languages. Stating the syntactic control issue in terms of the subject and the object of a transitive clause allows us to capture the fact that the difference between nominative and ergative patterns of syntactic control is not a difference in the fundamental properties of the grammatical relations of the transitive clause, but a difference in the distribution frequencies of syntactic control between those relations. This approach allows us to maintain the claim that regardless of which required argument controls the majority of the syntactic processes in a transitive clause, the subject will be the more agentive and more topical argument while the object will be the less agentive and less topical argument. The syntactic control issue is, thus, reduced to a question of whether in a transitive clause, the subject or the object controls a significant majority of the syntactic processes in a language.

The second reason for this approach is the problem of what to call the required argument of a single-argument clause. As the only required argument, this argument controls by default all syntactic processes occurring in the clause. If syntactic control consistently follows a nominative pattern, the required argument may be called a 'subject'; conversely, if syntactic control consistently follows an ergative pattern, the required argument may be called an 'object'. If, however, syntactic control follows a 'mixed' pattern, in which the required argument patterns with the transitive subject in some processes, but with the transitive object in other processes, then neither the label 'subject' nor 'object' is appropriate. For this reason, I will refrain from giving the required argument of the single-argument clause either label if Karao has a mixed pattern of syntactic control, as I suggest. Having laid the foundation for discussing grammatical relations and patterns of syntactic control, let us now consider what happens in Karao.

5. Coding properties

Of the three coding properties that commonly identify grammatical relations, Karao exhibits two: case marking and word order. Of these, case marking is the more straightforward property. As we have seen, case marking in Karao displays an ergative pattern. The pattern is given again in the following examples: (5) is a single-argument clause and (6) a transitive clause.

(5) man'ekad   'i   to'od   kolos
     man   -'ahad 'i   to'o -cha kolos
     ACT/AG/IMPFT-walk ABS person-OBL river
     'The person will walk to the river'.

(6) ketno'en   na   to'oy   pakod
     ketno-en   na   to'o -'i   pakod
     cut -ACT/TH/IMPFT ERG person-ABS rope
     'The person will cut the rope'.

Word order as a coding property is less straightforward. Karao has a relatively rigid VAT (Verb Agent Theme) (or VAP (Verb Agent Patient)) word order in transitive clauses. All NPs in basic transitive and single-argument clauses occur on the same side of the verb; consequently, word order has neither a nominative nor an ergative coding pattern. Later, however, I will suggest that word order is a coding property in that it consistently distinguishes between the absolutive NP and oblique NPs in single-argument clauses and between the ergative NP and the absolutive NP in transitive clauses.

Although Karao does not have verb agreement, it does have a language-specific coding property in which an affix on the verb cross-references the absolutive argument by identifying the semantic role of the argument. Verb cross-referencing of this type is one of the distinctive morphological features of Philippine languages. Consider *ʿakdo* 'to scoop (cooked rice)' in (7)-(9), for which all three semantic roles, Agent, Theme (Patient), and Location, can be the absolutive NP. (7) is an intransitive clause; (8) and (9) are transitive clauses.

(7) *manʿakdoy*   *biʿi*   *na*   *ʿinepoy cha pingkan*
     man   *-ʿakdo-ʿi*   *biʿi*   *na*   *ʿinepoy cha pingkan*
     ACT/AG/IMPFT-scoop-ABS woman OBL rice   OBL plate
     'The woman will scoop some rice onto the plate'.

(8) *ʿakdoʿen*   *na* *biʿiy*   *ʿinepoy cha pingkan*
     ʿakdo-en   *na* *biʿi* *-ʿi*   *ʿinepoy cha pingkan*
     scoop-ACT/TH/IMPFT ERG woman-ABS rice   OBL plate
     'The woman will scoop the rice onto the plate'.

(9) *ʿakdoʿan*   *na* *biʿiy*   *pingkan na* *ʿinepoy*
     ʿakdo-an   *na* *biʿi* *-ʿi*   *pingkan na* *ʿinepoy*
     scoop-ACT/LOC/IMPFT ERG woman-ABS plate   OBL rice
     'The woman will scoop rice onto the plate'.

Notice that the affix on the verb identifies the semantic role of the absolutive NP and only the absolutive NP in both intransitive and transitive clauses; thus, verb cross-referencing displays an ergative pattern.

To summarize, coding properties in Karao present a consistent pattern in that both case marking and verb cross-referencing follow an ergative pattern.

6. Relation-changing processes

Relation-changing processes are those processes which alter the grammatical relation that an argument bears to the verb. One of the characteristics of an argument bearing a relation to a verb is that it controls a syntactic process. It follows, then, that if an argument changes its relation to the verb, its eligibility to control such a process may also change. Thus, relation-changing processes provide a means of testing an argument for its ability to control a syntactic process, thereby establishing its identity as a grammatical relation or an oblique. These processes also provide a means of identifying an argument as a particular grammatical relation, such as subject or object, based on cross-linguistic patterns of control for these processes.

Relation-changing processes in Karao include: (1) promotion to direct object, (2) passivization, (3) antipassivization, and (4) raising. A general description will be given for each process as it normally occurs in a prototypical transitive clause in various languages.[15] Following the general description, an explanation will be given of the process as it occurs in Karao.

6.1. *Promotion to direct object*

Promotion to direct object is a process by which an oblique argument is promoted to direct object. If promotion to direct object occurs in a transitive clause, the semantic role that is normally the direct object, usually a Theme (Patient), is demoted to an oblique argument. Once an argument is promoted to direct object, it controls the same syntactic processes as does a direct object Theme (Patient).

In Karao, oblique arguments can be promoted to absolutive NP; these arguments are Location (Location or Recipient), Nonnuclear Theme (Instrument or Associative), and Nonnuclear Location (Source or Beneficiary). Once an oblique argument is promoted to absolutive NP, it controls the same syntactic processes as an absolutive Theme, e.g. passivization, antipassivization, relativization, and clefting. Promotion to absolutive NP occurs in intransitive as well as transitive clauses.

When an oblique argument is promoted to absolutive NP in an intransitive clause, only promotion takes place, and the intransitive clause becomes a transitive clause, as shown in (10) and (11).

(10)   Location as Oblique

   ʿontokkong   *ʿi*   *ngaʿnged*   *chetʿal*
   ʿon   *-tokkong* *ʿi*   *ngaʿnga-cha chetʿal*
   ACT/TH/IMPFT-sit   ABS child   -OBL floor
   'The child will sit on the floor'.

(11) Promotion of Location

> *tokkongan*   *na nga^cngiy*   *chet^cal*
> *tokkong-an*   *na nga^cnga-^ci*   *chet^cal*
> sit   -ACT/LOC/IMPFT ERG child   -ABS floor
> 'The child will sit on the floor'.

The oblique Location *chet^cal* 'floor' in (10) is promoted to absolute
NP in (11). Promotion of the argument is signaled by the change in its case
marker from *-d*, an allomorph of the oblique marker *cha*, to *-y*, an allomorph of the absolutive marker *^ci*. With promotion, the verb affix changes
to *-an*, identifying the absolutive NP as a Location. The Theme, *nga^cnga*
'child', remains a required argument, and (11) becomes a transitive clause.
Evidence that (11) is a transitive clause is that it has transitive word order
(i.e. V *na*-NP *^ci*-NP) and the *^ci*-NP is eligible for passivization, as we will
see shortly.[16]

When an oblique argument is promoted to absolutive NP in a transitive clause, promotion of the oblique argument is accompanied by demotion of the Theme (Patient): the promoted argument is preceded by the
absolutive marker *^ci*; the demoted Theme is preceded by the oblique marker
na; the affix on the verb changes to identify the semantic role of the promoted argument; and the demoted Theme optionally, but commonly, moves
to a position following the promoted argument, as shown in the following
pairs of transitive clauses.

(12) Location (Recipient) as Oblique

> *^ci^ckan*   *na to^coy*   *dibchod*   *nga^cnga*
> *^ci*   *-^cikan*   *na to^co -^ci*   *dibcho-cha nga^cnga*
> ACT/TH/IMPFT-give   ERG person-ABS book -OBL child
> 'The person will give the book to the child'.[17]

(13) Promotion of Location (Recipient)

> *^ci^ckanan*   *na to^coy*   *nga^cnga na dibcho*
> *^ci--an*   *-^cikan na to^co -^ci*   *nga^cnga na dibcho*
> ACT/LOC/IMPFT-give ERG person-ABS child   OBL book
> 'The person will give the child the book'.

(14) Nonnuclear Location (Beneficiary) as Oblique

tongkalen   *na to^coy*   *^camayo para*
tongkal-en   *na to^co -^ci   ^camayo para*
buy   -ACT/TH/IMPFT ERG person-ABS toy   for

nga^cnga
nga^cnga
child

'The person will buy the toy for the child'.

(15) Promotion of Nonnuclear Location (Beneficiary)

^citongkalan   *na to^coy*   *nga^cnga*
^ci--an   *-tongkal na to^co -^ci   nga^cnga*
ACT/NLOC/IMPFT-buy   ERG person-ABS child

na ^camayo
na ^camayo
OBL toy

'The person will buy the child the toy'.

In (13) and (15), the argument promoted to absolutive NP, *nga^cnga* 'child', moves closer to the verb while the demoted Theme (Patient), *dibcho* 'book' in (13) and *^camayo* 'toy' in (15), moves to the periphery of the clause; the ergative argument, *to^co* 'person', however, does not change position. The shift in position between the promoted argument and the demoted argument is optional (though common); thus, word order in a transitive clause does not distinguish between required absolutive arguments and oblique arguments.

Although these examples show that the absolutive NP controls promotion to absolutive NP, they do not actually show us that the promoted argument is an object. What we need to see is that any argument encoded as the absolutive NP of a transitive clause behaves like an object. For example, if the transitive absolutive NP is an object, it should play a central role in a process normally controlled by an object, such as passivization.

6.2. Passivization

When a transitive clause undergoes passivization, the subject is demoted, either by being encoded as an oblique argument or by being deleted altogether, and the object becomes the single required argument of the passive clause. The object may or may not change its relation to the verb, depending on the language.

If the transitive absolutive NP in Karao is indeed an object, we would expect it to be the single required argument of a corresponding passive clause. As a single required argument, it must be an absolutive NP; consequently, the case marking of the transitive absolutive NP should not change following passivization, and this is what we find.

When a prototypical transitive clause undergoes passivization in Karao, the ergative Agent is usually deleted, and the absolutive Theme (Patient) of the transitive clause is the single remaining required argument of the passive clause. Since the Theme is already encoded as the absolutive NP, no change occurs in its case marking. An example follows: (16) is a prototypical transitive clause; (17) is its passive counterpart. (18) shows that for *ketno* 'to cut', deletion of the ergative NP is obligatory.

(16) *ketno'en*   *na to'oy   pakod*
      ketno-en   *na to'o -'i   pakod*
      cut   -ACT/TH/IMPFT ERG person-ABS rope
      'The person will cut the rope'.

(17) *meketnoy   pakod*
      me   -ketno-'i   pakod
      PASS/IMPFT-cut   -ABS rope
      'The rope will be cut'.

(18) **meketnoy   pakod na   to'o*
      me   -ketno-'i   pakod na   to'o
      PASS/IMPFT-cut   -ABS rope OBL person
      'The rope will be cut by the person'.

In the passive clause in (17), *pakod* 'rope' remains the absolutive NP; *me-* signals that the event is a state, and the lack of a semantic role morpheme on the verb indicates that the semantic role of the absolutive NP is Theme (Patient).

One might argue that the absolutive NP of the passive is a subject. If the single argument of the passive clause were promoted to subject as part of the passivization process, we would expect it to be marked like the subject of a transitive clause. On the basis of semantic role and topicality, the Agent in a transitive clause is the best candidate for subject, and in Karao, a transitive Agent is encoded in a *na*-marked ergative NP. Since the required argument of a passive clause retains its absolutive case marking, we conclude that the absolutive NP is not a subject, and that the Karao passive is nonpromotional.

In Karao, any oblique argument that can be promoted to absolutive NP is eligible for passivization. This is true for oblique arguments of semantically intransitive verbs as well as semantically transitive ones. An example involving a semantically intransitive verb is given in (19)-(21). (19) is an intransitive clause in which the Location is an oblique NP; (20) is a transitive clause in which the Location has been promoted to absolutive NP; (21) is the passive counterpart of (20). (Parentheses signal that the presence of an argument is optional.)

(19)   *'ontokkong*   *'i   nga'nged   chet'al*
        'on   *-tokkong 'i   nga'nga-cha chet'al*
        ACT/TH/IMPFT-sit   ABS child   -OBL floor
        'The child will sit on the floor'.

(20)   *tokkongan*   *na nga'ngiy   chet'al*
        tokkong-an   *na nga'nga-'i chet'al*
        sit   -ACT/LOC/IMPFT ERG child   -ABS floor
        'The child will sit on the floor'.

(21)   *metokkongan*   *'i   chet'al (na   nga'nga)*
        me--an   *-tokkong 'i   chet'al na   nga'nga*
        PASS/LOC/IMPFT-sit   ABS floor   OBL child
        'The floor will be sat on (by the child)'.

Although the demoted ergative NP is normally obligatorily absent in a passive clause, some Karao speakers accept the presence of a demoted ergative NP in passives involving certain semantically intransitive verbs, such as *tokkong* 'to sit', *japtok* 'to jump', and *sada* 'to dance'. When the demoted ergative NP is present in the passive, as in (21), it is preceded by the oblique marker *na* and is obligatorily moved to the periphery of the clause, changing from transitive word order (V *na*-NP *'i*-NP) to single-argument order (V *'i*-NP *na*-NP). Thus, word order indicates that the *na*-NP in (21) is the oblique argument of a single-argument clause and not the required ergative argument of a transitive clause. In this respect, word order functions as a coding property distinguishing between required arguments and oblique arguments.

Any oblique argument of a semantically transitive verb that can be promoted to absolutive NP is also eligible for passivization. For all semantically transitive verbs, the demoted ergative NP is obligatorily absent in a passive clause.

For the verb *'ikan* 'to give', either a Theme or a Location (Recipient) can be the absolutive NP of a transitive clause. As the absolutive NP, both are eligible for passivization, as in:

(22) Theme (Patient) — Transitive Clause

'i^ckan *na to^coy* *dibchod* *nga^cnga*
'i *-'ikan na to^co -'i dibcho-cha nga^cnga*
ACT/TH/IMPFT-give ERG person-ABS book -OBL child
'The person will give the book to the child'.

(23) Theme (Patient) — Passive Clause

may'i^ckan *'i dibchod nga^cnga*
may *-'ikan 'i dibcho-cha nga^cnga*
PASS/TH/IMPFT-give ABS book -OBL child
'The book will be given to the child'.

(24) Location (Recipient) — Transitive Clause

'i^ckanan *na to^coy* *nga^cnga na dibcho*
'i--an *-'ikan na to^co -'i nga^cnga na dibcho*
ACT/LOC/IMPFT-give ERG person-ABS child OBL book
'The person will give the child the book'.

(25) Location (Recipient) — Passive Clause

may'i^ckanan *'i nga^cnga na dibcho*
may--an *-'ikan 'i nga^cnga na dibcho*
PASS/LOC/IMPFT-give ABS child OBL book
'The child will be given the book'.

For *tongkal* 'to buy', a Theme (Patient) or a Nonnuclear Location (Beneficiary) can be the absolutive NP, and as such, both are eligible for passivization.

(26) Theme (Patient) — Transitive Clause

tongkalen   *na toᶜoy*   *ᶜamayo*
tongkal-en   *na toᶜo -ᶜi*   *ᶜamayo*
buy   -ACT/TH/IMPFT ERG person-ABS toy

para ngaᶜnga
para ngaᶜnga
for   child

'The person will buy the toy for the child'.

(27) Theme (Patient) — Passive Clause

metongkal   *ᶜi*   *ᶜamayo para ngaᶜnga*
me   -tongkal ᶜi   *ᶜamayo para ngaᶜnga*
PASS/IMPFT-buy   ABS toy   for   child

'The toy will be bought for the child'.

(28) Nonnuclear Location (Beneficiary) — Transitive Clause

ᶜitongkalan   *na toᶜoy*   *ngaᶜnga*
ᶜi--an   -tongkal na toᶜo -ᶜi   *ngaᶜnga*
ACT/NLOC/IMPFT-buy   ERG person-ABS child

na ᶜamayo
na ᶜamayo
OBL toy

'The person will buy the child the toy'.

(29) Nonnuclear Location (Beneficiary) — Passive Clause

maytongkalan   *ᶜi*   *ngaᶜnga na ᶜamayo*
may--an   -tongkal ᶜi   *ngaᶜnga na ᶜamayo*
PASS/NLOC/IMPFT-buy   ABS child   OBL toy

'The child will be bought the toy'.

For *tegteg* 'to flatten', a core Theme (Patient) or a Nonnuclear Theme (Instrument) can be the transitive absolutive NP, and as such, are eligible for passivization.

(30) Theme (Patient) — Transitive Clause

tegtegen   *na ngaᶜngiy*   *ᶜaramdi*
tegteg-en   *na ngaᶜnga-ᶜi*   *ᶜaramdi*
flatten-ACT/TH/IMPFT ERG child   -ABS wire

na   batho
na   batho
OBL rock

'The child will flatten the wire with a rock'.

(31) Theme (Patient) — Passive Clause

metegteg   *'i   'aramdi na   batho*
me   *-tegteg 'i   'aramdi na   batho*
PASS/IMPFT-flatten ABS wire   OBL rock
'The wire will be flattened with a rock'.

(32) Nonnuclear Theme (Instrument) — Transitive Clause

'itegteg   *na   nga'ngiy   bathod*
'i   *-tegteg na   nga'nga-'i   batho-cha*
ACT/NTH/IMPFT-flatten ERG child   -ABS rock -OBL

'aramdi
'aramdi
wire

'The child will use the rock to flatten the wire'.

(33) Nonnuclear Theme (Instrument) — Passive Clause

maytegteg   *'i   bathod   'aramdi*
may   *-tegteg 'i   batho-cha 'aramdi*
PASS/NTH/IMPFT-flatten ABS rock -OBL wire
'The rock will be used to flatten the wire'.

Since objects play a central role in the passivization of transitive clauses, and since the absolutive NP of a transitive clause plays a such role in passivization in Karao, this is evidence that the transitive absolutive NP is an object. Furthermore, since any oblique argument can trigger passivization once it is promoted to absolutive NP in a transitive clause, this verifies that promotion to absolutive NP is, in fact, promotion to direct object.

6.3. *Antipassivization*

Antipassivization is a process in which the object of a transitive clause is demoted, either by being encoded as an oblique argument or by being deleted. Following antipassivization, the subject is the only remaining required argument, and may or may not change its syntactic relation with the verb, depending on the language.

If the absolutive Theme (Patient) in a prototypical transitive clause in Karao is an object, then we would expect it to be demoted following anti-passivization. Following demotion, we would also expect the Agent, the single remaining required argument, to change from an ergative NP to an absolutive NP, since the required argument of a single-argument clause must be an absolutive NP.

Following antipassivization in Karao, the absolutive Theme of the transitive clause is demoted as predicted. (34) is a transitive clause, and (35) an antipassive clause.

(34) *ketno⁽en*   *na to⁽oy*   *pakod*
     ketno-en   *na to⁽o -⁽i*   *pakod*
     cut -ACT/TH/IMPFT ERG person-ABS rope
     'The person will cut the rope'.

(35) *mengetnoy*   *to⁽o*   *na pakod*
     meN   -ketno-⁽i *to⁽o* *na pakod*
     ACT/AG/IMPFT-cut   -ABS person OBL rope
     'The person will cut a rope'.

In the antipassive clause in (35), the Theme *pakod* 'rope' is demoted and its case marking changes to the oblique marker *na*; case marking on the Agent *to⁽o* 'person' changes to *-y*, an allomorph of the absolutive marker *⁽i*; the affix on the verb changes to *meN-*, identifying the absolutive NP as Agent.

Notice that transitive word order V *na*-NP *⁽i*-NP in (34) changes to single-argument order V *⁽i*-NP *na*-NP in (35). Syntactic evidence that the *na*-marked Theme in (35) has been demoted is that it no longer governs syntactic processes normally controlled by a transitive absolutive NP.[18] (See (79) in Relativization 7.2 and (104) in Clefting 7.3.)

In Karao, a Theme (Patient) is normally the unmarked choice for absolutive NP for semantically transitive verbs; however, there are a few transitive verbs for which the unmarked choice is some argument other than Theme, such as Location or Nonnuclear Theme (Instrument), and so we are interested to see how antipassivization operates with these verbs. If an absolutive non-Theme (non-Patient) argument follows the same pattern as an absolutive Theme, then we have evidence that antipassivization is sensitive to a level of syntactic relations independent of semantic role.

The verb *pakchal* 'to build a ladder on (or add steps to) a structure' is a semantically transitive verb that takes a Location, rather than a Theme (Patient), as the unmarked choice for absolutive NP in a transitive clause.[19] (36) is a transitive clause; (37) is an antipassive clause.

(36) *pakchalan*   *na dahiy*   *batilja*
      pakchal-an   *na dahi-ʻi*   *batilja*
      ladder -ACT/LOC/IMPFT ERG man-ABS porch
      'The man will build steps on the porch'.

(37) *memakchal*   *ʻi dahi na batilja*
      meN   *-pakchal ʻi dahi na batilja*
      ACT/AG/IMPFT-ladder   ABS man OBL porch
      'The man will build steps on a porch'.

As these examples show, the absolutive Location of a transitive clause undergoes exactly the same alternations in antipassivization as an absolutive Theme (Patient), thus verifying that the process is controlled by a grammatical relation, and not a semantic role.

The verb *tegteg* 'to flatten' is one of several verbs that encode two propositions. With *-en* in (38), it encodes the proposition: 'someone flattens an object', and a core Theme (Patient) is the absolutive NP; with *ʻi-* in (39), it encodes the proposition 'someone uses an object (to flatten another object)', and a Nonnuclear Theme (Instrument) is the absolutive NP.

(38) *tegtegen*   *na ngaʻngiy*   *ʻaramdi na batho*
      tegteg-en   *na ngaʻnga-ʻi*   *ʻaramdi na batho*
      flatten-ACT/TH/IMPFT ERG child   -ABS wire   OBL rock
      'The child will flatten the wire with a rock'.

(39) *ʻitegteg*   *na ngaʻngiy*   *bathod*
      ʻi   *-tegteg na ngaʻnga-ʻi*   *batho-cha*
      ACT/NTH/IMPFT-flatten ERG child   -ABS rock -OBL
      ʻaramdi
      ʻaramdi
      wire
      'The child will use the rock to flatten the wire'.

What is of interest for the discussion of antipassivization is that verbs like *tegteg* appear to have two antipassive affixes: one that occurs with a demoted core Theme (Patient), as in (40), and another that occurs with a demoted Nonnuclear Theme (Instrument), as in (41). (The verb affixes themselves cross-reference the absolutive NP, identifying it as an Agent.)

(40) *menegteg*   *ʻi   ngaʻnga na   ʻaramdi*
      meN   *-tegteg ʻi   ngaʻnga na   ʻaramdi*
      ACT/AG/IMPFT-flatten ABS child   OBL wire

      na   batho
      na   batho
      OBL rock

      'The child will flatten the wire with a rock'.

(41) *mengitegteg*   *ʻi   ngaʻnga na   bathod*
      mengi   *-tegteg ʻi   ngaʻnga na   batho-cha*
      ACT/AG/IMPFT-flatten ABS child   OBL rock -OBL

      ʻaramdi
      ʻaramdi
      wire

      'The child will use a rock to flatten the wire'.

With *tegteg* 'to flatten', the contrast between the affixes *meN-* and *mengi-* signals different propositions, not different constructions; Karao has only one antipassive construction.[20]

To summarize, objects play a central role in antipassivization in many languages. Since the absolutive NP of a transitive clause plays a similar role in Karao, antipassivization supports the claim that the transitive absolutive NP is an object.

6.4. *Raising*

Raising is a process in which the subject or the object of a complement clause moves to the subject position of the main clause (raising-to-subject) or to the object position (raising-to-object).

Karao has a relation-changing process that resembles raising-to-object: The ergative NP or the absolutive NP of the complement clause can move to the absolutive position of a transitive main clause.[21] If the ergative NP of the complement clause and that of the main clause are not coreferential, only the ergative NP of the complement clause can be raised, as shown in (42)-(46). (44) is an unraised complement construction; (45) is a raised construction.[22]

(42) *mitak*   *ʿi*   *ngaʿnga*
      matha-iy- *-ko*   *ʿi*   *ngaʿnga*
      see   -ACT/PFT-1SG/ERG ABS child
      'I saw the child'.

(43) *biyosak*   *na*   *ngaʿngiy*   *ʿispiho*
      bosak-iy-   *na*   *ngaʿnga-ʿi*   *ʿispiho*
      break-ACT/PFT ERG child   -ABS mirror
      'The child broke the mirror'.

(44) *mitak*   *ʿa biyosak*
      matha-iy- *-ko*   *ʿa bosak-iy-*
      see   -ACT/PFT-1SG/ERG LK break-ACT/PFT

      na   *ngaʿngiy*   *ʿispiho*
      na   *ngaʿnga-ʿi*   *ʿispiho*
      ERG child   -ABS mirror

      'I saw that the child broke the mirror'.

(45) *mitak*   *ʿi*   *ngaʿngen*
      matha-iy-   *-ko*   *ʿi*   *ngaʿnga-ʿa*
      see   -ACT/PFT-1SG/ERG ABS child   -LK

      biyosak   *toy*   *ʿispiho*
      bosak-iy-   *to*   *-ʿi*   *ʿispiho*
      break-ACT/PFT 3SG/ERG-ABS mirror

      'I saw the child break the mirror'.[23]

(46) *mitak*   *ʿi*   *ʿispihon*
      matha-iy-   *-ko*   *ʿi*   *ʿisipho-ʿa*
      see   -ACT/PFT-1SG/ERG ABS mirror-LK

      biyosak   *na*   *ngaʿnga*
      bosak-iy-   *na*   *ngaʿnga*
      break-ACT/PFT ERG child

Change in word order and case marking provide evidence that *nga͑nga* 'child' is raised: *nga͑nga* 'child' moves from the complement clause in (44) to the main clause in (45), and its case marking changes from ergative *na* in (44) to absolute *͑i* in (45). An anaphoric pronoun is deposited in the ergative position of the complement clause, coreferencing the raised argument. (46) shows that the complement absolute NP cannot be raised if the ergative NP of the main clause and that of the complement clause are not coreferential.[24]

Notice that the raised construction in (45) implies that the referent of the ergative NP of the main clause, 'I', was present when the child broke the mirror. Conversely, the unraised construction in (44) is neutral with respect to whether or not the referent was present when the mirror was broken.

One might argue that the process just described is not "true" raising since an anaphoric pronoun is deposited in the ergative position of the complement clause, coreferencing the raised argument; however, deletion of the raised argument from the complement clause is not a requirement of raising. The use of an anaphoric pronoun versus deletion to recover the identity of a raised argument in the complement clause is an issue of coding; languages have different coding strategies for tracking repositioned arguments. The central issue for raising is, does a semantically required argument of the complement clause become a syntactic argument of the main clause? Both word order and case marking indicate that in Karao, a semantically required argument of a complement clause, namely an ergative NP, can become the syntactic argument of the main clause. We conclude, then, that the process shown in (45) is raising. Now consider the absolute NP of a complement clause.

If the ergative NP of the complement clause and that of the main clause are coreferential, the absolute NP of the complement clause can be raised to the absolute position of the main clause, as shown in (47)-(51). (49) is an unraised complement construction; (50) is a raised construction; and (51) shows that deletion of the absolute NP in the complement clause is obligatory.[25]

(47) *diningding*   *koy*   *dibcho*
      dingding-iy-   *ko*   -*͑i*   *dibcho*
      forget   -ACT/PFT 1SG/ERG-ABS book
      'I forgot the book'.

(48)   *konen*   *taha*
        kowan-en   *ta-ka*
        tell   -ACT/TH/IMPFT ??-2SG/ABS
        'I will tell you'.[26]

(49)   *diningding*   *kon*
        dingding-iy-   *ko*   *-ˤa*
        forget -ACT/PFT 1SG/ERG-LK

        konen   *ka*
        kowan-en   *ka*
        tell   -ACT/TH/IMPFT 2SG/ABS

        'I forgot that I would tell you'.

(50)   *diningding*   *tahen*
        dingding-iy-   *ta-ka*   *-ˤa*
        forget -ACT/PFT ??-2SG/ABS-LK

        konen
        kowan-en
        tell   -ACT/TH/IMPFT

        'I forgot to tell you'.

(51)   **diningding*   *tahen*
        dingding-iy-   *ta-ka*   *-ˤa*
        forget   -ACT/PFT ??-2SG/ABS-LK

        konen   *ka*
        kowan-en   *ka*
        tell   -ACT/TH/IMPFT 2SG/ABS

Here, change in word order provides evidence that the absolutive NP of the complement clause is raised to become a syntactic argument of a main clause; specifically, the absolutive argument *ka* 'you' moves from the complement clause in (49) to the main clause in (50). Since *ka* 'you' is an absolutive argument before it is raised to the absolutive position in the main clause, there is no change in its case marking. Following raising, the absolutive NP is deleted in the complement clause. (The coreferential ergative NP of the complement clause is also deleted as a result of equi-NP deletion. See 7.1.)

The following examples show that a raised ergative NP can encode a semantic role other than Agent. For *'awat* 'to understand', the ergative NP, the cognizer, is a Location (Experiencer).

(52) *piyan koy   dibcho*
     piyan ko   -ʕi dibcho
     want 1SG/ERG-ABS book
     'I want the book'.

(53) *'egwathan   moy   songbat*
     'awat   -an   mo   -ʕi songbat
     understand-ACT/TH/IMPFT 2SG/ERG-ABS answer
     'You will understand the answer'.

(54) *piyan kon   'egwathan*
     piyan ko   -ʕa 'awat   -an
     want 1SG/ERG-LK understand-ACT/TH/IMPFT

     moy   songbat
     mo   -ʕi songbat
     2SG/ERG-ABS answer

     'I want that you will understand the answer'.

(55) *piyan tahen   'egwathan*
     piyan ta-ka   -ʕa 'awat   -an
     want ??-2SG/ABS-LK understand-ACT/TH/IMPFT

     moy   songbat
     mo   -ʕi songbat
     2SG/ERG-ABS answer

     'I want you to understand the answer'.

Similarly, a raised absolutive NP can encode a semantic role other than Theme (Patient). In the examples below, the absolutive NP of *tongkal* 'to buy' is a Nonnuclear Location (Beneficiary).

(56) *diningding   koy   dibcho*
     dingding-iy-   ko   -ʕi dibcho
     forget   -ACT/PFT 1SG/ERG-ABS book
     'I forgot the book'.

(57) *'itongkalan*   *koy*   *nga'nga na dibcho*
     'i--an   *-tongkal ko*   *-'i nga'nga na dibcho*
     ACT/NLOC/IMPFT-buy   1SG/ERG-ABS child   OBL book
     'I will buy the child a book'.

(58) *diningding*   *kon*   *'itongkalan*
     dingding-iy-   *ko*   *-'a 'i--an*   *-tongkal*
     forget   -ACT/PFT 1SG/ERG-LK ACT/NLOC/IMPFT-buy

     'i   *nga'nga na dibcho*
     'i   *nga'nga na dibcho*
     ABS child   OBL book

     'I forgot to buy the child a book'.

(59) *diningding*   *koy*   *nga'ngen*
     dingding-iy-   *ko*   *-'i nga'nga-'a*
     forget   -ACT/PFT 1SG/ERG-ABS child   -LK

     'itongkalan   *na dibcho*
     'i--an   *-tongkal na dibcho*
     ACT/NLOC/IMPFT-buy   OBL book

     'I forgot to buy the child a book'.

In many languages subjects and objects play a central role in the raising of arguments from a complement clause to a main clause. Since both the ergative NP and the absolutive NP of a transitive complement clause in Karao can be raised to the absolutive position of a main clause, we have evidence that these arguments are grammatical relations. Furthermore, in many languages the subject outranks the object in eligibility for raising. In Karao, if the ergative NP of the main clause and that of the complement clause are not coreferential, only the ergative NP can be raised. On the other hand, if these arguments are coreferential, in which case the complement ergative NP is already present in the main clause by virtue of coreference, then the absolutive NP can also be raised. In this sense, the ergative NP outranks the absolutive NP in eligibility for raising in Karao, suggesting that the ergative NP is a subject.

6.5. *Summary of relation-changing processes*

Karao has four relation-changing processes: (1) promotion to direct object,
(2) passivization, (3) antipassivization, and (4) raising. For all four processes, the absolute *'i*-marked NP of a transitive clause plays a significant
role. For raising, the ergative *na*-marked NP also plays a significant role.
The findings are summarized in Table 1.

Table 1. *Relation-changing processes in Karao*

Process	Syntactic Control	
	na-NP (AG)	*'i*-NP (non-AG)
Promotion to Direct Object		X
Passivization		X
Antipassivization		X
Raising	X	X

Relation-changing processes show that the absolute NP of a transitive clause satisfies all four criteria for grammatical relations. The coding
and syntactic control criteria are satisfied in that the absolute NP, which
is uniquely and consistently marked by *'i*, has a significant role in all four
processes, and so by definition is a syntactic control. The exclusion criterion is satisfied in that only the absolute NP controls promotion to direct
object, passivization, and antipassivization. The multiple semantic role criterion is satisfied in that as the syntactic control for these processes, the
absolute NP can encode different semantic roles. Since the absolute NP
satisfies the criteria for grammatical relations, we conclude that it is a
grammatical relation. Furthermore, since the absolute NP is also the less
agentive and the less topical argument of a transitive clause and since it
controls relation-changing processes that by definition are controlled by objects,
we conclude that the absolute NP is an object.

In the same way, the ergative NP also satisfies all the criteria for grammatical relations. The coding criterion is satisfied in that of the two required
arguments in a transitive clause, the ergative NP is uniquely and consistently marked by *na*. The syntactic control criterion is satisfied in that the

ergative NP plays a significant role in raising, and so is a syntactic control for that process. The exclusion criterion is satisfied in that under certain conditions only the ergative NP controls raising. The multiple semantic role criterion is satisfied in that as the syntactic control for raising, the ergative NP can encode different semantic roles. Since the ergative NP satisfies the criteria for grammatical relations, we conclude that it is a grammatical relation. Since it is the more agentive and more topical argument of a transitive clause, and since it outranks the absolutive NP in eligibility for raising as do subjects in many languages, we conclude that the ergative NP is a subject. (Equi-NP deletion will provide further evidence that the ergative NP is a subject.)

7. Coreferential deletion processes

Coreferential deletion processes in Karao are: (1) equi-NP deletion, (2) relativization, (3) clefting, (4) zero anaphora in chained clauses, (5) coreference in imperatives, and (6) coreference in reflexives. All of these processes except coreference in imperatives and reflexives involve a sequence of clauses in which an argument in clause 1 is coreferential with another in clause 2, and the coreferential argument in clause 2 is deleted.

Coreferential deletion processes provide evidence for grammatical relations. If a uniquely coded coreferential argument in clause 2 is consistently and exclusively deleted, regardless of its semantic role, it is a grammatical relation.

These processes also provide evidence for patterns of syntactic control. If the ergative NP of transitive clause 1 is coreferential with a deleted absolutive NP in a single-argument clause 2, or a deleted ergative NP in a transitive clause 2, the coreferential deletion process has a nominative pattern of syntactic control. Conversely, if the absolutive NP of transitive clause 1 is coreferential with a deleted absolutive NP in a single-argument clause 2 or a transitive clause 2, the coreferential deletion process has an ergative pattern of control. These patterns are illustrated in Table 2. (Clause 2 is placed in square brackets.)

Table 2. *Patterns of syntactic control*

Nominative Patterns

V	na-NP$_i$	$'i$-NP$_j$	[V	0_i]	
V	na-NP$_i$	$'i$-NP$_j$	[V	0_i	$'i$-NP$_j$]

Ergative Patterns

V	na-NP$_i$	$'i$-NP$_j$	[V	0_j]	
V	na-NP$_i$	$'i$-NP$_j$	[V	na-NP$_i$	0_j]

Taken together, coreferential deletion processes allow us to see whether the subject or the object of a transitive clause is the dominant syntactic control in Karao. If a significant majority of these processes has a nominative pattern of control, then the ergative NP, the subject, will be the dominant syntactic control. If a significant majority of the processes has an ergative pattern of control, then the transitive absolutive NP, the object, will be the dominant syntactic control. On the other hand, if at least one process has an exclusively nominative pattern of control and at least one other process has an exclusively ergative pattern of control, then syntactic control is divided between the subject and object of a transitive clause, and Karao has a mixed pattern of control.[27]

7.1. *Equi-NP deletion*

Equi-NP deletion takes place between a main clause and a complement clause: when an argument in the main clause is coreferential with one in the complement clause, the coreferential complement argument is deleted. What is of importance here is the near-universal tendency for subjects to control equi-NP deletion; thus, if the ergative NP is a subject, it should control equi-NP deletion.

In Karao, when the ergative NP of a main clause is coreferential with the absolutive NP of a single-argument complement clause, the complement absolutive NP is deleted, as predicted. An example is given in (60)-(62). (63) verifies that equi-NP deletion is obligatory.

(60)   *piyan koy   dibcho*
        piyan ko   -ʻi   dibcho
        want 1SG/ERG-ABS book
        'I want the book'.

(61)   *manpasiyalak*
        man   -pasiyal-ak
        ACT/AG/IMPFT-go.visit-1SG/ABS
        'I will go visiting'.

(62)   *piyan kon   manpasiyal*
        piyan ko   -ʻa man   -pasiyal
        want 1SG/ERG-LK ACT/AG/IMPFT-go.visit
        'I want to go visiting'.

(63)   **piyan kon   manpasiyalak*
        piyan ko   -ʻa man   -pasiyal-ak
        want 1SG/ERG-LK ACT/AG/IMPFT-go.visit-1SG/ABS

When the ergative NP of a main clause is coreferential with the ergative NP of a transitive complement clause, the complement ergative NP is also deleted, as shown in (64) and (65). (66) verifies again that equi-NP deletion is obligatory.

(64)   *tongkalen   koy   dibcho*
        tongkal-en   ko   -ʻi dibcho
        buy   -ACT/TH/IMPFT 1SG/ERG-ABS book
        'I will buy the book'.

(65)   *piyan kon   tongkalen   ʻi   dibcho*
        piyan ko   -ʻa tongkal-en   ʻi   dibcho
        want 1SG/ERG-LK buy   -ACT/TH/IMPFT ABS book
        'I want to buy the book'.

(66)   **piyan kon   tongkalen*
        piyan ko   -ʻa tongkal-en
        want 1SG/ERG-LK buy   -ACT/TH/IMPFT

        koy   dibcho
        ko   -ʻi dibcho
        1SG/ERG -ABS book

(67)-(69) show that when the ergative NP of a main clause is coreferential with the absolutive NP of a transitive complement clause, the complement absolutive NP is not deleted.

(67)   *cha'cha'an*   *mo'ak*
       cha'cha-an   *mo   -ak*
       help   -ACT/TH/IMPFT 2SG/ERG-1SG/ABS
       'You will help me'.

(68)   *piyan kon*   *cha'cha'an*   *mo'ak*
       piyan ko   -'a cha'cha-an   *mo   -ak*
       want 1SG/ERG-LK help   -ACT/TH/IMPFT 2SG/ERG-1SG/ABS
       'I want that you will help me'.

(69)   **piyan kon*   *cha'cha'an*   *mo*
       piyan ko   -'a cha'cha-an   *mo*
       want 1SG/ERG-LK help   -ACT/TH/IMPFT 2SG/ERG

These examples demonstrate that equi-NP deletion follows a nominative pattern of syntactic control: the ergative NP in the main clause triggers
coreferential deletion of an absolutive NP in a single-argument complement
clause, and an ergative NP in a transitive complement clause.

In (62) and (65), the deleted coreferential argument is an Agent. The
following examples verify that the deleted argument in the complement
clause can encode semantic roles other than Agent, indicating that equi-NP
deletion is controlled by a grammatical relation, not a semantic role. (71)
has a single-argument complement clause, and the deleted coreferential
argument is a Theme (Experiencer).

(70)   *'onjo'kowak*
       'on   -jo'kow-ak
       ACT/TH/IMPFT-sleep -1SG/ABS
       'I will sleep'.

(71)   *piyan kon*   *'onjo'kow*
       piyan ko   -'a 'on   -jo'kow
       want 1SG/ERG-LK ACT/TH/IMPFT-sleep
       'I want to sleep'.

(73) has a transitive complement clause, and the deleted argument, the
cognizer, is a Location (Experiencer).

(72) ʿegwathan   koyˈ   songbat
     ʿawat   -an   ko   -ʿi   songbat
     understand-ACT/TH/IMPFT 1SG/ERG-ABS answer
     'I will understand the answer'.

(73) piyan kon   ʿegwathan
     piyan ko   -ʿa ʿawat   -an
     want 1SG/ERG-LK understand-ACT/TH/IMPFT

     ʿi   songbat
     ʿi   songbat
     ABS answer

     'I want to understand the answer'.

To summarize, equi-NP deletion follows a nominative pattern of syntactic control. The deleted coreferential argument can be the absolutive NP of a single-argument complement clause or the ergative NP of a transitive complement clause. These arguments satisfy the syntactic control criterion for grammatical relations in that as the deleted argument of equi-NP deletion, they are central to the operation of the process. The arguments satisfy the coding criterion in that they are always encoded as either the absolutive NP of a single-argument clause or the ergative NP of a transitive clause. The arguments satisfy the exclusion criterion in that only the absolutive NP of a single-argument clause and only the ergative NP of a transitive clause can be deleted in this process. Finally, the arguments satisfy the semantic role criterion in that as the syntactic control for this process, they can encode different semantic roles. Equi-NP deletion, then, verifies that the absolutive NP of a single-argument clause and the ergative NP of a transitive clause are grammatical relations. Furthermore, since it is a near-universal tendency for subjects to control equi-NP deletion, and since the ergative NP controls equi-NP deletion in Karao, this is direct support for the claim that the ergative NP is a subject.

7.2. Relativization

Relativization is a process by which a subordinate clause modifies an argument in a main clause; the subordinate clause is the relative clause, and the argument that it modifies is its head noun.

Karao has two types of relative clause, both of which share the same general structure: a head NP is joined to the subordinate clause by the linker *'a* (or its allomorph *-n*). The head NP is obligatorily moved to the front of the relative clause unless it is the absolutive NP of a transitive relative clause, in which case it can optionally remain in its normal position in the relative clause.

Relative Clause 1
Relative Clause 1 is the basic relative clause in Karao. The predicate of the main clause can be any finite verb. The only arguments that can be the head noun are the absolutive NP of the relative clause and the possessor of the absolutive NP.

In (74) and (75), the relative clause is a transitive clause, and the absolutive NP, a Theme (Patient), is the head noun. In (74), the head noun is fronted; in (75), it is not.

(74) *mitak*   *'i*   *'amayon*   *'iyomas*
      matha-iy-   *-ko*   *'i*   *'amayo-'a* *'omas-iy-*
      see   -ACT/PFT-1SG/ERG ABS toy   -LK break-ACT/PFT

      na   nga'nga
      na   nga'nga
      ERG child

      'I saw the toy that the child broke'.

(75) *mitak*   *'i*   *'iyomas*
      matha-iy-   *-ko*   *'i*   *'omas-iy-*
      see   -ACT/PFT-1SG/ERG ABS break-ACT/PFT

      na   nga'ngen   'amayo
      na   nga'nga-'a 'amayo
      ERG child   -LK toy

      'I saw the toy that the child broke'.

In order for the Agent in (74) and (75) to be the head noun, the transitive relative clause must first change to an antipassive construction so that the Agent is the absolutive NP, as in (76).

(76) mitak   ʿi   ngaʿngen
      matha-iy-   -ko   ʿi   ngaʿnga-ʿa
      see   -ACT/PFT-1SG/ERG ABS child   -LK

      ʿengomas   na   ʿamayo
      ʿeN   -ʿomas na   ʿamayo
      ACT/AG/PFT-break OBL toy

      'I saw the child who broke the toy'.

Notice that when an absolutive NP is the head noun, a deletion strategy is used to recover its identity in the relative clause: the absolutive NP is absent, and an affix on the verb in the relative clause identifies the semantic role of the missing NP.[28,29]

In (77), the relative clause is a passive construction, and the possessor of the absolutive NP is the head noun.

(77) mitak   ʿi   ngaʿngen
      matha-iy-   -ko   ʿi   ngaʿnga-ʿa
      see   -ACT/PFT-1SG/ERG ABS child   -LK

      ʿaʿomas   ʿi   ʿamayo to
      ʿe   -ʿomas ʿi   ʿamayo to
      PASS/PFT-break ABS toy   3SG/GEN

      'I saw the child whose toy had been broken'.

When a possessor of the absolutive NP is the head noun, a pronoun strategy is used to recover the identity of the head noun in the relative clause: an anaphoric pronoun is deposited in the relative clause, marking the position and the morphological case of the missing NP; the anaphoric pronoun agrees in person and number with the head noun.

Strictly speaking, possessors do not bear a relation to the verb, rather they bear a relation to another noun; consequently, they cannot be a grammatical relation since by definition a grammatical relation must bear a relation to a verb. I suggest that in Karao, a possessor may be the head of a relative clause only because it has a relation to the absolutive NP. It is the absolutive NP that is central to relativization, not the possessor. For these reasons, I will ignore possessor for the remainder of the discussion.

The following examples verify that only the absolutive NP can be the head of Relative Clause 1: (78) shows that the ergative NP cannot be the head of Relative Clause 1; (79) shows that a demoted absolutive NP also cannot be the head of Relative Clause 1.

(78) *mitak   ⁽i   ngaⁿngen
      matha-iy-   -ko   ⁽i   ngaⁿnga-ⁿa
      see   -ACT/PFT-1SG/ERG ABS child -LK

      ⁿiyomas   toy   ⁿamayo
      ⁿomas-iy-   to   -ⁿi   ⁿamayo
      break-ACT/PFT 3SG/ERG-ABS toy

      'I saw the child who broke the toy'.

(79) *mitak   ⁽i   ⁿamayon
      matha-iy-   -ko   ⁽i   ⁿamayo-ⁿa
      see   -ACT/PFT-1SG/ERG ABS toy   -LK

      ⁿengomas   ⁽i   ngaⁿnga
      ⁿeN   -ⁿomas ⁽i   ngaⁿnga
      ACT/AG/PFT-break ABS child

      'I saw the toy that the child broke'.

In (76) above, the relative clause is an antipassive, and the head noun is an Agent. In (80) below, the relative clause is an intransitive clause, and the head noun is a Theme (Patient), demonstrating that the head noun of a single-argument relative clause can encode different semantic roles.

(80) mitak   ⁽i   ⁿoleg ⁿa simekep
      matha-iy-   -ko   ⁽i   ⁿoleg ⁿa sekep-im-
      see   -ACT/PFT-1SG/ERG ABS snake LK enter -ACT/TH/PFT

      cha baliy
      cha baliy
      OBL house

      'I saw the snake that entered into the house'.

Oblique arguments can be the head of a relative clause if they are first promoted to direct object, in which case they automatically become absolutive NPs. Since promoted oblique arguments have a variety of semantic roles, this verifies that the syntactic control of a transitive relative clause can encode different semantic roles. In the following pairs of examples, the first example is an attested form in which the oblique argument has been

promoted before relativization; the second is an unattested form in which
the oblique argument has not been promoted before relativization.

(81) Location

    sejay ꞌi   bangkon   tokkongan   *na   ngaꞌnga*
    sejay ꞌi   bangko-ꞌa tokkong-an   *na   ngaꞌnga*
    this   ABS bench -LK sit   -ACT/LOC/IMPFT ERG child
    'This is the bench that the child will sit on'.

(82) **sejay ꞌi   bangkon   ꞌontokkong*   *ꞌi   ngaꞌnga*
    sejay ꞌi   bangko-ꞌa ꞌon   -tokkong ꞌi   ngaꞌnga
    this   ABS bench -LK ACT/TH/IMPFT-sit   ABS child

(83) Location (Recipient)

    sejay ꞌi   ngaꞌngen   ꞌiꞌkanan   *na   toꞌo*
    sejay ꞌi   ngaꞌnga-ꞌa ꞌi--an   -ꞌikan na   toꞌo
    this   ABS child   -LK ACT/LOC/IMPFT-give ERG person

    na   dibcho
    na   dibcho
    OBL book

    'This is the child who the person will give the book to'.

(84) **sejay ꞌi   ngaꞌngen   ꞌiꞌkan*   *na   toꞌoy*
    sejay ꞌi   ngaꞌnga-ꞌa ꞌi   -ꞌikan na   toꞌo
    this   ABS child   -LK ACT/TH/IMPFT-give ERG person

       dibcho
    -*ꞌi   dibcho*
    -ABS book

(85) Nonnuclear Theme (Instrument)

    sejay ꞌi   bathon   ꞌitegteg
    sejay ꞌi   batho-ꞌa ꞌi   -tegteg
    this   ABS rock -LK ACT/NTH/IMPFT-flatten

    na   ngaꞌnged   ꞌaramdi
    na   ngaꞌnga-cha ꞌaramdi
    ERG child   -OBL wire

    'This is the rock that the child will use to flatten the wire'.

(86) *sejay ⁽i   bathon   tegtegen*
      sejay ⁽i   batho-⁽a tegteg-en
      this ABS rock -LK flatten-ACT/TH/IMPFT

      na   nga⁽ngiy   ⁽aramdi
      na   nga⁽nga-⁽i   ⁽aramdi
      ERG child   -ABS wire

(87) Nonnuclear Location (Beneficiary)

      sejay ⁽i   nga⁽ngen   ⁽itongkalan   na to⁽o
      sejay ⁽i   nga⁽nga-⁽a ⁽i--an   -tongkal na to⁽o
      this ABS child   -LK ACT/NLOC/IMPFT-buy   ERG person

      na ⁽amayo
      na ⁽amayo
      OBL toy

      'This is the child who the person will buy the toy for'.

(88) *sejay ⁽i   nga⁽ngen   tongkalen*
      sejay ⁽i   nga⁽nga-⁽a tongkal-en
      this ABS child   -LK buy   -ACT/TH/IMPFT

      na to⁽oy   ⁽amayo
      na to⁽o   -⁽i ⁽amayo
      ERG person-ABS toy

Relative Clause 2

Relative Clause 2 modifies the argument of an existential clause, and the head noun can be either an ergative NP or an absolutive NP. When the ergative NP is the head noun, the pronoun strategy is used to recover the identity of the head noun in the relative clause: an anaphoric pronoun is deposited in the ergative position in the relative clause; the pronoun agrees in person and number with the head noun, as in (89).

(89) *gwara diy   ⁽iKadasan*
      gwara da -⁽i ⁽i   -Kadasan
      EXT   DIR-ABS person.of-Kadasan

      ⁽a ⁽in⁽anop   toy   ⁽aso tho
      ⁽a ⁽in   -⁽anop to   -⁽i ⁽aso to
      LK ACT/NTH/PFT-hunt 3SG/ERG-ABS dog 3SG/GEN

      'There was a person from Kadasan who went hunting with his dog'.

(90) confirms that the presence of the anaphoric ergative pronoun in the relative clause is obligatory.

(90) *gwara diy* *ʿiKadasan*
    gwara da -ʿi   *ʿi*   *-Kadasan*
    EXT   DIR-ABS person.of-Kadasan

    ʿa *ʿinʿanop*   *ʿi* *ʿaso tho*
    ʿa *ʿin*   *-ʿanop* *ʿi* *ʿaso to*
    LK ACT/NTH/PFT-hunt   ABS dog 3SG/GEN

In (89) above, the head noun is an Agent; in (91) below, it is a Location (Experiencer). These examples verify that as the head of Relative Clause 2, an ergative NP can encode different semantic roles.

(91) *gwara diy*   *ʿarin*   *diningding*   *toy*
    gwara da -ʿi   *ʿari -ʿa* *dingding-iy-*   *to*   *-ʿi*
    EXT   DIR-ABS king-LK forget   -ACT/PFT 3SG/ERG-ABS

    ngaran to
    ngaran to
    name   3SG/GEN

'There was a king who forgot his name'.

The difference between Relative Clause 1 and 2 may have its motivation in the discourse function of existential clauses: the preferred way to introduce an important participant in a narrative is to present the participant in an existential clause upon first mention. By allowing the ergative NP to be the head of a transitive relative clause, two key participants can be introduced simultaneously, with the more topical argument encoded in its usual ergative position. (89) is just such a presentation existential clause: it is the first sentence of a narrative and introduces simultaneously the hunter from Kadasan and his dog, the two participants that figure most prominently in the story. Although the difference between Relative Clause 1 and 2 may be motivated by discourse function, I have analyzed the clauses as two separate constructions because the main clause of each relative clause type takes a different predicate, and each clause type allows different arguments to be the head noun.

To summarize, Relative Clause 1 displays an unambiguous ergative pattern of syntactic control in that only the absolutive NP can be the head.

Relative Clause 2, on the other hand, can follow either an ergative or a nominative pattern of control since either the ergative NP or the absolutive NP can be the head of a transitive relative clause.

Since the ergative NP and the absolutive NP can be the head of a relative clause, this satisfies the syntactic control criterion for grammatical relations. Since only the absolutive NP can be the head of Relative Clause 1, this satisfies the coding and exclusion criteria for the absolutive NP. The fact that the ergative NP cannot be the head of Relative Clause 1, but can be the head of Relative Clause 2 demonstrates that relativization differentiates between the ergative NP and the absolutive NP. Since the pattern of inclusion and exclusion as syntactic control applies only to the ergative NP, this satisfies the coding and exclusion criteria for the ergative NP. Finally, since the absolutive NP and the ergative NP can encode different semantic roles as the head of a relative clause, this satisfies the semantic role criterion. Thus, relativization demonstrates that the absolutive NP and the ergative NP are grammatical relations.

7.3. *Clefting*

Cross-linguistically, the structure of relative clauses and cleft constructions tends to be similar, and this is true for Karao. In a cleft construction in Karao, the head noun occurs in the sentence initial position; the absolutive marker *'i* is inserted before the verb, nominalizing the remaining clause. (The nominalized clause is a headless relative clause.) The head noun is always coreferential with the deleted absolutive NP of the headless relative clause. An affix on the verb identifies the semantic role of the deleted NP. In cleft constructions, the headless relative clause can be a transitive clause, as in (92), or a single-argument clause, as in (93).[30]

> (92) *ngaʿngiy   kidat   na   ʿoleg*
>   *ngaʿnga -ʿi   kalat-iy-   na   ʿoleg*
>   child   -ABS bite -ACT/PFT ERG snake
>   'The child is who the snake bit'.

> (93) *ʿoleg ʿi   simekep   cha baliy*
>   *ʿoleg ʿi   sekep-im-   cha baliy*
>   snake ABS enter -ACT/TH/PFT OBL house
>   'The snake is what entered into the house'.

Oblique arguments can be the head of a cleft construction if they are first promoted to direct object, in which case they automatically become absolutive NPs, as the following pairs of examples show. In each pair, the first sentence is an attested form in which the oblique has been promoted before clefting; the second is an unattested form in which the oblique has not been promoted before clefting.

(94) Location

    bangkoy   tokkongan   na nga⁢nga
    bangko-⁢i   tokkong-an   na nga⁢nga
    bench -ABS sit   -ACT/LOC/IMPFT ERG child
    'The bench is what the child will sit on'.

(95) *bangkoy   ⁢ontokkong   ⁢i   nga⁢nga
    bangko-⁢i   ⁢on   -tokkong ⁢i   nga⁢nga
    bench -ABS ACT/TH/IMPFT-sit   ABS child

(96) Location (Recipient)

    nga⁢ngiy   ⁢i⁢kanan   na to⁢o
    nga⁢nga-⁢i ⁢i--an   -⁢ikan na to⁢o
    child   -ABS ACT/LOC/IMPFT-give ERG person

    na dibcho
    na dibcho
    OBL book

    'The child is who the person will give the book to'.

(97) *nga⁢ngiy   ⁢i⁢kan   na to⁢oy   dibcho
    nga⁢nga-⁢i ⁢i   -⁢ikan na to⁢o -⁢i dibcho
    child   -ABS ACT/TH IMPFT-give ERG person-ABS book

(98) Nonnuclear Theme (Instrument)

    bathoy   ⁢itegteg   na nga⁢nged
    batho-⁢i   ⁢i   -tegteg na nga⁢nga-cha
    rock -ABS ACT/NTH/IMPFT-flatten ERG child   -OBL

    ⁢aramdi
    ⁢aramdi
    wire

    'The rock is what the child will use to flatten the wire'.

(99) *bathoy   tegtegen   na   nga'ngiy
       batho-'i   tegteg-en   na   nga'nga-'i
       rock -ABS flatten-ACT/TH/IMPFT ERG child   -ABS

       'aramdi
       'aramdi
       wire

(100) Nonnuclear Location (Beneficiary)

       nga'ngiy   'itongkalan   na   to'o
       nga'nga-'i   'i--an   -tongkal na   to'o
       child   -ABS ACT/NLOC/IMPFT-buy   ERG person

       na   'amayo
       na   'amayo
       OBL toy

       'The child is who the person will buy the toy for'.

(101) *nga'ngiy   tongkalen   na   to'oy
       nga'nga-'i   tongkal-en   na   to'o -'i
       child   -ABS buy   -ACT/TH/IMPFT ERG person-ABS

       'amayo
       'amayo
       toy

The following examples verify that only the absolutive NP can be the
head of a cleft construction. (102) demonstrates that the ergative NP cannot be the head of a cleft construction.

(102) *'oleg 'i   kidat   toy   nga'nga
        'oleg 'i   kalat-iy-   to   -'i   nga'nga
       snake ABS bite -ACT/PFT 3SG/ERG-ABS child
       'The snake is what bit the child'.

In order for the Agent 'oleg 'snake' in (102) to be the head of a cleft construction, the verb has to change to its antipassive form so that the Agent
is the absolutive NP, as in (103).

(103) *'oleg 'i 'engalat   na nga'nga*
      'oleg 'i 'eN   -kalat na nga'nga
      snake ABS ACT/AG/PFT-bite   OBL child
      'The snake is what bit the child'.

(104) demonstrates that a demoted absolutive NP also cannot be the head
of a cleft construction.

(104) **nga'ngiy   'engalat   'i 'oleg*
      nga'nga-'i   'eN   -kalat 'i 'oleg
      child   -ABS ACT/AG/PFT-bite ABS snake
      'A child is what the snake bit'.

The preceding examples verify that the head noun, i.e. the syntactic
control, of a cleft construction can have different semantic roles, regardless
of whether the headless relative clause is a single-argument clause ((93) and
(103)) or a transitive clause ((92) and (94)-(101)).

These examples confirm that clefting has an unambiguous ergative pattern of syntactic control: only the absolutive argument can be the head of
a cleft construction. As the head of a cleft construction, the absolutive argument meets the syntactic control criterion for grammatical relations. It
meets the coding criterion in that the head of a cleft construction is always
encoded as an absolutive NP; it meets the exclusion criterion in that only
an absolutive argument can be the head of a cleft construction; and it meets
the semantic role criterion in that as the head of a cleft construction, the
absolutive NP can encode different semantic roles. Thus, clefting provides
evidence that the absolutive argument of either a single-argument or a transitive clause is a grammatical relation.

7.4. *Zero anaphora in chained clauses*

Zero anaphora in chained clauses involves conjoined or adjacent independent clauses that share coreferential arguments. An absent argument, i.e. a
zero anaphor, in the second clause is coreferential with an argument in the
first clause. Cooreman et al. (1984) give the following attested coreference
patterns for zero anaphora in chained clauses. In Table 3, clause 1 is a transitive clause; clause 2 can be either a transitive clause or an intransitive
clause (or any single-argument clause).

Table 3. *Coreference patterns for zero anaphora in chained clauses*

Transitive Clause 2

(i) Ergative Pattern
    John$_i$ saw Bill$_j$ and he$_i$ kicked 0$_j$
(ii) Nominative Pattern
    John$_i$ saw Bill$_j$ and 0$_i$ kicked him$_j$

Intransitive Clause 2

(i) Ergative Pattern
    John$_i$ saw Bill$_j$ and (then) 0$_j$ left
(ii) Nominative Pattern
    John$_i$ saw Bill$_j$ and (then) 0$_i$ left

In chained clauses, if clause 2 is a transitive clause, two argument slots are available and both arguments in clause 1 can be coreferenced, in which case the coreferential arguments are normally assigned to NPs in clause 2 in the same way as in clause 1. On the other hand, if clause 2 is an intransitive clause (or any single-argument clause), only one argument slot is available, and so only one argument in clause 1 can be coreferenced. If coreference follows an ergative pattern, the non-Agent of clause 1 is the antecedent of the zero anaphor in clause 2; if it follows a nominative pattern, the Agent of clause 1 is the antecedent.

Strictly speaking, there is no distinction between zero anaphora in chained clauses and zero pronominalization in Karao, since an anaphoric absolutive NP with a third person referent is normally encoded as a zero argument.[31] On the other hand, coreference in chained clauses is of interest in that Karao displays an ergative pattern when the second clause is intransitive. In (105) and (106), clause 2 is a transitive clause; the zero anaphor is a Theme (Patient) in (105) and a Nonnuclear Location (Beneficiary) in (106).[32]

(105) CLAUSE 1 (Transitive)

    ʻida   na   ngaʻngiy   mangka
    ʻala-iy-   na   ngaʻnga-ʻi   mangka
    get -ACT/PFT ERG child   -ABS mango

CLAUSE 2 (Transitive)

'et   kiyakan   to   0
'et   CV-kan-iy-   to   0
and R   -eat -ACT/PFT 3SG/ERG 0

'The child got the mango and he ate it [the mango]'.

(106) CLAUSE 1 (Transitive)

'iyodop   na   bi'iy   'anak tod   kantina
'olop-iy-   na   bi'i   -'i   'anak to   -cha kantina
take -ACT/PFT ERG woman-ABS child 3SG/GEN-OBL store

CLAUSE 2 (Transitive)

'et   'intongkalan   toy   0 na   kindi
'et   'in--an   -tongkal to   -'i   0 na   kindi
and ACT/NLOC/PFT-buy   3SG/ERG-ABS 0 OBL candy

'The woman took her child to the store and bought her some candy'.

In (107) and (108), clause 2 is a single-argument clause; the zero anaphor is an Agent in (107) and a Theme (Patient) in (108).

(107) CLAUSE 1 (Transitive)

'intoro   na   maistariy   nga'nga
'in   -toro na   maistara-'i   nga'nga
ACT/TH/PFT-point ERG teacher -ABS child

CLAUSE 2 (Intransitive)

'et   'iyankansiyon   0
'et   'iyan   -kansiyon 0
and ACT/AG/PFT-sing   0

'The teacher pointed at the child and she [the child] sang'.

(108) CLAUSE 1 (Transitive)

binirok   na   nga'ngiy   'osab
birok-iy-   na   nga'nga-'i   'osab
blow -ACT/PFT ERG child   -ABS bubble

CLAUSE 2 (Intransitive)

'et   timayab   0
'et   tayab   -im-   0
and blow.away-ACT/TH/PFT 0

'The child blew the bubble and it [the bubble] blew away'.

Zero anaphora in (105)-(108) displays a typical ergative coreference pattern. In (105) and (106), clause 2 is a transitive clause, and the anaphoric arguments are encoded in clause 2 in the same way as in clause 1. The antecedent of the zero anaphor in clause 2 is the absolutive NP in clause 1. In (107) and (108), clause 2 is a single-argument clause, and the antecedent of the zero anaphor in clause 2 is again the absolutive NP in clause 1.

Although the ergative coreference pattern is the most frequently occurring pattern for zero anaphora in chained clauses in Karao, it is not obligatory when clause 2 is transitive, as the following example shows.

(109) CLAUSE 1 (Transitive)

sinit   tos   'ahi   to;
senit -iy-   to   -si   'ahi   to
offend-ACT/PFT 3SG/ERG-ABS sibling 3SG/GEN

CLAUSE 2 (Transitive)

'isonga   'eg   to   tetetbalen   0
'isonga   'eg   to   CV -tebal   -en   0
that's.why NEG 3SG/ERG CONT-talk.with-ACT/TH/IMPFT 0

'He offended his brother; that's why he [his brother] never talks to him'.

In (109), clause 2 is transitive; the antecedent of the zero anaphor in clause 2 is the ergative Agent in clause 1, *to* 'he'; the antecedent for the ergative pronoun *to* 'he' in clause 2 is the absolutive Theme (Patient) in clause 1, *'ahi to* 'his brother'. Notice that in (109) both anaphoric arguments in clause 2 have third person singular antecedents. Since zero anaphora has more than one pattern of coreference when clause 2 is transitive, we assume that it is context that enables the listener to assign the correct antecedents to the arguments in clause 2.

The fact that Karao has two patterns of coreference for zero anaphora raises the question, which coreference pattern is favored in narrative text?

In his grammar of Dyirbal, Dixon (1972) argues that Dyirbal has syntactic ergativity because, among other things, coreferential arguments in chained clauses display an ergative pattern of coreference. In a later study of Dyirbal narrative text, Cooreman (1988) shows that coreference in chained clauses in Dyirbal actually follows a nominative pattern more often than an ergative pattern (nominative pattern — 48%; ergative pattern — 22%). Similarly, a claim has been made that coreferential arguments in chained clauses in Tagalog display an ergative pattern of coreference (Verhaar 1988). In a study of discourse ergativity, Cooreman et al. (1984) show that coreference in chained clauses in Tagalog narrative text follows an ergative pattern in only 48% of the total ergative transitive clauses. Since the ergative coreference pattern does not occur in the majority of chained clauses in either Dyirbal or Tagalog, we are interested to know what is the frequency of the two patterns in Karao narrative text.

To determine the frequency of these patterns, we will look at two quantitative measures. The first is the distribution frequency of nominative and ergative patterns of coreference in chained clauses in narrative text. The number of available narrative texts in Karao is quite limited; consequently, only 10 pairs of independent clauses displaying zero anaphora were identified. In these pairs, clause 1 is a transitive clause; clause 2 is either a transitive or a single-argument clause. For each pair of clauses, the antecedent of the zero anaphor in clause 2 was tallied. If Karao has a predominantly ergative pattern of coreference, we would expect the non-Agent of clause 1 (non-AG_1) to be the antecedent of the zero anaphor of clause 2 (0-NP_2) in the majority of the clause pairs. The results of the counts are given in Table 4.

Table 4. *Frequency distribution of antecedents for zero anaphora in chained clauses in Karao narrative text*

	Clause 2-Transitive		Clause 2-Single-Argument		Clause 2-Total	
	N	%	N	%	N	%
0-NP_2 = AG_1	0	0.0	0	0.0	0	0.0
0-NP_2 = Non-AG_1	6	100.0	4	100.0	10	100.0
Total	6	100.0	4	100.0	10	100.0

Note: 0-NP_2 is the zero argument in clause 2.
  AG_1 is the Agent in clause 1.
  Non-AG_1 is the non-Agent in clause 1.

For the 10 pairs of coreferential clauses, Table 4 shows the frequency with which the Agent and the non-Agent in clause 1 are the antecedents of the zero anaphor in clause 2; separate frequencies are listed for a transitive clause 2 and a single-argument clause 2. When clause 2 is transitive, the non-Agent in clause 1 is the antecedent of the zero anaphor in clause 2 in 100% of the occurrences (6 out of 6). When clause 2 is a single-argument clause, the non-Agent in clause 1 is also the antecedent of the zero anaphor in clause 2 in 100% of the occurrences (4 out of 4). Thus, the non-Agent in clause 1 is the antecedent of the zero anaphor in clause 2 in 100% of the occurrences (10 out of 10). These measures show that in Karao narrative text, the ergative coreference pattern occurs in 100% of the chained clauses with coreferential arguments. Since the number of chained clauses displaying zero anaphora is so limited, these figures are best taken as reflecting a general tendency rather than strict grammatical restrictions. Since a nonergative pattern of coreference is possible in Karao when clause 2 is transitive, we would expect that in a larger number of narrative texts, zero anaphora would follow a nonergative pattern in at least a small number of chained clauses, although we would still expect the process to follow an ergative pattern in the majority of the clauses.

The second quantitative measure is the frequency distribution of anaphoric arguments in three coding devices: zero argument (i.e. zero anaphor), pronoun, and full NP. The measure includes the 10 pairs of coreferential clauses in Table 4 plus 7 more for a total of 17 clause pairs. In Karao, if an anaphoric absolutive NP in clause 2 has a third person antecedent, it is always encoded as either a zero argument or a full NP; if the anaphoric absolutive argument in clause 2 has a first or second person antecedent, it is always encoded as a pronoun. Of the 17 clause pairs counted, 16 have an anaphoric argument in clause 2 that has a third person singular antecedent; 1 pair has an anaphoric argument that has a third person plural antecedent. If Karao follows a typical ergative pattern of coreference, the majority of the anaphoric arguments in clause 2 will be encoded as zero arguments, i.e. zero anaphors. The frequencies for coding devices are given in Table 5.

Table 5. *Frequency distribution of coding devices for anaphoric absolutive NPs in chained clauses in Karao narrative text*

Coding Device	N	%
Definite Full NP	6	35.4
Pronoun	1	5.8
0-NP	10	58.8
Total	17	100.0

Table 5 shows that the anaphoric argument in clause 2 is encoded as a zero argument in 58% of the clause pairs (10 out of 17). It is worth noting that of the 7 pairs of chained clauses that have corefential arguments, but which encode the coreferential absolutive argument in clause 2 as a pronoun or a full NP, all 7 follow an ergative pattern of coreference. In other words, all 17 pairs of chained clauses follow an ergative pattern. Taken together, the frequencies in Tables 4 and 5 provide clear evidence that the majority of chained clauses with coreferential arguments in Karao narrative text follow an ergative pattern of coreference.

To summarize, zero anaphora in chained clauses can follow either an ergative or a nominative pattern of syntactic control. Thus, both the ergative NP and the absolutive NP of a transitive clause satisfy the syntactic control criterion for grammatical relations. The arguments satisfy the coding criterion in that the syntactic control for zero anaphora in chained clauses is always encoded as either an ergative NP or an absolutive NP; the exclusion criterion is satisfied in that only the ergative NP or the absolutive NP can be the syntactic control for this process; and the semantic control criterion is satisfied in that as the syntactic control, these arguments can encode different semantic roles. Thus, zero anaphora in chained clauses verifies that the ergative NP and the absolutive NP of a transitive clause are grammatical relations.

7.5. *Coreference in imperatives*

Imperatives are constructions in which an argument of the clause is coreferential with the addressee; thus, the argument can be said to control coreference. The coreferential argument may be present in the surface structure,

usually as a second person pronoun, or it can be absent, depending on the
language.

Karao has three imperative constructions: a positive imperative, a negative imperative, and a first-person imperative. Each construction has a unique
structure.

Positive imperative
In the positive imperative, a second person pronoun coreferences the addressee.
In single-argument clauses, the absolutive NP is coreferential with the
addressee.

> (110) *kepejas*   *ka*
>   *ke*   -*payas*   *ka*
>   IMPER-stay.behind 2SG/ABS
>   'You stay behind'.

The verb in (110) corresponds to the stative form *mepejas* (*me*–+*payas*)
'to stay behind'. The lack of a semantic role morpheme on the verb indicates that the absolutive NP *ka* 'you' is a Theme (Patient).

> (111) *pansada*   *ka*
>   *pan*   -*sada*   *ka*
>   IMPER/AG-dance 2SG/ABS
>   'You dance'.

The verb in (111) corresponds with the intransitive form *mansada*
(*man*–+*sada*) 'to dance', and the semantic role of the absolutive NP is
Agent.

In transitive clauses, the ergative NP is coreferential with the addressee.

> (112) *ʿalam*   *ʿi*   *kompay*
>   *ʿala-mo*   *ʿi*   *kompay*
>   get -2SG/ERG ABS hand.hoe
>   'You get the hand hoe'.

The bare verb stem in (112) corresponds with the transitive form *ʿaʿdaʿen*
(*ʿala*+–*en*) 'to get'; the ergative NP is an Agent.

(113) *nemnem moy*   *songbat*
      nemnem mo   -*ʿi*   *songbat*
      think   2SG/ERG-ABS answer
      'You think of the answer'.

The bare verb stem in (113) corresponds with the transitive form *nemnemen* (*nemnem+–en*) 'to think'; the ergative NP is a Location (Experiencer).

In these examples, the absolutive NP in a single-argument clause and the ergative NP in a transitive clause are coreferential with the addressee, indicating that coreference in the positive imperative operates on a nominative pattern of control.

Negative imperative
The negative imperative follows the same coreference pattern as the positive imperative; however, in the negative imperative, the argument that is coreferential with the addressee is always absent. In single-argument clauses, the absent absolutive NP is coreferential with the addressee.

(114) *ʿenog ʿi*   *chanag*
      don't ABS worry
      'Don't worry'.

The bare verb stem in (114) corresponds to the intransitive form *ʿonchanag* (*ʿon–+chanag*) 'to worry'; the semantic role of the absent absolutive NP is a Theme (Experiencer).

(115) *ʿenog ʿi*   *dinis*
      don't ABS clean
      'Don't clean'.

The bare stem in (115) corresponds to the intransitive form *mandinis* (*man–+dinis*) 'to clean'; the absent absolutive NP is an Agent.

In transitive clauses, the argument that is coreferential with the addressee is the absent ergative NP. In (116), the absent ergative NP is an Agent; in (117), it is a Location (Experiencer).

(116) *ʿenog ʿi*   *kinibot*   *ʿi*   *manok*
      ʿenog ʿi   *kibot-iy-*   *ʿi*   *manok*
      don't ABS steal-ACT/PFT ABS chicken
      'Don't steal the chicken'.

(117) *'enog 'i   niyemnem   'i   digat   mo*
      'enog 'i   nemnem-iy-   'i   digat   mo
      don't ABS think   -ACT/PFT ABS difficulties 2SG/GEN
      'Don't think about your troubles'.

(114)-(117) show that deletion of the coreferential addressee in the
negative imperative follows a nominative pattern of control.

First-person imperative
The first-person imperative has two constructions: one for single-argument
verbs and another for transitive verbs. Single-argument verbs are encoded
in a single-argument clause, and the absolute first person dual pronoun
kiya 'we' is coreferential with the speaker and addressee.[33] In (118), the
semantic role of *kiya* 'we' is Agent; in (119), it is Theme (Patient). Note
that *mepejas* 'to stay behind' in (119) is a stative form, not a passive form.

(118) *man'ekad   kiya*
      man   -'ahad kiya
      ACT/AG/IMPFT-walk 1DL/ABS
      'Let's walk'.
      [Literally: 'We will walk'.]

(119) *mepejas   kiya*
      me   -payas   kiya
      STAT/IMPFT-stay.behind 1DL/ABS
      'Let's stay behind'.
      [Literally: 'We will stay behind'.]

In contrast to single-argument verbs, transitive verbs are encoded in a
passive clause, and the deleted ergative NP of the corresponding transitive
clause is coreferential with the speaker and addressee. In (120), the deleted
ergative NP is an Agent; in (121), it is a Location (Experiencer).

(120) *mesked   'ira*
      me   -seked 'ira
      PASS/IMPFT-wait 3PL/ABS
      'Let's wait for them'.
      [Literally: 'They will be waited for'.]

(121) *menemnem*   *ʿi* *ʿobda*
  me *-nemnem ʿi* *ʿobda*
  PASS/IMPFT-think ABS book
  'Let's think about the work'.
  [Literally: 'The work will be thought about'.]

In a passive clause, the demoted ergative NP is no longer a required argument of the verb; consequently, the first-person imperative is irrelevant for the issue of grammatical relations since a grammatical relation must be a required argument of the verb. It should be noted, however, that only the deleted ergative NP can be coreferential with the addressee and the speaker in this construction; thus, the coreferential pattern of the first-person imperative does not contradict the nominative coreference pattern displayed by the positive and the negative imperatives. For the remainder of this study, coreference in imperatives will refer only to the positive imperative and the negative imperative.

To summarize, addressee coreference in imperatives operates on a nominative pattern of control: the absolutive argument of a single-argument clause and the ergative argument of a transitive clause are coreferential with the addressee. Thus, the absolutive argument and the ergative argument satisfy the syntactic control criterion for grammatical relations. These arguments satisfy the coding criterion in that arguments that are coreferential with the addressee of imperatives are always encoded as the absolutive NP in a single-argument clause and the ergative NP in a transitive clause; they also satisfy the exclusion criterion in that only the absolutive argument of a single-argument clause and only the ergative argument of a transitive clause are coreferential with the addressee in imperatives; and they satisfy the semantic role criterion in that as the control for addressee coreference in imperatives, the arguments can encode different semantic roles. Thus, coreference in imperatives verifies that the absolutive NP of a single-argument clause and the ergative NP of a transitive clause are grammatical relations.[34]

7.6. *Coreference in reflexives*

Reflexives are constructions in which two arguments of a clause are coreferential, normally the Agent and the Theme (Patient). One of these arguments, usually the Theme, will be less distinctly coded. Depending on the language, the less distinctly coded argument can be a pronoun or a zero argument or an invariant noun, such as 'body'. The more distinctly coded argument can be said to control coreference.

Karao has two reflexive constructions: one for verbs that are inherently reflexive and another for verbs that are not. Verbs that are inherently reflexive are encoded in a single-argument clause. Only the Agent surfaces; the coreferential Theme (Patient) is a zero argument, as shown in (122).

(122) *ʿiyanʿemes   ʿi   ngaʿnga*
      ʿiyan   -ʿemes ʿi   ngaʿnga
      ACT/AG/PFT-bathe ABS child
      'The child bathed (himself)'.

For all of the inherently reflexive verbs identified to date, the absolutive NP is an Agent.

Verbs that are not inherently reflexive are encoded in a transitive clause, and the ergative NP and the absolutive NP are coreferential. The absolutive NP is always represented by the invariant noun *ʿangel* 'body'; a possessor pronoun on *ʿangel* is coreferential with the ergative NP and agrees with it in person and number, as in (123).[35]

(123) *ʿingked   na ngaʿngiy   ʿangel to*
      ʿeked-iy-   na ngaʿnga-ʿi   ʿangel to
      cut -ACT/PFT ERG child   -ABS body 3SG/GEN
      'The child cut himself'.

In (123), the ergative NP is an Agent; in (124), it is a Location (Experiencer), demonstrating that as the control for coreference in reflexives, the ergative NP can encode different semantic roles.

(124) *niyemnem   na toʿoy   ʿangel to*
      nemnem-iy-   na toʿo -ʿi ʿangel to
      think   -ACT/PFT ERG person-ABS body 3SG/GEN
      'The person thought about himself'.

To summarize, coreference in reflexives has a nominative pattern of syntactic control: the absolutive argument of a single-argument clause and the ergative argument of a transitive clause are the more distinctly coded arguments of the two coreferential arguments in a clause that refer to a participant who is performing a reflexive action. As the syntactic control for reflexives, the absolute NP of the single-argument clause and the ergative NP of a transitive clause satisfy the syntactic control criterion for grammatical relations. The arguments satisfy the coding criterion in that the syntactic control of coreference in a single-argument reflexive is always encoded as an absolute NP while the syntactic control in a transitive reflexive is always encoded as an ergative NP. The arguments satisfy the exclusion criterion in that only the absolute argument of a single-argument clause and only the ergative argument of a transitive clause control coreference in reflexives. The ergative argument satisfies the semantic role criterion in that as the syntactic control of coreference in reflexives, it can encode different semantic roles; however, the absolute argument of a single-argument clause has been found so far to encode only an Agent. Thus, we conclude that coreference in reflexives is evidence that the ergative argument of a transitive clause is a grammatical relation.

7.7. Summary of coreferential deletion processes

Six coreferential deletion processes in Karao have been examined: (1) equi-NP deletion, (2) relativization, (3) clefting, (4) zero anaphora in chained clauses, (5) coreference in imperatives, and (6) coreference in reflexives. These processes and their patterns of syntactic control are summarized in Table 6.

Table 6. *Coreferential deletion processes in Karao*

Process	Syntactic Control Pattern	
	NOM	ERG
Equi-NP Deletion	X	
Relativization 1		X
Relativization 2	X	X
Clefting		X
Zero Anaphora in Chained Clauses	X	X
Coreference in Imperatives	X	
Coreference in Reflexives	X	

Coreferential deletion processes provide evidence for patterns of syntactic control. Table 6 shows that two coreferential processes follow an ergative pattern exclusively: relativization 1 and clefting. For these processes, the absolutive argument of a single-argument clause or a transitive clause plays a central role in the operation of each process. Three processes follow a nominative pattern exclusively: equi-NP deletion, coreference in imperatives, and coreference in reflexives. For these processes, the absolutive NP of a single-argument clause and the ergative NP of a transitive clause play a central role in each process. Two processes can follow more than one pattern. Relativization 2 can follow either an ergative or a nominative pattern of control. Zero anpahora in chained clauses follows an ergative pattern exclusively when clause 2 is intransitive, and either an ergative or a non-ergative pattern when clause 2 is transitive. (For convenience, the 'non-ergative' pattern is grouped with 'nominative' patterns in Table 6). The fact that the ergative pattern is obligatory for relativization 1 and clefting and the nominative pattern is obligatory for equi-NP deletion and coreference in imperatives and reflexives provides indisputable evidence that Karao has a mixed pattern of syntactic control.

Coreferential deletion processes also offer evidence for grammatical relations. As the only required argument of a single-argument clause, the absolutive NP is assumed to be a grammatical relation. This is verified in that the absolutive NP in a single-argument clause meets the four criteria for grammatical relations. It satisfies the syntactic control criterion in that in a single-argument clause, the absolutive NP controls all the coreferential deletion processes in Table 6; it satisfies the coding criterion in that the argument that controls these processes in a single-argument clause is always encoded in an absolutive NP; it satisfies the exclusion criterion in that in a single-argument clause, only the absolutive NP controls these processes; and it satisfies the semantic role criterion in that as the syntactic control in a single-argument clause for all of these processes except coreference in reflexives, the absolutive NP can encode different semantic roles.

The ergative NP of a transitive clause also satisfies the criteria for grammatical relations. It satisfies the syntactic control criterion in that it controls equi-NP deletion, relativization 2, zero anaphora in chained clauses, and coreference in imperatives and reflexives; it satisfies the coding criterion in that in a transitive clause, the argument that exclusively controls equi-NP deletion, and coreference in imperatives and reflexives is always encoded in an ergative NP; it satisfies the exclusion criterion in that in a transitive clause, only the ergative NP controls these three processes; and it satisfies the semantic role criterion in that as a syntactic control, the ergative NP can encode different semantic roles.

Finally, the absolutive NP of a transitive clause also satisfies the criteria for grammatical relations. It satisfies the syntactic control criterion in that it controls relativization 1 and 2, clefting, and zero anaphora in chained clauses; it satisfies the coding criterion in that in a transitive clause, the argument that exclusively controls relativization 1 and clefting is always encoded in an absolutive NP; it satisfies the exclusion criterion in that in a transitive clause, only the absolutive NP controls these two processes; and it satisfies the semantic role criterion in that as a syntactic control in transitive clauses, the absolutive NP can encode different semantic roles.

From these findings, we conclude that the absolutive NP in a single-argument clause, and the ergative NP and the absolutive NP in a transitive clause are grammatical relations. We are now ready to consider the entire body of evidence for grammatical relations and patterns of syntactic control in Karao.

8. Summary of all coding properties and syntactic processes

We began this study with the observation that Karao is a morphologically ergative language and noted that this raises two important questions: (1) what are the grammatical relations of the language and (2) what pattern of syntactic control does it follow?

To answer the first question, we defined grammatical relations in terms of four general criteria: (1) unique coding, (2) syntactic control, (3) exclusion, and (4) multiple semantic roles. For Karao, we specified that an argument is a grammatical relation if: it is uniquely identified by at least one coding property, it controls at least one syntactic process to the exclusion of all other arguments, and as a syntactic control, it encodes different semantic roles. We proposed that the required argument of a single-argument clause would be a grammatical relation by default since it is the only required argument in the clause. We further proposed that if the two arguments of a transitive clause proved to be grammatical relations, then the ergative NP would be identified as a subject, since it is usually the more agentive and more topical argument; the absolutive NP, on the other hand, would be identified as an object, since it is usually the less agentive and less topical argument. We, then, investigated a range of coding properties and syntactic processes in an attempt to identify the grammatical relations of Karao. The results of the investigation are summarized in the tables below. Table 7 lists the coding properties in Karao.

Table 7. *Summary of coding properties in Karao*

Coding Property	Morphological Pattern	
	NOM	ERG
Case Marking		X
Verb Cross-Referencing		X

Karao has three coding properties: case marking, verb cross-referencing, and word order. Word order distinguishes between the two required arguments of a transitive clause, and between the required argument and oblique arguments in a single-argument clause; however, since all NPs occur on the same side of the verb in a basic verbal clause, word order does not establish an ergative or a nominative pattern, and so is irrelevant for this issue. Case marking and verb cross-referencing, on the other hand, follow an ergative pattern exclusively. Coding properties, then, offer evidence for grammatical relations by demonstrating that the two required arguments of a transitive clause are uniquely coded in the surface structure: the more agentive argument as the *na*-marked ergative NP and the less agentive argument as the *'i*-marked absolutive NP.

Relation-changing processes in Karao provide evidence for grammatical relations by demonstrating that an argument functions as the syntactic control for a process. Based on cross-linguistic patterns of control for relation-changing processes, these processes also help verify the identity of the subject and object in a transitive clause. The results of relation-changing processes are summarized in Table 8.

Table 8. *Summary of relation-changing processes in Karao*

Process	Syntactic Control	
	ERG-NP	ABS-NP
Promotion to Direct Object		X
Passivization		X
Antipassivization		X
Raising	X	X

Karao has four relation-changing processes: (1) promotion to direct object, (2) passivization, (3) antipassivization, and (4) raising. The investigation shows that the first three processes are controlled exclusively by the absolutive NP in a transitive clause. Since these processes are controlled by an object (i.e. the less agentive argument of a transitive clause) in many languages, this is direct evidence that the transitive absolutive NP in Karao is an object. Raising is controlled by both the ergative NP and the absolutive NP; however, the ergative NP outranks the absolutive NP in eligibility for raising. Since subjects (i.e. the more agentive argument of a transitive clause) outrank objects in eligibility for raising in many languages, this is evidence that the ergative NP is a subject.

To answer the question about pattern of syntactic control, we investigated a range of coreferential deletion processes. These processes establish patterns of syntactic control and offer additional evidence for grammatical relations. Coreferential deletion processes are summarized in Table 9.

Table 9. *Summary of coreferential deletion processes in Karao*

Process	Syntactic Control Pattern	
	NOM	ERG
Equi-NP Deletion	X	
Relativization 1		X
Relativization 2	X	X
Clefting		X
Zero Anaphora in Chained Clauses	X	X
Coreference in Imperatives	X	
Coreference in Reflexives	X	

Karao has six coreferential deletion processes: (1) equi-NP deletion, (2) relativization, (3) clefting, (4) zero anaphora in chained clauses, (5) coreference in imperatives, and (6) coreference in reflexives. Equi-NP deletion and coreference in imperatives and reflexives follow a nominative pattern exclusively; relativization 1 and clefting follow an ergative pattern exclusively. Relativization 2 and zero anaphora in chained clauses follow an ergative pattern, and a nominative pattern (for relativization 2) or a nonergative pattern (for zero anaphora). Since three processes follow a nominative pattern exclusively and two processes follow an ergative pattern exclusively, this establishes that Karao has a mixed pattern of syntactic control.

With respect to grammatical relations, those coreferential deletion processes that have an exclusively nominative pattern of syntactic control demonstrate that the ergative NP is a grammatical relation. Since one of these processes, equi-NP deletion, is almost universally controlled by a subject (i.e. the more agentive argument of a transitive clause) even in languages that display a mixed pattern or an ergative pattern of syntactic control, this is direct support for the claim that the ergative NP is a subject. On the other hand, those processes that have an exclusively ergative pattern of control provide evidence that the absolutive NP in a transitive clause is also a grammatical relation. If equi-NP deletion identifies the ergative NP as a subject, this implies that the absolutive NP is an object which agrees with findings from relation-changing processes. Finally, all coreferential deletion processes provide evidence that the absolutive NP of a single-argument clause is a grammatical relation; however, since this argument does not control any syntactic process that is not also controlled by the ergative NP or the absolutive NP of a transitive clause, I have proposed that Karao has only two grammatical relations: a subject and an object.

Taken together, coding properties and syntactic processes show that the absolutive NP of a single-argument clause, and the ergative NP and the absolutive NP of a transitive clause are uniquely coded arguments, each of which functions as the exclusive syntactic control for at least one syntactic process, thus satisfying the coding, exclusion, and syntactic control criteria for grammatical relations. We have also shown that as a syntactic control, each of these arguments can encode different semantic roles, thus satisfying the semantic role criterion.[36] These findings verify our claim that the two required arguments in a transitive clause are grammatical relations: the ergative NP is a subject, and the absolutive NP is an object. The findings also verify that the absolutive NP of a single-argument clause is a grammatical relation; however, since this argument does not pattern exclusively with the subject or the object of a transitive clause, we have refrained from calling it either 'subject' or 'object'.

Coreferential deletion processes also show that some processes follow a nominative pattern of syntactic control exclusively, some follow an ergative pattern of control exclusively, and still others follow both an ergative, and a nominative or nonergative pattern of control. This verifies our claim that Karao has a mixed pattern of syntactic control in which syntactic control is distributed more or less evenly between the subject and the object of the transitive clause. We conclude, then, that Karao, a morphologically ergative language, has two grammatical relations, a subject and an object, and a mixed pattern of syntactic control.

Abbreviations

ABS	absolutive	PFT	perfective
ACT	active	R	reduplicated segment(s)
AG	Agent	SAP	speech act participant
CONT	continuous	STAT	stative
DIR	directional	TH	Theme
ERG	ergative	TOP	topic
EXT	existential	VAP	'Verb Agent Patient' word
GEN	genitive		order
IMPER	imperative	VAT	'Verb Agent Theme' word
IMPFT	imperfective		order
LK	linker	0-NP	zero anaphor
LOC	Location	1SG	first person singular
NEG	negative	2SG	second person singular
NLOC	Nonnuclear Location	3SG	third person singular
NOM	nominative	3PL	third person plural
NTH	Nonnuclear Theme	1DL	first person dual
non-AG	non-Agent	1EX	first person plural exclusive
OBL	oblique	1IN	first person plural inclusive
PASS	passive	??	meaning unknown

Notes

1. Karao is a Southern Cordilleran language of the Northern Philippines. This study is based on data gathered in 1988-1990 and 1994-1995, while the author was living in the village of Karao, under the auspices of the Summer Institute of Linguistics. The data include elicited sentences and paradigms, a 3,000-entry dictionary, and 150 pages of natural text, including samples of narrative, expository (explanatory), procedural, and hortatory genres. The author would like to thank all the people of Karao who helped with the collection of the data. Special thanks goes to Mr. John Beray who helped check all the data included in this paper.

    The following is the Karao orthography. The consonants are: *b* [b], *ch* [č], *d* [d], *f* [ɸ], *g* [g], *gw* [gʷ], *h* [x], *j* [ǰ], *k* [k] and [k], *l* [l], *m* [m], *n* [n], *ng* [ŋ], *p* [p], *r* [ř], *s* [s], *t* [t], *th* [θ], *w* [w], *y* [y]. The vowels are: *i* [i] or [e], *o* [u] or [o], *a* [a], and *e* [ɨ]. Glottal stop is a phoneme and is represented by a single quotation mark, as in pa'dok [paʔdok] 'stream' and bay'ong [bayʔoŋ] 'market basket'. Intervocalic consonants following *e* [ɨ] are always geminates.

2. This question is important, of course, for all languages.

3. Single-argument clauses include intransitive, antipassive, stative, and passive clauses.

4. Karao has complex phonological alternations which result in extensive allomorphy. (See Brainard 1994a for details.) Most case markers have two surface forms, the selection of which is controlled by phonological rules. For example, the case markers *'i* and *cha* usually follow a consonant-final word (although they can follow a vowel-final word); their counterparts *-y* and *-d* always follow a vowel-final word.

    The element *na* has several homophonous forms. Of these, some forms alternate with *-n* and some do not. Each homophonous form which has a consistent and different function is treated as a separate morpheme. All case markers are given in the following table.

Karao Case Markers

	Topic	Absolute	Ergative/ Oblique	Oblique
Singular				
Common noun	*say*	*'i/-y*	*na*	*cha/-d*
Personal noun	*si*	*si/-s*	*0/-n*	*cha/-d*
Plural				
Common noun	*say*	*'iriy/chiy*	*'ira na/cha na*	*'ired/ched*
Personal noun	*si*	*'ires/ches*	*'iren /chen*	*'ired/ched*

The ergative/oblique case markers can function as either ergative markers or oblique markers. They are also homophonous with genitive markers.

There is some variation between speakers concerning the ergative/oblique case markers. For *'ira na*, some speakers use *'iren na*; for *cha na, chen na*. The absolutive markers *'iriy* and *'ires* follow verbs ending with either a vowel or a consonant; however, when these case markers are separated from the verb by a word ending with a vowel, they are replaced by *chiy* and *ches*.

5.   Case-marked NPs can be replaced by case-marked pronouns and deictics. There are three sets of pronouns, each of which corresponds to a particular case marker, as shown in the following tables. (In the tables, if a form has two allomorphs, the first one usually follows a consonant-final word; the second always follows a vowel-final word.)

Karao Pronouns

	Absolutive	Ergative/ Genitive	Oblique/ Topic
Singular			
1	ak	ko/k	si'kak
2	ka	mo/m	si'kam
3	0	to/tho	si'katho
Plural			
1DL	kiya	tayo/thayo	si'kathayo
1IN	kiyacha	tayocha/thayocha	si'kathayocha
1EX	kawi	mi/wi	si'kawi
2	kayo	jo/yo	si'kayo
3	'ira/cha	cha/ra	si'kara

Oblique/topic pronouns can function as either topic pronouns or as oblique pronouns. When an oblique/topic pronoun replaces a NP preceded by the topic marker *say*, no case marker occurs before the pronoun; however, when such a pronoun replaces a NP preceded by the oblique marker *cha*, *cha* also occurs before the pronoun. Ergative/genitive pronouns can function as ergative pronouns or genitive pronouns. In an independent verbal clause, oblique *na*-marked NPs cannot be replaced by personal pronouns; although, they can be replaced by deictics.

Noun phrases can also be replaced by one of three sets of deictics, each of which corresponds to a particular case marker. Deictics have three basic forms: *jay* 'this/here' (near the speaker), *tan* 'that/there' (near the hearer), and *man* 'that/there' (away from both speaker and hearer). Most of these forms combine with case markers; for example, the case marker *na* plus the basic form *jay* becomes *niyay* (following consonant-final words) or *-n jay* (following vowel-final words). The singular absolutive forms *jay*, *tan*, and *man*, however, do not combine with a case marker when they function as adjectives. Also, when deictics function as adjectives, the final consonant of the deictic is optionally deleted. Like case markers, most deictics have a singular and a plural form, and most of these forms have two allomorphs — one that follows consonant-final words, and another that follows vowel-final words. All deictic forms are listed in the tables below.

Karao Deictics-Singular Forms

Basic Form		Topic	Absolutive	Ergative/ Oblique	Oblique
jay	'near speaker'	*sejay*	ʿiyay/ *jay*	*niyay/* *-n jay*	*chiyay/* *-d jay*
tan	'near hearer'	*setan*	ʿithan/ *tan*	*nithan/* *-n tan*	*chithan/* *-d tan*
man	'away from speaker and hearer'	*seman*	ʿiwan/ *man*	*niwan/* *-n man*	*chiwan/* *-d man*

Karao Deictics-Plural Forms

Basic Form		Topic	Absolutive
jay	'near speaker'	*sejay* ʿira	ʿira jay/ *cha jay*
tan	'near hearer'	*setan* ʿira	ʿira tan/ *cha tan*
man	'away from speaker and hearer'	*seman* ʿira	ʿira man/ *cha man*

Basic Form		Ergative/ Oblique	Oblique
jay	'near speaker'	ʿiren jay/ *chen jay*	ʿired jay/ *ched jay*
tan	'near hearer'	ʿiren tan/ *chen tan*	ʿired tan/ *ched tan*
man	'away from speaker and hearer'	ʿiren man/ *chen man*	ʿired man/ *ched man*

6. A comprehensive analysis of verb classes, verb affixes, and semantic roles is found in Brainard (1994b).

7. DeLancey's version of localist case grammar is based on earlier models proposed by Anderson (1971), Diehl (1975), Gruber (1976), and Jackendoff (1983, 1990).

8. Within the localist model, Recipients are assumed to be human Locations.

9.   A list of perfective and imperfective verb affixes is given in the table below. The affixes are identified by a semantic role that they commonly identify. Many verb affixes have more than one surface form; the basic form is given first and alternate forms follow.

Karao Verb Affixes

			Active			
	IMPFT	PFT			IMPFT	PFT
Theme	*'on-*	*-im-*				
Agent	*man-*	*'iyan-*				
Agent	*meN-*	*'eN-/*	Theme		*-en*	*-iy-/*
		'iyaN-				*-i- /*
						-in-
			Location		*-an*	*-iy--an/*
						-i--an /
						-in--an
Agent	*mengi-*	*'engi-*	Nonnuclear Theme		*'i-*	*'in-*
			Nonnuclear Location		*'i--an*	*'in--an*

	Stative		
	IMPFT	PFT	
Theme	*me-/*	*'e-/*	
	ma-	*'a-/*	
		'iya-	
Location	*me--an/*	*'e--an/*	
	ma--an	*'a--an/*	
		'iya--an	
Nonnuclear Theme	*may-*	*'iyay-*	
Nonnuclear Location	*may--an*	*'iyay--an*	

The affixes *mengi-* and *'engi-*, and *may-* and *'iyay-* (and by extension *may--an* and *'iyay--an*) are structurally complex morphemes. *Mengi-* is composed of the morphemes *meN+'i*, and *'engi-* of *'eN+'i*; *may-* is composed of *me+'i*, and *'iyay-* of *'iya+'i* (underlyingly *'e+'i*).

10. Since Karao has complex phonological alternations, the underlying form of each morpheme is given in the second line of an example. For convenience, examples are often given in the imperfective aspect since verb forms in this aspect do not have infixes as do many perfective forms; case marking is not affected by changes in aspect. Also, the absolutive NP is usually definite; NPs marked by *na* or *cha* (or their allomorphs) may be definite or indefinite, depending on the context. To avoid multiple English translations, one representative translation is given for each example.

11. In the passive construction, the deletion of the ergative NP of its transitive counterpart is not obligatory for all verbs. See section 6.2 for a discussion of passivization.

12. The syntactic control and exclusion criteria are borrowed from Anderson's (1976) discussion of subject in ergative languages.

13. The term 'syntactic control' is adopted here as a convenience to refer to the required argument that plays a crucial role in the operation of a syntactic process. Arguments differ in the way in which they play that role: the controlling argument can be the trigger of the process, as is the object in passivization, or it can be a target, as is the object in antipassivization. Since our primary concern here is to identify the argument that appears to be crucial for the operation of a syntactic process, we will use the term 'syntactic control' to refer to such an argument regardless of whether it functions as a trigger or target.

14. The issues of semantic role and topicality of the ergative and the absolutive NP of a transitive clause are beyond the scope of the paper. A discussion of these issues is found in Brainard (1994b).

15. A prototypical transitive clause is defined here as a clause that encodes a semantically transitive verb, such as *crush* or *cut*, and has two required arguments: an Agent and a Theme (Patient).

16. Since only the absolutive argument of a transitive clause can trigger passivization in Karao, and since (11) can be a transitive clause only if it has two required arguments, we conclude that the *na*-NP must be an ergative argument.

17. With the addition of the affixes *ʻi-*, *mengi-*, and *ʻengi-*, *i* [i] of the verb stem *ʻikan* 'to give' is deleted. (The initial glottal stop of the stem is inserted epenthetically, and does not block phonological alternations in the underlying form.)

18. In his discussion of subject in Tagalog, Kroeger (1993) suggests that the Tagalog equivalent of the construction in (35) is not an antipassive because the demoted Theme (Patient) does not act like other obliques in Tagalog. He argues that this is evidence against the 'object' analysis presented here (or 'ergative' analysis in Kroeger's terms). Whether or not the demoted Theme acts like other obliques is an irrelevant issue. The central question for the construction in (35) is, does the Theme (Patient) act like an object? For Karao, the answer is no. The *na*-marked NP in (35) cannot control any of the syntactic processes that are controlled by the absolutive NP in a transitive clause, thus indicating that it is not a required argument.

19. *Pakchal* is a denominal verb; the Theme (Patient) is the noun *pakchal* 'ladder/steps' which has been lexicalized into the verb, thereby allowing the Location to be the absolutive NP.

20. Further support for this claim is the argument that the imperfective affix *mengi-* is the composite form *meN+ʻi*, and the perfective affix *ʻengi-*, the composite form *ʻeN+ʻi*. If this morphological analysis is correct, then the same affix, *meN-*, is added to the verb in (40) and (41) to signal antipassivization.

21. To date, I have not found any examples of raising-to-subject in Karao.

22. In a complement construction, the main clause and the complement clause are connected by one of two linkers, *ʕi* or *ʕa*. The linker *ʕi* has only one surface form (which distinguishes it from the absolute case marker which has two allomorphs, *ʕi* and *-y*). The linker *ʕa* has two allomorphs: *ʕa* and *-n*. The allomorph *ʕa* usually follows consonant-final words; the allomorph *-n* always follows vowel-final words. The form of these allomorphs suggests that they derive historically from a single form, such as **na*. Although *na* is an attested form that shows up seemingly everywhere in Karao, performing different functions in different syntactic structures, *na* never occurs as a linker between a main clause and a complement clause. The morpheme *ʕa* also functions as a linker connecting members of other constituents, such as a head noun and its modifiers or a head noun and its relative clause. In these constructions also, *na* never replaces *ʕa* (or its allomorph *-n*).

23. Those readers who are familiar with Philippine languages may wonder if (45) is not simply a main clause in which *ngaʕnga* 'child' is modified by a relative clause, since the linker *ʕa* also joins a head noun and its relative clause. The construction in (45), however, contrasts with a noun modified by a relative clause: in a basic relative clause, the head noun must be the absolutive NP of the relative clause, and the semantic role of the head noun is identified by an affix on the verb in the relative clause, as shown (125).

(125) *mitak*   *ʕi   ngaʕngen*
       matha-iy-   -ko   ʕi   ngaʕnga-ʕa
       see   -ACT/PFT-1SG/ERG ABS child   -LK

       ʕemosak   na   ʕispiho
       ʕeN   -bosak na   ʕispiho
       ACT/AG/PFT-break OBL   mirror

       'I saw the child who broke the mirror'.

In addition, Karao speakers confirm that the construction in (45) cannot have the meaning: 'I saw the child who broke the mirror'.

24. (46) is actually a grammatical construction: it is a transitive clause in which the absolutive NP *ʕisipho* 'mirror' is modified by a relative clause. As such, it has the meaning 'I saw the mirror that the child broke'. Karao speakers accept only this meaning for (46).

25. Since an absolutive NP having a third person singular referent is encoded as a zero argument, examples involving SAP (speech act participant) referents are given in order to verify that the absolutive NP is deleted as the result of the syntactic process.

26. *Taha* is a suppletive form and is the equivalent of *ko* (1SG/ERG) + *ka* (2SG/ABS).

27. This is an operational definition of mixed pattern of syntactic control. In actuality, we would expect control of coreferential deletion processes to be more or less evenly distributed between the subject and the object of a transitive clause in such a pattern, so that not just one, but several processes would have an exclusively nominative pattern of control while several others would have an exclusively ergative pattern of control.

28. A relative clause with SAP referents verifies that the absolutive NP is deleted in the relative clause, as shown in (126)-(128). (129) confirms that deletion of the absolutive NP is obligatory.

(126) kowan matha'iy nga'nga
   ko -an matha-a -'i nga'nga
   1SG/ERG-CONT see -TH-ABS child
   'I see the child'.

(127) 'engi'emot   ka na dibcho
   'engi -'emot ka na dibcho
   ACT/AG/PFT-hide 2SG/ABS OBL book
   'You hid the book'.

(128) kowan   matha'a ken
   ko -an matha-a -'i ka -'a
   1SG/ERG-CONT see -TH-ABS 2SG/ABS-LK

   'engi'emot   na dibcho
   'engi -'emot na dibcho
   ACT/AG/PFT-hide OBL book
   'I see you who hid the book'.

(129) *kowan   matha'a ken
   ko -an matha-a -'i ka -'a
   1SG/ERG-CONT see -TH-ABS 2SG/ABS-LK

   'engi'emot   ka na dibcho
   'engi -'emot ka na dibcho
   ACT/AG/PFT-hide 2SG/ABS OBL book

29. Notice also that the Theme *'amayo* 'toy' in (76) is definite. In the Karao antipassive, demoted absolutive NPs can be definite.

30. A cleft construction with SAP referents verifies that the absolutive NP is deleted in the headless relative clause. In (130)-(132), the headless relative clause is a single-argument clause; in (133)-(135), it is a transitive clause. (132) and (135) confirm that the deletion of the absolutive NP is obligatory.

(130) jimo'kowak
   jo'kow-im-   -ak
   sleep -ACT/TH/PFT-1SG/ABS
   'I slept'.

(131) si'kak 'i jimo'kow
   si'kak 'i jo'kow-im-
   1SG/TOP ABS sleep -ACT/TH/PFT
   'I am the one who slept'.

(132) *si'kak 'i jimo'kowak
   si'kak 'i jo'kow-im- -ak
   1SG/TOP ABS sleep -ACT/TH/PFT-1SG/ABS

(133)   *kidat*   *to'ak*   *na 'aso*
        kalat-iy-   *to*   *-ak*   *na 'aso*
        bite -ACT/PFT 3SG/ERG-1SG/ABS ERG dog
        'The dog bit me'.

(134)   *si'kak 'i   kidat*   *na 'aso*
        si'kak 'i   kalat-iy-   *na 'aso*
        1SG/TOP ABS bite -ACT/PFT ERG dog
        'I am the one who the dog bit'.

(135)   **si'kak 'i   kidat*   *to'ak*   *na 'aso*
        si'kak 'i   kalat-iy-   *to*   *-ak*   *na 'aso*
        1SG/TOP ABS bite -ACT/PFT 3SG/ERG-1SG/ABS ERG dog

31. In chained clauses in Karao, only an absolutive NP with a third person referent can be encoded as a zero anaphor; absolutive NPs having first and second person referents, and all ergative NPs must be encoded as pronouns or full NPs.

32. In (105), the absence of a semantic role morpheme on the verb in clause 2 indicates that the zero anaphor is a Theme (Patient).

33. The absolutive pronoun *kiya* 'first person dual' is often used in place of the absolutive pronoun *kiyacha* 'first person plural'.

34. There has been disagreement about what exactly coreference in imperatives (and reflexives) tests. One suggestion is that it is a test for subject; another suggestion is that it is a test for agentivity (Anderson 1979 among others); still another suggestion is that it is a test for control, or volition (Bresnan 1982 and Kroeger 1993 among others). A full discussion of this issue is beyond the scope of this study; however, the criteria for grammatical relations presented here clearly establish that an argument that controls coreference in imperatives in Karao is a grammatical relation, regardless of any other pragmatic or semantic properties it may also have. (The same holds true for coreference in reflexives, as we will see shortly.)

35. Certain verbs that are not inherently reflexive can also be encoded in a passive clause to signal accidental reflexive action. Compare the construction in (123) which is neutral about the Agent's intent to perform the action with (136) which indicates that the action is accidental.

(136)   *'iya'ked   'i   nga'nga*
        'e   -'eked 'i   nga'nga
        PASS/PFT-cut ABS child
        'The child cut himself (accidently)'.
        [Literally: 'The child was cut'.]

Here, the Theme (Patient) is the absolutive argument and the coreferential demoted Agent is absent.

36. The one exception, noted in 7.6, is the absolutive NP in a single-argument clause which, to date, has been found to encode only Agents when it is the syntactic control

for coreference in reflexives; however, all the other syntactic processes considered in this study leave no doubt that the absolutive argument of a single-argument clause is a grammatical relation.

References

Anderson, John M. 1971. *The Grammar of Case: Towards a Localistic Theory*. Cambridge: Cambridge University Press.

Anderson, John M. 1979. "On being without a subject." Bloomington, Indiana: Indiana University Linguistics Club.

Anderson, Stephen R. 1976. "On the notion of subject in ergative languages." In *Subject and Topic*, Charles N. Li (ed.), 1-23. New York: Academic Press.

Brainard, Sherri. 1994a. *The Phonology of Karao, the Philippines*. Pacific Linguistics, B-110.

Brainard, Sherri. 1994b. "Voice and ergativity in Karao." Unpublished University of Oregon doctoral dissertation.

Bresnan, Joan. 1982. "Control and complementation." *Linguistic Inquiry*, 13.3:343-434.

Comrie, Bernard. 1978. "Ergativity." In *Syntactic Typology: Studies in the Phenomenology of Language*, Winfred P. Lehmann (ed.), 329-394. Austin: University of Texas Press.

Cooreman, Ann. 1988. "Ergativity in Dyirbal discourse." *Linguistics* 26:717-746.

Cooreman, A., B. Fox, and T. Givón. 1984. "The discourse definition of ergativity." *Studies in Language* 8:1-34.

DeLancey, Scott. 1984. "Notes on agentivity and causation." *Studies in Language* 8:181-213.

DeLancey, Scott. 1985. "Agentivity and syntax." *Chicago Linguistic Society* 21.2:1-12.

DeLancey, Scott. 1991. "Event construal and case role assignment." *Berkeley Linguistics Society* 17:338-353.

Diehl, Lon. 1975. "Space case: Some principles and their implications concerning linear order in natural languages." *Working Papers of the Summer Institute of Linguistics, University of North Dakota Session* 19:93-150.

Dixon, R.M.W. 1972. *The Dyirbal Language of North Queensland*. Cambridge: Cambridge University Press.

Dixon, R.M.W. 1979. "Ergativity." *Language* 55:59-138.

Gruber, Jeffrey S. 1976. *Lexical Structures in Syntax and Semantics*. Amsterdam: North-Holland.

Jackendoff, Ray. 1983. *Semantics and Cognition*. Cambridge: MIT Press.

Jackendoff, Ray. 1990. *Semantic Structures*. Cambridge: MIT Press.

Keenan, Edward L. 1975. "Some universals of passive in relational grammar." *Chicago Linguistic Society* 11:340-352.

Keenan, Edward L. 1976. "Towards a universal definition of 'subject'." In *Subject and Topic*, Charles N. Li (ed.), 303-333. New York: Academic Press.

Kroeger, Paul. 1993. *Phrase Structure and Grammatical Relations in Tagalog.* Stanford, California: CSLI Publications (Center for the Study of Language and Information).
Van Valin, Jr., Robert D. 1981. "Grammatical relations in ergative languages." *Studies in Language* 5:361-394.
Verhaar, John W.M. 1988. Syntactic ergativity in contemporary Indonesian." In *Studies in Austronesian Linguistics*, Richard McGinn (ed.), 347-384. (Monographs in International Studies, Southeast Asia No. 76.) Ohio: Ohio University.

Evolution of Grammatical Relations in Cariban: How Functional Motivation Precedes Syntactic Change

Spike Gildea
Department of Linguistics
Rice University
and
DCH/Área de Linguística
Museu Paraense Emilio Goeldi

0. Introduction

This paper is a case-study in comparative syntax, reconstructing and then tracking the evolution of a Proto-Cariban verbal adjective through a chain of changes in modern languages, in which it is found as a verbal adjective, then in combination with a copula as passive, as inverse voice, and finally as a past/completive tense. As in the well-known cases in the Indo-Iranian branch of the Indo-European family, the verbal adjective becomes a participle, used in both passive and perfect constructions (for transitive and intransitive verbs, respectively); next, these participial constructions are used with increasing frequency, until they replace the etymologically active past tenses entirely. Since the same participle is used for both transitive and intransitive verbs, the new form of the past tense is precisely the etymological participial inflection of the verb; since the transitive participle was also passive, the etymologically oblique agent phrase of the passive becomes the ergative-marked subject of the new past tense clause, thus creating a tense/aspect based split ergative system.

Such an evolution has effects in three interlocked areas of grammar: (1) a marked voice (passive, then inverse) becomes the unmarked active; (2) a syntactically intransitive construction (passive) becomes transitive (active); and (3) the subject and oblique agent phrase of the passive clause become the (absolutive) direct object and (ergative) subject of the new active clause type. In the parallel evolution in intransitive clauses, only the first change is relevant: a marked analytical perfect construction becomes the unmarked past/completive. This paper examines exactly what happens as the grammatical relations of the passive construction evolve into the grammatical relations of the new active past tense construction. Four of the six Cariban languages treated here have already evolved beyond the simple passive use of the participle, each in a slightly different way, but all arguably to different points along the same continuum between a passive and an active-ergative clause type. The complex of pragmatic, syntactic, and morphological differences between these languages highlights the difficulty with defining grammatical relations solely in terms of syntactic criteria, or even with defining them as discrete, criterial categories in all grammatical constructions.

The first section is the meat of the paper, in which I lay out the actual database, showing the cognate verbal morphology (*t*-V-*se*) and common semantic/syntactic core of the construction for each language in question, then show how the construction has evolved in the various modern languages. In addition to morphological and syntactic properties of the construction, where available, pragmatic and semantic properties are also given. The second section approaches the changes in grammatical relations from the perspective of grammaticalization theory, first reviewing the problem of determining whether **reanalysis** has taken place in the absence of a clear syntactic **actualization** (Timberlake 1977; Harris and Campbell 1994), then concluding that we must reconcile ourselves to a significant amount of doubt if we rely only on morphosyntactic evidence. With the development of tools for diagnosing relative topicality of arguments in a clause (cf. Givón 1983, ed. 1994) and incorporating semantic and pragmatic evidence with the morpho-syntactic evidence into a richer **grammaticalization chain** (cf. Heine, et al. 1991; Heine 1992), it is possible to argue for reanalysis in at least one of the languages in the absence of syntactic confirmation. But even with the richer set of clues available to us, it remains questionable whether we should identify some discrete point prior to which the two participants in an event are oblique agent-phrase and subject, and after which they are subject and direct object. In section 3, I conclude with the suggestion that the morphosyntactic properties of change can be less central to our argumentation, especially in languages like those of the Cariban family, where the familiar "subject properties" of English and other more configurational languages have a very limited role in the grammar. Given this conclusion, it also follows that in determining grammatical relations of subject and object in a given synchronic language description, functional analyses of the distribution of construction types and participants in discourse should become a part of the tool-kit used in any good description. Finally, given that the categories of "subject" and "object" are in a state of flux as passive constructions become ergative, one must remain open to the possibility of analyses in which absolute, discrete categories of "subject" and "object" do not exist in a synchronic language, but are caught in a state of momentary flux between the two, with various pragmatic and morphosyntactic "subject properties" mixed between the two.

1. The t-*V*-se construction: verbal adjective to passive participle to active ergative verb

This section will document that cognate verbal morphology, referred to throughout as *t*-V-*se*, is attested in six modern Cariban languages (§1.1): Apalaí (Koehn and Koehn 1986; Koehn 1991), Carib of Surinam (Hoff 1968, 1991, 1995; Gildea 1994a), Hixkaryana (Derbyshire 1985), Katxuyana (Gildea 1995, author's field notes), Tiriyó (Meira 1994, 1995; Gildea 1994c, Meira's and author's field notes), and Wayana (Tavares 1994; Gildea 1994c; Tavares' and author's field notes).[1] In all six languages, the verb bearing this morphology can function as a participle with stative-resultative semantics, something like a verbal adjective. This function (and the morphosyntax associated with it) reconstructs back to Proto-Cariban. In §1.2 we see that, in five of the six languages, an innovative range of functions is attested for the *t*-V-*se* verb when it is the complement of a copular clause (attributive predicate) construction. In this construction, the participle has evolved through an eventive passive stage (unattested in any synchronic Cariban language in my database) to inverse voice in Carib of Surinam, some sort of pragmatically-marked active ergative construction in Apalaí, and to clear ergative in Tiriyó and Wayana (and in younger speakers of Katxuyana).

In this section we will look at a good amount of data, but given the space limitations on an article of this sort, the data on each language may appear somewhat sparse; I ask you to accept on faith that these represent a much larger body of data (and for ye of little faith, consult the original sources for Apalaí, Carib and Hixkaryana, or contact Meira, Tavares and me about our work in progress on Tiriyó, Wayana, and Katxuyana).

1.1. *Reconstructing* *t-V-ce *to Proto-Cariban as a participle*

Across the Cariban family, verbs are attested which bear a combination of a prefix *t-* and a suffix something like *-se*: on consonant-initial roots, the *t-* prefix becomes either *tu-* (before bilabial consonants) or *tɨ-* (elsewhere) and for most roots which begin with *e*, this *e* changes to either *o* (in Apalaí, Carib, Hixkaryana and Katxúyana) or *ə* (in Tiriyó and Wayana) following the *t-*; alloomorphs of the suffix range in phonological shape from *-se*, *-so*, *-ʃe*, *-ʧe*, *-ti*, and *-ye* to *-e*, *-i*, *-y* and *-Ø*, with, in each language, at least one allomorph which shows consonantal correspondences largely consistent with those which Girard (1971) reconstructs to Proto-Carib **c*. In most of these languages, the semantics and morphosyntax associated with this combination of affixes and the verb root are consistent with an analysis of the form as a verbal adjective; however, considering the general lack of a category "adjective" in Cariban languages, the form might be better called a participle (i.e. neither noun nor verb, but partaking of some of the properties of both). Restricting our attention to the six languages to be discussed here, the cognate *t-V-se* construction shows the following allomorphic variation:[2]

> (1) Hixkaryana: *t-V-so* when verb root ends in e or a; *t-V-ʃe* else-
>   where (D. 1985.183, 239)
>
> | *ono* | 'eat (meat)' | *t-ono-so* | 'edible, can be eaten, is to eat.' |
> |---|---|---|---|
> | *omokɨ* | 'come' | *to-moh-so* | 'coming' |
> | *arʸma* | 'throw out' | *t-arʸma-ʃe* | 'thrown out, discarded' |
> | *ahataka* | 'come out' | *t-ahataka-ʃe* | 'coming out' |
> | *ama* | 'cut down' | *t-ama-ʃe* | 'to be cut down, can be cut down' |
> | *eʃe* | 'be' | *t-eh-ʃe* | 'being' |

Regarding syntax, Derbyshire (1985: 46) states that neither S, A, nor O can occur with *t*-V-*so* or with nouns derived on the basis of *t*-V-*so*; as examples, he gives "pseudopassives", in which the participle is the complement of a copula, whose subject is coreferential with the patient of the participialized verb:[3]

(2)   Hixkaryana: Examples of simple stative/attributive meaning

     a.   Adj   COP   S

        tonoso   *naha*   *kyokyo*

        <u>t-ono-   so</u> naha   kyokyo

        t-eat.meat-so 3.Cop parrot

        'Parrot can be eaten.' (D. 1985.95)

     b.   Adj   COP   [S]

        tar^ymaʃe   *naha*   *ɨro tho*

        <u>t-ar^yma-ʃe</u>   naha   ɨro tho

        t-throw.out-so 3.Cop this Devalued

        'These old things are to be thrown out.' (D. 1985.95)

Parallel allomorphic patterns are seen in closely-related Katxuyana:

(3)   Katxuyana: *t*-V-*ʧe* when verb root ends in *e* or *a*; *t*-V-*so* elsewhere[4]

ohɨ	'come'	*t-oh-so*	'come'
to	'go'	*tɨ-to-so*	'gone'
renɨmɨ	'wander'	*tɨ-renɨm-so*	'wandered'
uru	'advise'	*t-uu-so*	'advised'
mɨʧi	'dive'	*tɨ-mɨ'-so*	'dived'
ene	'see'	*t-one-ʧe*	'seen'
ka	'say'	*tɨ-ka-ʧe*	'said'

(4)   Katxuyana: Examples of simple stative/attributive meaning

     a.   *to'ramenkaʧe*   *nasɨ*

        <u>t-o'-ramenka-ʧe</u> n-   a   -sɨ

        t-Detr-tangle.up-se 3-Cop-T/A

        'it's all tangled up'

     b.   *takɨhso*   *so*   *witasɨ*

        <u>t-akɨpɨ   -so</u> so   w-iti -ya -sɨ

        t-squeeze-se even 1Sa-go-Impf-T/A

        'Even squeezed, I'll go.'

In Apalaí, there is virtually no allomorphy:

(5)   Apalaí: *t*-V-*se* only (Koehn and Koehn 1986: 47-9, 100)

ori'	'die'	*t-ori'-se*	'dead' (K&K, p. 49)
ene	'see'	*t-one-se*	'seen' (K&K, p. 49)
anori	'dry'	*t-anori-se*	'dried' (K&K, p. 49)
eseka	'bite'	*t-oseka-se*	'bitten' (field notes)
enep	'bring'	*t-one'-se*	'brought' (field notes)
etapa	'beat'	*t-otapa-se*	'beaten' (field notes)

(6)   Apalaí: Examples of simple stative/attributive meaning

a. *moroto-ino   t- õnu'-se to'   mana*
    that   -after <u>t-go.up-se</u> 3Pl 3+be+Pres
    'After that they are gone up.'

b. *toori'se   kineʃine*
    <u>t-w-ori'-se</u> kɨn-eʃi-ne
    t-Sa-die-se 3Sa-be-Past
    'It was dead.'[5]

In the remaining three languages, Carib, Tiriyó and Wayana, the allomorphy for the suffixal portion of the *t*-V-*se* is complex:

(7)   Carib: *t*-V-*se* with reducing roots which lose an obstruent in the final syllable; *t*-V-*ye* with reducing roots which lose a sonorant, and *t*-V-*Ø* with nonreducing roots (Hoff 1968: 195-200)

kaapɨ	'make'	*tɨ-kaa-se*	'made'
ambootɨ	'break (tr)'	*t-amboo-se*	'broken'
poomɨ	'plant'	*tɨ-poi-ye*	'planted'
weei	'become'	*tu-wei-ye*	'having become'
ɨɨrɨ	'give, place'	*t-ɨɨ-ye*	'given, placed'
tunda	'arrive'	*tɨ-tunda-Ø*	'arrived'
aaro	'take with'	*t-aaro-Ø*	'taken'
ere'na	'faint'	*t-ore'na-Ø*	'fainted'
kuupi	'bathe'	*tɨ-kuupi-Ø*	'bathed'

Hoff (1968: 196) describes the meaning of the *t*-V-*se* construction as: "having undergone (transitive verbs) or having performed (intransitive verbs) the action designated by the corresponding monomorphemic verb".

(8) Carib: Examples of simple stative/attributive meaning
     a. Occurs as an manner adverbial in a sentence with a main
         verb of motion
         tokaanuiye   *kinoχsañ*
         t -ekaanumɨ-se   kɨ -n -oopɨ -ya   -ñ
         Ad-run   -Prtcp Evid-3S-come-NDur-Evid
         'He comes running.'

     b. *am   anuiye   tokaanuiye   miχsa*
         am   anumɨ-se   t -ekanumɨ-<u>se</u>   m -to-ya
         some get-Prtcp   Ad-run   -Prtcp 2S-go-Ndur
         'You will go to get some, running.'

     c. Occurs as the verb form which precedes the conditional par-
         ticle *aχta*:
         tuwootapoiye   *teraapa aχtaine*
         <u>tu-wot-apooi-se</u>   teraapa aχta-ʔne
         Ad-Detr-take -Prtcp   already Cond-Pl
         'as they had already taken each other'

(9) Tiriyó: *t*-V-*se* with reducing roots which lose an obstruent or *r*
     in the final syllable; *t*-V-*ye* with reducing roots which have a
     nasal or nonreducing roots ending in *i*; *t*-V-*e* following non-
     reducing vowels (except *e*); and *t*-V-*Ø* following nonreducing -*e*
     (Meira 1994).
     enapɨ   'eat (fruit)'   *t-əna-se*   'eaten (fruit)'
     onamɨ   'bury'   *t-onan-ye*   'buried'
     imoi   'obey, accept'   *t-ɨmoi-ye*   'obeyed, accepted'
     eta   'hear'   *t-əta-e*   'heard'
     ene   'see'   *t-əne-Ø*   'seen'

(10) Tiriyó: example of simple stative/attributive meaning (Meira 1995)[6]
     wəri   nɨ-tə-n   tɨ-pakoro-ta <u>t-əəka-e</u>   əkəi   ya
     woman 3-go-Evid 3RFL-house-All Adv-bite-Prt snake Agt
     'The woman went home *bitten by a snake/snake-bitten*'

(11) Wayana: *t*-V-*y* for non-reducing verb stems ending in vowels *a*,
     e, *o*, *ə*; *t*-V-*ʃe* for reducing verb stems that end in *t*, *t*-V-*he* for
     all other verb stems (Tavares p.c.; author's field notes):

tə(mə)	'go'	*ti-tə-y*	'gone'
ka	'say'	*ti-ka-y*	'said'
ene	'see'	*t-əne-y*	'seen'
uputu	'fill'	*t-uput-ʃe*	'full'
enati	'finish'	*t-ənat-ʃe*	'finished'
emtap	'yawn'	*t-emtap-he*	'yawned'
ipoki	'smell'	*t-ipok-he*	'smelt'
kəktimi	'shout'	*ti-kəktim-he*	'shouted'

Jackson (1972: 59) refers to this inflectional category as "stative verbs", denoting either "an ongoing state or a state that is the result of the completion of an action." These semantics are clear in the following text examples, for the word *t-ewakam-he* 'seated' in (12a) and for the word *t-uput-ʃe* 'full' in (12b). However, as can be seen from the two main verbs in (12b), *t-ətuput-ʃe* 'filled up (intr)' and *t-əəti-he* 'became', the same verbal morphology can also be used for eventive sentences (more on this soon).

(12)   Wayana: Examples of simple stative/attributive meaning
a.   S   Pred, S   Pred   Adv
tohohoho! wayana teren, məgrə terenuhnə təwakamhe
tohohoho wayana teren məgrə terenuhnə t-ewakam-he
Oh   person big   that   also.is   t -sit -se
'Oh! That person is really big, and also that (one who is) seated.'

b.   [S   ]   V ,   (S) Adv   V
əpi   muhere tətuputʃe,   Ø tuputʃe   təətihe
əpi   muhere t-ət -uput-ʃe Ø t-uput-ʃe t-əti   -he
magic amulet t-Detr-fill-se Ø t-fill-se   t-become-se
'The magic amulet filled up, (Ø) became full.' (yorok, p. 19)

Conclusion: the verbal adjective function is attested in all of the languages, sometimes as complement of the copula or the inchoative verb 'become', but most frequently as a manner adverbial modifying a verb of motion. As this function is attested in all modern Cariban languages of which I have knowledge, I reconstruct the same function for this construction in Proto-Cariban. In the next section, I will argue that for five of these six languages, when the *t-V-se* form is used as the complement of a copula it has entered into the well-known evolution from adjective to passive participle to active past-perfective verb in an ergative construction.

1.2. Evolution from verbal adjective to passive, inverse, and finally ergative

There is ample typological evidence for the fact that participles evolve into passive constructions and beyond (Shibatani 1985, ed. 1988; Givón 1979, 1990, ed. 1994; Estival and Myhill 1988; Haspelmath 1994). The logical first step of this evolution must be extending the use of the stative participle to describe the events which lead to the states. This seems to always occur in the syntactic context where the stative participle is the complement of a copula. The stative participle plus copula is what Estival and Myhill refer to as a "lexical passive"; when this construction gets extended to eventive readings, an agentless passive is born. Given that the participle plus copula combination is now sometimes used to refer to transitive events, it is just a matter of time before one of the pre-existing morphosyntactic means of indicating oblique agents is pulled analogically into the mix to create an agentive passive (Estival and Myhill's "transformational passive").

The simple stative participle is attested in all six Cariban languages treated here. In Hixkaryana, the stative participle occurs as the complement of a copula (a potential source construction for the subsequent evolution of a passive), but it appears to have evolved no further. The next two steps, an agentless passive and agentive passive, are as yet unattested in the Cariban family, and must be inferred from the further evolution of the construction in the remaining five languages (but see the dispute about the status of the Carib Inverse construction, §1.2.1). Estival and Myhill describe in intuitive terms the sorts of functional changes which the passive must go through in order to shift grammatical relations so as to become an unmarked active voice with ergative case-marking. Givón (1994) discusses the same sort of changes in a more quantifiable framework, using the term Inverse Voice for the intermediate step between passive and ergative. In Carib of Surinam, the *t*-V-*se* participle has taken this next step, becoming an inverse voice construction (§1.2.1). In Apalaí, the cognate construction is too frequent to consider a simple inverse, but not frequent enough to be considered the unmarked active voice, either — it seems a new term is needed (§1.2.2). In Tiriyó and Wayana, the cognate construction is the un-marked past tense, and occurs with great frequency in narrative (§1.2.3). In Katxuyana, the situation is confused by recent intense contact with Tiriyó, so that the (entirely bilingual) younger generations have apparently calqued the construction into Katxuyana as an ergative, which the older speakers understand, but do not use themselves in narrative discourse (§1.2.4).

1.2.1. t-*V*-se *as inverse voice in Carib of Surinam*

Hoff (1991) was the first unambiguous claim of passive status for the *t*-V-*se* construction in a Cariban language.[7] In Hoff (1995), the arguments are laid out carefully to support his claim that the *t*-V-*se* construction is a passive:

- the patient has the morphological properties of an intransitive sub-ject, being unmarked for case and controlling person marking on the copula
- the agent occurs as an optional oblique, the object of the dative postposition *?wa*
- the patient, as intransitive subject, controls coreference with the subject of a coordinate clause.[8]

Each of these properties is illustrated in examples (13)-(14) (Hoff 1995: 360, 362):

(13) "[S-ø]" [t-V-se] " t-V-se (Aux) "
    y-eemïi -rï tïi-ka-Ø t-aaro -Ø man maae
    1-daughter-Pssn t-say-se t-carry.off-se 3.be Interj
    'My daughter — she said — has been carried off, alas!'

(14) S$_j$ -ø V-passive Aux [[A$_j$] Obl] conj. s$_j$-V
    seeri t-owa?ma-Ø n -eei Baaku ?wa indombo n -oreh
    Silvia$_j$ t-embrace-s<u>e</u> 3$_j$-Cop Baaku Agt then 3$_j$-angry
    -ko -i
    -Inch-Tns
    'Silvia$_j$ was embraced by Baaku$_i$, then (she$_j$) became angry.'
    *'... then (he$_i$) became angry.' (Hoff 1995)

However, a functional analysis of this participial construction presented in Gildea (1994a) shows it has already moved through the prototypical passive phase, and on functional criteria would now be more appropriately labeled an inverse. The functional tests are given in Givón (ed. 1994) *inter alia*, especially Thompson (1994); here I repeat them only in abbreviated fashion:

- relative frequency in discourse (15-20% — like passive, a relatively infrequent, marked voice)
- relative frequency of overt agent expression (low for passive, high for inverse)
- relative topicality of agent and patient compared to standard active clauses (both passive and inverse patient more topical than active patient; passive agent totally nontopical, inverse agent less topical than active agent, but nearly as topical as inverse patient)

In Gildea (1994a), I found that the oblique agent appeared in virtually all cases of the *t*-V-*se* construction encountered in my text, and that in the two cases where it did not occur, it was both highly topical and identifiable from context. Further, the topicality profile of the agent and patient in the *t*-V-*se* construction fit exactly the profile of inverse voice. As Hoff (1995: 359-60) points out, in reviewing a larger body of texts, he has found cases in which the agent is neither explicit nor identifiable from context, a fact which appears to argue against a "pure" inverse analysis. I interpret this residue of "passive" function in the construction in much the same way that I interpret the continued existence of the stative participle in Carib: when a construction extends from its previous function/meaning into a related new function/meaning, it does not necessarily give up its old function, but it rather becomes polysemous for a time, until some phonological or morphosyntactic difference (correlated with the different functions) is introduced to distinguish the two. I will return to this point in the discussion of grammaticalization chains in §2.

Taking the functional shift to inverse as a given, it can be argued that the construction is now more "pragmatically transitive" than a simple passive, with its erstwhile oblique agent gaining some of the topicality properties of unmarked subjects of active clauses. It is thus no surprise to find that one subject property, the control of the reflexive possessive prefix, has been transferred in Carib from the erstwhile passive subject to the erstwhile oblique agent (Hoff 1995: 364):[9]

(15) a. The oblique agent controls the reflexive which possesses the
        patient-S
        [Refl$_i$-S]$_j$-ø   *t-V-se*   A$_i$-Obl Aux$_j$
        [*ti$_i$ -saano*]$_j$ *t-otaawa-ø i$_i$-?wa man*
        [3Refl$_i$-mother]$_j$ t-visit   -se 3$_i$-Agt 3$_j$.Cop
        'His$_i$ own mother$_j$ was$_j$ visited by him$_i$.'

     b. The patient-S of the passive cannot control a reflexive prefix
        possessing the agent
        $*t$-V-se   [[Refl$_j$-A]$_i$ Obl] Aux$_j$
        *$*t-otaawa-ø* [*t   -saano*]   *?wa man*
        visited   [3Refl$_j$-mother]$_i$ Agt 3$_j$.Cop
        ((he$_i$) was$_i$ visited by his$_i$ own mother$_j$)

With regard to word order, there appear to be no restrictions associated with grammatical role: Hoff (1995) states that the only grammatical
restriction is that the *t*-V-*se* participle must precede Aux, with any order
[including absence] of nominal arguments allowed; in text, the statistically
most frequent and stylistically least-marked order is Patient-V-Agent/VS.)
It is also noteworthy that the auxiliary, while grammatically not required,
nonetheless is almost uniformly retained in narrative text (these facts will
play a role in later discussion). To conclude our discussion of the Carib
inverse: by one syntactic test, control of coreference in coordinate clauses,
the patient is the subject (and the clause is therefore syntactically intransitive, a passive); by the only other test, control of coreference with the third
person reflexive possessive prefix, the agent phrase is the subject (and the
clause is therefore syntactically transitive, an incipient ergative).[10] This contradiction is resolved in the next four languages by the simple expedient of
losing the rule of coreference, leaving the only remaining subject property
firmly aligned with the agent phrase.

1.2.2. *Between inverse and active ergative: the* t-V-se *construction in Apalaí*

As mentioned above (note 7), Koehn and Koehn (1986) seem somewhat
undecided about what to call the *t*-V-*se* in Apalaí: it has some of the same
surface morphosyntax of a passive seen in Carib (*viz.* auxiliary agreement
with patient, oblique marking on the agent), but it occurs with great frequency in discourse (on both transitive and intransitive verbs), and native
speakers frequently translate it into an active past tense clause. Because of

these latter properties, E. Koehn (1991) investigated further and concluded that it might be better to call the *t*-V-*se* an ergative construction rather than passive. It appears that while the copular auxiliary is allowed to occur in the *t*-V-*se* clause, it does not occur frequently (judging from the paucity of auxiliaries in Koehn's (1991) examples and in my own elicited data). The construction is illustrated with an intransitive verb in (16) and with a transitive verb in (17).

(16) *t*-V-*se*   S-ø
toetɨwɨkase   rokẽ kurumu
t-e-tɨwɨka-se rokẽ kurumu
t-Refl-humiliate-se only vulture
'The vulture just hung it's head (i.e. felt humiliated)' (Koehn 1991's 9, p. 3)

(17) Ø*ᵢ*   *t*-V-*se*   Aux*ᵢ*   [A-Erg]*ⱼ*
tone'se   ase   João a
t-onep-se ase   João a
t-bring-se 1.Cop John Erg
'John brought me.'

Turning now to my own elicited data, as in Carib, the agent phrase controls the reflexive possessive marker when in competition with the erstwhile passive subject (18a) and even when the item possessed is the patient (18b). To drive home the difference from the English passive, consider that it is not possible to utilize the reflexive possessive prefix on the ergative agent, although the passive translation sounds fine in English (18c).

(18) Ergative A controls coreference with reflexive possessive prefix
a. *Pauru tone'se   João a tɨtapɨi   taka*
Pauru t-enep-se João a t-tapɨ-i taka
Paulo t-bring-se John Erg 3R-house-Pssn to
John*ᵢ* brought Paulo*ⱼ* to his*ᵢ* house (*to his*ⱼ* house)'

b. *tɨse   tonese   eɨa*
t-ɨse t-ene-se e-a
3R-mother t-see-se 3-Erg
'He saw his own mother'

c. **tonese tɨse a*
(he was seen by his own mother)

Unlike Carib, the rule of coreference has been lost even in etymologically active clauses (compare 19 and 20), and similarly in *t*-V-*se* clauses there is no apparent rule (cf. the ambiguity in 21):[11]

(19) O/S (passive/absolutive) pivot with the etymologically active clause type

A_i O_j V   // 3_j-V

Pauru João apoino niekitapano

Pauru João apoi-no ni-ekitapa -no

Paulo John hug-Past 3S-get.angry-past

'Paul embraced John and (John) got angry' ("probably Paulo squeezed too hard")

(20) A/S (active/nominative) pivot with the etymologically active clause type

$Ø_i$ O_j V   // 3_i-V

João etapano nitoropa

João etapa-no ni-to-no-ropa

John hit-Past 3S-go-Past-repet

'(he$_i$) hit John$_j$ and (he$_i$) left.'

(21) Ambiguous pivot with the *t*-V-*se* clause first

O_i *t*-V-*se*   [A-Erg]$_j$ // $3_?$-V

João tapoise Pauru a niekitapano

João t-apoi-se Pauru a ni-ekitapa-no

John t-hug-se Paulo Erg 3S-get.angry-Past

'Paulo hugged John and (someone) got angry' ("it can't be said who got angry")

Returning to Koehn's 1991 data, when the first clause is intransitive and the second transitive, the expectation might be for obligatory coreference with the following A (cf. English *He arrived and Ø set down his backpack* versus **he arrived and bill hit Ø*) or O, but according to Koehn this is not the case. He offers examples of both S/A and S/O pivots (with both clauses of the *t*-V-*se* type):

(22) An S/A (active/nominative) pivot

        t-V-*se*   **S**$_i$ -ø

    tẽẽ rokene tiporo?se   *inororo.*

    tẽẽ rokene <u>t-poro?-se</u>   inoro-ro

    shortly only t-sit.down-se he-?

    Refl$_i$-O-ø   *t*-V-*se*   (**A**$_i$)

    tikataorĩ   *tiporo?kase.*

    t-katauri-ni <u>t-poro?ka-se</u>

    3R-backpack-POS t-set.down-se

    'That very moment he$_i$ sat down. (He$_i$) set down his$_i$ backpack.'

    (K's 23-4, p. 6)

(23) An S/O (passive/absolutive) pivot

    S$_i$ -ø   *t*-V-*se*   // (**O**$_i$) *t*-V-*se* [A-Erg]

    mame arimi tooe?se   *rahkene,*   *tuose*   *eya*   *šine*

    mame arimi <u>t-oe?-se</u>   rahkene   <u>t-wo-se</u> e-ya   šine

    after monkey t-come-se consumation t-kill-se 3-Erg Pl

    'The monkey$_i$ came and they shot (it$_i$)' (K's 25, p. 6)

Not only does a grammatical rule not exist in elicitation, but Koehn (1991) reports that the overall percentages of S/A versus S/O pivots varied tremendously in the two texts he analyzed (by different speakers); in neither case can the pattern be interpreted as governed by the kind of simple syntactic rule which might be used to help identify either an absolutive (passive) or nominative (active) subject for transitive verbs.

Table 1. *Percentage of S/A versus S/O pivots in Apalaí narrative*

	Story 1:		Story 2:	
	S/A	*S/O*	*S/A*	*S/O*
n =	12	14	22	7
	46%	54%	76%	24%

In future work, I intend to collect unambiguous examples of sentence-internal pivots (cf. the possible sentence boundary between the two clauses in 22), as well as examples of all sequences of transitive and intransitive clauses along with combinations of etymologically active clauses and *t*-V-*se* clauses. Ideally, such examples would come from text, as the intuitions of

native speakers are not always reliable on such tests (cf. note 11 and the
Wayana data in the next section). I anticipate that Apalaí will be similar to
Wayana, Tiriyó, and Katxuyana, showing no evidence for any rule of syntactic pivot, either nominative or absolutive. In the absence of published
analyzed text, I cannot offer quantifiable evidence of the relative topicality
of participants in the various clause types of Apalaí; based on the impressionistic distinctions between etymological active clauses and *t*-V-*se* clauses
reported by Koehn (1991: 22, 25), such counts would likely give very interesting results. The following is my summary of Koehn's (1991) description
of the functions of the *t*-V-*se* clause type (as opposed to those of the etymologically active clause type).

(24)   Claimed functional properties of *t*-V-*se* as opposed to etymologi-
       cally active verbs

t-V-*se*	*etymologically active*
non-eyewitness	eye-witness
reporting non-direct speech	quoting direct speech
background information	foreground information
used with "non-prominent A"	used with "prominent A"
enhance topicality of O	
downplay personal achievement	
quote tag for quoted direct speech	

Like both inverse and passive, the *t*-V-*se* clause is used to enhance the
topicality of O. In a passivelike way, the *t*-V-*se* clause can be used to
downplay personal achievement (making the A less topical/salient), and is
used with a "non-prominent A". However, in his discussion, Koehn makes
it clear that the term "less prominent A" is not to be understood as referring to an A that is totally nontopical (as it would be in a passive); rather,
Koehn uses this term to distinguish between the two globally most-topical
participants, in which the etymological active voice is most commonly used
when the intuitively "most-prominent" participant is the A, and the *t*-V-*se*
clause is most commonly used when the intuitively "second-most-promi-
nent" participant is the A (apparently regardless of the identity of the O
participant). In this sense, Koehn likens the alternation between the two
constructions to a kind of switch reference system, in which (if necessary)

one could almost disambiguate a third person agent pronoun simply by noting in which construction it occurs: when you see the unmarked (nominative) A pronoun in the etymologically active construction, likely the agent is the most prominent participant; when you see the ergative A pronoun in the *t*-V-*se* clause, probably the agent is the less-prominent participant.

The other functional distinctions which Koehn impressionistically associates with this "voice" alternation are still less voice-like: reporting an event in an etymologically active clause indicates that the speaker is an eyewitness to the event, whereas reporting the same event in a *t*-V-*se* clause indicates lack of eyewitness knowledge (while not indicating the actual source of the information).[12] Quoted speech in a narrative is usually a quoted conversation between participants, in which the "speakers" are discussing more immediate events that they either have just witnessed or are in the process of witnessing; thus, there is a strong tendency for quoted speech to contain the etymologically finite clause types.[13] Finally, it seems to be a lexical idiosyncrasy of the verb of quoted speech, *ka*, that it always occurs inflected with *t*-V-*se* in Apalaí narrative.

Even granting the need to test the impressionistic nature of these patterns, we can reach the tentative conclusion that the *t*-V-*se* clause in Apalaí has been reanalyzed as active and transitive, but that it is still in competition with the other active past-completive tenses, as seen by the fact that it is still used in (just) less than half of the apparently appropriate temporal situations. Further, the patient has lost both of the two abstract syntactic properties which would identify it as "subject of passive" in an earlier stage: as in Carib, the oblique A controls coreference with the reflexive possessive prefix; unlike Carib, the control of obligatory coreference with the subject of a coordinate clause is no longer an operating rule in Apalaí, and the O has thereby lost this property without the oblique A gaining it. On the other hand, one would not want to call the *t*-V-*se* an unmarked active clause, either, given that it does not show the kind of statistical dominance one would like to see in an unmarked active (cf. Givón 1994). One might consider the possibility of comparing the *t*-V-*se* clause to the "goal-focus" voice system described for Philippine languages, in which there is arguably no clear-cut "active" voice to serve as the standard against which other voice distinctions are measured (cf. Shibatani 1988; Comrie 1988). But even here, the functional profile of the *t*-V-*se* clause does not seem to match Shibatani's (1988) definitions (which actually concide much better with

Givón's (1994) definition of inverse voice). While these indeterminate syntactic and functional properties make sense from a diachronic perspective (as will be argued in §2), more research is definitely in order on the synchronic function(s) of the Apalaí *t*-V-*se* clause.

1.2.3. *The unmarked active (ergative) past-completive in Wayana and Tiriyó*

In Wayana and Tiriyó we have two cases in which the *t*-V-*se* clause has become an unmarked active clause type with ergative case-marking on the A. The morphosyntactic properties of the *t*-V-*se* construction in Apalaí also hold in both Wayana and Tiriyó, with S and O unmarked, A bearing an ergative marker *ya*, and the optional copular auxiliary agreeing with the absolutive for person, but almost never being used. The ergative A controls the third person reflexive prefix and coreference in coordinate clauses is apparently pragmatically, rather than syntactically, determined. All orders of A, O, and V are attested, with OVA and VS being statistically the most frequent. In Wayana, this exhausts the properties described for the system to date (§1.2.3.1); in Tiriyó, some additional properties have been discovered which further cement the ergative analysis (§1.2.3.2).

1.2.3.1. *The Wayana active ergative past-completive*

The Wayana examples come from Petronila Tavares' and my field work, first reported in Gildea (1994c). While the auxiliaries illustrated in (25a-b) are acceptable in elicitation, in a medium-length narrative text only ten cases were found (around 4%).

(25) Sample *t*-V-*se* clauses in Wayana (Gildea 1994c)

    a. t-V-he S-ø

        tɨtəy *(way)*

        t-tə-he way

        t-go-he 1Cop

        'I went.'

    b. O-ø   t-V-he   (Aux) A-Erg

        kuraʃi *tɨpanaŋmay*   *(man)* *ɨya*

        kuraʃi t-panaŋma-he man   ɨ-ya

        rooster_i t-hear-he   3_i.Cop 1-Agt

        'I heard the rooster (crow).'

As in Carib and Apalaí, the ergative A controls coreference with the reflexive possessive prefix:

(26) Control of coreference with the reflexive possessive prefix
   a. The ergative A controls in text examples
      [3R$_i$- Loc]　　　　V　　　　A-Erg$_i$　[Possr$_j$ O]$_k$
      tipehnak　　*tipimihe*　*eya*　*yorok pitpə*
      t-peh-nak　　<u>t-pimi-he</u>　e-ya　yorok pitpə
      3Refl-forehead-Loc t-tie.up-he 3-Agt spirit skin
      'On his$_i$ forehead he$_i$ tied up the skin$_j$ of the spirit$_k$'
   b. The rule is confirmed in elicitation with nine speakers
      Ariko-ya　ti-arə-y　Kurune ti-pakoro-n-tak
      Ariko$_i$-Agt <u>t-take-se</u> Kurune$_j$ 3R$_i$-house-Pssn-Loc
      'Ariko$_i$ took Kurune$_j$ to his$_i$ house (Ariko's)' (*Kurune's, *some-
      one else's)

Unlike Carib, but like Apalaí, it appears that there is no rule of control for coreference in coordinate clauses. Interestingly, rather than simply stating that the example was ambiguous, speakers chose instead to interpret each example according to some context which they had cooked up to make sense of the utterance. Thus, while each speaker was emphatic that any other interpretation was wrong, every single speaker showed a variation in the syntactic pattern of coreference on at least one example from the set. My guess is that the speakers who did not allow certain sentences were simply unable to imagine the participants in question carrying out the events described. Examples (27-29) show the mixed results obtained in elicitation, and example (30) shows a clear case of the nominative pivot from a text example:

(27)　　*kurasi　ti-panaŋmə-y Anakari-ya　ni-tə-imə-Ø*
　　　　rooster <u>t-hear-se</u>　　Anakari-Agt 3S-go-Repet-Rec.Past
   (6) 'Anakari heard the rooster and then (Anakari) left.' (Agent controls: ergative)
   (2) 'Anakari heard the rooster and then (the rooster) left.' (Patient controls: passive)
   (2) no interpretation: sentence not acceptable

(28)   *Anakari -ya Ariko tɨ-ene-y nɨ-tə-imə-Ø*
         Anakari-Agt Ariko <u>t-sèe-se</u> 3S-go-Repet-Rec.Past
   (1) 'Anakari saw Ariko and (Anakari) left.' (Agent controls: ergative)
   (5) 'Anakari saw Ariko and (Ariko) left.' (patient controls: passive)
   (3) no interpretation: sentence not acceptable

(29)   *Ariko tɨ-ene-y rep Anakari-ya nɨ-tə-imə-Ø*
         Ariko <u>t-see-se</u> then Anakari-Agt 3S-go-Repet-Rec.Past
   (1) 'Anakari saw Ariko and then (Anakari) left.' (ergative)
   (4) 'Anakari saw Ariko and then (Ariko) left.' (passive)
   (1) 'Anakari saw Ariko and (the two) left.' (??)

(30)   *tɨpɨmɨhe, hemik   təhemikay*
         t-pɨmɨ-he [hemik]   t-hemika-y
         <u>t-tie.up-se</u> [disappear] <u>t-disappear-se</u>
         '(he$_i$) tied (it$_j$) up and (he$_i$) disappeared.' (Yorok)

On the functional side, the *t*-V-*se* clause type appears to be the unmarked active in Wayana narrative, occurring in 79% of all main clauses; in conversation, the *t*-V-*se* clause type was less frequent, 34% compared to 66% for the etymologically active clause type. As might be expected, the only non-*t*-V-*se* clauses in the narrative were exactly those clauses in which conversations were being quoted or in which the narrator was departing temporarily from his role to explain something to the listeners (i.e. when he was conversing with his interlocutors rather than narrating to them).[14] In terms of argument structure, the ergative agent phrase is syntactically optional, but it is omitted in situations where it is obvious from context rather than in situations where it is unknown, nontopical, or being suppressed for some other reason.

1.2.3.2. *The Tiriyó active ergative past-completive*

Regarding the *t*-V-*se* in Tiriyó, Meira (1995) gives an excellent summary of the morpho-syntactic properties of the *t*-V-*se* clause as part of a paper in which he argues that it has become a new past tense inflection. He summarizes the now-familiar passive-like properties of the construction as case marking (O and S both unmarked, like intransitive subjects; Agent of transitive apparently an optional oblique, relatively infrequent) and agreement (the optional copula/auxiliary agrees with S and O, as though both were intransitive subjects). Although he has not (yet) conducted the quantified measurements of topicality in Tiriyó discourse, in a first look, Meira found that the *t-V-se* clause predominated: 70% of all pasts in narratives, and almost 100% when quoted speech is removed from the database (cf. note 13). This discourse distribution must call the passive analysis into question, and in a diligent search for syntactic evidence in favor of either analysis, Meira was rewarded with a morphological asymmetry which indicates that the *t-V-se* verb is gaining an independent tense value, and then with an additional subject property which accrues to the ergative agent of the *t-V-se* clause.

The morphological asymmetry is that the copula/auxiliary does not have the same inflectional possibilities when in combination with the erstwhile passive participle (the *t-V-se*) as it does when combined with other adverbial forms: the copula/auxiliary can only occur in its present tense form with the participle (which unlike the parallel form in English, then yields a past tense reading):

(31) Copular forms contrasted with auxiliary forms in Tiriyó (Meira 1995):

Normal copular sentences	*t-V-se* **sentences**
a. *kure n-ai* good 3-be.Pres 's/he/it is good'	*wəri n-ai t-əəka-e* woman 3-be.Pres t-bite-se 'The woman was bitten' '(Someone) bit the woman'
b. *kure n-ei-Ø* good 3-be-Rec.Past 's/he/it was good'	**wəri n-ei-Ø t-əəka-e* (the woman was bitten)
c. *kure kɨn-ei* good 3:Dist.Past-be 's/he/it was good'	**wəri kɨn-ei t-əəka-e* (the woman was bitten)
d. *kure n-eh-ta-n* good 3-be-Fut-Evid 's/he/it will be good'	**wəri n-eh-ta-n t-əəka-e* (the woman will be bitten)
e. *kure t-ee-se* good <u>t-be-se</u> 's/he/it was good'	**wəri t-ee-se t-əəka-e* (the woman was bitten)

f. *kure eh-kə*   **t-əəka-e eh-kə*
    good be-Imper   (be bitten!)
    'Be good!'

g. *kure yi-w-eh-to*   **t-əəka-e yi-w-eh-to*
    good 1-w-be-Nmlzr   (my being bitten)
    'My being good'

Meira interprets this restriction on the form of the auxiliary as a function of the reanalysis of the participle to an active verb tense — as the *t-V-se* leaves behind the final vestiges of its etymological passive identity to become a past tense in its own right, it will no longer be able to take various tense values from an auxiliary, and thus will lose the ability to co-occur with the full variety of copular inflections. In fact, there are almost no attested cases of an overt auxiliary in recorded narrative text, and as it becomes ever more limited in terms of actual discourse frequency, it is on the verge of being lost altogether (and taking with it one of the remaining subject properties of the absolutive, *viz.* auxiliary agreement). Next, Meira shows the now familiar fact that the ergative A controls coreference with the reflexive possessive prefix:

(32) O_j *t-V-se* [A-Erg]$_i$ [3R$_i$- Loc]
      yi-pawana t-əne-Ø pahko ya   ti-pakoro-htao
      1-friend   t-see-<u>se</u> father Agt 3R-house-LOC
      'My father$_i$ saw my friend$_j$ in his$_i$ house'

Since coreference in conjoined clauses is as messy in Tiriyó as it is in Wayana, Meira went in search of subordinate clause types that might yield a syntactic pivot rule — he found an innovative subordinate clause type which allows finite verbal morphology (one of very few attested in the Cariban family), the *ahtaw* 'while' clause. The nominative subject of the etymologically active clause type controls coreference with the intransitive S of an *ahtaw* clause (33), and similarly, the ergative A of a *t-V-se* main clause controls coreference with the intransitive subject of of an *ahtaw* clause (34):

(33) With an etymologically active main clause: nominative A controls coreference

3_i-V while // A$_i$ V   O$_j$

[n-urakanun-ya-n   *ahtao] pahko   n-ene yi-pawana*

3_i-walk:around-Prog-Evid while 1:father$_i$ 3_i-see 1-friend$_j$

'While (he$_i$ was) walking around, my father$_i$ saw my friend$_j$.'

*'While (he$_j$ was) walking around, my friend$_i$ was seen by my father$_j$.'

(34) With a *t-V-se* clause: ergative A controls coreference

3_i-V while // O$_i$ *t-V-se* [A-Erg]$_j$

[n-urakanun-ya-n   *ahtao] yi-pawana t-əne-Ø pahko   ya*

3_i-walk:around-Prog-Evid while 1-friend$_j$ <u>t-see-se</u> 1:father$_i$ Agt

'While (he$_i$ was) walking around, my father$_i$ saw my friend$_j$.'

*'While (he$_j$ was) walking around, my friend$_j$ was seen by my father$_i$.'

With the cases of Tiriyó and Wayana, we have now documented the final stages of the evolution from verbal adjective through passive participle to active past-perfective verb tense. In the next section we will take a brief look at the case of Katxuyana, in which the *t-V-se* clause type has apparently arrived at ergativity by a more accelerated path.

1.2.4. t-V-se *in Katxuyana: all of the above?*

Katxuyana is genetically very closely related to Hixkaryana, in which it appears that the *t-V-se* construction has not even taken the first step on the road to ergativity. This branch of the family is quite differentiated from any branch which might include the other four languages. One might expect, then, that the Katxuyana *t-V-se* construction would be more stative/passive, like Hixkaryana, and less eventive/active, like the other four. While working with a young Xikuyana woman in 1994,[15] I was surprised to discover that *t-V-se* clauses kept popping up in elicitation, just like they did in Tiriyó, and in the one brief narrative she told me, nine of the 12 clauses referring to past events used the *t-V-se* construction (the other three were all copulas). This led me to think of the fact that, since 1968, the great majority of the Katxuyana have been living in intimate contact with the Tiriyó at Missão Tiriyó, and all but the oldest are now fully bilingual (as was this young Xikuyana woman); further, the older speakers of Katxuyana consistently complain about how the younger generation is "changing" or "ruining" the language, making it more like Tiriyó. Thus, I modified my hypothesis about the similarities between Katxuyana and Hixkaryana grammar, limiting it perhaps to the oldest speakers. In a stretch of conversation preceding a narrative, three men aged 35-50 produced 20 standard etymologically active sentences, with only five *t*-V-*se* forms at all, and two of these stative. In 1996, I transcribed and translated a portion of an epic tale told in 1994 by the second-oldest living Katxuyana (since deceased); as anticipated, in 161 clauses I encountered only five instances of a verb bearing the *t*-V-*se* morphology, none with agent phrases, and all possibly interpretable as stative/passive.

A serious socio-linguistic investigation is in order before determining the place of the Kaxuyana *t*-V-*se* construction in the evolutionary scenario developed above. My preliminary hypothesis is that the two older speakers who are not fluent in Tiriyó will show patterns very like that of Hixkaryana, the middle-aged speakers with Tiriyó spouses (adolescents when they arrived at Missão Tiriyó) will not use *t*-V-*se* frequently, but will use it with an agent phrase at times; speakers 30 years of age and younger (bilingual in Tiriyó from birth) will have calqued the Tiriyó ergative use of *t*-V-*se* clauses into their sociolect of Katxuyana. This syntactic difference between the generations would presumably be one of the features of the speech of the younger generations about which the older speakers complain. Since such a hypothesis is not testable without a great deal more research, here I simply illustrate that the *t*-V-*se* does have an eventive reading, an agent phrase, and the option of occurring with no copular auxiliary (at least for some younger speakers):

(35) Active uses of the Kaxuyana *t*-V-*se*
    a. Adv S-ø *t*-V-*se*
        soro ana tooso
        soro ana t̲-ehɨ-s̲o̲
        today 1.Pl.Excl t-come-se
        'Today we (excl) arrived.'

    b. [A   Erg] O-ø *t*-V-*se*
        suriana wɨya sesu tomoʔkaʃe
        suriana wɨya sesu t-emoʔka-ʃe̲
        Juliana Erg Sérgio t-teach-se
        'Juliana taught Sérgio'

In summary, we have a series of cognate morphology which marks a stative participle in Hixkaryana, an inverse voice verb in Carib, a past-perfective verb (which takes ergative morphosyntax) in Tiriyó, and something apparently in between these last two in Apalaí and Wayana. Before discussing how to best model the obvious evolution which has taken place here, we need a brief detour to a discussion of the theory and methodology of diagnosing diachronic changes in syntax.

2. Is there a discrete point at which syntactic reanalysis takes place?

This section addresses the interrelations between syntax, morphology, semantics and pragmatics in determining both the synchronic status of grammatical relations, and the status of grammatical relations as they change during reanalysis. §2.1 considers the syntactic evidence for reanalysis, §2.2, the pragmatic and semantic evidence for reanalysis, and §2.3 then brings together both sides into a grammaticalization chain (a la Heine 1992), from which I conclude (in §3) that there is no natural *point* of reanalysis, but that there appears to be a period in which grammatical relations might reasonably be seen as in flux, somewhere between their starting and ending points.

2.1. *Morphological and syntactic evidence for reanalysis*

In a syntactically-oriented view of grammaticalization, a major problem is the distinction between what Timberlake (1977) has called reanalysis and actualization (cf. also Harris and Campbell's 1994 discussion). In Timberlake's conceptualization of the problem, **reanalysis** occurs when children learning a language take as input from older speakers a surface string of words, but analyze the underlying structure of that surface string differently than the older speakers (presumably motivated by some functional evolution in progress).[16] After reanalysis, the surface string of words remains unchanged, so we are unable to detect that reanalysis has occurred for some indeterminate period of time, until a further generation of speakers inherits the new underlying structure and adds some alteration to the actual surface structure (some innovative syntactic rule which would ideally be a consequence of the new underlying structure). This change in the surface structure would then be the **actualization**, and would be the first evidence *available to linguists* that the posited reanalysis had actually taken place. The problem then becomes to determine when it is that reanalysis has taken place, and further to determine how much — of what kinds of — syntactic change will qualify as sufficient evidence for the actualization of reanalysis. The syntactic properties of the *t-V-se* construction in Hixkaryana, Carib, Apalaí, Wayana, and Tiriyó are summarized in Figure 1:

	Hixkaryana	Carib of Surinam	Apalaí	Wayana	Tiriyó
-Agent phrase	No	Optional	Anaphorically Deleted	Anaphorically Deleted	Anaphorically Deleted
-Control of coreference w/ refl. possr.	O	A	A	A	A
-Control of coreference w/S of coordinate clause	O	O	>NA<	>NA<	>NA<
-Control of coreference w/S of *ahtaw* clause	>NA<	>NA<	>NA<	>NA<	A

Figure 1. *Syntactic properties of* t-V-se *argument structure*

The evidence summarized above applies to (at least) two distinct stages of change: the reanalysis from verbal adjective to passive participle in a passive construction, and the reanalysis from passive to active ergative. To the extent that word order, verb agreement and case-marking are involved, they identify the patient (O) of the transitive *t-V-se* participle with the sole argument (S) of the intransitive *t-V-se* participle, but this identification is inherited from the source construction, in which either S or O is the subject of the copula, and then linked to the verbal adjective *cum* participle via the predicational semantics of the copula. The sole syntactic argument for the reanalysis of the verbal adjective plus copula into a passive participle plus auxiliary is the introduction of the agent phrase — a step which occurred somewhere between Hixkaryana and Carib of Surinam.[17]

In the evolution from passive to ergative, we can no longer trust the agreement morphology of the copula nor the oblique case-marking of the agent to guide us in identifying subject and oblique status, respectively, since these markers are purportedly being reanalyzed as indicating absolutive and ergative, respectively. In Carib of Surinam, we have only two syntactic properties to guide us: control of coreference with the reflexive possessive prefix, and control of coreference with the subject of a coordinate clause (cf. Figure 1). Both of these properties rest with the nominative in the more conservative languages, and in the source construction I thus infer that these properties both rested with the subject of the copula (the S and O). With the reanalysis to passive, these properties presumably remained with the subject of passive (S and O). However, in the Carib passive, the control of coreference with the reflexive possessive prefix shifts to the erstwhile oblique A. However, control of coreference with subject of a coordinate clause remains with the O, as the erstwhile subject of passive. Is this change sufficient to convince a skeptic that we are seeing actualization of a pre-existing reanalysis of grammatical relations? If so, we must ask if the reanalysis is all the way to transitive ergative already, or if inverse voice represents a transitional stage in which the clause has become syntactically transitive, but the agent and patient are not subject and object, respectively. A skeptic might suggest that this second property combined with the first still does not justify treating the *t*-V-*se* clause as anything other than an idiosyncrative VP in which the V is a copula and the predicate is an adverb derived from a transitive verb, and in which only two ad hoc notes are required to list two idiosyncratic properties of a certain optional oblique adjunct phrase; another skeptic might suggest that this is a standard passive, except that the oblique A has acquired an idiosyncratic property, which can be modeled somewhere in the grammar without resorting to calling it by a new name. With only two syntactic subject properties in evidence, and these two divided between the two participants of the clause, it is difficult to imagine resolution coming solely from an analysis of the syntax.

At the next stages, Apalaí and Wayana have lost the global rule by which subject controls coreference with the subject of a coordinate clause — there is no such rule for any clause type yet investigated. For these two languages, then, the ambiguity is not resolved: the skeptic need list no further rules in order to describe the "idiosyncracies" of the *t*-V-*se* clauses, but only to remove the last remaining syntactic rule which argues for the subject status

.

of the erstwhile subject of passive, leaving the determination of subject to rest solely on morphological grounds. Since the coreference rule has been lost for all clause types, and is therefore not unique to the *t*-V-*se* clause, it is possible to argue that this change cannot be considered evidence for the actualization of a passive to ergative reanalysis, nor even (for the extreme skeptic) as evidence for the reanalysis from verbal adjective in a copular clause to passive.

Only when we arrive at Tiriyó, where coreference with a third person subject of the innovative *ahtaw* 'when' clause is controlled by the agent-phrase of the *t*-V-*se* clause, do we finally have two syntactic rules combining to unambiguously indicate the agent-phrase as subject (and thereby indicating the arrival of the *t*-V-*se* clause type as active ergative). Further, the paradigm of the copula is greatly restricted just in the case that it is combined with the *t*-V-*se* verb. The analysis of the *t*-V-*se* clause as an active ergative past-perfective makes sense of both of these innovative facts, whereas any other analysis is forced to posit a number of ad hoc rules which idiosyncratically affect just this one clause type.

To the extent that clear morphosyntactic criteria are required to argue for reanalysis, we have a weak case for Carib, Apalaí and Wayana. But given the comparative context, it is clear that these languages occupy medial stages of a single evolutionary chain, beginning with resultative verbal adjective/participle in a copular clause and resulting in a past-perfective inflected finite verb. We need some clear way to identify the roots of the later changes in the synchronic ground of the intermediate stages, some reliable methodology to capture the intuition that the changes in question are more than autonomous shifts in morphosyntax, but are actually reflections of shifting cognitive processes.

2.2. *The evolution of semantics and pragmatics*

In my own early work (Gildea 1989), influenced by second language acquisition studies, I framed my discussion of syntactic evolution as an evolution of function (reanalysis) which then triggered a subsequent evolution of form (actualization). It is, I think, generally accepted in grammaticalization theory that innovative constructions first extend their functional load into new domains without immediate consequences in the (surface) formal structures of grammar; then, like the languages of two groups which split off from the same speech community and lose contact, the grammar of the independent functions begins to evolve independently, introducing formal differences, creating evidence that we have not merely two distinct functions for the same grammatical construction, but two distinct grammatical constructions. The problem then becomes finding some non-arbitrary way to identify: (a) cases of functional change which ought to have consequences for grammar (i.e. which motivate reanalysis), and (b) which sorts of grammatical change are consonant with particular functional changes. Having identified these things, on a case-by-case basis, given a clear functional change which *ought* to have syntactic consequences, the first, most minimal syntactic change which is plausibly related to a reanalysis motivated by a functional shift should be sufficient evidence to establish the prior existence of the reanalysis.

Givón (1994: 10-12), identifies the following quantitative measures as correlating with synchronic function: the topicality measures of referential distance and topic persistence, the frequency distribution of construction types in text, and the frequency of non-anaphoric agent deletion (for antipassive, patient deletion) in actual discourse production. All of these measures are taken in basically a single genre of discourse, that of an individual narrating a story, with minimal interaction from interlocutors/audience. See Givón (ed. 1994 *inter alia*), Zavala (1994, In press) for case studies which illustrate that these measures are reliable cross-linguistically, are useful in synchronic studies to identify constructions which correlate with certain functional profiles, and can independently identify synchronic functional profiles for individual constructions. In the remainder of this section, I discuss the synchronic functional profiles of the various Cariban *t-V-se* clauses in comparative perspective.

First, the frequency of non-anaphoric agent deletion. This particular test seems useful primarily in distinguishing between passive and inverse, and would thus be more useful to the present study if we had some Cariban language(s) in which the *t-V-se* construction were attested as a passive. Extrapolating from Derbyshire's (1985) categorical statement about the absence of agent phrases in the *t-V-se* construction in Hixkaryana, we could assume that 100% of agents are deleted there. Based on Gildea's (1994a) measurements for Carib of Surinam, non-anaphoric deletion of agents approaches Ø (although Hoff 1995: 359-60) encountered at least two cases in a larger sample of text). Although we have no measurements in the other languages, I assume that non-anaphoric deletion of agents will be virtually nonexistent, yielding the following (relatively uninteresting) scale:

Table 2. *Frequency of non-anaphoric agent deletion*

Hixkaryana:	(100%)
Carib:	<5%
Apalaí:	(Ø)
Wayana:	(Ø)
Tiriyó:	(Ø)

Turning to the frequency distribution of the *t*-V-*se* construction type in text, Givón predicts that the unmarked active voice construction will occur in some 65-80% of clauses, whereas marked voice constructions, like passive or inverse, will occur only in some 15-20% of clauses. For the purposes of these counts, it is important to define the "construction" in such a way as to count only the frequency of the innovative voice construction (in Estival and Myhill's 1988 terms, the "transformational passives") while excluding reflexes of the etymologically prior stative participle (Estival and Myhill's "lexical passives"). This is simple for most cases, since all occurrences of a verb bearing *t*-V-*se* morphology in combination with main verbs other than copulas are unquestionably stative participles serving as adjuncts; when a *t*-V-*se* occurs with a copula, the only distinguishing characteristic is the semantics (like in English): stative = participle, eventive = passive. Again, we do not have the counts for Hixkaryana, but relying on Derbyshire's categorical statement that the Hixkaryana *t*-V-*se* plus copula is unattested with eventive meaning, we can safely assign it a frequency of Ø in narrative text. The numbers for Carib come from Gildea (1994a), those for Apalaí from Koehn (1991), those for Tiriyó from Meira (1995), and those for Wayana from Gildea (1994c). Although the gross numbers for Tiriyó and Wayana might appear to place Tiriyó between Apalaí and Wayana, when the confounding variables of quoted speech and aside comments to interlocutors are removed, Wayana and Tiriyó appear to be identical.

Table 3. *Frequency distribution of eventive* t-V-se *clauses*

Hixkaryana:	Ø%
Carib:	17%
Apalaí:	<47%
Wayana:	100% (79% before removing quoted speech and asides)
Tiriyó:	100% (70% before removing quoted speech)

The topicality measures of referential distance and topic persistence are used to distinguish the relative topicality of the agent and patient participants in any given transitive event in a narrative (cf., Givón ed. 1994 *inter alia* for discussion and illustration of the counting procedure and analysis of topicality based on these counts — the following discussion assumes these steps). First a base-line measurement is taken from the relative topicality values of agent and patient participants in active clauses (that is, the statistically most frequent clause type). Then measurements are taken of the participants in all other clause types, and participants are ranked according to degree of topicality: completely nontopical ($\downarrow\downarrow$), relatively nontopical ($\downarrow$), a secondary topic ($\uparrow$), and a primary topic ($\uparrow\uparrow$). The relative rankings of the agent and patient in any given clause type is then compared against the following functional profiles (adapted from Thompson 1989):

Table 4. *Functional profiles of the major voices*

Active	Agentless Passive	Agentive Passive	Inverse	Antipassive
$\uparrow\uparrow$Agt	$\downarrow\downarrow$Agt	$\downarrow$Agt	$\uparrow$Agt	$\uparrow\uparrow$Agt
$\uparrow$Pat	$\uparrow\uparrow$Pat	$\uparrow\uparrow$Pat	[$\uparrow$]$\uparrow$Pat	$\downarrow\downarrow$Pat

In the Cariban languages discussed here, such a study has only been carried out for the *t-V-se* clause found in Carib of Surinam, which fell squarely into the inverse category (Gildea 1994a). Taking Derbyshire's categorical statements about Hixkaryana as a guide, I assume a pre-passive stage in which, since the construction does not invoke the event, the Agent does not even exist semantically for its pragmatic status to be measured. Reviewing Koehn and Koehn's (1986) section on the *t-V-se* construction as a passive, and then Koehn's (1991) impressionistic discussion of the pragmatic status of arguments in what he called the *t-V-se* ergative clause, it is difficult to guess the probable outcome of topicality counts. I assume they would show a construction pragmatically somewhere in transition between inverse and active ergative. Counts on Wayana and Tiriyó will doubtless confirm the status of the *t-V-se* clause as an unmarked active. I combine these hypotheses into a single chain as follows (where the symbol [↑]↑ for agent and patient in Apalaí represents some indeterminate middle ground between inverse and active):

Table 5. *Functional profiles of Agt and Pat participants in* t-V-se *clauses*

Hixkaryana	Carib	Apalaí	Tiriyó Wayana
Ø Agt	↑Agt	[↑]↑Agt	↑↑Agt
↑↑Pat	[↑]↑Pat	[↑]↑Pat	↑Pat

We are now ready to combine this pragmatic information with the semantic, syntactic, and morphological information into a single picture to create a scenario of the overall change from the Hixkaryana verbal adjective to the Tiriyó active ergative, after which we can discuss the implications of each functional change in this richer context.

2.3. *The integrated grammaticalization chain*

Given this richer perspective, we can see each of the morphosyntactic changes in the evolution of the *t-V-se* clauses as a natural consequence of the new function which these clauses are serving. The first two changes — from the incipient passive of Hixkaryana to an agentless passive and then to an agentive passive — are not actually attested in modern Cariban languages (these two columns are in italic print to serve as a reminder that their properties are inferred from typological studies). The subsequent columns represent the different properties of the synchronic languages as described above.

When the *t-V-se* participle in a copular clause, previously used only to describe states which result from events (cf. English *the window was broken for six months*), is extended to use in situations where it is describing

the event itself (cf. English *just then, the window was broken*), this creates
a functional pressure to include some means of referring to the other participant in the event, the one who caused the change of state in the patient.
The syntactic addition of the agent phrase (with all the selectional restrictions of the subject of an active clause) should then count as a clear case
of actualization, i.e. an argument that the semantic extension was accompanied by a syntactic reanalysis, *viz.* from a participle in a copular clause
to a passive plus auxiliary. Presumably this syntactic reanalysis did not take
place until such time as the eventive use of the participle was fairly frequent, motivating people to think of the new use as different in some significant
way from its stative source.

Similarly, in pre-Carib, the erstwhile passive began to be used more
frequently in situations where the agent was less nontopical, and the agent
phrase thus began to be used more frequently than not. This created a statistically more transitive clause type, with both agent and patient not just
semantically implied, but pragmatically salient as well. As more and more
topical participants were allowed to occur in the erstwhile agent phrase, the
more topicality-sensitive syntactic rules — which rested with the patient as
the primary topic of the passive — would begin to come under pressure to
shift to the increasingly topical agent. The first syntactic recognition of this
functional shift is the switch of a subject property: the "oblique" A gains
control of coreference with the reflexive possessive prefix. While this
change is a clear indicator of an increase in saliency on the part of the erstwhile oblique A (and thus an increase in transitivity in the overall clause),
it is not clear that we can talk of the oblique A as the *subject* of the clause,
since: (a) it does not have the topic persistence profile of the subject of an
active clause, and (b) the other syntactic subject property, control of coreference of the subject of a coordinate clause, remains with the patient, the
erstwhile subject of passive.

As we turn to Apalaí, the functional profile of the *t-V-se* construction
appears to have moved beyond that of the Carib inverse, towards a semi-
active ergative clause type. Most significantly, the discourse frequency of
the *t-V-se* clause is much higher than would be expected for a marked
voice; and while Koehn's (1991) assertions about functional distinctions
between *t-V-se* clauses and its 'active' counterpart remain in need of veri-
fication, they are uncontroversially outside the domain of what we normally
think of as voice (i.e. they do not point us to a Philippine-style goal-focus

Stage:	I HIXKARYANA Incipient Passive	II >not attested< Agentless Passive	III >not attested< Passive plus Agent Phrase	IV CARIB OF SURINAM Inverse Voice	V APALAÍ Marked Active past-completive verb (Ergative)	VI WAYANA Active past- completive verb (Ergative)	VII TIRIYÓ Active past- completive verb (Ergative)
Dimensions of Change:							
Semantics							
- Eventiveness	Stative	Stative/ Eventive	Stative/ Eventive	Eventive	Eventive	Eventive	Eventive
- Transitivity	Patient	Patient (Agent?)	Patient Agent	Patient Agent	Patient Agent	Patient Agent	Patient Agent
- temporal profile	-stative/ resultative	-resultative/ completive	-resultative/ completive	-(resultative/) completive (-past?)	-completive -distant past	-completive -past	-completive -distant past
Pragmatics							
- Relative Topicality of A and O	(A↓↓) O↑↑	(A↓↓) O↑↑	A↓ O↑↑	A↑ O↑↑	A(↑)↑ O(↑)↑	A↑↑ O↑	A↑↑ O↑
- Frequency of A-Deletion	100% (no Agt)	100% (no Agt)	<15-20%>	<5%	(∅)	(∅)	(∅)
- Frequency of eventive *t-V-se*	∅ (all stative)	<15-20%>	<15-20%>	17%	<47%	≈100%	≈100%
Syntax							
- Agent phrase	No	No	Optional	Optional	Anaphorically Deleted	Anaphorically Deleted	Anaphorically Deleted
- Control of coreference w/ refl. possr.	O	O	O	A	A	A	A

cont...

- Control of coreference w/ S of coordinate clause	O	O	O	>NA<	>NA<	>NA<
- Control of coreference w/ subject of *ahtaw* 'when' clause	>NA<	>NA<	>NA<	>NA<	>NA<	A
Morphology						
- markedness of verb form *vis-à-vis* active	-no agreement -no tense/ aspect	-no agreement -no tense/ aspect	-no agreement -completive aspect -distant past tense	-no agreement -completive aspect -past tense	-no agreement -completive aspect -past tense	-no agreement -completive aspect -past tense
- use of auxiliary	100% (copula)	100% (auxiliary)	near 100% (not quantified)	rare (not quantified)	4%	near Ø% -restricted paradigm for auxiliary

Figure 2. *Grammaticalization chain for comparative Cariban t-V-se: from stative participle to active ergative*

analysis). Thus, we would expect the preponderance of syntactic properties to indicate that the O of the *t*-V-*se* clause is no longer a subject of passive; while this functional change does not motivate its loss in active clauses as well, it is not surprising that the subject property of control of coreference in coordinate clauses no longer treats the patient of *t*-V-*se* clauses as subject.

By the time we arrive at Wayana and Tiriyó, the discourse frequency of the *t*-V-*se* clauses is so overwhelming that we are almost forced *a priori* to call them ergative or risk ridicule as recreating the errors of the early Eurocentric grammarians who spoke of the Caucasian "passive languages". Surprisingly, we have yet to find any additional syntactic change between Apalaí and Wayana,[18] but for Tiriyó, the additional changes are conclusive: only a single conjugation of the copula can occur in the *t*-V-*se* clause, and the agent phrase of the *t*-V-*se* clause controls coreference with the subject of a subordinated *ahtaw* 'while' clause. Both are motivated by the obvious function of the *t*-V-*se* clause as an active, transitive, past-perfective predication.

3. Conclusion

The picture which emerges from this case study shows that a simple syntactic determination of grammatical relations will miss a great deal in these Cariban languages. Compare the *t*-V-*se* clauses in Wayana with those in Apalaí on the one side and Tiriyó on the other. The syntactic profiles of Wayana and Apalaí are identical, whereas the Tiriyó *t*-V-*se* clause has developed two new properties which we can call actualization, and which we thereby can use to argue for a prior reanalysis. In contrast, the functional profiles of Wayana and Tiriyó are virtually identical, as fully transitive, active clauses, whereas the Apalaí *t*-V-*se* clause remains a pragmatically marked alternant of the etymologically active clause type.

If a skeptic insists that Carib and Apalaí do not show sufficient syntactic evidence for reanalysis, then it must follow that Wayana also would not show such evidence. In fact, the general paucity of syntactic constituents and rules in the Cariban languages makes it difficult to ever argue for reanalysis solely on the basis of syntactic evidence. Yet I suspect that most linguists would not hesitate to join me in considering the Wayana *t*-V-*se* clause an active ergative clause type, solely on the basis of its discourse frequency — it is simply the unmarked past tense inflection. Yet if we are to justify this functionally obvious conclusion in syntactic terms, we must affirm that a single syntactic test — control of coreference with the reflexive possessive prefix — is sufficient evidence for actualization, and thus is sufficient to argue for the reanalysis of the etymological passive as an active transitive clause type. We are then caught in a formal bind when we turn to Apalaí and Carib of Surinam, where this sole syntactic test has exactly the same behavior, singling out the agent phrase of the *t*-V-*se* clause (presumably as the subject of a transitive active clause).

The clear differences between the *t*-V-*se* construction from Carib to Tiriyó do not seem to lend themselves to the standard labels used by linguists: for example, what do we call the *t*-V-*se* construction in Apalaí? From the perspective of the entire chain of reanalysis, it could be characterized as a transitional stage between the inverse voice of Carib and the active ergative of Wayana and Tiriyó, a transition which is captured synchronically simply because we happened to describe the construction at exactly this moment in its evolution. Had we encountered the construction a bit earlier or later in the transition, presumably it would have looked a bit different, but still without being either an inverse or an active clause type. This possibility raises the question of just how discretely we should define boundaries between the stages. And if the boundaries between the stages look less discrete as we consider a broader spectrum of properties associated with them, the existence of a "point" of transition between the extremes, passive and ergative, also begins to look a bit doubtful. If our metaphor for the transition between passive and ergative spreads out from a point into a continuum, spanning not just inverse, but also any number of transitional stages similar to the one seen in Apalaí, then we must be prepared to accept indeterminacy in what we want to call subject and object as we attempt to give synchronic descriptions of these constructions in flux.

Acknowledgements

Earlier versions of this paper were previously presented at the Conference on Functional Approaches to Grammar, Albuquerque, NM, July 1995, and in my course at the Australian Linguistic Institute, July 1996. Some Apalaí data and all Katxuyana, Tiriyó and Wayana data were collected under the auspices of the Northern Brazilian Cariban Languages

Documentation Project (Projeto Karíb), financed by National Science Foundation grant no. DBS-9210130, with the institutional support of Rice University and the Museu Paraense Emílio Goeldi, and with permission from the Brazilian National Research Council (CNPq) to conduct a research project in Brazil, and with permission from the Foundation for the Indian (FUNAI), the Brazilian Air Force (FAB), and the local communities of speakers to enter the Indigenous Areas where the research was carried out. Without the support of all the institutions listed above, this research would not have been possible — a sincere thanks to all. All data were collected either in Belém, at the Museu Goeldi, in Icoaraci and Macapá at the respective Casa do Índio of FUNAI in each city, or in the Área Indígena Parque do Tumucumaque, Wayana data in Aldeia Bona and Tiriyó data in either Matawaré or Missão Tiriyó, in various visits in 1994 and 1996. My personal thanks to the following language teachers: Merekuku Apalaí, Trindade Apalaí, Anakari Wayana, João Aranha (Tuwarinke) Wayana, Mikiri Wayana, Francisco Wayana, Arikó Wayana, Teu Wayana, Warema Wayana, Paturi Wayana, Tïpïn Tiriyó, Niyo Tiriyó, Wanatïimo Sikuyana, Weriki Sikuyana, Awakuku Katxuyana, Irinama Katxuyana, Pikirirwa Katxuyana, Mosoku Katxuyana, Kuhewiri Katxuyana, Wanaruku Katxuyana, Sebastião Katxuyana, Tawarika Katxuyana, Wiriya Kahyana, and Roseni Kahyana. Obviously, comparative work of this sort requires cooperation from other colleagues involved in descriptive work: thanks to Edward Koehn for providing an unpublished manuscript of his work in Apalaí, to Berend Hoff for meticulously detailed description and for countless suggestions and corrections to this paper (and to all my ongoing comparative work), and especially to Petronila Tavares and Sérgio Meira, for ongoing inspiration, and for providing the debates and arguments that renew my excitement in the goals of field work every time I wonder if it's worth facing yet another bureaucratic nightmare. On the theoretical front, thanks to Denny Moore for extremely articulate (and productive) skepticism, to Sérgio for not accepting half-baked answers, and to T. Givón, Scott DeLancey, Alice Harris and Bernd Heine for theoretical inspiration. I take full responsibility for all mistakes.

Notes

1. Tentative genetic sub-grouping of the six Cariban languages in question:

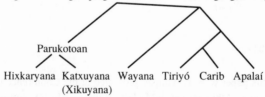

One socio-linguistic variable which might be relevant in understanding parallel patterns between languages is that all speakers of the Wayana and Apalaí data used here are fully fluent in both languages (Both the Koehns' and our data were collected in Aldeia Bona, on the upper Rio Paru do Leste, where the two groups live together with a great degree of intermarriage and full bilingualism amongst all but the oldest speakers); similarly, all speakers of the Kaxuyana data cited here are bilingual in Tiriyó, although not all from birth (the 40 surviving Katxuyana immigrated to Missão Tiriyó in 1968, and nearly all of the 100 Katxuyana speakers born since then are products of mixed marriages, Tiriyó-Katxuyana, and are equally fluent in both languages). While our data on these three languages come exclusively from bilingual speakers, there are Katxuyana in Área Indígena Nhamundá-Mapuera (Brazil) who do not speak Tiriyó, Wayana in Surinam and French Guiana who do not speak Apalaí, and presumably there are speakers of Apalaí somewhere who do not speak Wayana. With luck, in the future we will be able to collect data from different dialects of these languages and thereby better identify the potential effects of contact on the phenomena discussed in this paper.

2. Each linguist uses different orthography for what are roughly the same sounds — if all examples were to be presented in each author's original orthography, the non-specialist would find it extremely difficult to remember which symbol represents which sound in a given example. As such, I have substituted my own uniform orthography for examples in this paper. The chart below shows my own orthographic symbols on the left, then correlates this orthography to that of the original authors in the various columns to the right: Derbyshire (1985) for Hixkaryana, the official Katxuyana orthography (author's work in progress), Koehn and Koehn (1986) for Apalaí, Hoff (1968) for Carib of Surinam, Meira (1994) for Tiriyó, and the official Wayana orthography (Tavares' work in progress).

Phonet.	Hixkaryana	Katxuyana	Apalaí	Carib	Tiriyó	Wayana
h	h	h			h	h
ʔ		'	h	ʔ		
χ				x		
ʃ	x	tx	x		s	s
ʧ	tx	tx				
dʸ	dy					
ñ	ny					
r	r	r	r	r	r	l
rʸ	ry	ry				
y	y	y	j	y	y	j
ɨ	ɨ	ɨ	y	ï	ï	ï
ə					ë	ë

194

3.　To avoid drawing analytical conclusions before presenting all the relevant information, I will gloss the *t-* and the *-se* of all *t*-V-*se* verbs as simply *t-* and *-se* rather than, say, 'participial' or 'passive' or 'past-completive'.

4.　The single exception so far is *eʧi* 'be', which surprisingly takes the suffix *-ʧe*; it is interesting to note that the cognate form in Hixkaryana, *eʃe*, takes the cognate suffix *-ʃe* as well.

5.　This morphemic analysis is not from Koehn and Koehn, but is my own. The morpheme *w-* 'Sa' is the subject of another comparative Cariban investigation, that of the origin of Active-Stative systems in the family. The long vowel at the start of this form is a vestige of the etymological *w-* prefix which I tentatively reconstruct as marking all Sa verbs in the *t*-V-*se* construction in Proto-Cariban (cf. Gildea, 1994b; Tavares 1994; Meira 1997 for further information).

6.　The use of the agent phrase with this stative *t*-V-*se* is surprising, since such a use is not reported with the stative *t*-V-*se* in any other Cariban language. It is clear that this agent is generic, and is included only to modify the nature of the state into which the patient enters after the event of biting (which is quite different after being bitten by a snake than, say, a dog). In future research, we hope to test whether the stative *t*-V-*se* accepts generic agents of this sort in the other languages studied here.

7.　Koehn and Koehn (1986) did write a section on *t*-V-*se* as passive in their 1986 grammar sketch, but they also included the same form in the chart of verb conjugations as a "nonfinite tense", which clouded the picture some. In the absence of extensive exemplification and syntactic argumentation for the status of the construction, it was impossible to evaluate this analysis. cf. §1.2.2 for my current hypothesis.

8.　Note: third person is marked independently on the verb of the coordinate clause in this example and all others to follow in this paper. Had the mark been for another person, there would have been no question of controlling coreference. The test functions only in this unique case, where there are two third persons in the first clause and the intransitive verb of the second clause is marked for third person without indicating anything further about the identity of the subject. In this case, the subject of the second clause could logically be coreferential with either of the third person referents in the first clause, or with neither (i.e. with some other third person referent). If native speakers insist on the interpretation that the second subject is coreferential with either the A or the O of the preceding clause, I agree with Hoff that this should constitute a syntactic pivot rule.

9.　Note that Hoff 1995.364 considers this potential subject test "fundamentally different" from the other subject test (doubtless at least in part because it gives different results). He argues that control of coreference with the reflexive possessive prefix diagnoses the inherent *activity* of a participant, rather than indicating anything about its potential status as subject.

10.　For the skeptical, I affirm Hoff's (1995: 362, note 19) observations as true for a number of other Cariban languages as well: "Other observations [subject tests — SG] are precluded by the particular properties of Carib grammar: there are no relative pronouns and no conjunctions, and dependent (nonfinite) verbs contain personal prefixes too, including two third-person prefixes distinguishing identity or non-identity with a participant referent of the main verb. Also, question words can easily reconcile their location in front position with any grammatical role."

11. Methodological note: these examples must be taken with a grain of salt, as these are the intuitive judgements of a single Apalaí speaker in a single elicitation session, with no confirmation either from other sessions with the same speaker, other sessions with other speakers, nor from any sort of recorded spontaneous discourse. I include these data only because they are consistent with the claims made by Koehn (1991), which are based on discourse data and a base of more than 20 years working with the language.

12. Evidential distinctions have been encountered in several Cariban languages, including Carib (Hoff 1986), Hixkaryana (Derbyshire 1985: 255-6), Katxuyana (author's field notes), Panare (author's field notes, Payne, Payne and Gildea 1992), Tiriyó (Meira, p.c.). and Wayana (Tavares p.c.). In both Panare and Apalaí, the etymologically active clauses are in competition with extremely frequent innovative clause types, and in each case it is the etymologically active clause type which gives the eyewitness reading, as opposed to the innovative clause type, which is apparently neutral with regard to source of evidence.

13. I suspect that the heavy use of visual experience evidentials is a characteristic of conversation as a genre in Cariban languages, and I further suspect that this led to one of our most complicated problems in field work on Panare: speakers apparently considered elicitation sessions to be a form of conversation, and so the grammar which we were eliciting did not match at all well with the grammar found in the narrative texts we collected (except for several snippets of quoted conversation embedded in these texts). Our suspicions were apparently confirmed when we finally transcribed and analyzed a conversation, where the forms we had been collecting in elicitation finally showed up in some reasonable quantity. This same skewed distribution has shown up in Wayana (Tavares p.c.), Tiriyó (Meira 1995), and in Katxuyana (where it is compounded by age-related sociolinguistic variation). I hope to gather sufficiently detailed information on this problem in one or more of the languages above to address it in future discourse studies or sociolinguistically-oriented work.

14. Cf. notes 12 and 13.

15. As noted in note 1, Xikuyana and Katxuyana can be considered the same language: although they are clearly from distinct social communities and the Xikuyana insist that the languages are "completely different", the Katxuyana insist that Xikuyana is "the same Katxuyana, just smoother". Investigation of the differences is complicated by the fact that no speakers of Xikuyana are fluent in Portuguese, and thus the majority of my work on Xikuyana has been mediated by my halting Tiriyó or Katxuyana (use of the latter perhaps leading me to find more parallelism between Xikuyana and Katxuyana than I would have found if I could have used a more neutral third language). This caveat aside, having done preliminary investigations with the young Xikuyana woman and an older Xikuyana man and compared the results to Katxuyana speakers of parallel age groups, I have been unable to identify any phonological differences,

only a handful of lexical differences, one minor morphological difference, and no syntactic differences between Xikuyana and Katxuyana. Thus, for the purposes of this paper, I treat Katxuyana and Xikuyana data equally as Katxuyana.

16. For the record, I do not believe it is necessary to assume that language change is a function of child language acquisition, but this paper is not the vehicle to argue that point.

17. I have actually had arguments with linguists who adhere more strictly to the notion that syntax is autonomous from meaning/function, in which it was pointed out that the agent phrase could be seen as just an oblique adjunct, like any other, and since all predicates allow the addition of oblique adjuncts, the semantic content of the adjunct (i.e. the identification of the object of the postposition as the *agent* of the *t*-V-*se* verb) does not constitute *syntactic* evidence for reanalysis. However, even the most extreme autonomous syntacticians admit the relevance of selectional restrictions imposed by the verb on its *subject* (a syntactic role, not to be confused with the semantic notion of agent if you want to argue successfully on autonomous grounds). Presumably a study of the selectional restrictions which the passivized verb imposes on the types of participant allowed in the agent phrase would confirm that they are identical to the selectional restrictions imposed on the subject of the same verb in an active clause, and the syntactic status of the rule would be accepted. In the absence of such a study, I will assert that the semantic identification of the agent is sufficient for our purposes.

18. If we do not uncover any in future research, we might speculate whether the syntactic parallelism between Wayana and Apalaí does not have something to do with the fact that virtually all speakers of each language are bilingual in the other.

References

Comrie, Bernard. 1988. "Passive and Voice." In Shibatani (ed.) 1988: 9-23.

Derbyshire, Desmond C. 1985. *Hixkaryana and Linguistic Typology*. Dallas: Summer Institute of Linguistics.

Estival, Dominique and John Myhill. 1988. "Formal and functional aspects of the development from passive to ergative systems." In Shibatani (ed.) 1988: 441-492.

Fox, Barbara and Paul Hopper. 1994. *Voice: Form and Function*. Amsterdam: John Benjamins [Typological Studies in Language 27].

Gildea, Spike. 1989. Simple and Relative Clauses in Panare. University of Oregon Master's Thesis.

Gildea, Spike. 1994a. "Semantic and Pragmatic Inverse — Inverse alignment and inverse voice — in Carib of Surinam." In Givón (ed.) 1994 187-232.

Gildea, Spike. 1994b. "Gramática comparativa como meio de entender análise sincrônica: o prefixo *w-* e sistemas ativos-estativos em línguas Karibe." Presented at the Museu Goeldi "Quintas Lingüísticas" Colloquium, May 1994.

Gildea, Spike. 1994c. "A evolução da ergatividade nas línguas Karibe do norte do Pará." Presented at Nono Encontro da ANPOLL, Caxambu, June.

Gildea, Spike. 1995. "Tracking grammaticalization: the evolution of function versus the evolution of syntactic rules." Presented at Conference on Functional Approaches to Grammar, Albuquerque, New Mexico, July.

Girard, Victor. 1971. *Proto-Carib Phonology*. PhD dissertation, University of California, Berkeley.

Givón, T. 1979. *On understanding grammar*. New York: Academic Press.

Givón, T. (ed.) 1983. *Topic Continuity in Discourse: Quantitative Cross-Language Studies*, vol. 5. Amsterdam: John Benjamins [Typological Studies in Language 3].

Givón, T. 1990. *Syntax: a functional typological introduction*, vol. 2. Amsterdam/Philadelphia: John Benjamins.

Givón, T. 1994. "Introduction." In T. Givón (ed.) 1994: 3-44.

Givón, T. (ed.) 1994. *Voice and Inversion*. Amsterdam: John Benjamins [Typological Studies in Language 28].

Harris, Alice and Lyle Campbell. 1994. *Diachronic Syntax*. Cambridge: Cambridge University Press.

Haspelmath, Martin. 1994. "Passive participles across languages." In B. Fox and P. Hopper (eds) 1994.

Heine, Bernd. 1992. *Auxiliaries*. Chicago: University of Chicago Press.

Heine, Bernd, Ulrike Claudi, and Friederike Hünnemayer. 1991. *Grammaticalization: a Conceptual Framework*. Chicago: University of Chicago Press.

Hoff, Berend. 1968. *The Carib language*. The Hague: Martinus Nijhoff.

Hoff, Berend J. 1986. "Evidentiality in Carib." *Lingua* 69.49-103.

Hoff, Berend J. 1991. "Configurationality and non-configurationality in the Carib language of Surinam." Presented at the Tupi-Guarani/Cariban Linguistics Symposium of the 47th Congress of Americanists, New Orleans.

Hoff, Berend. 1995. "Configurationality and non-configurationality in the Carib language of Surinam." *International Journal of American Linguistics* 61.347-77.

Jackson, Walter S. 1972. "A Wayana grammar." In J.E. Grimes (ed.) 1972: 47-77.

Koehn, Edward. E. 1991. "Ergativity and the split case system of Apalaí." Paper from the Tupi-Guarani/Cariban Linguistics Symposium, 47th Congress of Americanists, New Orleans.

Koehn, Edward E. and Sally S. Koehn. 1986. "Apalai." In *Handbook of Amazonian Languages*, vol. 1, D.C. Derbyshire and G. Pullum (eds), 33-127. Berlin: Mouton de Gruyter.

Li, Charles N. (ed.) 1977. *Mechanisms of Syntactic Change*. Austin: University of Texas Press.

Meira, Sérgio. 1994. "O morfema -se/-ye/-e/-0 em Tiriyó." Presented at Nono Encontro da ANPOLL, Caxambu, June; Rice University (ms).

Meira, Sérgio. 1995. "From Adverbializer to Verb Tense in Tiriyó (Cariban)." Presented at the Summer Meeting of the Society for the Study of the Indigenous Languages of the Americas (SSILA), July 7, Albuquerque, NM.

Meira, Sérgio. 1997. "The Evolution of an epi-phenomenal Split-S system in the Cariban family". Rice University MA thesis.

Payne, Thomas, Doris Payne and Spike Gildea. 1992. "Panare Reference Grammar". Final Report to the National Science Foundation 400 pp. ms.

Shibatani, Masayoshi. 1985. "Passive and related construction: a prototype analysis." *Language* 821-48.

Shibatani, Masayoshi. 1988. "Voice in Philippine languages." In Shibatani (ed.) 1988: 85-142.

Shibatani, Masayoshi (ed.) 1988. *Passive and Voice*. Philadelphia: John Benjamins.

Tavares, Petronila. 1994. "O sistema ativo-estativo em Wayana." Presented at Nono Encontro da ANPOLL, Caxambu, June; Rice University (ms) (in English).

Thompson, Chad. 1989. *Voice and Obviation in Athapaskan and Other Languages*. PhD dissertation, University of Oregon.

Thompson, Chad. 1994. "Passive and inverse constructions." In T. Givón (ed.) 1994: 47-63.

Timberlake, Alan. 1977. "Reanalysis and actualization in language change." In C.N. Li (ed.) 1977: 141-177.

Zavala, Roberto. 1994. "Inverse alignment in Huastec." *Función* 27-81.

Zavala, Roberto. In press. "La pragmática de las voces en akateko." Presented at Memorias del III Congresso de Lingüística en el Noroeste, Hermosillo.

Grammaticalization, Clause Union and Grammatical Relations in Ecuadorian Highland Spanish

Marleen Haboud
Linguistics Department
University of Oregon
and
Universidad Católica
Quito, Ecuador

1. Introduction*

A peculiar set of periphrastic constructions can be observed in the Spanish spoken by monolingual speakers in the Ecuadorian Highlands (henceforth HS). This dialect probably arose through long contact between the variety of Standard Spanish (henceforth SS) spoken in the region and the indigenous language of the area, Quichua.[1] The variety of Spanish arising through such substratum contact displays, in addition to many features of Standard Spanish, a number of peculiarities not attested elsewhere in Spanish. Most relevant to this paper, HS shows peculiar uses of gerund-marked verbs, uses that resemble SS superficially, but in fact represent considerable innovation and syntactic-semantic reanalysis. As a brief illustration consider:

(1) *Le boté pegando*
him throw-I hit-GER
HS: 'I hit him/her *unintentionally*'
SS: *'I threw him out hitting (him)'

Construction (1) is ungrammatical in SS, but its semantic interpretation — if possible — would have tagged the gerund-marked second verb as an adverial subordinate clause, with *botar* 'throw' remaining the semantically main verb. In contrast, the semantic interpretation of (1) in HS tags the gerund-marked *pegar* as the main verb, and the finite *botar* as a **grammaticalized auxiliary** that now carries the adverbial sense 'unintentionally'. In this division between a finite but de-semanticized auxiliary and the non-finite but semantically vigorous complement, HS two-verb constructions such as (1) follow superficially the familiar auxiliary-main-verb pattern of SS, as in:

(2)   *Le estaba pegando*
      him be/IMPF/I hit-GER
      'I was hitting him'

In this paper I will first survey the range of periphrastic construction in HS that follow the morpho-syntactic pattern of (1). I will show the various types of semantic reanalysis — or de-semanticization — undergone by the various finite auxiliary verbs involved.[2] I will then survey several syntactic properties of these complex clauses, showing that they have indeed undergone **clause union**. And further, that clause union is clearly reflected in the reanalyzed grammatical relations of the merged clause. The data for this study come from texts, informal conversations with monolingual speakers of HS Spanish, and direct elicitation.

2.   The variety of grammaticalized gerund constructions in HS

Examples (3) below illustrate the variety of grammaticalized periphrastic constructions in HS to be discussed in this paper:[3]

(3)   a.   *Voy llorando*
           go-I cry-GER
           SS: 'I cry while going'
           HS: 'Having cried I go'

      b.   *Vengo llorando*
           come-I cry-GER
           SS: 'I cry while coming'
           HS: 'Having cried I come'

c. *Le dejé matando*
   him leave-I kill-GER
   SS: '*I left him killing'
   HS: 'I killed him/her (and abandoned him)'

d. *Le mandé hablando*
   him order-I speak-GER
   SS: '*I sent/order him speaking'
   HS: 'I scolded him'

e. *Le boté pegando*
   him throw-I hit-GER
   SS: '*I threw him out hitting him'
   HS: 'I hit him/her (unintentionally)'

f. *Le doy cocinando*
   him give-I cook-GER
   SS: '*I give him cooking'
   HS: 'I cook for/instead of him'

On the syntactic surface, it seems, HS does not distort the standard pattern of finite auxiliary plus gerund-marked complement. Semantically however, all the HS constructions display considerable semantic reanalysis, so that many of them (e.g. (3c-f)) are ungrammatical in SS.

Further, the verbs *mandar* 'send'/'order' (3d), and *botar* 'throw'/ 'drop' (3a,e) have different selectional restrictions in the two varieties of Spanish. In SS, gerund complements cannot be used with these two verbs (4a,b). Both can take nominal (or pronominal) objects (4c,d), and *mandar* as a manipulation verb can also take an infinitival verbal complement, as in (4e):

(4)   a. **Te mando enviando el paquete*
         you send-I send-GER the package

      b. **Te boto enviando el paquete*
         you throw-I send-GER the package

      c. *Te mandó el paquete (por avión)*
         you send-PAST/3s the package (by air)
         'He sent you the package (by plane)'

      d. *Ya boté la basura*
         already throw-PAST/I the garbage
         'I already threw the garbage away'

    e. *Me mandó   a callar*
         me order-PAST/3s to be.quiet/INF
         'He ordered me to be quiet'

Further, in SS *dar* 'give' cannot take a gerund verbal complement (5a), but takes nominal or pronominal objects as a simple bi-transitive (5b). As a causative verb, it may also take an infinitival verbal complement (5c):

(5)   a. **Te doy comiendo*
         you give-I eat-GER

      b. *Le doy el vestido a María*
          her give-I the dress   to María
          'I give the dress to Maria'

      c. *Doy de comer a los animales*
          give-I of eat/INF to the animals
          'I feed the animals'
          (Lit.: 'I give to eat to the animals')

3. Grammaticalization

In treating the HS construction discussed here as cases of grammaticalized finite main verb, I follow Givón (1971, 1973, 1975, 1979, 1995), Heine (1990, 1993), Heine and Reh (1982), Heine et al. (1991), and Traugott and Heine (1991). Within the theoretically-oriented framework of grammaticalization, the pattern described here for HS is viewed as the product of a unidirectional diachronic development whereby lexical words change into grammatical morphemes (Givón 1971, 1975, 1979; Heine 1993; Lehman 1982; Silva-Corvalán 1994; Traugott and Ekkehar 1991).

    A number of distinct parallel changes are most commonly involved in such grammaticalization, chief of which are:

    a. functional-semantic re-analysis ('de-semanticization')
    b. syntactic-categorial change ('re-categorization')
    c. phonological reduction
    d. cliticization
    e. clause union ('clause integration')

De-semanticization is the process by which a lexical word loses its lexical meaning and acquires a grammatical function. **Re-categorization** is the process by which a lexical word loses its erstwhile syntactic category (noun, verb, adjective) and is then reassigned into a new grammatical morpheme category. **Phonological reduction** involves first de-stressing and then phonological attrition (bleaching) and shortening of the erstwhile lexical stem. **Cliticization**, which invariable follows phonological reduction, involves the adjustment of the morphemic status of the grammaticalized word — from free lexical stem to a bound morpheme, first a clitic, then affix, eventually an inflection. Finally, **clause integration** is not involved in all cases of grammaticalization, but is an essential ingredient when the grammaticalized verb had a verbal complement. In clause union, two erstwhile independent clauses, each with each own set of grammatical relations, merged as a result of the grammaticalization of one of the two verbs, to form a single clause with a single set of grammatical relations (Givón 1980, 1990: ch. 13, 1995: ch. 6).

It is important to note that the parallel processes associated with grammaticalization do not proceed at the same pace. Functional and semantic reanalysis (a) is the earliest manifestation of grammaticalization (Givón 1975, 1979). While the more formal syntactic, morphemic and phonological adjustments (b), (c), (d), (e) proceed at a much slower pace.

What is more, all five processes may — at least in principle — procede gradually through multiple stages (Lehmann 1982, 1985; Bybee 1988).

Clause integration (e) is of particular relevance to this study, since the grammaticalization of modality verbs that take equi-subject complements is the main diachronic source of grammaticalized tense-aspect-modal morphemes (TAMs), as well as of other types of grammatical morphology (Givón 1971, 1973, 1979; Heine 1993). In an embedding language such as Spanish, the initial syntactic configuration that gives rise to TAM auxiliaries is precisely such an equi-subject complementation configuration. In such a configuration, an erstwhile main verb can become a de-semanticized auxiliary, and the complement verb then takes over as the semantic main verb of the merged clause, as in:

(6) a. *se-lo-estamos explicando*
         him-it-be-we explain-GER
         'We are explaining it to him'

b. *se-lo-han   dado*
    her-it-have-3p give-PART
    'They have given it to her'

The rise of tense-aspect-modal morphology in embedding languages, via clause union of an equi-subject complementation, often proceeds through an intermediate diachronic stage of **auxiliary verbs**. In this stage, the finite main verb, already re-analyzed as a TAM marker, still retains the finite morphology that characterized it as a main verb. While the complement verb, already re-semanticized as a the main verb of the merged clause, retains its non-finite complement morphology. In Spanish this is particularly glaring with respect to the subject and object pronominal inflections. Those remain cliticized to the auxiliary even after ceasing to bear grammatical relation to it (6a,b).[4] In this way, grammaticalized auxiliaries continue to resemble complement-taking modality verbs that have not been grammaticalized, as in:

(7) *Los niños   siguen cantando*
     the children follow singing
     'The children continue to sing'

In this paper I will show how HS utilizes an existing SS morpho-syntactic pattern in forming its new de-semanticized auxiliaries.

What is unique to HS is that many of the lexical verbs that develop into auxiliaries do not likewise grammaticalize in any other dialect of SS. I will then suggest that in many respects Heine's (1993) 'transparency principle' ("one word, one function") is reflected in the HS grammaticalization. So that reanalysis of the formal (morpho-syntactic) properties of the grammaticalized verb follows a three-stage progression:

(8) **Gradual morpho-syntactic change:**

Stage:	early	intermediate	late
formal status of main verb:	Verbal	Verbal	
		Grammatical	Grammatical

4. Semantic re-analysis

The grammaticalized main verbs in HS are both intransitive motion verbs ('go', 'come') and transitive verbs ('leave', 'order', 'throw', 'give'). In this section I discuss the semantic reanalysis of the grammaticalized two-verb constructions in HS by contrasting them with their SS equivalents. The discussion will be divided into two subsections, dealing first with grammaticalized intransitive motion verbs, then with grammaticalized transitive main verbs.

4.1. *Grammaticalized intransitive motion verbs*

In Both SS and HS, *ir* 'go' and *venir* 'come' denote motion away or toward a reference point:

(9)   a. *Me voy a las siete*
           me go-I at the seven
           'I (will) leave at seven'

        b. *Vengo a las siete*
           come-I at the seven
           'I (will) come (over) at seven'

As main verbs taking equi-subject complements, these verbs can function in SS usage, in Ecuador and elsewhere, as auxiliaries. When the second-clause verb is marked as gerund, the sense of two simultaneous events two is conveyed.

In HS, however, these construction also convey two consecutive events, with the one coded by the second, gerund-mark verb *preceding* the one coded by the main motion verb:[5]

(10)   a. *Voy llorando*
           go-I cry-GER
           'Having cried I leave (go)' (HS)
           'I go crying' (SS)

       b. *Vengo llorando*
           'Having cried I come' (HS)
           'I come crying' (SS)

c. *Voy pegándole*
go-I hit-GER-3s
'Having hit her I leave (go)' (HS)
'I go hitting her' (SS)

In some grammaticalized gerund constructions, HS shows no semantic restrictions over the second (gerund) verb. This makes constructions such as (11a,b) perfectly accepted by HS, but pragmatically odd in SS:[6]

(11) a. *Me voy operando dos casos graves*
me go-I operating two cases dangerous
'Having operated two dangerous cases I leave (go)' (HS)
'*I leave operating . . .' (SS)

b. *Vendrás arreglando todos los problemas legales*
come-FUT/2s fixing all the problems legal
'Come after fixing all the legal problems' (HS)
'*Come fixing the legal problems' (SS)

4.2. *Grammaticalized transitive verbs*

4.2.1. Dejar *'leave'/'abandon'*
In both SS and HS, the verb *dejar* 'leave', 'abandon' in simple clauses codes agent-initiated motion away initiated by an agent:

(12) a. *Dejé la casa a las siete*
leave-PAST/I the house at the seven
'I left the house at 7'

b. *Dejé mi abrigo en la casa*
leave-PAST/I my coat in the house
'I left my coat at home'

c. *Le dejé a Juan en la estación*
him leave-PAST/I OB Juan in the station
'I left Juan at the station'

d. *Le dejé por borracho*
him leave-PAST/I because drunk
'I left him because he was alcoholic'

In complex two-verb constructions in both SS and HS, 'dejar' may be followed by a verb marked either by the perfect (13a) which assumes a causative, or the gerund (13b) which describes two simultaneous events:

(13) a. *Te dejé   dormido*
        you leave-PAST/I sleep-PERF
        'I left you asleep'

    b. *Te dejé   durmiendo*
        you leave-PAST/I sleep-GER
        'I left you sleeping'

However, *dejar* in such a construction may also assume a *causative* sense similar to (13a), as in:[7]

(14) a. *Te dejó   durmiendo*
        you leave-past/3s sleep-GER
        'She left you sleeping' (SS, HS)
        'She made you sleep' (HS)

    b. *Le dejé   llorando*
        him leave-PAST/I cry-GER
        'I left him crying' (SS, HS)
        'I made him cry' (HS)

Example (15) below, taken from natural conversation, illustrate the fact that in early stages of grammaticalization usage may be ambiguous, in this case carrying both the original motion sense and the later causative sense of *dejar* 'leave'. The speaker describes here how by the time she left the family she used to work for, the baby she had cared for had learned — from her — to walk well:

(15) *Conmigo nació el Santi,*
     with-me born   the Santi(ago)
     '. . . Santi(ago) was born with me;

     me fui   porque estaba   esperando yo también,
     me go-PAST/I because be-IMF/I expecting I   also
     I left because I was expecting too;

     yo caminando bien le   dejé
     I walk-GER   well him leave-PAST/I
     I left him walking well 3ACC . . .' [RN.01.95]

It is precisely such cases, where the two senses are not in conflict but rather are semantically complementary, that characterize the beginning of the gradual process of semantic re-analysis.

In its grammaticalized capacity in HS, *dejar* in (16a) below involves an equi-subject chain. In SS, (16a) is ungrammatical as it stands, unless clarified with an explicit direct object for the second, as in (16b), whereby it clearly displays a switch-subject chain.

(16) a. *Le   dejé   pegándole*
         him leave-PAST/I hit-GER-him
         HS: 'I left him after first hitting him'
         SS: '*I left him (while he was) hitting'

      b. *Le   dejé   pegándole a Juan*
         him leave-PAST/I hit-GER-him OB Juan
         HS: 'I left Juan after first hitting him'
         SS: 'I left him (while he was) hitting John'[8]

The sense of 'motion away' of *dejar* is still preserved in the HS examples (17a,b):

(17) a. *Voy a verle   a este sinverguenza ...*
         go-I to see-INF-3s to this shameless
         'I'm going to see this shameless guy ...'

         le he   de dejar   castigando
         3s have-I of leave-INF punish-GER
         'I will leave him after first punishing him'
         (Lit.: 'I am going to see this shameless guy, I will leave him
               punishing')

      b. *Dejarás   limpiando todo*
         leave-FUT/2s clean-GER all
         'Clean everything before leaving'
         (Lit.: 'You will leave cleaning it all up')

As an illustration of the effect of the grammaticalized *dejar*, contrast the two HS examples in (18), (18a) without *dejar* and (18b) with it:

(18) a. *Mamá me encargó   unas pastillas*
         mom me ask-PAST/3s some pills
         'Mom asked me to get her some pills'
         (> no knowledge of Mom's movement is implied)

b. *Mi antigua vecina   me dejó   encargando*
my old   neighbor me leave-PAST/3s ask-GER
'My old neighbor (while still here) asked me to get her

unas pastillas
some pills
some pills (she is gone now)'

The grammaticalized (18b) may be rendered in SS with an explicit adverbial clause:

(19) *Antes de irse,   mi vecina   me encargó unas pastillas.*
before of leaving my neighbor me-asked   some pills
'Before leaving, my neighbor asked me for some pills'

4.2.2. Mandar *'send'/'order'*
In its sense of 'send', *mandar* in simple clauses in SS is a bi-transitive verb of in caused motion of a PAT toward a goal, as in:

(20) *Yo mandé   una carta a la Universidad*
I   send-PAST/I a   letter to the University
'I sent a letter to the University'

In its manipulative sense of 'tell' or 'order', it takes either an infinitival (21a) or a subjunctive (21b) complement, as in:

(21) a. *A esa lora, le mandé   que hable*
to that parrot her order-PAST/I SUB speak-SUBJUN/3s
'I told that parrot that it should speak'

b. *A esa lora, le mandé   a hablar*
to that parrot her order-PAST/I to speak-INF
'I ordered that parrot to speak'

In HS, *mandar* 'send' with a gerund-marked verbal complement functions as a causative verb, thus presumably extending the SS caused-motion sense. This is the case with intransitive complement verbs, as in:

(22) a. *Me manda llorando*
me send-3s cry-GER
'S/he makes me cry'
(Lit.: 'She sends me crying')

b. *Qué buen doctor, entré   casi   muerta*
    what good doctor enter/PAST/I almost dead
    'What a good doctor! I entered his office half dead

    y   me mandó   caminando
    and me send-PAST/3s walk-GER
    and he made me walk' [FO.05.95]
    (Lit.: '.... he sent me walking')

An even more extreme case of semantic reanalysis may be seen in complements with *hablar* 'speak', yielding the combined sense of 'send-speak' as 'reprimand' or 'scold':

(23) *Todavía no entiendo   porque*
      yet   NEG understand-I why
      'I still don't understand why

      la señora me mandó   hablando
      the lady   me send-PAST/3s speaking
      lady scolded me' [NR.13.04.95]
      (Lit.: 'I still don't understand why the lady sent me speaking')

With transitive verbs as complements, the sense of causation is not evident, although it may well be that some vestige of the sense of 'motion away' of the patient of 'send' is retained, especially in (24d). Thus contrast:

(24) a. *Me dio   flores*
          me give-PAST/3s flowers
          'She gave me flowers'

      b. *Me mandó   regalando flores*
          me send-PAST/3s give-GER   flowers
          'She gave me flowers' (> as I was leaving)

      c. *Me pegó*
          me hit-PAST/3s
          'She hit me'

      d. *Me mandó   pegando*
          me send-PAST/3s hit-GER
          'By hitting me she caused me to leave'

HS *mandar* constructions emphasize on the causer while *dejar* constructions emphasize on the causee.

4.2.3. Botar *'throw'*, *'drop'*

The use of *botar* 'throw', 'drop' in simple clauses in SS may be seen in:

(25) a. *Boté   la basura ayer*
          throw-PAST/I the garbage yesterday
          'I threw out the garbage yesterday'

      b. *Le boté   al   niño*
          him drop-PAST/I OB-the child
          'I dropped the child (down)'

This use of *botar* in simple clauses is retained in HS. In addition, however, *botar* can also occur as a grammaticalized auxiliary before transitive gerund-marked complement verbs. This use is characteristic with verbs involving a negative effect to the patient, such as *pegar* 'hit', *patear* 'kick', *matar* 'kill', *destruir* 'destroy', *quemar* 'burn', etc. In this capacity, *botar* conveys the sense of an **unintended result**, as in:

(26) a. *Estaba   planchando bien*
          be/IMPFV-3s iron-GER   well
          'She was ironing well

        y   le botó   dañando (la plancha)
          and it throw-PAST/3s ruin-GER (the iron)
          and wound up ruining it (the iron)'

      b. *le ha   botado   matando a la mujer*
          her have-3s throw-PERF kill-GER OB the wife
          'He accidentally/unintentionally killed his wife'

      c. *Me han   botado   quemando la casa*
          me have-3p throw-PERF burn-GER   the house
          'Accidentally, someone has burned my house'

In this construction, *botar* follows the pattern of equi-subject auxiliaries in SS. The development of the grammaticalized sense 'unintentionally', 'accidentally' may be due to the conflation of two factors:

- The detrimental sense of 'drop' vis-a-vis the patient
- The detrimental sense associated with the complement verbs.

4.2.4. Dar *'give'*

In simple clauses in both SS and HS, *dar* 'give' retains its original bi-transitive sense, as in:

(27) a. *Te doy dinero cada semana*
    you give-I money each week
    'I give you money every week'

But in addition, *dar* can be used in HS as a grammaticalized auxiliary. The added sense here is a **benefactive** one, but with the inference of 'subject doing the action instead of the beneficiary'. Thus consider:

(28) a. *Te doy cocinando los domingos*
    you give-I cook-GER the sundays
    'I do you the favor of cooking for you on Sundays (instead of you doing it)'
    (Lit.: 'I give you cooking on Sundays')

   b. *Dame haciendo el pan mientras duermo*
    Give/IMP-me make-GER the bread while sleep-I
    'Would you do me the favor of baking the bread for me while I sleep?' (instead of me doing it)
    (Lit.: 'Give me making the bread....')

The complement verb may itself be transitive, as above, or intransitive, when it carries the sense of transitivity as in:

(29) *Dame saliendo del juego,*
    give/IMP-me leave-GER from-the game

   no entiendo nada
    NEG understand-I nothing

   'Would you do me the favor of finishing this game, I don't understand anything' [XZ.12.95]
   (Lit.: 'Give me leaving from the game, ...')

or even bi-transitive, including 'give' itself:

(30) a. *Dame   vendiendo el libro a María*
       give/IMP-me sell-GER   the book to Maria
       'Would you do me the favor of selling the book to Maria
       (instead of me)'
       (Lit.: 'Give me selling the book to Maria')

    b. *Me dió   comprando el libro para María*
       me give-PAST/3s sell-GER   the book for   Maria
       'He did me the favor of buying the book for Maria (instead
       of me)'
       (Lit.: 'He gave me buying the book for Maria')

    c. *El nos da   dando   la ropa   a la costurera*
       he us   give/IMP give-GER the clothes to the dressmaker
       'He is doing us the favor of giving the clothes to the dress-
       maker (instead of us)'
       (Lit.: 'He gave us giving the clothes to the dressmaker')

The development of benefactive senses out of 'give' is a near universal tendency in grammaticalization, though it is most commonly associated
with verb serialization (Givón 1975). It is, further, also found in the Quichua substratum of HS (Haboud 1995; Taylor 1982; Van de Kerke 1994).
What is of course of interest in HS is that this development occurs in an
embedding — complementation — syntactic configuration.

5. Clause union and grammatical relations

It is clear that the complex clauses described above in HS, with various
auxiliaries followed by a gerund-mark complement verb, have undergone
the kind of extensive semantic reanalysis normally associated with grammaticalization. In this section I suggest that these constructions have also
undergone considerable syntactic reanalysis, along the process of clause
integration ('clause union').

And further, that part of the transition toward clause union involves a
reanalysis of grammatical relations. I will begin by outlining the formal criteria that may be used to demonstrate clause union.

5.1. *Criteria for clause union*

Clause union is a complex diachronic development involving a number of morpho-syntactic features (Givón 1980, 1990: ch. 13). For this and other reasons, it cannot be a discrete (either/or) change, but is rather a gradual development. Therefore, as a synchronic product of a gradual multi-featured diachronic process, clause union is likewise a matter of degree. When one of the two verbs in an erstwhile periphrastic construction grammaticalizes semantically, syntactic clause union is then the formal reflection of the fact that what was construed earlier as two separate events is now construed as an integrated single event.

The formal morpho-syntactic criteria used here to determine the degree of clause union of HS two-verb constructions have been adapted from Givón (1980, 1990: ch. 13) as modified by Zavala (1993) and will be discussed in order. They are:

- Scope of negation
- Preposing the gerund clause
- The presence and interpretation of adverbials
- The position and reference of pronominal clitics.

5.2. *Scope of negation*

Contrast first the scope of negation in the SS and HS interpretations of (30a,b). The events in HS are interpreted as having occurred in the immediate past:

(31) a. *No va   comiendo el pobre*
        NEG go-3s eat-GER   the poor
        HS: 'The poor thing *didn't eat* before going'
        SS: 'He *is not eating* while going'

     b. *No vengo comiendo nada*
        NEG come-I eat-GER   nothing
        HS: 'I *didn't eat anything* before coming'
        SS: 'I *am not eating* while coming'

Likewise in (32a,b) where the SS are semantically odd:

(32) a. *No va   limpiando la casa*
      NEG go-3s clean-GER the house
      HS: 'He *did not clean the house* before leaving'
      SS: '?He *isn't cleaning the house* while leaving'

   b. *No viene   enterrando el caballo*
      NEG come-3s bury-GER   the horse
      HS: 'He *didn't bury the horse* before coming'
      SS: '?He *doesn't come* while burying the horse'

In the case of the intransitive auxiliaries above, the equi-subject condition makes it theoretically possible to have an interpretation of such negative clauses in SS. This is not possible anymore with the transitive grammaticalized auxiliaries of HS. In the case of *dejar*, the negation test is not decisive because the verb is causative-implicative verb. The scope of negation in such a case necessarily spreads over both verbs. That is:

(33) a. *No le dejé   llorando*
      NEG her leave-PAST/I cry-GER
      HS: 'I *didn't make her cry* (before leaving her)'
      SS: 'When I left, she was not crying'

   b. *No le dejó   rompiendo el brazo,*
      NEG his throw-PAST/3s breaking   the arm

      solo torciéndole
      only twist-GER-it
      HS: 'He *didn't break his arm* (before leaving him), just twisted it'
      SS: *'He didn't leave him breaking the arm, only twisting it'

When causative senses are not involved, the exclusion of any independent sense of the grammaticalized verb from the scope of negation is more obvious. This is evident in the case of *mandar-hablar* 'scold':

(34) *No le mandó   hablando, mas bien regalando plata*
     NEG him send-PAST/3s speak-GER more well give-GER   money
     'He *didn't scold him*, but rather gave him money'

Likewise with *botar* and *dar*:

(35) a. *No   le   botó   matando, solo asustándole*
NEG him throw-PAST/3s kill-GER, only scare-GER-him
'He didn't kill him, just scared him'

b. *No   te   doy   cocinando nada*
NEG you give-I cook-GER nothing
'I don't do you the favor of cooking anything for you (instead of you)'

5.3. *Preposing the gerund-marked clause*

In SS, gerund ADV-clauses can be preposed for pragmatic effects, as in:

(36) *todavía buscando a   su caballo, regresó*
still   seach-GER OB his horse   return-PAST/3s

a   la   casa
to the house

'Still looking for his horse, he returned home'

When the grammaticalized construction in HS involves the intransitives *ir* and *venir*, preposing of the gerund clause is still possible, since two event clauses are still involved. If the construction is negative then, the scope of negation falls over the gerund clause alone:

(37) *Enterrando el   caballo, no   viene*
Burying   the horse, NEG come+3SPr
'He *didn't bury the horse* before coming'
SS: '*Burying the horse, he *isn't coming*'

The transitive grammaticalized auxiliaries in HS allow preposing of the gerund-marked subordinate clause for emphatic purposes. This is presumably because there are no two independent events here, each with its own independent temporality. This is most striking when negation is also involved. Thus compare:

(38) a. *No   le   dejé   pegando*
NEG him leave-PAST/I hit-GER
'I didn't leave him after first hitting him' (HS)

b. *?Pegando(le), no le deje*
hit-GER-(him) NEG him leave-PAST/I
(possible as a defense from false accusation)

c. *No le mandé hablando*
NEG him send-PAST/I speak-GER
'I didn't scold him'

d. *?Hablándo(le), no le mandé*
speak-GER-(him) NEG him send-PAST/I
(possible as a defense from false accusation)

The more advanced in the process of grammaticalization the motion verb is, the more restricted pre-posing of the gerund-marked subordinate clause becomes:

e. *No le boté rompiendo*
NEG it drop-PAST/I break-GER
'I didn't break it (not even unintentionally)'

f. **Rompiéndo(le), no le boté*
break-GER-(it), NEG it drop-PAST/I

g. *No le doy cocinando*
NEG her give-I cook-GER
'I am not cooking for her'

h. **Cocinando, no le doy*
cook-GER NEG her give-I

One might as well note that the behavior of these grammaticalized one-event constructions in HS follows the behavior of grammaticalized TAM auxiliaries in SS, both with and without negation:

(39) a. *Está durmiendo*
be-3s sleep-GER
'He is asleep'

b. *?durmiendo, está*
sleep-GER be-3s

c. *No está durmiendo*
NEG be-3s sleep-GER
'He is not asleep'

   d. *?Durmiendo, no está*
      sleep-GER   NEG be-3s

   e. **No durmiendo, está*
      NEG sleep-GER   be-3s

(40) a. *Ha   dormido*
        have-3s sleep-PERF
        'She has slept'

   b. **dormido, ha*
      sleep-PERF have-3s

   c. *No ha   dormido*
      NEG have-3s sleep-GER
      'She hasn't slept'

   d. **Dormido, no ha*
      sleep-PERF NEG have-3s

   e. **No dormido, ha*
      NEG sleep-PERF have-3s

5.4. *The presence and interpretation of adverbials*

In the SS usage of *ir* 'go' followed by a gerund adverbial, either verb can
be modified by a semantically-appropriate adverbial. Thus:

(41) SS: a. *Se fue   muy rápido(,) comiendo*
            REF go-PAST/3s very fast   eat-GER
            'He took off very quickly, eating'

     b. *Se fue   comiendo muy rápido*
        REF go-PAST/3s eat-GER   very fast
        'He left, eating very fast'

   With the auxiliaries 'go' and 'come', which retain the sense of two
separate — consecutive — events, this variation is also possible in HS,
although to ensure the HS semantics, (42b,c) are preferred:

(42) HS: a. *Se fue   muy rápido(,) comiendo*
            REF go-PAST/3s very fast   eat-GER
            'Having eaten, he left very quickly'

    b. *Se fue   comiendo muy rápido*
        REF go-PAST/3s eat-GER   very fast
        'Having eaten very fast, he left'

    c. *Comiendo muy rápido se fue*
        eat-GER   very fast   REF go-PAST/3s
        'Having eaten very fast, he left'

The constructions with the auxiliaries 'come' and 'go' are thus shown, once again, to be less grammaticalized.

With the transitive auxiliaries in HS, modifying the auxiliary verb by an adverbial becomes impossible. Consider first the causative *dejar*, as in:

(43) a. *Le dejaron   hiriendo   con un cuchillote*
        him leave-PAST/3p wound-GER with a big.knife
        'They wounded him with a big knife (and then abandoned him)'

    b. *Con un cuchillote, le   dejaron   hiriendo*
        with a big.knife   him leave-PAST/3p wound-GER
        'With a big knife they wounded him and (then abandon him)'
        SS: 'With a big knife they left him wounding'

    c. *?Le dejaron,   con un cuchillote, hiriendo*
        him leave-PAST/3p with a big.knife   wound-GER[9]
        (possible as an emphatic, as in e.g. news headlines)

Consider next the combination *mandar-hablar* 'scold':

(44) a. *Le mando hablando como a   tonto*
        him send-I speaking like OBJ fool
        'I scold (treat) him like a fool'

    b. *Como a   tonto le   mando hablando*
        like OBJ fool him send-I speak-GER
        'As if he were a fool I scold (treat) him'
        (possible as an emphatic)
        SS: '*As if he were a fool I send him speaking'

    c. *?Le mando, como a   tonto, hablando*
        him send-I like OBJ fool speak-GER
        (possible as an emphatic)

Similarly with *botar*:

(45) a. *Le   botó   rompiendo como papel*
          him drop-PAST/3s break-GER like   paper
          'She tore it (the blouse) like paper'

      b. *Como papel le botó   compiendo*
          like   paper it drop-PAST/3s break-GER
          'Like paper she tore it'
          SS: '*Like paper she dropped it tearing'

      c. *?Le botó,   como papel, rompiendo*
          him drop-PAST/3s like   paper break-GER

And likewise with *dar*:

(46) a. *Le da   cocinando como a   reina*
          her give-3s cook-GER like OBJ queen
          'He cooks for her as for a queen'

      b. *Como a   reina le da   cocinando*
          like OBJ queen her give cook-GER
          'As for a queen he cooks for her'
          '*As for a queen he gives her cooking'

      c. *?Le da,   como a   reina, cocinando*
          her give-3s like OBJ queen cook-GER

While the test of adverbial placement and interpretation seems syntactic, it is transparently a semantic test.

5.5. *Clitic pronouns, clause union and grammatical relations*

5.5.1. *Preamble*
As is well known elsewhere (Keenan 1975, 1976; Givón 1995, This volume), pronominal agreement on the verb is one of the most common overt coding properties of grammatical relation, both subject and object. When two verbal clauses undergo clause union as a result of the grammaticalization of one of the verbs, especially in an embedding language, the realignment of the clitic pronouns, and often their consolidation around one of the two verbs, is part and parcel of the syntactic reanalysis accompanying clause union (Aissen and Perlmutter 1976; Rizzi 1976; Givón, This volume). This

process is driven by two parallel factors. First, semantically, the grammaticalized verb, as part of its de-semanticization, loses its original grammatical relation to arguments in the condensed clause. And second, syntactically — at least in embedding languages — the complementation configuration that gives rise to clause union marks one of the two verbs (main verb) as finite, the other (complement) as non-finite or nominalized.

Clitic pronouns, in conformance with the common rule for simple finite clauses, tend to gravitate in such configurations to the finite verb even before full clause union. This happens in spite of the fact that upon clause union, the finite verb is the one that most commonly becomes the grammaticalized auxiliary.

In this section I will suggest that the realignment of object clitics around the grammaticalized finite auxiliary in the HS constructions surveyed here follows precisely such a pattern. We will begin with surveying the placement of object clitics in SS.

5.5.2. *Clitic object pronouns in SS*
While the tendency for object clitics to gravitate to the finite auxiliary is well-established in SS, a certain residual variation remains in their placement in some grammatical contexts. The general rules governing the placement of clitics are summarized below (see also Silva-Corvalán 1994).

a. **Finite main verb — the default choice:**
When the verb to which a pronouns bear object relation is finite, and no grammaticalized finite auxiliary is present, the clitics appear prefixed to that finite verb:

> (47) *me-lo-compró*
> **me-it**-buy-PAST/3s
> 'She bought it for me'

b. **Imperative verb:**
When the verb is in the imperative, and thus cannot take an auxiliary, its object pronoun always appears as a suffix:

> (48) *cóme-te-lo*
> eat-**you-it**
> 'It it up!'

c. **Following the finite perfect auxiliary 'have':**

When the semantic main verb is marked as perfect and is preceded by the finite auxiliary 'have', the pronouns referring to its semantic objects appear as prefixes on the finite auxiliary:

(49) *Ya*   ***se-la**-he*   *comprado*
      already **her-it**-have-I buy-PERF
      'I have already bought it for her'

d. **Following the finite progressive auxiliary 'be':**

When the semantic main verb is marked as gerund and follows the auxiliary 'be' (or other progressive auxiliaries), the clitic can be placed as either a prefix on the auxiliary or a suffix on the gerund-marked verb:

(50) a. ***te-lo**-estoy contando*
         you-it-be-I tell-GER
         'I am telling it to you'

      b. *Estoy contándo-**te-lo***
         be-I   tell-GER-**you-it**
         'I am telling it to you it'

When the gerund-marked verb appears without an auxiliary, naturally only the suffix option (50b) can be exercised:

(51) *Viéndo-**la**   te   acordarás   de ella*
      see-GER-**her** REF remember-FUT/2s of her
      'Seeing her you'll remember her'

e. **Infinitive-marked complement after a finite main verb:**

When a finite verb is followed by an infinitive-marked complement, pronouns referring to the objects of the complement may appear as either prefixes on the main verb or suffixes on the complement:

(52) a. ***te**-vine   a hablar*
         you-come-PAST/I to talk-INF
         'I came to talk to you'

      b. *vine   a hablar-**te***
         come-PAST/I to talk-INF-**you**
         'I came to talk to you'

c. *te-quiero ver*
you-want-I see-INF
'I want to see you'

d. *quiero ver-te*
want-I see-**you**
'I want to see you'

e. *me-hizo   abrir-la*
me-make-PAST/3s open-INF-**it**
'He made me open it (the window)'

f. *me-la-hizo   abrir*
me-**it**-make-PAST/3s open-INF
'I saw him break it (the window)'

5.5.3. Clitic pronouns in HS grammaticalized clauses

As seen above, in SS gerund complement verbs following the finite progressive auxiliary 'be' allow the option of either taking their object pronouns as suffixes or ceding them as prefixes on the finite auxiliary. In HS (except with 'go' and 'come' still in the first stages of grammaticalization), only one option is preserved — all object pronouns that refer to semantic arguments of the complement verb must be prefixed to the finite auxiliary.

(53) a. *María le(lo)-dejó   matando*[10]
María **him**-leave-PAST/3s kill-GER
'Maria killed him (and then left)'

b. **María dejo matándo-le*

c. *Juan le-botó   pegando*
Juan **her**-drop-PAST/3s hit-GER her
'Juan hit her unexpectedly'

d. **Juan botó pegándo-le*

e. *María le-mandó   hablando*
Maria **him**-send-PAST/3s talk-GER
'Maria insulted him'

f. **María mando hablándo-le*

g. *Juan (0)-le-dió   escribiendo*
Juan **her-it**-give-PAST/3s write-GER
'Juan wrote it for her (instead of her)'

h. **Juan dió escribiéndo-le*

i. *María le-vino   pegando a   Juan*
   Maria **him**-come-PAST/3s hit-GER   OB Juan
   'Maria came after hitting Juan'

j. *María vino   pegando-le* (a   Juan)
   Maria come/PAST/3s hit-GER-**him** (OB Juan)
   'Maria came after hitting him (Juan)'

Note, finally, the presence of **clitic doubling** and in HS, so that the same object pronoun may appear on *both* verbs. Such uses may be considered sub-standard even in HS:[11]

(54) a. *?Le-dejó   pegándo-le*
         him-leave-PAST/3s hit-GER-**him**
         'He hit him (and left)'

      b. *?Le-botó   pegándo-le*
         him-drop-PAST/3s hit-GER-**him**
         'He hit him (accidently)'

      c. *?Te-doy   cocinándo-te*
         you-give-I cook-GER-**you**
         'I cook for you (instead of you)'

      d. *?Se-viene   comiéndo-se*
         REF-come-3s eat-**REF**
         'He comes after eating'

6. Discussion

6.1. *De-semanticization*

The conflation of all the evidence suggests that the periphrastic two-verb construction in HS are syntactically all highly grammaticalized. But the concomitant de-semanticization has not advanced at the same pace for all verbs. Thus, the intransitive auxiliaries *venir* 'come' and *ir* 'go' still retain the sense of motion verb, as well as the sense of two separate events, one following the other.

In the cases of the transitive *mandar* 'send' and *dejar* 'leave' their original lexical meaning, of motion, is retained, at least in some uses. But that sense is almost lost in other uses. The grammaticalized sense that becomes is now that of causation.

And in some combinations, such as e.g. *mandar* + *hablar* to yield 'scold', the original lexical sense of 'send' is almost entirely gone.

At the top of the de-semanticization scale, the transitives *botar* 'drop' and '*dar* 'give' have just about lost their original lexical meaning. *Botar* now adds the meaning 'unintentionally', and *dar* that of 'benefactive'.

One may thus view these verbs along a continuum of semantic re-analysis:

(55) **Continuum of de-semanticization of HS auxiliaries:**

least	....	**most**
ir	.... mandar	botar
venir	.... dejar	dar

6.2. Syntactic re-analysis

6.2.1. Scope of negation
The negation test suggest that even in the least grammaticalized *ir* and *venir*, the two clauses are so well integrated semantically that only a single sense of negation may be obtained. That sense, however, centers on the gerund-marked complement, excluding the grammaticalized auxiliary. This contrast sharply with the morphologically-similar SS construction, where the scope of negation of the main verb covers *both* clauses. In the case of the further de-semanticized transitive auxiliaries of HS, the scope of negation, rather expectedly, excludes the auxiliary, covering only the gerund-marked verb.

6.2.2. Preposing of the gerund-marked clause
All the grammaticalized HS surveyed here resist preposing the gerund-marked VP. This contrasts sharply with SS gerund adverbial clauses, which are readily preposed. The removal of freedom of pre-posing suggests that the HS construction is not a loose parataxis, but rather a rigid syntactic

configuration displaying a considerable measure of syntactic integration — i.e., clause union.

6.2.3. *Interpretation of adverbials*

Only with the least grammaticalized auxiliaries *ir* and *venir* can one modify both clauses with an adverbial. With the more grammaticalized transitive auxiliaries, the adverbial can only modify the gerund-marked semantic main verb, never the grammaticalized and largely de-semanticized auxiliary.

6.2.4. *Clitic object pronouns and grammatical relations*

Spanish, both SS and HS, follows the general trend of embedding languages (Givón 1995, This volume), whereby in complement constructions, most finite morphology gravitates to the main verb. This tendency remains strong in the grammaticalization of main verbs into TAM auxiliaries in SS, although some variation is still allow in two non-finite verb forms, gerund and infinitive. But in the case of the progressive auxiliary followed by a gerund-marked verb, object clitics can only appear as prefixes on the grammaticalized finite verb — the tail end of the clause-union process.

One could of course raise the obvious question — is the general tendency in Spanish and other embedding languages counter intuitive? That is, how come the verb that de-semanticizes and grammaticalizes nonetheless winds up with all finite marking, including tense-aspect modality, subject pronominal agreement and object clitic pronouns? The answer to this ought to be rather obvious, although it is perennially obscured by linguists' abiding attachment to the writing systems of languages such as English or Spanish: In clause union associated with grammaticalized auxiliaries, not only does the auxiliary wind up with all finite morphology for the merged clause, but it itself also cliticizes on the non-finite semantic main verb.

In the process of clause union in embedding languages, the finite morphology — including the grammaticalized auxiliary — winds up being re-attached precisely where it should be, to the *now finite* semantic main verb. Since all grammatical relations are now relevant to that verb alone, the assignment of object clitics as prefix on that verb, riding piggyback on the erstwhile auxiliary, is a return to the default rule of simple main clauses. It simply reasserts that it is to the finite semantic-mail verb that all grammatical roles now bear their grammatical relations. That is, that the merged clause now has a merged single set of grammatical relations.

Abbreviated Grammatical Terms

COND	Conditional
FUT	Future
GER	Gerund
HS	Highland Spanish
IMP	Imperative
INF	Infinitive
NEG	Negative
OBJ	Object
PERF	Perfect
PAST	Past
REFL	Reflexive
SS	Standard Spanish
3p	third person plural
3s	third person singular
SUBJUN	Subjunctive
TAM	tense-aspect-modality

Notes

*   I am indebted to T. Givón and Roberto Zavala for comments on earlier versions of
       the manuscript.

1.   For the language contact situation in the Ecuador Highlands, see Toscano (1953),
       Niño-Murcia (1988), or Haboud (1994, 1995, 1996).

2.   These are known in the linguistic literature as 'aspect auxiliaries', 'aspectuals' (García
       1967), 'co-verbs', 'quasi auxiliaries' (Bolinger 1980: 297; Heine 1993: 15), or 'semi
       auxiliaries' (Green 1987b: 261; Silva-Corvalán 1994; Myhill 1988).

3.   Most of my data on HS were collected between May 1992 and January 1993 as well
       as summer 1993. Much of the data is based on text from various sources, including
       Moya (1992), Perez-Torres (1991) and Stolen (1987). Most of my oral text elicitations
       took place on the campus of the Universidad Católica de Ecuador in Quito, or during
       social, family and taxi-riding occasions. During 1994 and 1995, e-mail correspond-
       ences with other native speakers of HS augmented my textual data-base.

4.   This is the so-called "affix climbing" of Romance languages, see Aissen and Perl-
       mutter (1986).

5.   Previous studies suggest that the perfectivity associated with these constructions is due
       to the influence of the Quichua substratum (Haboud 1994; Niño-Murcia 1988; Toscano
       1953).

6.   The morphological future in HS can also function as an informal (familiar) *impera-
       tive* (Haboud 1995).

7.   According to JG (native HS speaker), (13a) also implies that the action-event has been
       totally completed while (14a) the end result may be uncertain. Further research is
       needed to draw specific conclusions.

8.   See Yépez (1986), and Suñer and Yépez (1988) for analyses of clitic doubling and
       clitic deletion in Quiteño Spanish.

9.   Example (43b,c) may be used for extreme emphatic purposes as headlines of small
       local newspapers.

10.   The region focus of this study (Central Ecuadorian Highlands) is characterized as
       leista because of the use of the pronouns *le/les* replacing *lo/la* in all contexts. Nevertheless,
       Niño-Murcia (1995) accounts for similar constructions on the Northern Ecuadorian
       Highlands which are mainly *loistas* (use of *lo/los* in all contexts), as in: *darámelo
       leyendo* 'Read it to/for me' (1995: 90).

11.   This double-clitic pattern is characteristic of bilingual Quichua-Spanish speakers as
       shown by Muysken (1977).

References

Alcina, Juan and Jose M. Blecua. 1980. *Gramática Española*. Barcelona: Ed. Ariel.

Aissen, Judy and D. Perlmutter. 1986. "Clause reduction in Spanish", In *Studies in Relational Grammar*, D. Perlmutter, (ed.), 1, (360-404). Chicago: University of Chicago Press.

Bolinger, Dwight. 1988. "*Wanna* and the gradience of auxiliaries." In G. Brettschneider and C. Lehman (eds) 1980, 292-299.

Bybee, Joan, W. Pagliuca and Revere Perkins. 1991. "Back to the Future." In E. Traugott and B. Heine (eds) 1991: II, 17-58.

Campos, Héctor. 1993. *De la Oración simple a la oración compuesta*. Washington: Georgetown University Press.

Dixon, R.M.W. 1991. *A New approach to English Grammar, on Semantic Principles*, Oxford: Clarendon Press.

Emonds, J. 1976. *A transformational approach to English Syntax*. New York: Academic Press.

Freed, Alice. 1979. *The semantics of English complementation*, Dordrecht, Boston, and London: D. Reidel.

Garcia, Erica. 1967. "Auxiliaries and the criterion of simplicity." *Language* 43,4: 853-70.

Garcia, Erica. 1985. "Quantity into quality: synchronic indeterminacy and language change." *Lingua* 65: 275-306.

Givón, T. 1971. "Historical syntax and synchronic morphology: An archaeologist's field trip." In *CLAS 7*. Chicago: University of Chicago, Chicago Linguistics Society.

Givón, T. 1973. "The time-axis phenomenon." *Language* 49.4.

Givón, T. 1975. "Serial verbs and syntactic change: Niger-Congo." In *Word Order and Word Order Change*, C. Li (ed.). Austin: University of Texas Press.

Givón, T. 1979. *On Understanding Grammar*. New York: Academic Press.

Givón, T. 1980. "The Binding hierarchy and the typology of complements." *Studies in Language* 4:3:333-377.

Givón, T. 1984. *Syntax: A functional Typological Introduction*, vol. I. Amsterdam: John Benjamins.

Givón, T. 1990. *Syntax: A Functional-Typological Introduction*, vol. II. Amsterdam: John Benjamins.

Givón, T. 1995. *Functionalism and Grammar*. Amsterdam: John Benjamins.

Gómez-Torrego, Leonardo. 1986. *Teoría y Práctica de la Sintaxis*. Madrid: Ed. Alhambra.

Green, John. 1987a. "The status of Romance auxiliaries of voice." In N. Vincent and R. Ramat (eds) 1987: 97-138.

Green, J. 1987b. "The evolution of Romance auxiliaries: Criteria and chronology." In N. Vincent and R. Ramat (eds) 1987: 257-67.

Haboud, Marleen. 1994. "On language contact and grammatical changes in Highland Ecuadorian Spanish", University of Oregon (ms).

Haboud, Marleen. 1995. "Semantic Transfer in Highland Ecuadorian Spanish", Paper presented at the Conference: Lenguas del Sur del Río Bravo. Tulane University. Tulane (January 1995) (ms).

Haboud, Marleen. 1996. Quichua and Spanish in the Ecuadorian Highlands: The Effects of Long-term Contact. PhD. dissertation, University of Oregon.

Heine, B. 1990. "Grammaticalization chains as linguistic categories." *Studies in Language* 16.2:335-68.

Heine, B. 1993. *Auxiliaries: Cognitive Forces and Grammaticalization*. Oxford: Oxford University Press.

Heine, Bernd, U. Claudi, and F. Hünnemeyer. 1991. *Grammaticalization: A Conceptual Framework*, Chicago: The University of Chicago Press.

Heine, B. and M. Reh. 1982. *Patterns of Grammaticalization in African Languages*, *AKUP 47*, University of Koeln.

Hopper, P. and S.A. Thompson. 1984. "The discourse basis for lexical categories in universal grammar." *Language* 60:703-752.

Kany, Charles. 1976. *Sintaxis Hispanoamericana* (version espanola de Martin Blanco Alvarez) Biblioteca Románica Hispánica. Madrid: Ed. Gredos.

Keenan, E.L. 1975. "Some universals of passives and relational grammar", *CLS 11*, University of Chicago, Chicago Linguistics Society.

Keenan, E.L. 1976. "On the notion 'subject' in universal grammar." In *Subject and Topic*, C.N. Li (ed.). New York: Academic Press.

Lehman, Christian. 1982. "Thoughts on grammaticalization: A programmatic sketch." I, *AKUP 48*, Cologne: Institut für Sprachwissenschaft.

Levin, Beth. 1993. *English Verb classes and alternations*, Chicago: University of Chicago Press.

Moya, Ruth, 1992. "El Bilingüismo del Maestro y del Niño en la Escuela Quichua-Castellano." Ponencia presentada al seminario Bilingüismo y Educación. Tema 3. Perspectivas Pedagógicas y Bilingüismo. Academia de Educación Indigena, Universidad Pedagógica Nacional, México.

Muysken, Pieter. 1977. *Syntactic Developments in the Verb Phrase of Ecuadorian Quechua*. Dordrecht: Foris.

Myhll, John. 1988. "The grammaticalization of auxiliaries: Spanish clitic climbing." *BLS* 14:352-363. Berkeley: Berkeley Linguistics Society.

Niño-Murcia, Mercedes. 1988. *Construcciones verbales del español andino: Interacción quec hua-española enla frontera colombo-ecuatoriana*, PhD dissertation, University of Michigan.

Niño-Murcia, Mercedes. 1995. "The Gerund in the Spanish of the North Andean region." In Silva-Corvalán (ed.). 1995:83-100.

Palmer, F.R. 1974. *The English Verb*. London: Longman.

Payne, Thomas. 1994. "The pragmatics of voice in a Philippine language: Actor-focus and goal-focus in Cebuano narrative." In *Voice and Inversion*, T. Givón (ed.). Amsterdam: John Benjamins [Typological Studies in Languages 28].

Pérez Torres, Raúl. 1991. *Cuentos Escogidos*, Colección Antares. Quito: Libresa.

Rizzi, Luigi. 1976. "Ristrutturazione: Rivista di Grammatic Generativa" (ms).

Silva-Corvalán, Carmen. 1994. *Spanish in Los Angeles*. Cambridge: Cambridge University Press.

Silva-Corvalán, Carmen. 1995. *Spanish in four continents: studies in language contact and bilingualism.* Washington, D.C.: Georgetown University Press [Studies in Language Contact and Bilingualism].

Stolen, Kristi A. 1987. *A Media Voz: Ser Mujer Campesina en la Sierra Ecuatoriana.* Quito: CEPLAES.

Subirats-Rüggeberg, Carlos. 1987. "Sentential Complementation in Spanish: A lexico-grammatical study of three classes of verbs." *Lingüística Investigaciones Supplementa*, 14. Amsterdam: John Benjamins.

Suñer, Margarita and María Yépez. 1988. "Null Definite Objects in Quiteño." *Linguistic Inquiry* 19:3. Cambridge, MA.

Talmy, Leonard. 1985. "Lexicalization patterns: semantic structure in lexical forms." In *Language typology and Syntactic Description*, vol. III, T. Shopen (ed.), 57-149. Cambridge: Cambridge University Press.

Toscano, Matheus. 1953. *El español en el Ecuador*, Madrid.

Traugott, Elizabeth and Bernd Heine (eds) 1991. *Approaches to Grammaticalization*, I, II. Amsterdam: John Benjamins [Typological Studies in Language 19].

Traugott, Elizabeth and Ekkehar Konig. 1991. "The Semantics-pragmatics of grammaticalization revisited." In E. Traugott and B. Heine (eds) 1991: vol. I.

Taylor, Gerald. 1982. "Le morpheme de respect /-pa-/ dans les parlers quechuas de la sierra équatorienne." *Amerindia Paris: Centre de Recherche de l'Université de Paris VIII* 7:55-61.

Twadell, W. Freeman. 1963. *The English Verb Auxiliaries*, 2nd edition. Providence, RI: Brown University Press.

Van de Kerke, Simon. 1994. "Mismatches between affix order and interpretation: Quechua *chi-*, *-mu*, and *-pu* revisited." in *Language in the Andes*, P. Cole, G. Hermonand and M. Martín (eds), 231-245. Delaware: University of Delaware.

Vincent, Nigel and M. Harris (eds). 1987. *Studies in the Romance Verb.* London: Croom Helm.

Yépez, María. 1986. "Direct Object Clitics in Quiteño Spanish." Cornell University, MA Thesis.

Zavala, Roberto. 1993. *Clause Integration with Verbs of Motion in Mayan Languages*, MA Thesis, University of Oregon, Eugene.

The Direct Object in Bi-transitive Clauses in Indonesian

Bambang Kaswanti Purwo
Atma Jaya Language Institute, Jakarta

1. Introduction*

The bi-transitive verbs 'give' and 'buy' show, in English, an identical pattern of syntactic variation of the rather familiar "dative-shifting" sort. One variant codes the patient as the direct object and the dative or benefactive as the indirect object (1a, 2a). The other variants reverses this pattern, "promoting" the dative or the benefactive to direct object (1b, 2b):

(1) a. John gave a/the book to Mary
     b. John gave Mary a book

(2) a. John bought a/the book for Mary
     b. John bought Mary a book

The "promotion" (1b, 2b) involves removing the dative ('to') or benefactive ('for') preposition and placing "promoted" object directly after the verb.

The similarity in the behavior of 'give' and 'buy' in English stretches only up to a point. For example, in some fundamental way both objects of 'give' are obligatory participant in the giving transaction as it is normally framed, so that dispensing with either one of the participants yields odd, semantically incomplete event clauses. In contrast, only the patient object of 'buy' seems to be semantically obligatory in the normal framing of buying transactions. The benefactive — or source, or price — seem optional. Thus compare:[1]

(3)   a.   *John gave a book
      b.   *John gave (to) Mary
      c.   John bought a book
      d.   *John bought (for) Mary
      e.   *John bought from Bill
      f.   *John bought for twelve dollars

Indonesian displays a dative-shifting pattern that, superficially, resembles that of English, but with some peculiar twists. What this paper shows is that behind the superficial resemblence lies considerable typological differences in the grammatical organization of the relation "object".

In both English and Indonesian, the presence vs. absence of a preposition and proximity of the object to the verb constitute important signals ('criteria') of direct objecthood.

In addition, Indonesian uses specific verb morphology to amplify the differences between variants (1a) vs. (1b) or (2a) vs. (2b). In this respect, Indonesian is to some extent reminiscent of the "promotional" patterns described for KinyaRwanda (Kimenyi 1976) and Nez Perce (Rude 1987). In addition, however, verb morphology in Indonesian marks not only the distinction between (1a) vs. (1b) or (2a) vs. (2b), but also between (1a) and (2a). That is, Indonesian treats differentially the dative-shifting patterns of 'give' and that 'buy'. The two patterns may thus be viewed as prototypes, vis-a-vis which the behavior of other bi-transitive verbs in Indonesian may be described.

In this paper, I investigate the differences between five groups of seemingly-bi-transitive verbs, first the two 'give'-like and 'buy'-like prototypes, then three others. I show that a systematic clustering of grammatical properties can be identified in each case, a clustering that correlates with the distribution of the verb suffixes *-kan* and *-i*. Among the conclusions I draw from the Indonesian data, two are of particular interest.

First, 'give'-like verbs are true bi-transitives, with two semantically-obligatory objects, in the variant corresponding to (1a) as well as in the variant corresponding to (1b). 'Buy'-like verbs, on the other hand, are monotransitive. Their indirect ('oblique') object is thus optional, in the variant corresponding to (2a). But in the variant corresponding to (2b) 'buy'-like verbs seem to be bi-transitives, with neither of the two objects being oblique.

Second, different verb-types select different semantic roles as their **default direct object**. 'Give'-like verbs select the dative as their default DO. 'Buy'-like verbs select the benefactive as their default DO. The behavior of the two other verb-types fits well within this perspective, albeit with some specific variations.

My conclusions are at considerable variance from those presented in Chung's (1976) and others who have relied on her data (Dik 1980; Hopper and Thompson 1980). They are consonant however, up to a point, with some of Dryer's (1986) suggestions, albeit without necessarily subscribing to his typology of of "primary" vs. "direct" object.

2. The 'give' and 'buy' prototypes

The verb suffix *-kan* is used in Indonesian to distinguish between the two variants in dative-shifted verb pairs. The use of this suffix is, however, the exact opposite for 'give' and 'buy'. With 'give', the suffix *-kan* is used when the patient is the direct object, as in (4a) below. With 'buy', *-kan* is used when the benefactive is the direct object, as in (5b).

(4)   a.   *John mem-beri-**kan** buku itu **kepada** Mary*
           J.   MEN-give-**KAN** book that **to**   M.
           'John gave the book to Mary'

      b.   *John mem-beri² Mary buku itu*
           J.   MEN-give-**I** M.   book that
           'John gave Mary the book'

(5)   a.   *John mem-beli² buku itu **untuk** Mary*
           J.   MEN-buy   book that **for**   M.
           'John bought the book for Mary'

      b.   *John mem-beli-**kan** Mary buku itu*
           J.   MEN-buy-**KAN** M.   book that
           'John bought Mary the book'

This opposite use of *-kan* for 'give' and 'buy' is somewhat surprising, particularly in view of the many languages that treat the obligatory dative of 'give'-like verbs and the optional benefactive of 'buy'-like verbs the same way morpho-syntactically. Thus, the "obligatorily-promoted" datives and benefactives in Bantu (KinyaRwanda; Kimenyi 1976), in Nez Perce (Rude 1987) or Mayan (Aissen 1975) display the very same "promotional" suffix on the verb.

Other verbs that follow the 'give' pattern are *mengirim(-kan)* 'send', *menyerah-kan* 'hand over', *menghadiah-kan*, 'give a present', *menawar-kan* 'offer', *meminjam-kan*, 'lend'. The use of the suffix *-kan* with these verbs may be optional in the variant corresponding to (4a), but the suffix *-i* always alternates with it in the variant corresponding to (4b).[3]

Other verbs that follow the 'buy' pattern are *membuat-kan* 'make', *memasak-kan* 'cook', *membawa-kan* 'bring, carry', *menangkap-kan* 'catch', as well as hosts of other mono-transitive verbs. The presence of *-kan* in these verbs is obligatory in the variant corresponding to (5b). In the variant corresponding to (5a), these verbs are suffixless.[4]

Unlike 'give'-like verbs then, where the pairwise alternation is from the verb suffixed with *-kan* (4a) to that suffixed with *-i* (4b), with 'buy'-like verbs the alternation is from the suffixless verb (5a) to the verb suffixed with *-kan* (5b). The presence of *-kan* thus seems to mark the (5b) variant of 'buy'-like verbs as bi-transitive.

3.   Verbs with a locative-instrumental alternation

Another group of bi-transitive verbs also exists in Indonesian, with an alternation that marks the indirect object as either locative or instrumental. These verbs correspond to the English paired 'pour'/'fill', 'stick'/'stab' or 'spread'/'cover' in:

		IO coded as
(6)		
a.	She *poured* the water into the cup	(LOC)
b.	She *filled* the cup with water	(INSTR)
c.	She *stuck* the knife into him	(LOC)
d.	She *stabbed* him with a knife	(INSTR)
e.	She *spread* the cloth over the table	(LOC)
f.	She *covered* the table with cloth	(INSTR)

In English, such pairwise alternations most commonly require different lexical stems. In Indonesian, on the other hand, the same lexical stem is used in each pair, thus following the pattern described by Givón (1972,

1984b: ch. 4) for Bemba. These verbs seem semantically as bi-transitive as 'give', in the sense that both objects seem obligatory for normal event framing. Although presumably one of the object can be omitted under anaphoric or anti-passive contexts. That is:

(7) a. ?She poured the water
     b. ?She filled the cup
     c. *She stuck the knife
     d.   She stabbed him
     e. ?She spread the cloth
     f. ?She covered the table

In Indonesian, verbs in this group are treated as follows: The suffix *-kan* is used when the locative argument is coded as the indirect object (8a), (9a), and the suffix *-i* (or the suffix-less form) is used when the instrument is coded as the indirect object (8b), (9b). That is:

(8) a. *Mary menuang(-kan) air ke ember*
         M.   MEN-pour-KAN water LOC bucket
         'Mary poured water into the bucket'

     b. *Mary menuang-i ember dengan air*
         M.   MEN-pour-I bucket INSTR water
         'Mary filled the bucket with water'.

(9) a. *John menikam-kan belati ke perut harimau*
         J.   MEN-stab-KAN dagger LOC belly tiger
         'John stuck the dagger into the tiger's belly'

     b. *John menikam perut harimau dengan belati*
         J.   MEN-stab belly tiger   INSTR dagger
         'John stabbed the tiger's belly with a dagger'

In one respect, these verbs may be further split into 'give'-like and 'buy'-like sub-types. The verb 'pour'/'fill' displays the suffix *-i* when the instrumental is coded as indirect object (8b), thus resembling 'give'.

The verb 'stick'/'stab', on the other hand, is suffixless in the corresponding variant (9b), thus resembling 'buy'. The use of the suffix *-kan*, however, is identical in both types, showing up when the locative is coded as indirect object.

Other verbs in this group that use the suffix *-i* (and in this respect are

'give'-like) are listed in (10) below. Other that are *-i*-less (and in this respect
are 'buy'-like) are listed in (11).

(10) *menempel(-kan)/-i*   'stick X on Y'/'patch Y with X'
      melengket-kan/-i   'glue X on Y'/'fix Y with X'
      menumpah-kan/-i   'spill X on Y'/'wet Y with X'

(11) *memukul-kan/-0*   'slap X on Y'/'hit Y with X'
      menyemprot-kan/-0   'spray X on Y'/'spray Y with X'
      menyumbang-kan/-0   'donate X to Y'/'supply Y with X'
      membalut-kan/-0   'wrap X around Y'/'bandage Y with X'

4. 'Partial dative' verbs

Verbs such as 'show' and 'tell' in English closely resemble 'give', in let-
ting the dative object to be most commonly the direct object, as in (12b,d)
below (Givón 1984a):

(12) a. John showed the house to Mary
      b. John showed **Mary** a house
      c. Mary told the story to John
      d. Mary told **John** a story

While in the appropriate discourse context one can omit one of the objects, it is fairly clear that this can be done only if the missing object has
been anaphorically established. In this sense these verbs thus again resemble 'give', where both objects are semantically obligatory.

(13) a. *John showed Mary
      b. ?John showed the house
      c. *John showed to Mary
      d. ?Mary told the story
      e. *Mary told to John
      f. ?Mary told John

In Indonesian, verbs in this group include *menunjuk-kan* 'show', *men-
jelas-kan* 'explain, clarify', *menerang-kan* 'explain, clarify', *mengurai-kan*
'explain, analyze', *menggambar-kan* 'describe', and *menjanji-kan* 'pro-

mise'. These verbs show partial resemblance to 'give', in that the suffix -*kan* must be used when the dative is the indirect object.

However, they differ from 'give' in that the dative argument cannot be promoted to direct object, so that the variant with the suffix -*i*, as in (14b) and (14d) below, cannot be used. That is:

(14) a.   *John menunjuk-**kan** foto   itu **kepada** Mary*
       J.   MEN-show-KAN photo the **to**   M.
       'John showed the photograph to Mary'

     b.   **John menunjuk-i** Mary foto   itu*
       J.   MEN-show-**I** M.   photo the
       ('John showed Mary the photograph')

     c.   *John menjelas-**kan**   persoalannya **kepada** Mary*
       J.   MEN-explain-KAN problem-the **to**   M.
       'John explained the problem to Mary'

     d.   **John menjelas-i**   Mary berita   itu*
       John MEN-explain-**I** M.   problem the
       (*'John explained Mary the problem')

5.   Interim summary

In the preceding sections I have identified five groups of seemingly bi-transitive verbs, each with the following distribution of the suffixes -*kan* and -*i* in the two related variant structures. That distribution can be expressed in terms of the choice of suffix as related to the semantic role of the direct object.

(15)   *Summary of the distribution of the* -kan *and* -i *suffixes as correlated with the semantic role of the direct object*

verb type	-0 suffix	-i suffix	-kan suffix
I. 'give' (DAT)	////////	dative DO	patient DO
II. 'buy' (BEN)	patient DO	////////	benefactive DO
III. 'pour'/'fill'	////////	locative DO	instrument DO
VI. 'stick'/'stab'	locative DO	////////	instrument DO
V. partial-DAT	////////	////////	patient DO

The question that now begs resolution is this: Is the choice of the verb suffix in each verb-group merely arbitrary, or does it reveal a coherent principle?

Before proceeding to answer this question, we must establish in a more formal way criteria for the grammatical relation "direct object" in Indonesian.

6. The passivization test for direct objecthood

As the Indonesian data suggest, two of Keenan's (1976) overt coding properties are relevant to direct objecthood of Indonesian, in much the same way as in English:

a. **Word order**: the DO directly follows the verb
b. **Nominal case marking**: the DO is unmarked

In this section I would like to show that rule-governed ("behavior-and-control") properties also single out the unmarked post-verbal argument as the direct in Indonesian.

Indirect objects in many languages are inaccessible to being made subject-of-passive. English is one such language. In some languages with a similar constraint, such as KinyaRwanda (Kimenyi 1976) or Nez Perce (Rude 1987), indirect objects can be "promoted" to DO and then become accessible to the subject-of-passive role (see also Givón 1979: ch. 4).

Indonesian also exhibits the "DO-only constraint" on passivization.[5] Thus, in the two variants of 'give', only the dative is accessible to subject-of-passive status in the *-i* (16) variant, and only the patient in the *-kan* variant (17):

(16) a.   *John **mem**-beri Mary buku itu*
           J.   MEN-give-I M.   book that
           'John gave Mary the book'.

      b.   *Mary **di**-beri   buku itu oleh John*
           M.   PASS-give-I book that by   J.
           'Mary was given the book by John'

      c.   **Buku itu **di**-beri   Mary oleh John*
           Book that PASS-give-I M.   by   J.
           (*'The book was given (to) Mary by John')

(17) a. *John **mem**-beri-**kan** buku itu   kepada Mary*
       J.   MEN-give-KAN book that to   M.
       'John gave the book to Mary'

      b. *Buku itu **di**-beri-**kan**   kepada Mary oleh John*
       book that PASS-give-KAN to   M.   by   J.
       'The book was given to Mary by John'

      c. **Mary **di**-beri-**kan**   buku itu oleh John*
       M.   PASS-give-KAN book that by   J.
       (*'Mary was given the book by John')

With the verb 'buy', on the other hand, the benefactive DO is accessible to becoming subject-of-passive in the *-kan* variant (18), and the patient DO in the *-0* variant (19):

(18) a. *John **mem**-beli-**kan** Mary buku itu*
       J.   MEN-buy-KAN M.   book that
       'John bought Mary the book'

      b. *Mary **di**-beli-**kan**   buku itu oleh John*
       M.   PASS-buy-KAN book that by   J.
       lit.: 'Mary was bought the book by John'

      c. **Buku itu **di**-beli-**kan**   Mary oleh John*
       book that PASS-buy-KAN M.   by   J.
       (*'The book was bought (for) Mary by John')

(19) a. *John **mem**-beli buku itu untuk Mary*
       J.   MEN-buy-0 book that for   M.
       'John bought the book for Mary'

      b. *Buku itu **di**-beli   untuk Mary oleh John*
       book that PASS-buy-0 for   M.   by   J.
       'The book was bought for Mary by John'

      c. **Mary **di**-beli   buku itu oleh John*
       M.   PASS-buy-0 book that by   J.
       (*'Mary was bought the book by John')

Locative-instrumental verbs display similar restrictions. The locative object can be promoted to subject-of-passive only in the *-i* or *-0* variant (20), (22). And the instrumental object can only be promoted to subject-of-passive in the *-kan* variant (21), (23):

(20) a.   *Mary **menuang-i** ember dengan air*
      M.   MEN-pour-**I** bucket with   water
      'Mary filled the bucket with water'

    b.   *Ember itu **di**-tuang-**i**   dengan air   oleh Mary*
      bucket that PASS-pour-**I** with   water by   M.
      'The bucket was filled with water by Mary'

    c.   **Air   itu **di**-tuang-**i** ember itu oleh Mary*
      water that PASS-pour-**I** bucket that by   M.
      (*'The water was filled the bucket (with) by Mary')

(21) a.   *Mary **menuang(-kan)** air   itu ke   ember*
      M.   MEN-pour-**(KAN)** water that LOC bucket
      'Mary poured the water into the bucket'

    b.   *Air   itu **di**-tuang(-**kan**) ke   ember oleh Mary*
      water that PASS-pour(-**KAN**) LOC bucket by   M.
      'The water was poured into the bucket by Mary'

    c.   **Ember itu **di**-tuang(-**kan**)   air   itu oleh Mary*
      bucket that PASS-pour(-**KAN**) water that by   M.
      (*'The bucket was poured water (into) by Mary')

(22) a.   *John **menikam**   perut harimau dengan belati*
      J.   MEN-stab-**0** belly tiger   INSTR   dagger
      'John stabbed the tiger's belly with a dagger'

    b.   *Perut harimau **di**-tikam   dengan belati oleh John*
      belly tiger   PASS-stab-**0** INSTR   dagger by   J.
      'The tiger's belly was stabbed with a dagger by John'

    c.   **Belati itu **di**-tikam   perut harimau oleh John*
      dagger that PASS-stab-**0** belly tiger   by   J.
      (*'The dagger was stabbed the tiger's belly (with) by John')

(23) a.   *John **menikam-kan** belati ke   perut harimau*
      J.   MEN-stab-**KAN** dagger LOC belly tiger
      'John stuck the dagger into the tiger's belly'

    b.   *Belati itu **di**-tikam-**kan**   ke   perut harimau oleh John*
      dagger that PASS-stuck-**KAN** LOC belly tiger   by   J.
      'The dagger was stuck into the tiger's belly by John'

    c.   **Perut harimau **di**-tikam-**kan**   belati   oleh John.*
       belly tiger   PASS-stuck-KAN dagger by   J.
       (*'The tiger's belly was stuck (with) a dagger by John')

Finally, "semi-dative" verbs, in which only the *-kan* variant is possible, allow only the patient to become the subject-of-passive:

    (24)   a.   *John **menunjuk-kan** foto   itu kepada Mary*
             J.   MEN-show-KAN photo the to   M.
             'John showed the photograph to Mary'

        b.   **John **menunjuk-i** Mary foto   itu*
             J.   MEN-show-**I** M.   photo the
             (*'John showed Mary the photograph')

        c.   *Foto   itu   **di**-tunjuk-**kan**   kepada Mary oleh John*
             photo that PASS-show-KAN to   M.   by   J.
             'The photo was shown to Mary by John'

        d.   **Mary **di**-tunjuk-**kan**   foto   itu   oleh John*
             M.   PASS-show-KAN photo that by   J.
             (*'Mary was shown the photo by John')

        e.   **Mary **di**-tunjuk-**i**   foto   itu   oleh John*
             M.   PASS-show-**I** photo that by   J.
             (*'Mary was shown the photo by John')

The constrains on passivization in Indonesian thus single out, rather coherently, the unmarked object directly adjacent to the verb as the only one accessible to promotion to subject-of-passive. The conclusion that this unmarked post-verbal NP is the grammatical direct object in Indonesian is thus supported by rule-governed behavior. This conclusion is consonant with the facts of other languages with similar restrictions, such as English, KinyaRwanda and Nez Perce.

7.   "Lexical passives" with and without the suffix *-kan*

A group of verb in Indonesian seem to yield a passive-like structure without the use of the preffix *di-*. In other respects, though, the construction parallels the promotional passives with *di-*. Verbs in this group may be further divided to 'give'-like and 'buy'-like verbs.

Consider first the 'give'-like verb 'lend'. In the variant with the suffix *-kan*, the patient is the direct object of this verb. In the variant with *-i*, the dative is direct object. In normal ('syntactic') passivization with *di-*, this verb adheres to the "DO-only constraint", so that only the patient is accessible to be subject-of-passive in the *-kan* variant (25c), and only the dative in the *-i* variant (25d):

(25) a. *Mary **mem**injam-**kan** buku-nya pada saya*
       M.   MEN-lend-KAN book-her to   me
       'Mary lent her book to me'

     b. *Mary **mem**injam-**i** saya buku-nya*
       M.   MEN-lend-**I** me book-her
       'Mary lent me her book'

     c. *Buku Mary **di**-pinjam-**kan** pada saya*
       book M. PASS-lend-KAN to   me
       'Mary's book was lent to me'

     d. *Saya **di**-pinjam-**i** (oleh) Mary buku-nya*
       I   PASS-lend-**I** by   M.   book her
       'I was lent her book by Mary'

The lexical passive counterpart of this verb, easily translatable as the English 'borrow', is suffixless, and may be thus considered to be marked with the *-0* suffix equivalent of *-i*. Only the dative can be made the subject of this verb:

(26) *Saya **mem**injam   buku-nya*
     I   MEN-borrow-**0** book-her
     'I borrowed her book'

Similarly with the 'give'-like verb 'rent out', which (unlike 'lend') cannot have an active *-i* variant with the dative as DO:

(27) a. **Active:**
       *John **men**yewa-**kan**   mobil-nya pada orang-asing*
       J.   MEN-rent.out-KAN car-his   to   foreigner
       'John rents his car out to foreigners'

     b. **John **men**yewa-**i**   orang asing mobil-nya*
       J.   MEN-rent.out-**I** foreigner   car-his
       (*'John rents foreigners his car')

c. **Di- passive:**
   mobil John di-sewa-kan pada orang-asing
   car   John PASS-rent.out to   foreigner
   'John's car is rented out to foreigners'

d. **Orang-asing di-sewa-i   mobil John*
   foreigner   PASS-rent.out-I car   John
   (*'Foreigners are rented-out John's car')

e. **Lexical passive:**
   Orang asing menyewa   mobil-nya.
   foreigners   MEN-rent-0 car-his
   'Foreigners rent his car'

Simple transitive verbs such as 'sew (for)', on the other hand, follow the syntactic behavior of 'buy'. Just like 'buy', the variant with the patient DO is -0 suffixed (28a). And the variant with the benefactive DO is marked by -*kan* (28b). Predictably, the patient is accessible to be subject of the 'syntactic' *di*-marked passive in the -0 variant (28c), and the benefactive in the -*kan* variant (28d):

(28) a. *Ibu   men-jahit baju itu   untuk saya*
        mother MEN-sew-0 shirt that for   me
        'Mother sewed the shirt for me'

     b. *Ibu   men-jahit-kan saya baju*
        mother MEN-sew-KAN me   shirt
        'Mother sewed me a shirt'

     c. *Baju itu di-jahit   oleh ibu   untuk saya*
        shirt that PASS-sew-0 by   mother for   me
        'The shirt was sewed by mother for me'

     d. *Saya di-jahit-kan   baju oleh ibu.*
        I   PASS-sew-KAN shirt by   mother
        'I was sewed a shirt by mother'

The lexical passive of 'sew' is suffixed with -*kan*. And only the benefactive can be the subject of this lexical passive:

(29) *Saya men-jahit-kan baju itu ke tailor*
     I   MEN-sew-KAN shirt the to tailor
     'I had the shirt made by a tailor'
     (*lit.*: 'I was made-a-shirt-for to a tailor')

8. Non-standard use (or non-use) of the suffix *-kan*

One would be remiss if one did not mention the fact that Indonesian speakers often display a certain range of variability in the use or non-use of the suffix *-kan*. While prescriptive grammarians regard such violations as 'grammatically deviant', such deviations are often produced in conversation by native speakers. However, the pattern of such deviation is highly biased. Thus, speakers may render the grammatical use of 'give', as in (30a), by the 'deviant' (30b) in which *-kan* has been omitted. However, the corresponding passive requires *-kan*, as is evident from the unacceptability of (30d):

(30) a. *John **mem**-beri-**kan** buku itu kepada Mary*
          J.   MEN-give-KAN book that to   M.
          'John gave the book to Mary'

      b. *John **mem**-beri buku itu kepada Mary*
          J.   MEN-beri-**I** book that to   M.
          'John gave the book to Mary'

      c. *Buku itu **di**-beri-**kan**   kepada Mary (oleh John)*
          book that PASS-give-KAN to   M.   (by   J.)
          'The book was given to Mary by John'

      d. **Buku itu **di**-beri   kepada Mary (oleh John)*
          book that PASS-give-**I** to   M.   (by   J.)

Likewise with 'buy'-like verbs, the grammatical (31a) may also be rendered by (31b) with an 'inappropriate' *-kan*, but not in the corresponding passive (31d):

(31) a. *John **mem**-beli buku itu untuk Mary*
          J.   MEN-buy-**0** book that for   M.
          'John bought the book for Mary'

      b. *John **mem**-beli-**kan** buku itu untuk Mary*
          J.   MEN-beli-KAN book that to   M.
          'John bought the book for Mary'

      c. *Buku itu **di**-beli   untuk Mary (oleh John)*
          book that PASS-buy-**0** for   M.   (by   J.)
          'The book was bought for Mary (by John)'

    d.   **Buku itu* **di-beli-kan**   *untuk Mary (oleh John)*
        book that PASS-buy-KAN for   M.   (by   J.)

Further, while the 'non-standard' (30b) and (31b) are attested, with the dative or benefactive marked with prepositions, the converse 'non-standard' usage — with the dative and benefactive as direct objects — is never attested. That is:

(32) a.   *John* **mem**-*beri*   *Mary buku*
          J.   MEN-give-**I** M.   book
          'John gave Mary a book'

      b.   **John* **mem**-*beri*-**kan** *Mary buku*
          J.   MEN-give-KAN M.   book

(33) a.   *John* **mem**-*beli*-**kan** *Mary buku*
          J.   MEN-buy-KAN M.   book
          'John bought Mary a book'

      b.   **John* **mem**-*beli*   *Mary buku*
          J.   MEN-buy-**0** M.   book

The biased distribution of 'non-standard' uses of *-kan* suggests that tampering with the standard grammatical pattern is tolerated better when the semantic role of the non-patient object — be it dative or benefactive — is marked explicitly by nominal case-markers, i.e. when it is coded as indirect objects. The bias against the non-standard usage in the passive suggests that deviations are tolerated better in simple clauses, where the semantic roles of the participants are better coded.

In complex clauses, where the change of grammatical roles renders the interpretation of semantic roles more difficult, deviations are less tolerated (see Givón 1979: ch. 4).

9. Discussion

9.1. *Summary*

The distribution of the verbal suffixes *-kan* and *-i /-0* in Indonesian bi-transitive clauses suggests that the language divides bi-transitive verbs into two major types. The first, 'give'-type verbs, are truely bi-transitive with a semantically obligatory dative object, in addition to the patient. The second, 'buy'-type verbs, are fundamentally mono-transitive when the patient is the DO, but may be rendered bi-transitive when the benefactive is the DO.

Many languages — Tzotzil, KinyaRwanda, Nez Perce, English — treat these groups roughly alike, in that:

a. the overwhelming tendency in discourse is to code the dative and benefactive argument as the direct object; and

b. if the verb is marked by a suffix that signals a non-patient direct object, it is the very same suffix for the dative and benefactive.

In Indonesian, however, the obligatory dative and the optional benefactive are treated rather differently, and the use of the suffix *-kan* is central for understanding the difference. I would like to propose that in Indonesian the *zero* or *-i* suffixes marks the **norm** direct object for verbs, while the *-kan* suffix marks the **counter-norm** direct object. For 'give'-like verbs, the obligatory dative in 'give'-like verbs is the 'norm' DO, the patient the 'counter norm'. But 'buy' and verbs like it are inherently mono-transitive. Their patient is their 'norm' DO, with *-0* suffix. Their optional benefactive is thus the 'counter-norm' DO, marked by the 'counter norm' suffix *-kan*.

If this generalization is valid, then the verbs in the locative/instrumental group, such as 'pour/fill' and 'stab/stick', behave as if the their *locative* argument is the 'norm' DO, requiring as DO the *-0* or *-i* suffix; while their *instrumental* argument is the 'counter-norm' DO, requiring as DO the *-kan* suffix.

The group of 'dative-like' verbs follow, in most important detail, the morpho-syntactic pattern of the 'give'. When the patient is the DO ('counter norm'), they are marked with *-kan*. However, unlike 'give' these verbs do not have a variant where the dative is the DO.

Lexical passives are shown to follow either the 'give' or 'buy' pattern. The subject of the 'give'-like lexical passive is the obligatory dative, and the verb — as expected with the 'norm' dative DO — is *zero*-marked. The subject of the 'buy'-like lexical passive is the optional benefactive, and the verb — as expected with the 'counter-norm' benefactive DO — is marked with *-kan*.

Finally, the 'grammatically deviant' uses or non-uses of *-kan* also divide into two types. One type follows the 'give' pattern, the other the 'buy' pattern. Verbs of the former drop the *-kan* suffix, those of the latter retain the *-kan* suffix.

9.2. *Interpretation*

As noted earlier, many languages treat the dative and benefactive arguments similarly, in obligatory assignment of DO status and in identical verb morphology. In Indonesian the frequency of coding the — highly topical, human — dative and benefactive argument as direct object may be equally high. Still, the alternation of *-kan* and *-i/-0* suggests that this language insists on an added distinction, one reminiscent of Dryer's (1986) concept of **primary object**. When the extra object is optional and not a semantically obligatory dative, the *patient* object is considered the 'norm' DO. When the extra object is the obligatory dative, it is considered the 'norm' DO.

Since most bi-transitive verbs in Indonesian allow some 'dative-shift' variation, the suffixes *-i/-0* vs. *-kan* signal whether the DO is the 'norm' or counter-norm, respectively.

Does the Indonesian data support Dryer's suggestion (1986: 808) that:

(34) a. "... rules in some languages are sensitive to the distinction between direct objects and indirect objects; but in others, they are sensitive to a distinction between primary and secondary object ..."

b. "... a Primary Object is an Indirect Object in a ditransitive clause or a Direct Object in a monotransitive clause, while a Secondary Object is the Direct Object in a ditransitive clause ..."

Paradoxically, the answer is both yes and no. The Indonesian data suggests that the distinction between primary ('norm') and secondary ('counternorm') is useful in languages such as Indonesian. However, this distinction does not replace the notions of direct and indirect object in such languages, but rather supplements it.

The morphologically-unmarked post-verbal object is just as much a direct object in Indonesian as it is in KinyaRwanda, Tzotzil or English. It controls syntactic processes (e.g. passivization) in very much the same way, regardless of whether it is 'primary' or 'secondary'.

What the data of all these languages taken together suggest, is that Dryer's (1986) characterization of both direct and indirect objects in the (34b) is semantic rather than grammatical. One may thus suggest that a more accurate way of phrasing Dryer's generalization would have been:

> ... the primary direct object is the dative argument of the bi-transitive clause and the patient object of the monotransitive clause ...

Notes

*   I am indebted to Werner Abraham, Anne-Marie Diller, Abby Cohn, and my editor T. Givón for their comments on an earlier version of this paper. None of them, however, should be held accountable for my views or mistakes.

1.   Dispensing with one of the objects of 'give' is of course acceptable under either anaphoric or antipassive conditions:

> 'We know who he gave it to, but what did he give'?
> 'He gave a book'
> 'We know he gives money to many deserving causes, but which ones'?
> 'He gives to charity, primarily'

2.   The apparent absence of *-i* in *memberi* (4b) is due to a simple phonological process in verbs whose stem ends with /i/. This is clear from consonant-final verbs; see Dardjowidjojo (1974: 380ff.) for a similar analysis. Thus compare:

> *mengirim(-kan)/mengirim-i* 'send'
> *menyerah-kan/mengirim-i* 'hand'
> *menghadiah-kan/menghadiah-i* 'give a present'
> *menawar-kan/menawar-i* 'offer'
> *meminjam-kan/meminjam-i* 'lend'

However, *membeli* in (5a) is *-0* suffixed. Compare the verbs belonging to 'buy'-like verbs:

> *membuat/membuat-kan* 'make'
> *memasak/memasak-kan* 'cook'
> *membawa/membawa-kan* 'bring, carry'
> *menangkap/menangkap-kan* 'catch'

3.   It is true, as Chung (1976: 55) notes, that the presence of *-kan* in mengirim 'send' is optional, as is also the case with *mengajar(kan)* 'teach'. She is wrong, however, in stating that "... the use of *-kan* ... disappeared from the speech of younger Indonesians ..." in sentences like

> ... *mengirim(-kan) surat kepada wanita itu*
> ... sent a letter to the woman

The dropping of *-kan* has nothing to do with the age of the speakers, but rather with the formal and non-formal use of the language. Careful speakers tend not to drop *-kan*, especially in a formal setting. This *-kan* dropping is peculiar only to a few verbs like *mengirim(kan)* 'send' and *mengajar(kan)* 'teach'.

4.   The presence of *-kan* in a 'buy'-like verb such as 'close' in (ib) below, according to Hopper and Thompson (1980: 261), indicates that "... the door is more affected, the action is carried out more completely, or is done with more force ...".

There indeed exists such use of *-kan* in Indonesian, the so-called 'transitivizing' *-kan*, as in (ii) below. But it is not the same usage of *-kan* as in 'buy'-like verbs.

(i)   a.   *Tutup pintu itu!*
            close door that
            'Close the door'!

       b.   *Tutup-kan pintu itu!*
            close-KAN door that
            'Close the door'!

(ii)   a.   *mendengar* ('hear')
                  vs.
            mendengarkan ('listen to')

       b.   *merasa dingin* ('feel cold')
                  vs.
            merasakan dinginnya malam ('feel the cool of the night')

5.   The term 'passive' here must not be taken literally. The Indonesian di-marked clause is translated into either the English active or passive, depending on the context (Kaswanti 1988). A negative command "Don't eat that!", which is active in English, must be coded in Indonesian in with a di-marked verb. Verhaar (1983) analyzes the di-marked verbs with the "active" interpretation as "ergative". One may also note that the frequency of di-marked clauses in written Indonesian fiction is 30%-40% (Kaswanti 1987), as against the reported 9% frequency of English passives (see Givón (1979: ch. 2).

References

Aissen, J. 1975. "Obligatory promotion in Tzotzil" (ms).

Chung, Sandra. 1976. "An object-creating rule in Bahasa Indonesia." *Linguistic Inquiry* 7.1:41-87.

Dik, Simon C. 1981. *Functional Grammar* Dordrecht: Foris Publications.

Dryer, M. 1986. "Primary objects, secondary objects and antidative." *Language* 62.4:808-845.

Dardjowidjojo, Soenjono. 1974. "The role of overt markers in some Indonesian and Javanese passive sentences." *Oceanic Linguistics* 13.1/2:371-389.

Foley, W.A. and Van Valin, R.D. 1985. "Information packaging in the clause." In *Language Typology and Syntactic Description*, vol. I, Timothy Shopen (ed.). Cambridge: Cambridge University Press.

Givón, T. 1972. *Studies in ChiBemba and Bantu Grammar*, supplement #3, *Studies in African Linguistics*.

Givón, T. 1979. *On understanding grammar*. New York: Academic Press.

Givón, T. 1983. "Topic continuity in discourse: An introduction." In *Topic Continuity in Discourse: A Quantitative Cross-Language Study*, T. Givón (ed.), Amsterdam: John Benjamins.

Givón, T. 1984a "Direct object and dative shifting: Semantic and pragmatic case." In *Objects: Towards a Theory of Grammatical Relations*, F. Plank (ed.), 151-182. London: Academic Press.

Givón, T. 1984b. *Syntax: A Functional-Typological Introduction*, vol. I. Amsterdam: John Benjamins.

Hopper, P.J. and S.A. Thompson. 1980. "Transitivity in grammar and discourse", *Language* 56.2:251-319.

Kaswanti Purwo, Bambang. 1987. "Sensitivity to person in Indonesian: Grammar and discourse." In *Proceedings of the Fourteenth International Congress of Linguists*, W. Bahner, J. Schildt and D. Viehwerger (eds), 2139-2145. Berlin: Akademie-Verlag.

Kaswanti Purwo, Bambang. 1988. "Voice in Indonesian: A discourse study." In *Passive and voice*, M. Shibatani, (ed.), 195-241. Amsterdam: John Benjamins.

Kaswanti Purwo, Bambang. 1991. "Motion verbs in Indonesian." *Workshop on Concepts of Space and Spatial Reference in Austronesian and Papuan Languages*, Max-Planck-Institut für Psycholinguistik, Nijmegen, September 30-October 1, 1991. [To appear in Gunter Senft (ed.)]

Kimenyi, A. 1976. *A Relational Grammar of KinyaRwanda*, PhD dissertation, UCLA (ms).

Rude, N. 1987. *Studies in Nez Perce Grammar and Discourse*, PhD dissertation, University of Oregon, Eugene (ms).

Verhaar, John W.M. 1978. "Some notes on the verbal passives in Indonesian." In *NUSA: Linguistic Studies in Indonesian and Languages in Indonesia*, J.W.M. Verhaar (ed.), 6: 11-19, Jakarta: Badan Penyelenggara Seri NUSA.

Verhaar, J.W.M. 1980. *Teori linguistik dan Bahasa Indonesia*. Yogyakarta: Kanisius.

Verhaar, J.W.M. 1983. "Syntactic ergativity in Contemporary Indonesian." In *Proceedings of the Third Eastern Conference on Austronesian Linguistics*, Ohio University, Athens.

Serial Verbs and Grammatical Relations in Akan

E.K. Osam
Linguistics Department
University of Oregon
and
University of Zimbabwe
Harare, Zimbabwe

1. Preamble

The purpose of this paper is to describe the grammatical relations that exist in Akan.[1] Studies on Akan have always appealed to notions like subject, object, and indirect object, but no study, to my knowledge, has offered a systematic description of these relations. The approach adopted in this paper follows in the main Keenan (1975, 1976), Anderson (1976), Comrie (1982), Borg and Comrie (1984) and Hyman and Duranti (1982), contrasting overt coding properties with behavior-and-control properties (see also Givón 1995, in this volume). The paper is organized as follows: Section 2 presents an overview of the cross-linguistic properties of subjects and objects. Sections 3 and 4 discuss properties relevant to Akan. Section 5 focuses on the problem of double objects in bi-transitive constructions. Section 6 is the conclusion.

2. Properties of grammatical subjects and objects

Keenan (1975, 1976) groups the formal properties of grammatical subjects and objects into two clusters — overt coding properties and behavioral properties. Overt coding properties involve grammatical word order, verb and/or pronominal agreement, and nominal case-marking. Behavioral properties involve syntactic processes ('rules') governed by the grammatical relations of subject and object, including:

a. constraints on coreferential deletion, as in:
   - relativization
   - equi-NP deletion in complementation
   - anaphora in participial adverbials
   - zero anaphora in clause chaining
b. constraints on case-changing rules, as in:
   - passive/inverse
   - antipassive
   - raising
   - dative shifting.

Not all criteria for grammatical subjecthood and objecthood are relevant to Akan. Of the overt coding properties, only word order and pronominalization are relevant, since Akan has little case-marking morphology. Of the behavioral properties, only the following are relevant:

- zero anaphora in clause chaining
- relativization
- equi-NP deletion
- raising

3. Overt coding properties in Akan

3.1. *Word-order*

Two overt coding criteria are relevant to both subject and object in Akan — word order and pronominalization. Akan is a nominative language with a rigid SVO word order. The following examples illustrate word order in simple clauses:

(1) **Transitive:**
a. *Banyin no bE-daadaa · okunafo no*
   man the FUT-deceive widow the
   'The man will deceive the widow'

b. *Banyin no hu-u   okunafo no*
   man the see-PAST widow the
   'The man saw the widow'

(2) **Intransitive:**
a. *Abofra no bE-yar*
   child the FUT-sick
   'The child will be sick'

b. *Maame no bo-guan*
   woman the FUT-run
   'The woman will run away'

3.2. *Pronominalization*

Subject pronouns precede the verb in Akan, and direct-object pronouns follow. Their position thus conforms to the SVO order with full NPs. The forms of nominative (subject) and accusative (direct object) pronouns are listed in (3) below. Those to the left side of the slash are used in the Fante dialect, and those to the right are used in the Twi dialects. Where the dialects agree, only one form is given. Note, however, that inanimate subject pronouns are used only in Twi.

(3) *Subject and object pronouns in Akan*

	subject	**direct object**
1sg	me-	me
2sg	i-/wo-	wo
3 (an.)	O-	no
(inan.)	E-	(no)
1pl	yE-	hEn/yEn
2pl	hom-/mo-	hom/mo
3 (an.)	wO-	hOn/wOn
(inan.)	E-	(no)

Example (4b) below illustrates pronominalization in a transitive clause,
and (5b) in an intransitive clause:

(4)   a.   *Abofra no bo-ku   ewi   no*
             child   the FUT-kill thief the
             'The child will kill the thief'

       b.   *O-bo-ku   no²*
             3sg-FUT-kill 3sg
             'S/he will kill him/her'

(5)   *a.*   *Abofra no bo-wu*
             child   the FUT-die
             'The child will die'

       b.   *O-bo-wu*
             3sg-FUT-die
             'S/he will die'

3.3. *Animacy and object pronoun*

Inanimate objects can only be pronominalized as *zero* in Akan. Thus
compare:[3]

(6)   a.   *Kofi bO-wosow dua no*
             Kofi FUT-shake tree the
             'Kofi will shake the tree'

       b.   *Kofi bO-wosow [0]*
             Kofi FUT-shake
             'Kofi will shake it (the tree)'
             *'Kofi will shake him/her'

(7)   a.   *Kofi bO-wosow abofra no*
             Kofi FUT-shake child   the
             'Kofi will shake the child'

       b.   *Kofi bO-wosow **no***
             Kofi FUT-shake **3sg**
             'Kofi will shake him/her'
             *'Kofi will shake it'

4. Behavioral (rule-governed) criteria

In this section I will deal with behavioral criteria in two steps, first those that distinguish the grammatical subject from the direct object, and those that distinguish the grammatical direct object from indirect objects.

4.1. *Telling subject from direct object*

4.1.1. *Coreference and zero anaphora in clause chaining*

The subject in Akan controls zero pronominalization under coreference in clause chaining.[4] In contrast, objects — unless they are inanimate (see above) — require explicit pronouns. Thus compare:

(8) a. *Araba kyer-r   abofra no* **[0]**-*kyekyer*
           Araba catch-PAST child   the **3sg**-tie-PAST

          no **[0]**-*bor-r*   **no**
          3sg 3sg-beat-PAST **3sg**

          'Araba caught the child, tied him/her, and beat him/her up'

    b. *Araba tO-O   guan,* **[0]**-*nyEn-n*   **no** **[0]**-*tOn-n*   **no**
          Araba buy-PAST sheep **3sg**-rear-PAST **3sg 3sg**-sell-PAST **3sg**

          [0]-*nya-a   sika*
          3s-get-PAST money

          'Araba bought a sheep, reared it, sold it, and had money'

As noted above, inanimate objects do pronominalize as *zero*:

(9) a. *Araba tO-O   dwow, kyew-e* **[0]**-*tOn-e*   **[0]**
          Araba buy-PAST yam   fry-PAST **3sg**-sell-PAST **3sg**
          'Araba bought yam, fried it, and sold it'

    b. **Araba tO-O   dwow kyew-e* **no** *tOn-n*   **no**
          Araba buy-PAST yam   fry-PAST **3sg** sell-PAST **3sg**
          ('Araba bought yam fried it and sold it')

Some verbs in Akan require an overt object pronoun even if it refers to an inanimate. This is why (10a) is grammatical but (10b) is not.

(10) a. *Kofi a-tsew   kraataa no a-hyew   **no** a-sEe   **no***
       Kofi PERF-tear paper   the PERF-burn **3sg** PERF-destroy **3sg**
       'Kofi has torn the paper, burnt it, and destroyed it'

   b. **Kofi a-tsew   kraataa no a-hyew   [0] a-sEe   [0]*
       Kofi PERF-tear paper   the PERF-burn **3sg** PERF-destroy **3sg**
       'Kofi has torn the paper, burnt it, and destroyed it'

With the exception of inanimate objects, then, zero anaphora is a behavioral property of subjects but not of objects.

4.1.2. *Overt Conjunction and Marked Subject Pronouns*
Chained clauses in Akan can be conjoined with or without the conjunction *na* 'and'. As seen above, when they are conjoined without *na*, coreferent subjects are marked as *zero*. With *na*, however, overt subject pronouns must be used. Thus compare:

(11) a. *Araba kyer-r   abofra no, kyekyer **no** bor-r   **no***
       Araba catch-PAST child   the, tie/PAST **3sg** beat-PAST **3sg**
       'Araba caught the child, tied him/her up and beat him/her'

   b. *Araba kyer-r abofra no **na** O-kyekyer-r **no***
       Araba caught child   the **and 3sg**-tied   **3sg**

   na** O-bor-r **no
   and 3sg-beat **3sg**

   'Araba caught the child, and she tied him/her up, and she beat him/her'

This interaction between anaphora and conjunction again distinguishes the behavior of the grammatical subject from that of the object.

4.1.3. *Relativization*
Subject relativization and object relativization follow different rules in Akan. Relative clauses follow the head noun and are separated from it by the relative subordinator *a*.[5]

    In both subject and object relativization, if the head noun is definite, the definite article appears again as clitic at the end of the REL clause (12c,d,e). An exception to this is subject REL-clauses with a definite object (12b), where a definite article is already there. It thus appears that the sequence DEF-DEF is shunned.

In both subject REL-clauses (12b) and object REL-clauses (12c,d), resumptive-anaphoric pronouns must be used.

(12) a. *Banyin no hyia-a   abofra no*
man   the meet-PAST child   the
'The man met the child'

b. **Subject REL-clause (DEF-object):**
Banyin no a   o-hyia-a   abofra no e-wu
man   the REL 3sg-meet-PAST child   the PERF-die
'The man who met the child has died'

c. **Object REL-clause:**
Abofra no a   banyin no hyia-a   no no   e-wu
child   the REL man   the meet-PAST 3sg DEF PERF-die
'The child that the man met has died'

d. **Subject REL-clause (INDEF-object):**
Banyin no a   o-bu   ndua no   e-wu
man   the REL 3sg-cut trees DEF PERF-die
'The man who fells trees has died'

e. **Subject REL-clause (no object):**
Banyin no a   O-ba-a   ha no   e-wu
man   the REL 3sg-come-PAST here DEF PERF-die
'The man who came here is dead'

4.1.4. *Raising out of complement clauses*

When raising is possible in Akan, only the subject of the complement clause can be 'raised' to object of the main clause. Thus compare:

(14) a. *Kofi hu-u   dE Esi re-twe   abofra no*
Kofi see-PAST SUB Esi PROG-pull child   the
'Kofi saw that Esi was pulling the child'

b. *Kofi hu-u   Esi dE O-re-twe   abofra no*
Kofi see-PAST Esi that 3sg-PROG-pull child   the
'Kofi saw Esi pulling the child'
(lit.: 'Kofi saw that Esi that she was pulling the child')

c. *Kofi hu-u   abofra no **dE** Esi re-twe   no
Kofi see-PAST child   the SUB Esi PROG-pull 3sg
*'Kofi saw the child being pulled by Esi'
(lit.: *'Kofi saw the child that Esi was pulling it')

In sum, both overt coding criteria and behavior-and-control criteria differentiate adequately between the grammatical subject and object in Akan.

5. Direct vs. indirect object

Since Akan is largely devoid of overt case-markers, the differentiation between
direct and indirect object, both of which follow the verb, is not always
clear. This is a problem especially when a verb takes two objects, both
unmarked for case. To resolve their status, three direct-objecthood criteria
will be considered:

- proximity to the verb
- accessibility to pronominalization
- accessibility to relativization

I will discuss the various types of bi-transitive verbs in order.

5.1. *The prototype bi-transitive verb 'give'*

Bi-transitive verbs such as 'give' or 'bring' may be considered prototypical bi-transitive verbs, with a concrete — typically non-human — patient
and a human recipient-dative. In Akan, such verbs can appear in two types
of clauses:

- simple clauses with a single verb
- serial clauses with two verbs

As illustration compare:

(15) a. *Kofi ma-a   papa no sika*
Kofi give-PAST man the money
'Kofi gave the man money'

    b.   *Kofi de⁶ sika   no ma-a   papa no*
        Kofi take money the give-PAST man the
        'Kofi gave the money to the man'
        (lit.: 'Kofi took the money and gave (it) to the man')

    c.   **Kofi ma-a   sika   papa no*
        Kofi give-PAST money man DEF
        (lit.: *'Kofi gave money to the man')

The restriction on indefinite patients in the PAT-DAT order will be discussed in section 5.3. below.

5.1.2. *Proximity to the verbs*
If proximity is considered a criterion for direct objecthood, then in the non-serial construction (15a) the dative NP is the direct object. When the test is applied to the non-serial (15b), each object directly follows a verb, so that by this criterion both are direct objects, albeit of different verbs.

5.1.3. *Access to pronominalization*
The dative object of the non-serial bi-transitive clause can be pronominalized (16a), but the patient cannot (16b):

  (16) a.   *Kofi ma-a   **no** sika*
           Kofi give-PAST **3sg** money
           'Kofi gave him/her money'

       b.   **Kofi ma-a   papa no* [0]
           Kofi give-PAST man the [0]
           (*'Kofi gave the man it')

In contrast, both object in the serial bi-transitive clause can be pronominalized:

  (17) a.   *Kofi de   sika   no ma-a   **no***
           Kofi take money the give-PAST **3sg**
           'Kofi gave the money to him/her'

       b.   *Kofi de [0] ma-a   papa no*
           Kofi take [0] give-PAST man the
           'Kofi gave it to the man'

5.1.4. *Access to relativization*

When the relativization test is applied to the simple bi-transitive clause, only the dative NP is accessible (18a), the patient is not (18b):

(18) a. *Papa no **a*** *Kofi ma-a* **no** *sika   no a-ba*
       man the REL Kofi give-PAST **3sg** money DEF PERF-come
       'The man Kofi gave money to has come'

   b. **Sika   a   Kofi ma-a   papa no a-yera*
       money REL Kofi give-PAST man the PERF-be.lost
       (*'Money Kofi gave (to) the man is lost')

In contrast, both objects in the serial clause can be relativized:

(19) a. *Papa no **a*** *Kofi de   sika   no ma-a*
       man the REL Kofi take money the give-PAST

    no *no a-ba*
    3sg DEF PERF-come

    'The man Kofi gave the money to has come'

   b. *Sika   no **a**   Kofi de   ma-a   [0] papa no a-yera*
       money the REL Kofi take give-PAST [0] man the PERF-be.lost
       'The money Kofi gave to the man is lost'

The relativization test again suggests that the simple bi-transitive clause has only one direct object, the dative NP, while the serial clause has two direct objects.[7]

5.2. *Other bi-transitive verbs with a dative object*

A group of bi-transitive verbs turns out to behave differently from 'give'. They are *kyerE* 'teach', *srE* 'beg/request', *kyerEw* 'write', *gye* 'charge'.

5.2.1. *Proximity to the verb*

In terms of proximity to the verb, these verbs follow the pattern of 'give', up to a point, allowing only the dative NP to directly follow the verb. However, the patients may then be either definite or indefinite. Thus:

(20) a. **DAT-PAT order:**
   Kofi kyerE-E   mbofra no   ndwom
   Kofi teach-PAST children DEF   song
   'Kofi taught the children a song'

   b. ***PAT-DAT order — INDEF-patient:**
   *Kofi kyerE-E   ndwom mbofra no
   Kofi teach-PAST song   children DEF
   (*'Kofi taught a song to the children')

   c. **DAT-PAT order — DEF-patient:**
   *Kofi kyerE-E   mbofra no ndwom **no***
   Kofi teach-PAST children DEF song   **DEF**
   'Kofi taught the children the song'

   d. **DAT-PAT order — INDEF-patient:**
   Kofi bisa-a   maame no asEm
   Kofi ask-PAST woman DEF question
   'Kofi asked the woman a question'

   e. **PAT-DAT oder — INDEF-patient:**
   *Kofi bisa-a   asEm   maame no
   Kofi ask-PAST question woman DEF
   (*'Kofi asked a question of the woman')

   f. **DAT-PAT order — DEF-patient:**
   *Kofi bisa-a   maame no asEm   **no***
   Kofi ask-PAST woman DEF question **DEF**
   'Kofi asked the woman about the issue'

While these verbs have no serial clause variant and allow only the DAT-PAT order, they allow the patient to be either definite or indefinite. This is important for both pronominalization and relativization.

5.2.2. Pronominalization
The bi-transitive verbs in this group allow both the dative and patient objects to be pronominalized:

(21) a. *Kofi kyerE-E   **hOn** ndwom*
   Kofi teach-PAST **3pl** song
   'Kofi taught them a song'

b. *Kofi kyerE-E   mbofra no* **[0]**
   Kofi teach-PAST children the **[0]**
   'Kofi taught it to the children'

One would suspect that the two pronominal patterns correspond to the two patterns of definite object — the DAT-PAT order with indefinite patient for the pronominalized dative (21a), and the DAT-PAT order with definite patient for the pronominalized patient (21b).

5.2.3. Relativization

Likewise, both the dative and patient NPs can be relativized in clauses with these 'teach'-like verbs:

(23) a. *Mbofra no **a**   Kofi kyerE-E   hOn ndwom no*
        children DEF **REL** Kofi teach-PAST them song   DEF

        a-ba   skuul
        PERF-come school

        'The children Kofi taught the song to have come to school'

   b. *Ndwom **a**   Kofi kyerE-E   mbofra no nn-yE dE*
        song   **REL** Kofi teach-PAST children the NEG-be sweet
        'The song Kofi taught the children is not nice'

It is clear from these illustrations that with the 'teach'-type verbs both the DAT NP and the PAT NP can be relativized, even when the latter is indefinite.

There remains the delicate question, however, of conflict in our criteria for direct objecthood: By the verb-proximity criterion, the patient is never the direct object in these clauses. By the pronominalization and relativization criteria, however, either the dative or the patient can become the direct object. Since the problem is intimately connected with the assignment of definiteness and thus topicality, we will examine it in the following section.

5.3. Definite patient objects and verb serialization

As seen above, the prototype simple bi-transitive clause of the 'give' pattern allows only the dative object to be definite. The patient in that clause must be indefinite. This restriction holds regardless of varying orders of the two objects following the verb. That is:

(24) a. **Kofi ma-a   papa no sika **no***
      Kofi give-PAST man DEF money DEF
      (lit.: *'Kofi gave the man the money')

b. **Kofi ma-a   sika **no** papa no*
      Kofi give-PAST money PAST man DEF
      (lit.: *'Kofi gave the money to the man')

c. **Kofi brE-E   abofra no ekutu **no***
      Kofi bring-PAST child   the orange DEF
      (lit.: *'Kofi brought the child the orange')

d. **Kofi brE-E   ekutu **no** abofra no*
      Kofi bring-PAST orange DEF child   DEF
      (lit.: *'Kofi brought the orange to the child')

This restriction on indefinite objects of 'give' is asymmetrical: It does not apply to dative object, which can be either definite or indefinite in these clauses:

(25) a. *Kofi ma-a   papa **no** sika*
      Kofi give-PAST man **DEF** money
      'Kofi gave **the man** money'

b. *Kofi ma-a   papa **bi** sika*
      Kofi give-PAST man **one** money
      'Kofi gave **a man** money'

To definitize a patient in the bi-transitive clause — and place it before the dative, one must resort to the use of verb serialization in Akan.

In the serial clause, the patient is now the direct object of the *de* 'take'/ 'hold'. Thus recall:

(26) a. *Kofi de sika   no ma-a   papa no*
      Kofi take money DEF give-PAST man DEF
      'Kofi gave the money to the man'

b. *Kofi de ekutu no brE-E   abofra no*
      Kofi take orange DEF bring-PAST child   DEF
      'Kofi brought the orange to the child'

This interaction between verb serialization and definitization of the patient object only applies to prototype bi-transitives such as 'give' or 'bring'. As noted above, bi-transitive of the 'teach'-type do not have a serial-clause variant, but rather allow their patient — in the invariant DAT-PAT order — to be either definite or indefinite. Thus recall:

(27) a. **INDEF-patient:**
Kofi kyerE-E mbofra no ndwom
Kofi teach-PAST children DEF song
'Kofi taught the children a song'

b. **DEF-patient:**
Kofi kyerE-E mbofra no ndwom no
Kofi teach-PAST children DEF song DEF
'Kofi taught the children the song'

c. **INDEF-patient:**
Kofi bisa-a maame no asEm
Kofi ask-PAST woman DEF question
'Kofi asked the woman a question'

d. **DEF-patient:**
Kofi bisa-a maame no asEm no
Kofi ask-PAST woman DEF question the
'Kofi asked him about the issue'

Unlike the prototype bi-transitive 'give' and 'bring', bi-transitives of the 'teach', 'ask' group do not have a serial variant with *de* 'take/'hold' to code the definite-patient alternation. One may suggest, for the moment tentatively, that the serial-verb pattern with the concrete *de* 'take'/'hold' began with verbs with concrete patients, such as 'give' and 'bring', and has not yet spread to bi-transitive verbs with more abstract patients (song, question, story) such as 'teach' and 'ask'. The serial pattern is thus, in essence, a fronting of the topical object. Definitization is involved because of its strong association with topicalization.

And direct objecthood is involved because, as is well established, the direct object is the more topical object in the bi-transitive clause (Givón 1984a, 1984b).

5.4. *Bi-transitive verbs with locative objects*

Some bi-transitive verbs take obligatory locative objects. In English these are verbs such as 'put ... on/in', 'take ... from', 'carry ... to', etc. Akan semantic equivalent of such clauses, all of them serial, may be seen in:

(28) a. *Esi de   ekutu   no   to-o   famu*[8]
 Esi take orange DEF put-PAST floor
 'Esi put the orange on (the) floor'

 b. *Kofi yi-i   tam   no   fi-i   pon   no   do*
 Kofi take-PAST cloth DEF leave-PAST table DEF on
 'Kofi took the cloth off the table'

 c. *Ebo soa-a   adaka no   kO-O   skuul*
 Ebo carry-PAST box   the go-PAST school
 'Ebo carried the box to school'

Which of the two post-verbal NPs in these serial clause is the direct object? By the proximity criterion, both objects directly follow a verb, albeit each a different verb. We will thus proceed to the two remaining tests, pronominalization and relativization.

5.4.1. *Pronominalization*
Both objects are equally accessible to pronominalization:

(29) a. *Kofi yi-i   [0] fi-i   pon   no   do*
 Kofi take-PAST [0] leave-PAST table DEF on
 'Kofi took it off the table'

 b. *Kofi yi-i   tam   no   fi-i   [0] do*
 Kofi take-PAST cloth DEF leave-PAST [0] on
 'Kofi took the cloth off it'

By the pronominalization test then, both the patient and locative are direct objects, albeit most likely of different verbs.[9]

5.4.2. *Relativization*
Both objects in the locative bi-transitive clause are also accessible to relativization:

(30) a. *Tam no a   Kofi yi-i   fi-i   pon   no   do no*
 cloth DEF **REL** Kofi take-PAST leave-PAST table DEF on DEF

 a-yew
 PERF-lost

 'The cloth Kofi took off the table is lost'

b. *Pon   no   a   Kofi yi-i   tam no fi-i   do no*
Table DEF **REL** Kofi take-PAST cloth DEF leave-PAST on DEF

e-bu
PERF-break

'The table Kofi took the cloth off has broken'

By the relativization test, both patient and locative are direct objects, although most likely of different verbs.

Our three criteria thus suggest that in the serial-verb clause, each nominal participant is the direct object of the verb that directly precedes it.

5.5. *Bi-transitive clauses with the instrumental-locative alternation*

Verbs in this group may appear in two variant clauses. In one, one of the object seems to be the patient, the other a locative. In the other, the erstwhile locative becomes the patient, and the erstwhile patient an instrumental object. In English, this pattern most commonly also requires alternation of paired lexical stems, such as 'pour X into-Y' vs. 'fill Y with-X', 'spread X on-Y' vs. 'cover Y with-X', 'tie X around-Y' vs. 'tie Y with-X', 'pour X out-of-Y' vs. 'empty Y of-X', 'remove X from-Y' vs. 'deprive Y of X'.

In many other languages (see Givón 1979, 1984b), the lexical verb remains the same in such alternations. Akan is in this respect more like English, in the sense that both serial verbs must change in this alternation. Thus consider:

(31) a. **Locative variant:**
          Esi hue-e   nsu gu-u   ankora no mu
          Esi pour-PAST water put-PAST barrel DEF in
          'Esi poured water **into** the barrel'

      b. **Instrumental variant:**
          Esi hyE-E   ankora no nsu   ma
          Esi fill-PAST barrel DEF water full
          'Esi filled the barrel **with** water'

5.5.1. *Proximity to the verb*
Considering first out verb proximity criterion, one may note that in variant (31a) both objects follow a verb. In variant (31b), on the other hand, only

the first object follows a verb. The second one does not, though it is itself followed by the adjectival predicate 'full'. By our verb proximity criterion, the locative variant (31a) has two direct objects, but the instrumental variant (31b) has only one.

5.5.2. *Pronominalization*
Both objects turn out to be equally accessible to pronominalization in both variants:

(33) a. *Esi hue-e*   **[0]** *gu-u*   *ankora no* *mu*
      Esi pour-PAST **[0]** place-PAST barrel DEF in
      'Esi poured it (= water) into the barrel'

    b. *Esi hue-e*   *nsu*   *gu-u*   **[0]** *mu*
      Esi pour-PAST water put-PAST **[0]** in
      'Esi poured water into it (= barrel)'

    c. *Esi hyE-E*   **no** *nsu*   *ma*
      Esi fill-PAST **3sg** water full
      'Esi filled it (= barrel) with water'

    d. *Esi hyE-E*   *ankora no* **[0]** *ma*
      Esi fill-PAST barrel DEF **[0]** full
      'Esi filled the barrel with it (= water)'

By the pronominalization test, then, each of the two variant clauses has two direct objects.

5.5.3. *Relativization*
The relativization test suggest a different story. Both object NPs in the more serial variant (locative), where both objects directly follow the verb, are indeed equally accessible to relativization:

(34) a. *Ankora no* **a** *Esi hue-e*   *nsu* *gu-u*   *mu no*
      barrel DEF **REL** Esi pour-PAST water place-PAST in DEF

      a-yew
      PERF-lost

      'The barrel Esi poured water into is lost'

b. *Nsu   a   Esi hue-e   gu-u   ankora no mu no*
water **REL** Esi pour-PAST place-PAST barrel DEF in DEF

a-sa
PERF-finish

'The water which Esi poured into the barrel is all gone'

In contrast, only the post-verbal object in the other (instrumental) variant
is accessible:

(35) a. *Ankora-no a   Esi hyE-E   no nsu   ma no a-yew*
         barrel-DEF **REL** Esi fill-PAST 3sg water full DEF PERF-lose
         'The barrel Esi filled with water is lost'

   d. **Nsu   a   Esi hyE-E   ankora no ma no a-sa*
       water **REL** Esi fill-PAST barrel   DEF full DEF PERF-finish
       (*'The water which Esi filled the barrel with is finished')

The pronominalization test does not discriminate here between the status of the various objects, all of which are equally accessible to relativization in both variant clauses. The verb proximity and relativization criteria,
on the other hand, go hand in hand here in discriminating between the two
clause types. Only in the truly serial clause (locative variant) do both
objects behave, equally, like direct objects. In the less-serial clause (instrumental variant), the object that directly follows a verb indeed behaves like
a direct object. The second object, however, the one that precedes the adjectival *ma* 'full', bears an object relation neither to the first verb 'fill' nor to
the adjective 'full'.

From a historical semantic perspective, the status of the instrumental
variant clause of course makes perfect sense. The historical — clause-
chaining — source for 'Esi filled the barrel with water' was probably 'Esi
filled the barrel (with) water, (till) it was full'. In such a chain, 'water' is
the indirect object of 'fill' as well as the *subject* of 'full'.

5.6. *Bi-transitive with optional participants*

The bi-transitive clauses surveyed thus far all involved verbs which require
both a patient and another object, be it dative or a locative (or an instrumental, in the variant of the latter). But bi-transitive clauses can also occur
when one adds an optional participant to simple transitive verbs that require

only a patient. All such added arguments are inserted into the transitive clause in Akan with serial verbs. In this section we probe into the grammatical status of both objects in such clauses.

5.6.1. *Benefactive objects*

An optional benefactive NP can be introduced through serialization:

(36) a. *Esi tur-r   abofra no ma-a   maame no*
      Esi carry-PAST child   DEF give-PAST woman DEF
      'Esi carried the child for the woman'

   b. *Esi twitwa-a Kofi **ne**   tsir ma-a   **no***
      Esi cut-PAST Kofi **3sg** Poss hair give-PAST **3sg**
      'Esi cut Kofi's hair for him'

In terms of verb proximity, each of the two objects in (36a,b) directly follows a verb. Both objects are equally accessible to pronominalization:

(37) a. *Esi tur-r   **no** ma-a   maame no*
      Esi carry-PAST **3sg** give-PAST woman DEF
      'Esi carried **him/her** for the woman'

   b. *Esi tur-r   abofra no ma-a   **no***
      Esi carry-PAST child   DEF give-PAST **3sg**
      'Esi carried the child for him/her'

Likewise, both objects are equally accessible to relativization:

(38) a. *Abofra no **a**   Esi tur-r   **no** ma-a   maame no*
      child   DEF **REL** Esi carry-PAST **3sg** give-PAST woman DEF

      a-yew
      PERF-missing

      'The child Esi carried for the woman is missing'

   b. *Maame no **a**   Esi tur-r   abofra no ma-a   **no***
      woman DEF **REL** Esi carry-PAST child   DEF give-PAST **3sg**

      no a-yew
      DEF PERF-missing

      'The woman Esi carried the child for is missing'

By all three criteria, then, both objects in the benefactive serial clause display direct objecthood.

5.6.2. *Instrumental objects*

Optional instrumental objects in Akan are put into the clause with the serial verb *de* 'take'/'hold':

(39) a. *Kofi de   sekan no   twa-a   ahoma no*
       Kofi take knife DEF cut-PAST rope   DEF
       'Kofi cut the rope with the knife'

   b. *Kofi de   akuma no bu-u   dua no*
       Kofi take axe   DEF fell-PAST tree DEF
       'Kofi felled the tree with the axe'

   c. *Kofi de   abaa no hwe-e   abofra no*
       Kofi take stick DEF whip-PAST child   DEF
       'Kofi whipped the child with the stick'

Each of the objects in this serial construction directly follows a verb. Further, both are equally accessible to pronominalization:

(40) a. *Kofi de   [0] hwe-e   abofra no*
       Kofi take [0] whip-PAST child   DEF
       'Kofi whipped the child with it (= stick)'

   b. *Kofi de   abaa no hwe-e   **no***
       Kofi take stick DEF whip-PAST **3sg**
       'Kofi whipped him/her with the stick'

Likewise, both objects are equally accessible to relativization:

(41) a. *Abaa no **a** Kofi de   hwe-e   abofra no   e-bu*
       stick DEF **REL** Kofi take whip-PAST child   DEF PERF-break
       'The stick Kofi whipped the child with is broken'

   b. *Abofra no **a** Kofi de   abaa no hwe-e   no no*
       child   DEF **REL** Kofi take stick DEF whip-PAST 3sg DEF

       a-yew
       PERF-missing

       'The child who Kofi whipped with the stick is missing'

All three criteria again suggest that both the patient and instrumental objects are direct objects.

5.6.3. *Associative objects*

Optional associative objects in Akan are introduced into the clause with the serial verb *nye* 'accompany'/'join':[10]

(42) a. *Kofi nye   aberwa   no   dzi-i   edziban no*
      Kofi join/PAST old.woman DEF eat-PAST food   DEF
      'Kofi ate the food with the old woman'

    b. *Kofi nye   **ne**   ba   no   twitwa-a ndua no*
      Kofi join/PAST **3sg** Poss child DEF cut-PAST trees DEF
      'Kofi cut the trees with his child'

Both objects in this constructions directly follow a verb. Both are equally accessible to pronominalization:

(43) a. *Kofi nye   **no** dzi-i   edziban no*
      Kofi join/PAST **3sg** eat-PAST food   DEF
      'Kofi ate the food with him/her'

    b. *Kofi nye   aberwa   no   dzi-i   **[0]***
      Kofi join/PAST old.woman DEF eat-PAST **[0]**
      'Kofi ate it (= food) with the old woman'

Similarly, both objects are equally accessible to relativization:

(44) a. *Aberwa   no   **a**   Kofi nye   **no** dzi-i   edziban no*
      old.woman DEF **REL** Kofi join/PAST **3sg** eat-PAST food   DEF
      e-wu
      PERF-die
      'The old woman Kofi ate the food with is dead'

    b. *Edziban no   **a**   Kofi nye   aberwa   no   dzi-i   no*
      food   DEF **REL** Kofi join/PAST old.woman DEF eat-PAST DEF
      nn-yE dE
      NEG-be sweet
      'The food Kofi ate with the old woman did not taste good'

Once again, both the patient and benefactive in this construction display direct-object properties.

5.6.4. *Manner adverbs*

Optional manner adverbs are inserted into the clause with the same serial verb *de* 'take'/'hold' used for instrumental objects:

(45) a. *Maame no de   aningye we-e   nam no*
        woman DEF take joy   chew-PAST fish DEF
        'The woman ate the fish with relish'

     b. *Akosua de   abotare twitwa-a ntEtea no*
        Akosua take patience cut-PAST ant   DEF
        'Akosua dissected the ant patiently'

Again, both objects directly follow a verb. Using (45a) I will illustrate the pronominalization test (46). However, only the patient is accessible to pronominalization, not the manner adverb. The clause with zero-anaphoric inanimate object of 'take' is fine, but the zero could not refer to the manner adverb, only to an **associate inanimate patient**:

(46) a. *Maame no de   [0] we-e   nam no*
        woman DEF take [0] chew-PAST fish DEF
        *'The woman ate the fish with **it** (= joy)'
        'The woman ate the fish with **it** (= e.g. onions)'

     b. *Maame no de   aningye we-e   [0]*
        woman DEF take joy   chew-PAST [0]
        'The woman ate it (= fish) with joy'

In the same vein, the manner adverb is not accessible to relativization either:

(47) a. *?Aningye a   maame no de   we-e   nam no*
        Joy   REL woman DEF take chew-PAST fish DEF

        yE-E   me nwanwa
        be-PAST 1sg surprise

        ('The joy with which the woman ate the fish was a surprise to me')

     b. *Nam no a   maame no de   aningye we-e   no bOn*
        fish DEF REL woman DEF take joy   chew-PAST DEF smell
        'The fish the woman ate with joy had a bad smell'

In sum, despite their superficial similarity to other objects that directly follow a serial verb, manner adverbs in Akan do not possess rule-governed properties of direct objects. The fact that they can not be pronominalized and have doubtful relativization status is no doubt related to the fact that they are a non-referring, non-topical participant in the clause.

6. Conclusion

The formal distinction in Akan grammar between subjects and direct objects is amply supported by both overt coding and behavior-and-control properties. In contrast, in serial-verb clauses in Akan, the presence of a single, unique direct object is not supported. This is certainly true in serial bitransitive clauses with an obligatory dative, locative or instrumental object.

But it is also true when the extra argument — be it benefactive, instrumental, locative or associative — is added optionally. All such optional arguments, which have no direct-object properties in English, have the same direct-object properties in Akan as does the patient.

The lone exception among serially-introduced arguments is manner adverb, which superficially follows the very same serial verb as the instrumental object, but does not display other direct-object syntactic properties. I suggest that semantic-pragmatic status of manner adverbs as indefinite, non-referring, non-topical participants probably accounts for their syntactic behavior.

If a clause has two syntactic direct objects, each follows its own verb, it most likely has two verb phrase nodes, each governing its own cluster of verb and object. This seems to be the conclusion drawn by others who have studied the formal properties of serial-verb clauses (Sebba 1987; Byrne 1987, 1992; Larson 1991; Givón 1995). Whether there is any syntactic support for assuming that all the VPs in the serial clause are indeed governed by a single "dominating" VP node (as suggested by Sebba 1987 or Larson 1991) remains to be seen.

Serial-verb clauses are the product of diachronic clause-union, a grammaticalization process arising from an erstwhile clause-chaining configuration (Givón 1995). While semantically the serial clause is fully integrated, it does retain many of the formal syntactic properties of its paratactic source. The fact that serial clauses formally retain two direct objects is fully in consonant with the fact that in grammaicalization, functional change precedes structural readjustment (Givón 1979; Heine et al. 1991; Haboud, in this volume).

Notes

* I am grateful to Colette Craig, Tom Payne, Doris Payne, Felix Ameka and T. Givón for helpful suggestions and comments. An earlier version of this paper was presented at the Linguistics Department Colloquium, University of Oregon, in 1993. Another appeared as a chapter in my dissertation (Osam 1994b).

1. Akan is spoken in Ghana and it is a member of the Kwa subbranch of Niger-Congo. There are no reliable figures as to the exact number of speakers, but it is estimated that the total number of speakers is about 40-45% of the national population. This means that there are about between 6 and 6.75 million speakers. The language has different dialects, but three of these are normally referred to as being the major dialects of the language. These are Asante, Akuapem, and Fante. The first two together with their subdialects are referred to as Twi, and I will use this term when I am referring to this cluster of dialects. Throughout this paper I will try to be as cross-dialectal as possible in the data to be cited. Where it is crucial a specific dialect may be referred to, otherwise most of the examples will be presented in such a way that they will reflect a cross-dialectal perspective.

2. The variation in the form of the subject clitic (between *O-* and *o-*) is the result of vowel harmony. Akan has the Advanced Tongue Root (ATR) harmony and the Fante dialect has, in addition, the Rounding harmony. For more detailed discussions of Akan vowel harmony readers are referred to the following: Berry (1957), Boadi (1963), Clements (1984, 1985), Dolphyne (1988), Schachter and Fromkin (1968), Stewart (1970, 1983).

3. One of the issues involved here is that not all transitive verbs behave this way. There are some verbs which require the overt expression of the object pronoun when its antecedent is an inanimate noun. Examples of such verbs are *sEe* 'destroy', *bu* 'break', *hyew* 'burn', *kyea* 'bend', *tsen* 'straighten'. Another interesting feature of the inanimate object pronoun is that if the sentence has an adverbial element after the object, the pronoun is required. These and related issues are the discussed in full in Osam (1994b).

4. The construction I refer to as clause chaining is equivalent to Bamgbose's (1974) "linking" type of serialization.

5. For a more detailed discussion of relativization in Akan see Saah (1990).

6. The position I take in this paper regarding the verbal status of verbs used in serialization runs counter to the trend in the works of Lord (1973, 1982, 1989/1993). I have shown in Osam (1994a) that there is no language internal evidence for the view that verbs in such constructions in Akan are prepositions. I grant that some of the verbs, especially *de* 'take, hold', *wO* 'be at', *nye* 'accompany'do not possess full verbal properties. In other words these may not be prototypical verbs, but neither are they prepositions. The verb *de* 'take, hold' has two forms in Akan determined by dialectal usage. While the Twi dialects use *de*, the Fante dialect uses *dze*. Throughout this paper the Twi variant will be used even though the sentence in which it occurs may be from the Fante dialect.

7. The results of these tests show that the long standing view in Akan studies that recipient NPs in bi-transitive constructions are indirect object (see for example Christaller 1875, Stewart 1963, and Saah 1990) is not supported by the facts of the grammar of Akan. The analysis of these NPs as indirect objects follows the traditional treatment of such NPs by some English grammarians as indirect object, an analysis which is strictly based on not differentiating grammatical relations from semantic roles.

8. This word is the lexicalization of the noun *efa* 'earth' and the postposition *mu* 'in'. This illustrates a process going on in Akan in which postpositions are cliticizing on preceding nouns. In fact in speech, the word *famu* is pronounced without the final vowel. This process is similar to the cliticization of 3SG object pronoun on verbs. For example, when the sentence

    Me-hyia-a   no
    1sg-meet-PAST 3sg
    'I met him/her'

    is spoken, the vowel of *no* is not articulated (especially in the Fante dialect). The spoken version of this sentence will therefore come out as

    Me-hyia-a-n
    1sg-meet-PAST-3sg
    'I met him/her'.

9. These locative NPs can also be replaced by certain pro-forms, specifically, by the deitic forms *ha* 'here' or *hO* 'there'. So instead of (a) we can have (b).

    a. *Kofi yi-i   ekutu no fi-i   fie*
        Kofi take-PAST orange the leave-PAST home
        'Kofi took the orange from home'

    b. *Kofi yi-i   ekutu no fi-i   hO*
        Kofi take-PAST orange the leave-PAST there
        'Kofi took the orange from there (there = home)'.

    These deitic forms, *ha* 'here' and *hO* 'there', however, are not restricted to the object position since the same forms can be used for locative NPs in subject position. In effect, though the permissibility of these pro-forms as replacement for the locative NPs makes it possible for us to assign some type of object status to them, they are not at the same rank of objecthood as prototypical objects.

10. The verb *nye* in Fante has the variant *ne* in the Twi dialects. I use the Fante form here because it is in Fante that the verbal status is distinctive.

References

Anderson, S. 1976. "On the notion of subject in ergative languages." In C. Li (ed.) 1976: 1-23.

Bamgbose, A. 1974. "On serial verbs and verbal status." *Journal of West African Languages* 9.1:17-48.

Berry, J. 1957. "Vowel harmony in Twi." *Bulletin of School of Oriental and African Studies* 19:124-130.

Boadi, L. 1963. "Palatality as a factor in Twi vowel harmony." *Journal of African Languages* 2.2:133-138.

Borg, A.J. and B. Comrie. 1984. "Object diffuseness in Maltese." In F. Plank (ed.) 1984: 109-116.

Byrne, F. 1987. *Grammatical Relations in a Radical Creole*. Amsterdam: John Benjamins [Creole Language Library 3].

Byrne, F. 1992. "Tense, scope and spreading in Saramaccan." *Journal of Pidgins and Creoles* 7.2:195-221.

Christaller, J. 1875. *A Grammar of the Asante and Fante Language called Twi*. Basel: Basel Evangelical Missionary Society.

Clements, G.N. 1984. "Vowel harmony in Akan: a consideration of Stewart's word structure conditions." *Studies in African Linguistics* 15.3:321-337.

Clements, G.N. 1985. "Akan vowel harmony: A nonlinear analysis." In *African Linguistics*, D.L. Goyvaerts (ed.), 55-98, Amsterdam: John Benjamins.

Comrie, B. 1982. "Grammatical relations in Huichol." In *Studies in Transitivity*, P. Hopper and S. Thompson (eds), 95-115. New York: Academic Press.

Dolphyne, F. 1988. *The Akan (Twi-Fante) Language: Its Sound Systems and Tonal Structure*. Accra: Ghana Universities Press.

Givón, T. 1979. *On Understanding Grammar*. New York: Academic Press.

Givón, T. 1984a. "Direct object and dative shifting: The pragmatics of case." In F. Plank (ed.) 1984.

Givón, T. 1984b. *Syntax: A Functional-Typological Introduction*, vol. I. Amsterdam: John Benjamins.

Givón, T. 1995. *Functionalism and Grammar*. Amsterdam: John Benjamins.

Heine, B., U. Claudi and F. Hünnemeyer. 1991. *Grammaticalization: A Conceptual Framework*. Chicago: University of Chicago Press.

Hopper, P. and S. Thompson (eds) 1982. *Studies in Transitivity, Syntax and Semantics* 15. New York: Academic Press.

Hyman, L. and A. Duranti. 1982. "On the object relation in Bantu." In *Studies in Transitivity*, P. Hopper and S. Thompson (eds), 217-239. New York: Academic Press.

Keenan, E.L. 1975. "Some universals of passive in relational grammar." *CLS 11*. University of Chicago: Chicago Linguistics Society.

Keenan, E.L. 1976. "Towards a universal definition of 'subject'." In C. Li (ed.) 1976: 303-334.

Keenan, E.L., and B. Comrie. 1977. "Noun phrase accessibility and universal grammar." *Linguistic Inquiry* 8:63-100.

Kemmer, S. 1988/1993. *The Middle Voice: A Typological and Diachronic Study.* Amsterdam: John Benjamins [Typological Studies in Language 23].

Larson, R.K. 1991. "Some issues in verb serialization." In *Serial Verbs: Grammatical, Comparative and Cognitive Approaches,* C. Lefebvre (ed.). Amsterdam: John Benjamins [SSLS #8].

Li, C. (ed.) 1976. *Subject and Topic.* New York: Academic Press.

Lord, C. 1973. "Serial verbs in transition." *Studies in African Linguistics* 4.3:269-296.

Lord, C. 1982. "The development of object markers in serial verb languages." In P. Hopper and S. Thompson (eds) 1982: 277-299.

Lord, C. 1989/1993. *Historical Change in Serial Verb Constructions.* Amsterdam: John Benjamins [Typological Studies in Language 26].

Osam, E.K. 1993. "The loss of the noun class system in Akan." *Acta Linguistica Hafniensia* 26:81-106.

Osam, E.K. 1994a. "From serial verbs to prepositions and the road between." *STUFF* 47.1:16-36.

Osam, E.K. 1994b. *Aspects of Akan grammar: A Functional Perspective,* PhD dissertation, University of Oregon, Eugene.

Plank, F. (ed.) 1984. *Objects: Toward a Theory of Grammatical Relations.* New York: Academic Press.

Saah, K. 1990. "Relative clauses in Akan", paper presented at the *19th West African Languages Congress,* University of Ghana, Legon, April 1990 (ms).

Schachter, P. and V. Fromkin. 1968. *A phonology of Akan: Akuapem, Asante and Fante, UCLA Working Papers in Phonetics* 9.

Stewart, J.M. 1963. "Some restrictions on objects in Twi." *Journal of African Languages* 2.2:145-149.

Stewart, J.M. 1967. "Tongue root position in Akan vowel harmony." *Phonetica* 16:185-204.

Stewart, J.M. 1983. "Akan vowel harmony: The word structure conditions and the floating vowels." *Studies in African Linguistics* 14:2:111-139.

Zero Anaphora and Grammatical Relations in Mandarin[1]

Ming-Ming Pu

Northern State University

1. Introduction

For the past three decades, Chinese pronominalization has aroused the interest of many linguists (Chen 1986; Huang 1984; Li 1985; Li and Thompson 1979; Luk 1977; Xu 1986) because of the fact that in Chinese, noun phrases used anaphorically that are understood from context are frequently left unspecified. Unlike English which uses anaphoric pronouns extensively and zero anaphora in syntactically more constrained circumstances, Chinese makes a much lesser use of lexical pronouns in tracking reference and a principal use of zero anaphora in discourse. The prevalence of zero anaphora in Chinese discourse has been investigated to some extent from two general perspectives: a pure syntactic approach and a semantic-pragmatic approach. Huang (1984), for example, advocates a pure syntactic analysis. He examines the distribution of Chinese zero anaphora within GB framework and contends that the occurrence of zero anaphora is governed by syntactic factors in terms of grammatical relations and functions. Luk (1977), along the same line but more moderately, approaches the problem by examining the syntactic environment in which the alternation between full noun phrase (NP) and pronoun/zero occurs. He argues for a coreference relation between lexical/zero pronouns and their possible referents when they occur in simplex, complex and coordinate sentences. He claims that in the same discourse a nominal in a sentence closer to the occurrence of pronoun/zero is preferred over one in a more remote sentence; in the same sentence a nominal in the main clause is preferred over one in a subordinate clause.

Li and Thompson (1979), on the other hand, take a semantic-pragmatic approach to the problem. They state that the crucial factor determining the appearance of a lexical or a zero pronoun is *conjoinability*, the extent to which a given clause constitutes a single grammatical unit with the preceding clause. The more "connected" the two consecutive clauses are, the more likely a zero anaphora will occur in the second clause. The conjoinability, they state, contains variables of syntactic and semantic properties of those clauses as well as the speaker's perception of the pragmatic situation. Similarly, Chen (1986) argues that anaphoric choice of a zero, a lexical pronoun or a NP is correlated with different assumptions about the identifiability and saliency of the referent under concern. According to Chen, the more identifiable and more negligible (little need to emphasize the identity of the referent) the referent, the more likely it is to be encoded by a zero anaphor in discourse. These studies have shed light on the phenomenon and mechanism of Chinese pronominalization, but neither approach has provided a full account of the occurrence and distribution of zero anaphora in Chinese discourse. Whereas the syntactic analysis dwells on the structural properties of the clause and makes zero anaphora appear more constrained than it is, the semantic-pragmatic analysis overemphasizes the free-occurrence of zero anaphora in discourse and makes it appear more widespread than it is.

While sharing the view that zero anaphora is a discourse phenomenon in Chinese, the present study departs from the prior research in several ways. It recognizes the complexity of the problem, and attempts to explore the phenomenon from an interactive perspective. The study attempts to examine factors determining the occurrence and distribution of zero anaphora: cognitive constraints, discourse context, pragmatic and semantic information, and speaker/writer-audience interaction. After all, it is the speaker/ writer who decides to make ellipsis in a certain place at a given moment in discourse production, and it is the hearer/reader who is assumed to have the ability and background knowledge to successfully interpret the referents for those ellipses in discourse comprehension.

The paper is organized as follows. Section 2 focuses on cognitive basis underlying the use of zero anaphora; Section 3 discusses the distribution of zero anaphora in Chinese discourse, taking into consideration pragmatic and discourse factors; Section 4 proposes a discourse-pragmatic principle governing the alternative use of lexical versus zero pronouns, and illustrates how speaker/writers differentiate between the two types of anaphors to convey their discourse organization to the audience. While concentrating on the occurrence and distribution of Chinese zero anaphora, this study compares, from time to time, the same phenomenon between English and Chinese, the two historically unrelated languages. The study attempts to show, to a certain extent, that the two languages do exhibit similar patterns of the occurrence of zero anaphora in discourse even though these are considered to be two very different languages with respect to the pro-drop phenomenon.

2. Cognitive basis

The cognitive activities underlying reference tracking in discourse processing have been discussed extensively in the literature of linguistics, cognitive science and discourse analysis because of the fundamental relationship between language and cognition. If the human mind is capable of dealing with only a limited number of explicit or implicit references at a time (e.g., short-term memory constraints), then this limitation will surely play a part in determining the nature of the "rules" for reference tracking in any language. Indeed, many studies (Chafe 1987; Clark and Clark 1977; Karmiloff-Smith 1980; Pu 1995; Tomlin 1987; Tomlin and Pu 1991; Tyler and Marslen-Wilson 1982) have demonstrated the cognitive properties of selective attention and memory activation underlying reference management in discourse processing. Chafe (1987), for example, claims that a particular concept, at a particular time, may be in any one of the three different activation states: active, semi-active, and inactive, which can be considered to correspond to "focus of attention", "activated memory", and "long-term memory" respectively in a cognitive model. It has been found that an entity that is being focused on or currently in a speaker's consciousness tends to get pronominalized, and entities outside the speaker's focal attention or consciousness tend to get nominalized. This makes perfect processing sense since an entity or a referent that is currently active in the speaker's consciousness is most readily accessible and hence a less explicit syntactic form or a *less marking material* (terminology Givón's, 1983) such as a lexical pronoun or a zero anaphor is sufficient to code the entity or referent. On the other hand, an entity or a referent that is currently inactive in the speaker's consciousness is less readily accessible and hence a more explicit syntactic form or *more marking material* is required to trigger the immediate activation of the entity or referent (Gernsbacher 1990).

Not only is speakers' referential choice governed by their own cognitive activities, but it is also based partially on their assessment of the hearers' knowledge with respect to a particular referent. Speakers provide guidance for the hearers to uniquely identify each given referent through the use of anaphoric form. If speakers believe that a concept has already been "activated" or is resident in the hearers' consciousness, they will treat that concept in an attenuated manner, most likely pronominalizing it. If speakers believe that the concept has not yet been activated or needs to be reactivated for their hearers, they will treat it in a less attenuated manner, most probably nominalizing it. The cognitive activities of the speaker and the speaker-hearer interaction are well captured by Givón's general psychological principle in language processing: "Expend only as much energy on a task as is required for its performance" (1983: 18).

In written discourse, however, a writer seems to be relatively freed from cognitive constraints because he "may look over what he has already written, pause between each word with no fear of his interlocutor interrupting him, take his time in choosing a particular word, even looking it up in the dictionary if necessary, check his progress with his notes, reorder what he has written, and even change his mind about what he wants to say" (Brown and Yule 1983: 5). Nevertheless, writers write for an audience. They would also empathize with their readers' need by using appropriate anaphors to help them successfully tracking reference through discourse just as speakers do.

Moreover, while written and spoken texts may be produced and heard/ read in a linear fashion, they are nevertheless processed hierarchically. This fact also controls the differential use of anaphors in discourse production. In order to facilitate comprehension and successfully convey the intended message, speakers/writers chunk the overall discourse into sizable, comprehensible thematic units of different levels, and try to help the audience build a discourse representation congruent with their own by signaling to the audience the different thematic units. Within a thematic unit when incoming information coheres with the previously presented information, comprehenders map the current information onto a developing structure; between the thematic units when incoming information is less coherent, comprehenders shift from actively building one structure to start another (Gernsbacher 1990). The process of shifting costs more mental effort than mapping, and comprehenders have more difficulty accessing information that occur after a unit boundary than before a boundary (Anderson, Garrod, and Sanford 1983). Therefore at the beginning of a unit, the speaker/writer will try to facilitate the audience's shifting process and reduce their cognitive burden by using a more self-defining NP, which immediately activate or reactivate the given referent. However, the speaker/writer will use a pronominal to maintain referential continuity within a thematic unit, when and where mapping demands less cognitive efforts.

Example (1) below illustrates how discourse structure serves as a function of alternative use of NPs and pronominals.

(1) *He Ting-de lian-shang yijiu duizhe qin-mi-wu-jian-de xiao,*
     (name) 's face-on   still pile intimate   smile

     φ *xin li que xiang: dengze qiao ba!*
     heart in but think wait   see (exclamation)

     He Ting an-xia   xin, φ zai   qu da   ta-de dianhua. . . .
              put-down heart   continue go make her   phone-call

     Fang-xia dianhua zhihou, ta chang-chang-di tule
     put-down receiver after she long-long   breathe-out

     yi-kou   qi. φ wanyao shi-qi di-shang-de wenjian,
     a-mouth breath bend   pick-up floor-on   document

     biji-ben. φ na   kuai mabu, φ kai-gan zhuo-mian
     note-book take a cloth   mop-off desk-face

     'He Ting was still all smiles, yet φ thought: wait and see!
     He Ting calmed down and continued to finish her phone call.
     Putting down the receiver, she took a deep breath, φ bent to pick
     up the documents and note-books on the floor, φ then dried the
     desk'.

This passage consists of two thematic units (which happen to be two paragraphs): the first one interrupts the action sequence of the story and describes the character's inner thoughts, and the second one resumes the story line. Although the referent remains the same and no potential referential ambiguity exists in the discourse context, the thematic continuity between the two units is temporarily disrupted. Hence the writer/speaker, at this point, cues the hearer/reader of this minor thematic gap by reinstating the referent with an NP, while within each unit the referent is maintained by a pronominal.

In summary, the alternation between NP and pronoun/zero in Chinese discourse is both speaker/writer motivated and audience-directed. It is constrained by cognitive processes and reflects discourse organization. Within a discourse unit where thematic continuity is largely maintained, an activated referent will most likely be coded by a zero anaphor, and an inactive referent will be coded by an NP; at the beginning of a discourse unit (i.e., between discourse units) when thematic coherence is broken, a referent will also be coded by an NP even though it was just activated in the preceding unit. The alternative use of lexical and zero pronoun will be explored in detail in Section 4.

3. The distribution of zero anaphora

In their article discussing third-person pronouns and zero anaphora in Chinese discourse, Li and Thompson (1979) point out: "zero-pronouns can occur in any grammatical slot on the basis of coreferentiality with an antecedent that itself may be in any grammatical slot, at some distance, or not even present" (p. 320). While sharing the view with Li and Thompson that the occurrence of zero anaphora is not controlled by pure syntactic factors, the present paper argues, with a quantitative discourse analysis, that the distribution of zero anaphora is constrained, to a large extent, by pragmatic, semantic and discourse factors, and the free occurrence of zero anaphora in Chinese discourse is more apparent than real.

In this section, we employ several quantitative measurements to assess the occurrence and distribution of zero anaphora in Chinese written narratives, using data collected from three contemporary Chinese novels: (1) The Aged (Chen Rong 1991), (2) The Years That Slipped By (Ye Xin 1982), and (3) The Leaden Wings (Zhang Jie 1984). All the examples appeared in this paper are rendered in Chinese *pinyin* (phonetic alphabet) with their English word-for-word gloss. The English translation follows each example with the original anaphora intact. The data used for the quantitative analysis comprised first 25 pages of each of the narratives. Four measurements were applied to these 75 pages of texts: (1) the overall frequency distribution of NPs, pronouns, and zero anaphora, (2) the frequency distribution of the three types of anaphors in various grammatical positions, (3) the factor of humanness and zero anaphora, and (4) the factor of topicality and zero anaphora. The first was simply counting the numerical distribution of all anaphors, and the results are presented in Table 1 below.

Table 1. *Overall anaphoric distribution*

Author	NP		PRON		ZERO		Total	
	N	%	N	%	N	%	N	%
Cheng	638	55.2	146	17.6	293	27.2	1077	100.0
Ye	653	60.5	124	11.4	303	26.1	1080	100.0
Zhang	704	59.4	193	16.3	288	24.3	1185	100.0

The second measurement was to compare the frequency distributions of zero anaphor, lexical pronoun and NP in the various grammatical positions such as subject, direct object, and prepositional or postpositional object, and then calculating the proportion of zero anaphora occurring in each position. The results are presented in Tables 2-4 below.

Table 2. *Anaphora and subjects*

Author	NP		PRON		ZERO		Total	
	N	%	N	%	N	%	N	%
Cheng	274	40.1	135	19.8	274	**40.1**	683	100.0
Ye	273	41.1	107	16.1	284	**42.8**	664	100.0
Zhang	275	39.4	156	22.3	268	**38.3**	699	100.0

Table 3. *Anaphora and direct objects*

Author	NP		PRON		ZERO		Total	
	N	%	N	%	N	%	N	%
Cheng	187	87.8	11	5.2	15	**7.0**	213	100.0
Ye	173	84.8	17	8.3	14	**6.9**	204	100.0
Zhang	288	84.0	37	10.8	18	**5.2**	343	100.0

Table 4. *Anaphora and prepositional objects*

Author	NP		PRON		ZERO		Total	
	N	%	N	%	N	%	N	%
Cheng	177	97.8	0	0.0	4	**2.2**	181	100.0
Ye	207	97.6	0	0.0	5	**2.4**	212	100.0
Zhang	144	98.6	0	0.0	2	**1.4**	143	100.0

The tables reveal that while the object positions are taken predominantly by NPs (ranging from 84% to 99%), the subject position has only about 40% of NPs. Zero anaphora, however, codes subject as frequently as NP does (see Table 5, the pooled results). On the other hand, zero direct object occurs much less frequently (6% of all object tokens), and other zeroes such as prepositional or postpositional object even more rarely (2% of all tokens of the type).

Table 5. *Pooled results*

Gram. Roles	NP		PRON		ZERO		Total	
	N	%	N	%	N	%	N	%
Subject	822	40.2	398	19.4	826	**40.4**	2046	100.0
Object	648	85.3	65	8.5	47	**6.2**	760	100.0
Other	525	97.9	0	0.0	11	**2.1**	536	100.0

3.1. *Zero anaphora and grammatical relations*

Table 5 shows that the difference between zero subject and object is striking in terms of frequency distributions. This difference is recaptured in Table 6, where the zero anaphor distributions in the three grammatical roles are measured. The following examples illustrate zero anaphora as subject, direct object and prepositional/postpositional object respectively.

(2)   zero subject
       Xia Zhuyun cong qian-jia li chou-chu yi-zhang chaopiao,
       (name)   from purse   in take-out   a   bill

φ *ba   ta di-gei Liu*
(OM)[2] it pass-to (name)

'Xia Zhuyun took a bill from (her) purse, φ pass it to Liu'

(3) zero object
Yurong kanzhongle yi-jian chenyi, dan Jianchun jianjue bu
(name) like   a   shirt but (name) firmly not

rang ta mai φ
let her buy

'Yurong wanted to buy a shirt, but Bizhou wouldn't let her buy φ'

(4) zero postpositional object
zhuo-shang fangzhe yi-ben shu, φ limian jiazhe yige shu-qian
desk-on   put   a   book   inside place a   book-mark
'On the desk is a book, a bookmark is placed in φ'

Table 6 shows that 94% of all zero pronouns appear as subjects, while only 5% as direct objects and only about 1% as others. Since the occurrence of zero prepositional object is marginal, I will focus my discussion on the distribution and occurrence of subject and object zero anaphora in the remainder of the study.

Table 6. *Frequency distribution of zero anaphora and grammatical roles*

Author	SUBJECT		D.O.		OTHERS		Total	
	N	%	N	%	N	%	N	%
Cheng	274	93.5	15	5.1	4	1.4	293	100.0
Ye	284	93.7	14	4.6	5	1.7	303	100.0
Zhang	268	93.1	18	6.2	2	0.7	288	100.0
Pooled	826	**93.5**	47	**5.3**	11	**1.2**	884	100.0

The table clearly indicates that the distribution of zero anaphora is not as free and unconstrained as many studies have claimed. While zero subject is overwhelming in frequency of occurrence, zero object is rare. The occurrence of zero subject in Chinese discourse, therefore, seems to be a grammaticalized phenomenon. In fact, the striking difference (94% versus 5%) between the occurrence of zero subject and zero object is not surprising, since it is a manifestation of syntactic correlates of semantic and discourse-pragmatic functions in discourse processing. As demonstrated by many studies (Ariel 1985; Brown 1983; Clark and Clark 1977; Givón 1979, 1989, 1992; Keenan 1976), factors such as topicality, humanness, agentivity, givenness, definiteness of a given referent correlate strongly with the grammatical subject, and these factors often interact to warrant the highest degree of referential coherence and/or thematic continuity of the subject, and hence the most frequent occurrence of zero subjects in discourse. The bias toward zero subject in discourse is not specific to Chinese, the phenomenon occurs in other languages like English as well, where zero anaphora is syntactically constrained to a large extent. Of 50 pages taken from an English narrative (Denker 1985), about 20% of grammatical subjects are zero anaphora, and the occurrence of zero anaphora is extremely rare in other grammatical positions.

3.2. *Humanness and zero anaphora*

Among various semantic, pragmatic and discourse factors, humanness seems to strongly affect the syntactic coding of a referent because in narrative discourse, a referent that is human is more often topical, agentive, given and definite than a non-human referent, and is more likely to be coded by grammatical subject and hence zero anaphora. To quantitatively assess how humanness affects the occurrence of ellipsis, the third measurement was applied to count the text frequency of human versus non-human referents encoded by zero anaphora. The pooled results are presented in Table 7.

Table 7. *Humanness, grammatical roles and zero anaphora*

	Subject		Object	
	N	%	N	%
Human	778	94.2	9	19.1
Non-human	48	5.8	38	80.9
TOTAL	826	100.0	47	100.0

Table 7 shows that of 826 tokens of zero subjects, 778 (94%) code human referents. The results support the claim made by many studies (Brown

1983; Kuno and Kaburaki 1978) that human referents tend to be coded by grammatical subject in narrative discourse, the one that is most likely to be talked about and therefore to recur in discourse. Since the grammatical subject tends to maintain thematic and referential continuity in discourse, the minimal coding material — zero anaphora — is frequently employed for that position.

3.3. *Topicality and zero subjects*

Although humanness is an important factor, it is not always necessary nor sufficient in determining the occurrence of zero anaphora in Chinese discourse. Humanness does not seem to affect the occurrence of zero objects, i.e., in the object position, zero anaphora codes non-human much more frequently than human referents (81% versus 19%). What prevails is topicality, which permits the extensive use of zero subject and governs the restricted use of zero object in Chinese discourse. A topical participant/referent is always the focus and the thread of a thematic unit, it is most likely to be activated and remain activated across a chain of clauses and hence most likely to be coded by zero anaphora once the topic is established in discourse. Since the grammatical subject tends to be the most topical clause participant (Givón 1992), it is coded most frequently by zero anaphora in discourse. The correlation between topic, subject and syntactic codings has been well captured by Du Bois (1985), who argues that the tendency in narrative discourse to maintain one particular referent as topic is ultimately responsible for the observed *dispreference* for NP subject, and the *preference* for NP objects. Repeated topics (usually realized by grammatical subjects) are typically given and definite, and hence can be coded with less explicit forms than NPs. On the other hand, "given that the roster of patients that are acted upon by a single thematic protagonist tends to shift frequently through a single narrative, patients are often new. Since patients are typically direct objects, we expect direct objects to be manifested in full noun phrase" (Du Bois 1985: 351). The factor of topicality well characterizes the dispreference for zero objects (6% in our text count) in Chinese discourse.

The claim that topicality governs the occurrence of zero anaphora can be substantiated by a further quantitative analysis — *Topic Persistence*, which refers to the number of times a referent recur within the next 10 clauses following the point in which it is first introduced (Wright and Givón

1987: 17). Table 8 below gives the topicality assessment for grammatical roles of referents, which is measured by the *Topic Persistence* of each referent. The results are expressed as the contrast in frequency between low-persistence referents (those that persist only 0-2 times in the following 10 clauses), and high-persistence referents (>2).

Table 8. *The topical-persistence of subject and object*

| | Occurrences in the following 10 clauses | | | | | |
| | 0-2 | | >2 | | Total | |
Author	N	%	N	%	N	%
Cheng						
Subject	142	20.8	541	**79.2**	683	100.0
Object	185	**86.9**	28	13.1	213	100.0
Ye						
Subject	133	20.0	531	**80.0**	664	100.0
Object	171	**83.8**	33	16.2	204	100.0
Zhang						
Subject	155	22.2	544	**77.8**	699	100.0
Object	303	**88.3**	40	11.7	343	100.0
Pooled						
Subject	430	21.0	1616	**79.0**	2046	100.0
Object	659	**86.7**	101	13.3	760	100.0

Comparing the topicality score between subject and object, we see that the subject persists much longer than the object. In general, about 79% of subject are high-persistence referents, while about 87% of objects are low-persistence referents. Since the object is much less topical and much more strongly associated with novel information and thematic discontinuity in discourse (Givón 1979), the minimal marking material — zero anaphora — is not preferred and the more explicit form — NPs — is normally required for its coding.

Topicality as the major determining factor for the distribution and occurrence of zero anaphora is manifest most conspicuously by the topic chain, a very common phenomenon in Chinese narratives, where the topic established in the first clause serves as the referent for the subsequent ellipted topics in the following chain of clauses. The two passages below exemplify the notion of topic chain.

(5)   *ta zhan-qi-shen,   φ zou-jin   qin-shi,   φ da-kai mu-xiang,*
      he stand-up   walk-in bed-room   open   wood-box

      φ zhao-chu yi-tiao zhanxin-de lan-bai-tiao   maojin, ranhou
      find-out a   brand-new blue-white-stripe towel   then

      φ na-chu   lian-pen,   φ yaole dian shui
      take-out wash-bowl   pour   some water

      'He stood up, φ walked into the bedroom, φ opened a wooden-
      box, φ took out a brand new, blue and white striped towel, and
      then φ poured some water into a washbowl'

(6)   *naxie wang-shi   zong   xiang yingzi   yiyang chuxian,*
      those past-things always like   shadow   same   appear

      φ jinjin-di gengsuizhe ta,   φ jiuchanzhe ta,   φ bu ken   he
      closely follow   him   pester   him   not willing from

      ta   fenli,   φ gei   ta   zengtianle xuduo fannao
      him separate give him add   much   trouble

      'The past was like a shadow, φ closely followed him, φ pestered
      him, φ never intended to leave him alone, and φ brought him a
      great deal of trouble'

Each of the two passages is a thematic unit, where the referent (subject NP) is what is being talked about in the span of discourse. It is topical, continuous, and being kept in focus across the chain of clauses, and
hence no elaboration is needed for its identification in discourse processing.
The topic chain exhibits the most frequent occurring zero anaphora in Chinese discourse.

The similar phenomenon can also be found in English. When a referent is important, recurrent and being talked about in a multi-clause span in
discourse, it is topical and often coded by zero anaphora. The following
two passages taken from the English narrative provide good examples:

(7)   He sprang from Susan's side, φ forced his way into the aisle, and
      φ headed toward the front of the auditorium.

(8)   She began pacing up and down the aisle, φ listening, φ watching,
      φ making mental notes as the scene progressed.

3.4. *Topicality and zero objects*

The effect of topicality on the occurrence of zero anaphora can be further explicated by examining the distribution of zero versus NP objects in various constructions. Basically, the direct object in a Chinese sentence can appear in one of the three positions: (1) following the verb in the structure of SVO, (2) preceding the verb in the construction of S*ba*OV (commonly referred to as the *ba*-construction), or (3) in the topic position preceding the entire sentence in the structure of OSV. An example of each of the three constructions is found in (9)-(11).

(9)   the direct object in SVO
      ta zhaole liang po   banche
      he find   a   broken cart
      'He found a broken cart'

(10) the direct object in SbaOV
      ta ba qian   di-gei   lao xiang
      he   money pass-give old farmer
      'He gave the money back to the farmer'

(11) the direct object in OSV
      maizi ta ca   hao le
      wheat he wash well
      'The wheat, he washed well'

As shown in Table 6, the grammatical object is rarely coded by zero anaphora since it is associated more strongly with new information and thematic discontinuity. However, we would expect a preference for zero object immediately following the construction of OSV and/or the *ba*-construction, in which the object is being topicalized and/or foregrounded and very likely to be kept in focus and recurring in a span of discourse. This prediction is borne out in our next text measurement, where frequency distributions of the object in each of the three object constructions and the zero object following each construction are calculated. The results are given in Table 9 below.

Table 9. *Frequency distribution of zero object*

Structure	NP		PRON		ZERO		Total	
	N	%	N	%	N	%	N	%
SVO	607	89.5	56	8.3	15	**2.2**	678	100.0
S*ba*OV	31	54.4	9	15.8	17	**29.8**	57	100.0
OSV	10	40.0	0	0.0	15	**60.0**	25	100.0
Pooled	648	85.3	65	8.6	47	6.2	760	100.0

The table reveals several interesting results. First, zero object in either OSV or S*ba*OV word order occurs much more frequently than in SVO order. Second, both of the marked structures S*ba*OV and OSV are employed to serve various discourse functions, as pointed out by Bolinger (1979: 19), "it is not normal for a language to waste its resources", and "if a language permits a contrast in form to survive, it ought to be for a purpose". While the object in the sentence-initial position (OSV) is being brought to focus, topicalized, and tends to remain activated, the object is positioned preverbally in the *ba*-construction to foreground the object entity (Pu and Wang 1993), or to get an emphatic/contrastive reading (Sun and Givón 1985). As a result, once the object is topicalized and stays in focus, it is most likely to be coded by zero anaphora (about 60% following the OSV construction); once the object is foregrounded, it is thematically more important and thus more likely to be coded by zero anaphora (about 30% following the *ba*-construction); when the object remains in its normal postverbal position, it is both thematically and referentially discontinuous and hence rarely coded by zero anaphora (only about 2% in the SVO structure). The following examples illustrate the structure of OSV, where the object is referred to by zero anaphora in the subsequent clauses after it is topicalized.

(12) *zhe gushi ta gousile haojiu,   zao jiu xiang xie* φ, *ke*
this story he compose very-long early yet want write   but

jiushi mei shijian xie φ
just   not time   write

'This story he had been composing for some time and wanted to write φ ever since, but just had no time to write φ'

(13) *qian   hen   zang,*   φ *erqian zhou-zhou-ba-ba, Xia Zhuyun*
      bill   very dirty   also   crumpled   (name)

      xiane-di   jie-guo   φ, yong zhi-jian   niezhe φ
      disgustedly take-over   use   finger-tip hold

      'The dollar-bills were dirty and crumpled, Xia took φ with a
      frown and held φ with the tips of her fingers'

Moreover, the property of being foregrounded or topical makes the
object in each of these construction persist longer than the object in the normal word order structure. Indeed, object in either OSV or *ba*-construction
persists much longer than object in the normal SVO construction, as shown
in Table 10 below.

Table 10. *Topic persistence of objects*

	Occurrences in the following 10 clauses					
Author	0-2		>2		Total	
	N	%	N	%	N	%
SVO	640	94.4	38	**5.6**	678	100.0
S*ba*OV	25	43.5	32	**56.5**	57	100.0
OSV	7	28.0	18	**72.0**	25	100.0
Pooled	672	88.4	88	11.6	760	100.0

Not only do objects in both S*ba*OV and OSV constructions persist
longer than those in the SVO structure, the high topicality and referential
continuity of these preverbal objects can also be quantified by *referential
distance* (RD), which measures the distance (namely, number of clauses)
between a referent and its antecedent in a discourse (Givón 1983). Based
on the fundamental assumption of this assessment, i.e., the more topical and
continuous a referent, the shorter the distance between the referent and its
antecedent, and hence the less coding material, we would expect a much
shorter referential distance for the preverbal object than the object in SVO
in Chinese discourse. This is verified by our next text measurement reported
in Table 11, which presents the mean referential distance values and degree
of categorial distribution for objects in each of the three constructions.

Table 11. *Referential distance value of objects*

Construction	Mean RD (# of clauses)	Degree of categorial distribution
SVO	10.23	14% between 1-3
		21% between 4-10
		20% between 10-19
		45% between 20+
S*ba*OV	3.26	30% at 1
		42% between 2-3
		28% between 4-8
OSV	2.18	54% at 1
		26% between 2-3
		20% between 4-6

Note in this table, the majority of objects in OSV (80%) and S*ba*OV (72%) refer back to their antecedents within the preceding 1 to 3 clauses, while only 14% of objects in the SVO construction have the same referential distance. The results of the quantitative assessments have demonstrated that the object in the preverbal position is referentially more continuous and topically more persistent than its counterpart in the normal postverbal position (SVO), and is hence more likely to be coded by zero anaphora.

The similar phenomenon, i.e., the preposed zero object, is also found in English discourse, where the object is important, topical and recur in a chain of subordinate clauses. For example,

(14)   All she wanted was a baby to love, φ to care for, φ to cherish.

In summary, the topicality of nominal referents seems to be one of the most prominent factors for ellipsis in Chinese discourse, which reflects mental activation of referents and coherence of the corresponding mental structures. Though being grammatically manifest at the clause level, topicality is a discourse phenomenon. What makes a clause participant topical is not its grammatical status of subject or object, but rather, its thematic importance, recurrence, or continuity in discourse (Givón 1992: 202).

4. The differential use of zero versus lexical pronoun

As shown in our text measurements, zero anaphora occurs much more frequently in Chinese discourse than lexical pronouns (of 1336 tokens of both
subject and direct object pronominals in our text count, 873 (65%) are zero
anaphora, see Table 5). Zero anaphora has a wider distribution in discourse
than lexical pronouns because (1) a zero anaphor often exhibits a closer referential bound with its antecedent than does a lexical pronoun, which may
cause referential ambiguity, (2) zero anaphora often assumes a higher
degree of topical coherence, and (3) zero anaphora is preferred in a multi-
clause span when thematic continuity is maintained simply because "if the
presence of a word is not needed to make the sense clearer, it is not needed
at all" (Henderson 1943: 9). Let us consider some examples.

(15) a. *Yang Qing jian le Li Yu,* φ *niu tou   jiu   zou*
          (name)   see   (name)   turn head just leave
          As soon as Yang Qing saw Li Yu, (he) took off.

      b. *Yang Qing jianle Li Yu, ta   niu tou   jiu   zou*
          (name)   see   (name) she turn head just leave

The zero anaphor in (15a) unambiguously refers to *Yang Qing*, the topical
referent in the preceding clause, but the lexical pronoun in (15b) is three-way
ambiguous in that it can refer to both subject and object of the preceding
clause or a third person in the preceding discourse context. Another example follows:

(16) *chao-guo ta za   le, (ta) yishi you mai-bu-dao (yige). (ta)*
      fry-pan   he break   he now just buy-not   one   he

      zhihao xuezhe bu-ye-bu φ zai   yong φ
      have-to learn mend   again use

      'The wok he broke, and (he) couldn't buy (one) anywhere for the
      time being. (He) had to learn to mend φ so that (he) could use
      φ again'.

In (16), all three zero objects refer to the topic of the passage *chao-guo*
(the wok). However if these are replaced by lexical pronouns, the passage
reads very awkward and has a very low acceptability to native speakers of
Chinese.

Not only can a zero anaphor refer to an antecedent in the preceding clause or discourse, it can also refer to an antecedent not explicitly expressed in the preceding discourse. For example,

(17) *Lu Yeming zhua-zhu bu-dai-kou,   lun φ shang jian,*
       (name)   grasp   cloth-sack-mouth throw up   shoulder

      zhunbei kang φ qu mo   main
      ready   carry   go grind flour

      'Lu Yeming took the sack-opening, throw φ (the sack) onto his shoulder, and carried φ (the wheat) to the mill to grind'

(18) *Huar   ku le, Xiao-Chi mang wu-zhu ta-de zui,   ta pa*
       (name) cry   (name)   busy cover-up her   mouth he fear

      die   niang   tingjian φ
      father mother hear

      'Huar started to cry, Xiao Chi quickly covered her mouth. He was afraid his parents would hear φ (the cry)'

In (17), the first zero object refers to 'the sack', and the second zero object is interpreted as referring to the content of the sack, i.e., the wheat in the sack. There is no explicit antecedent for either of the zero objects; the object in the first clause only serves as a partial antecedent for both. Nevertheless, the pragmatic knowledge available to the hearer as well as the speaker makes it obvious that the zero anaphors refer to the sack and the wheat respectively. It is the same situation with (18), where the zero anaphor is interpreted as 'the cry'. Although the zero anaphor has no antecedent in the preceding discourse, its referent can be readily inferred from the immediate discourse context, i.e., 'started to cry'. These implicit references are evoked by schemas or scripts, which "allow for new references to objects within them just as if these objects had been previously mentioned" (Schank and Abelson 1977: 41). Once they become activated and accessible to the hearer at the moment, zero anaphors are most appropriate for their encodings. In the above examples, the replacement of either lexical pronouns or full noun phrases for the zero anaphors would be less acceptable: lexical pronouns would sound unnatural and confusing as to their referents; full noun phrases would be redundant, and yet would not make the sense clearer at all.

The above discussion has illustrated that zero anaphora is normally used within a discourse unit when the topicality of the referent is high, and the referential continuity and thematic coherence are maintained. In other words, zero anaphora is used more frequently than lexical pronouns in a discourse unit because this minimal coding material assumes the maximum degree of topicality and thematic coherence, and its reference is most recoverable, identifiable and inferable on the part of the hearer during discourse processing.

Nevertheless, lexical pronouns are still found used within discourse units when the substitution of zero anaphors does not seem to hinder readers' interpretation of the referents, especially in the situation where there is only one referent involved. What, then, motivates the speaker/writer to employ a more explicit referential form to code a referent just mentioned in the same discourse unit at the expense of sacrificing the charge to be "quick and easy" in discourse production? The motivation comes from the speaker/writer's empathy with the hearer/reader's needs to be "clear." Within a discourse unit, there still exists minor thematic incoherence such as an interruption in referential, spatial, temporal or action continuity, or a change in local topics or perspectives, etc. (cf. Givón 1992: 320). It is precisely these types of local incoherence or minor thematic discontinuity that trigger the use of lexical pronouns because the speaker/writer wants to make the comprehension easier by coding referents with more marking material at such a local discourse gap. In other words, when local thematic continuity is high (i.e., when the incoming information is more coherent with the preceding information), the recoverability and identifiability of reference is also high, and hence a minimal marking material is sufficient for the hearer/reader to decode the referent; when local thematic continuity is low, recoverability and identifiability of referent is also low, and hence a more explicit coding form is required for the hearer/reader. Thus I propose a discourse-pragmatic principle governing the occurrence of lexical pronouns and zero anaphora in Chinese discourse, which states:

> Local thematic coherence controls pronominalization in Chinese discourse. The higher the degree of thematic coherence, the higher the degree of referential accessibility, and therefore the more likely the occurrence of a zero anaphor. When the local thematic coherence is impaired, a lexical pronoun is preferred over a zero anaphor.

In what follows, I will elaborate local thematic incoherence in two environments: single-referent environment which do not involve referential ambiguity, and two-referent environment, especially same gender environment, which often requires referential ambiguity resolution. Generally, there are six types of local thematic discontinuity observed in the first environment.

1. local topic change
2. weakened topicality
3. weak semantic link
4. story-line interruption
5. intervening materials
6. referential emphasis

Within a thematic unit when any of the above occurs, local thematic continuity is impaired and a lexical pronoun is expected to be used. I will use examples from the three narratives to illustrate each case.

1. *Local topic change.* Local thematic coherence is often maintained by topic chains, where a single referent remains topical for a multi-clause span in discourse. A topic chain normally describes a continued event or action sequence, or a character's appearance, personality, attitude, etc. Once the description is completed, the topic chain ends and another local topic occurs. The break of a topic chain usually marks the beginning of another substructure of discourse, which triggers the use of lexical pronoun. Consider the following.

(19) *Zeng Huixin dingzhe chuan-xin-tou-gu-de   han-feng,*
      (name)   head   pierce-heart-cut-bone cold-wind

   φ *yong-jin-di*   *tui-zhe xiao-che,*   φ *wai-wai-xie-xie-di*
      put-forth-strength push   small-cart   staggeringly

   xing-jin zai   qi-qu-bu-ping-de tu-lu   shang, ta
   walk   along rugged   dirt-road on   she

   gan-bu-dao leng
   feel-not   cold

   'Zeng Huixin braved the cold wind, φ pushed the cart with full strength, and φ staggered along the rugged mountain path. She didn't feel cold, ...'

In this passage, the first few clauses describe an action sequence, i.e., what the topical referent did, and the referent is maintained by zero anaphors. The topic chain ends when the perspective shifts in the last clause, which describes what the referent felt.

Moreover, the break of a topic chain is often accompanied by a time or locative phrase, which itself is a topic change device in discourse (Li and Thompson 1981; van Dijk and Kintsch 1983). The adverbial phrases 'early in the morning', 'in the afternoon' and 'back at home' in (20) below exemplify such topic-change devices, which are used to signal the advent of a new topic.

(20) *zhe-tian yi-da-zao,   Sima   qin-zi zuo che qu Wangfujing*
      this-day early-morning (name) self   take bus go (place)

      mai-hui shuiguo, nantang ji   su-shi-dianxin, φ bing rao-dao
      buy-back fruits   candies and su-style-cookies   and detour

      Congwenmen hua-dian, φ mai-hui xian-hua   yi-shu, . . .
      (place)   flower-shop buy-back fresh-flower one-bouquet

      xiawu   ta you   paole yi-tang Wangfujing, φ wei Zeng
      afternoon he again go   once   (place)   for (name)

      maile jin-nian-de xin-cha, φ wei Sheng Lanni maile zui
      buy   this-year   new-tea   for (name)   buy most

      gui-de   gua-zi,   hui-dao jia,   ta you   tuo-diao wai-yi,
      expensive melon-seeds back   home he again take-off coat

      φ qinzi tuo diban, φ ca   zhuo-yi
      self   mop floor   wipe table-chair

      'Early in the morning, Sima went to Wangfujing Street to buy fruits, candies, and cookies, φ made a detour to Congwenmen flower-shop and φ bought a bouquet of flowers, . . . In the afternoon, he went to Wangfujing again, φ bought the best new tea for Zeng, φ bought the most expensive melon seeds for Sheng. Arriving home, he immediately took off his coat, φ mopped the floor and wiped furnitures, . . .'

2. *Weakened topicality.* A topical referent can be temporarily moved out of focus when another entity becomes topicalized and 'promoted' to the sentence-initial position. When this happens, the former topical referent will be coded

by a lexical pronoun and tentatively moved to non-topical position. In the following excerpt, the topic continuity is broken by the topicalization of the object entity *translation*, i.e., *this* (the topic of the last clause). The human topical referent is temporarily out of focus and 'demoted' from the sentence-initial position. This shift of focus weakens the topicality of the human referent, and a lexical pronoun is used instead of the expected zero anaphor.

(21) *tuixiu yilai, ta   dui ziji-de shenghuo zuole jingxin-de anpai.*
     retire since she for self   life   make careful   plan

   shang-ban-tian   φ qu tushuguan, . . ., xia-ban-tian gao
   early-half-day   go library   late-half-day do

   *fanyi,   suiran **zhejian shi**   ta̲   congwei zuoguo, . . .*
   translation though this   thing she never   do

   'Since (her) retirement, she had had a busy schedule for herself. φ went to the library in the morning, . . . and φ tried to do some translation in the afternoon. Although this (the translation) she had never done before, . . .'

The passage below provides another example.

(22) *weile jia,   Liu Yuying fangqile yiqie nuren   ai-mei-de*
     for   home (name)   give-up all   women love-beauty

   tianxing. ta   hen shao ti ziji hua   qian,   φ zongshi xian
   desire   she very rarely for self spend money   always first

   xiangzhe zhangfu he   haizi, . . . danshi suoyou zhexie jiannan
   think-of husband and children but   all   these hardship

   xiang shi ta̲ gai   shou de
   like   is she should endure

   'For the sake of (her) family, Liu gave up all women's desire for beauty. She rarely spent any money on (her)self, φ always gave first priority to (her) husband and children. . . . But it seemed that all these hardships were what she ought to endure'.

3. *Weak semantic link.* A lexical pronoun is preferred over a zero anaphor when the semantic link between the two consecutive clauses is weak. For example, semantic link becomes loose when the speaker/writer modulates back and forth from one type of description to another such as from char-

acterization of discourse participants to externalizing characters' thoughts or state of mind, from foreground information to background information, or from conversation back to narration, etc. The following passage provides an example to illustrate the weak semantic link within a thematic unit.

(23) *Mo Zheng yi   bu-zai   shi nage chuanzhe qian-lai-se*
      (name)   already not-again is that wear   light-blue

      falanrong yi-ku   de xiao nanhai. ta chengle ge piaoliang-de
      flannel   clothes of little boy   he become a fine

      nanzihan, φ gaogezi kuan jianbang, φ fang   xiaba, fengman
      man   tall   broad shoulder   square   chin   full

      er   xiantiao qingxi-de zui,   rouruan-de hei   fa, bizhi-de
      and line   clear   mouth soft   black hair straight

      meimao. ta shi na-zhong rang nuhaizi yi-jian-zhong-qing-de
      eye-brow he is that-kind let girl   first-sight-fall-in-love

      nan-ren
      man

      'Mo Zheng was no longer a little boy in light-blue flannel. He had turned into a fine young man, φ was tall and strong, φ had a square-chin, a full and even mouth, soft black hair and straight eyebrows. He was certainly the kind that girls fell in love with at first sight'.

This passage first describes Mo's appearance and then shifts to an author-ial comment about the character. Even though the referential continuity is not broken in the passage, the thematic incoherence still triggers the use of lexical pronoun at the transition point. Consider the next example.

(24) *guniang zuo-zai chuang-yan, φ yanjing hong-zhong, φ dizhe*
      girl   sit-at bed-edge   eye   red-swollen   lower

      tou, φ renran bu-zhu-di chouqi. dang ta   natian zaocheng
      head still   no-stop sob   when she that morning

      bei   dai jinlai de shihou, ...
      (passive) take in   of time

      'The girl sat on the edge of the bed, (her) eyes were red and swollen, φ hung (her) head, φ was still weeping and sobbing. When she was taken in that morning, ...'

The first three clauses provide the foreground information, the character's current situation, and the last clause provides background information. Zero anaphors are used to code the character until the shift from foreground to background information occurs, where a lexical pronoun is used to indicate the switch.

4. *Story-line interruption.* It is often the case in both written and spoken narratives that the main story line is interrupted by descriptions of off-event-line materials. The story-line disruption impairs the local thematic continuity, which blocks the use of zero anaphora. Consider the following example,

(25)   *cha shiwu fen   ba   dian,   Tian Shoucheng maizhe*
     less fifteen minutes eight o'clock (name)   stroll

     cong-cong-rong-rong, si-ping-ba-wen-de buzi zou-jin
     calm-and-unhurried   very-steady   steps walk-in

     bangongshi, φ bian zou hai bian he φ ying-tou
     office   while walk and while to   head-on

     pengshang-de xiao-zi-bei-de gongzuo renyuan kai yi-liang-ju
     meet   young   working men   make one-or-two

     wu-shang-ta-ya-de wanxiao. <u>ta</u> mei-tian   ruci, bu-xiang qitade
     harmless   joke   he every-day so   not-like other

     buzhang, chang-chang zai ba-dian   yihou, qiche cai
     minister frequently at eight-o'clock after car   just

     shi-jin   bujiguande dayuan
     drive-in department compound

     'At precisely a quarter to eight, Tian Shoucheng strolled casually and confidently to (his) office. While walking, φ made jokes with the young people φ met on the way. He did so every working day, unlike other ministers, whose cars frequently arrived at the compounds after eight o'clock.'

Another instance of the use of lexical pronoun under the same circumstance is given below.

(26)   φ *huidao ziji wu-li, Xiuqing sui yi   hen pijuanle,*
     return self room-in (name) though already very tired

dan φ renran xiguandi zhan-zai Fang Yuan-de zhaopian qian
but   still   as-usual stand-by (name)   's picture front

φ zhushile yi-huir,   φ ranhou zuo-zai shuzhuangtai qian shu
 watch   a-while   then   sit-at   dresser   front comb

tou. xiayishi-di,   <u>ta</u> xiangqile hen-jiu   yiqian φ he
head subconsciously she think-of very-long ago   with

Fang Yuan yiqi   duguo-de rizi
(name)   together spend   days

'Xiuqing was tired when φ finally came back to (her) own room,
but φ stood as usual in front of Fang Yuan's picture, φ looked
at (it) for a while, and then φ sat in front of the dresser to comb
(her) hair. Subconsciously, she thought of the time φ spent with
Fang a long time ago'.

The first two sentences in the passage describe the referent's current ac-
tions, which was interrupted by an off-story-line description of the referent's
habitual daily activity. The story-line interruption thus creates a minor thematic gap in the discourse unit, and triggers the use of a lexical pronoun.

5. Intervening materials. Local thematic continuity is impaired when there
is some intervening material (non-human interference) separating two mentions of a referent. When this happens, zero anaphors are not preferred and
lexical pronouns are used instead to code the referent after the intervening material. In each of the following passages, for example, the topical
referent's activity is continuous, but the material separating the references,
though not off-event-line, blocks the occurrence of a zero anaphor, and a
lexical pronoun is used instead.

(27) *Ke Bizhou zhuan-guo tou,   φ kanzhe wu-jiao.   nar fangzhe*
     (name)   turn-over head   see   room-corner there put

     yi-dui shui-tong.   na   shi jiti-hu-de   caichan. <u>ta</u>
     a-pair water-bucket those is collective-family's property he

     zhan-qi-shen,   φ zou-jin qin-shi,   φ dakai mu-xiang, . . .
     stand-up   walk-in bedroom   open   wood-box

'Ke Bizhou turned (his) head and φ looked away at the corner of the house. There sat a pair of buckets, and those belonged to the collective family. He stood up, φ walked into the bedroom, φ opened a wooden-box, . . .'

(28) *ta   dakai meiyige shouti, meiyige chouti dou shi yiyang-di*
        she open every   drawer every   drawer all is same

      za-luan-wu-zhang: riji-ben, xinjian, tuzhang, xinfeng, pijiazi,
       mess   diary   letter stamps envelope wallet

      zhengjian, yanjing, yaopian-he, . . . ta zai zhe yi-dui
       ID-cards eyeglass pill-box   she in this a-pile

      luan-qi-ba-zao-de wujian li zhao-bu-dao renhe you-yong-de
       all-in-a-muddle stuff in find-not   any useful

      dongxi
       thing

'She opened every drawer, and every drawer was a big mess: diary, letters, stamps, envelopes, wallets, ID cards, eye-glasses, pill boxes, . . . she couldn't find anything useful in such a jumble'.

In either of these passages, the intervening material between the two mentions of the referent creates a slight referential gap, which "induces" the use of a lexical pronoun.

6. *Referential emphasis.* Within a discourse unit when local thematic coherence seems to be maintained, the speaker/writer may still want to overtly repeat a referent to achieve stylistic or emphatic effect. This overt repetition has to be done by explicit coding materials such as lexical pronouns or full NPs. For example,

(29) *yingwei ta shi jizhe,   yingwei ta shen-shen-di tongqing*
       because she is reporter because she deeply   sympathize

      naxie shoule yuanqu-de ren, yingwei ta tonghen
       those suffer injustice   man because she hate

      sheng-huo-zhong-de yiqie choue
       life-in   all ugliness

'Because she was a reporter; because she sympathized deeply
with those who were done injustice; because she was indignant
over all ugliness in life; ...'

Here the topical referent is coded by repeated lexical pronouns in the passage, where we could have expected zero anaphors. The three lexical pronouns are used stylistically by the writer to break the thematic coherence
of the unit in order to achieve the emphatic effect. Another instance of this
pattern is given below.

(30) *weile sheng ji-fen-qian, ta   conglai bu mai miantiao,*
      for   save a-few-cents she always not buy noodle

      φ *zongshi ziji gan, ... weile sheng ji-fen-qian, ta   conglai bu*
        always self make   for save a-few-cents she always not

      mai xinxian sucai,   φ zongshi qu tiao naxie pianyi dan
      buy fresh   vegetable always go pick those cheap but

      bu-zai   xian-lu-de dongxi, ... weile sheng ji-fen-qian, ta
      no-longer fresh-green stuff   for save a-few-cents she

      zongshi chongfeng liyong meiyi-shao xiyifen, φ xianshi xi
      always fully   use   every-scoop detergent first   wash

      qian-se-de yifu,   ranhou φ xi   shen-se-de, zai   ranhou
      light-color clothes then   wash dark-color again then

      φ *xi   xie, zhuihou* φ *xi   tuoba,* ...
        wash shoe finally   wash mop

      'In order to save a few cents, she never bought noodles, φ always
      made (them) herself, ...
      In order to save a few cents, she never bought fresh-picked vege-
      tables, φ always chose those cheaper but half-spoiled, not-so-
      green stuff, ...
      In order to save a few cents, she always made full use of a scoop
      of detergent, φ first washed light colored clothes, then φ washed
      dark colored ones, after that φ washed shoes, and finally φ
      washed mops. ...'

We have just explicated how, in a single-referent environment, a zero
anaphor is employed to maintain local thematic coherence and a lexical
pronoun to mark thematic discontinuity. For the 75 pages of the narratives

analyzed in the present study, lexical pronouns used to mark minor thematic discontinuity as represented by the above six patterns amount to about 61% of the total. Table 12 below gives the numerical distribution of lexical pronouns in each of the above six categories and their respective proportions.

Table 12. *The frequency distribution of lexical pronouns*

Category	Lexical Pronouns (Total # = 443)	Proportion
Local topic change	54	12%
Weak Topicality	47	11%
Weak Semantic Link	71	16%
Story-line Interruption	32	7%
Intervening Materials	37	8%
Referential Emphasis	29	7%
Total	270	61%

While lexical pronouns are employed when local thematic coherence is impaired in a single-referent environment, NPs are sometimes used to mark the discontinuity in a two-referent environment when the two referent under concern are involved in a close interaction of some kind (e.g., in events or action sequences, in physical or mental contacts, etc.). First, we will consider the environment of different-gender references. In written Chinese discourse when two characters of different gender interact, lexical pronouns "he/she" are employed to disambiguate reference even when thematic continuity is maintained. However, when thematic coherence is impaired in different-gender environment, both discourse participants would be coded by full NPs if they are not distinguished in the degree of topicality, i.e., both are topical. Consider the following passage:

(31) *pingchang*, Ye Zhiqiu *henshao he   He Jiabing lianxi. ta*
     usually   (name)   rarely   with (name)   contact she

   mang, ta ye   mang. zhishi dang ta   you ji-shi   shi,
   busy he also busy   only   when she have urgent-thing time

   ta cai gei ta   da-dianhua. tamen shi lao pengyou le, mei
   she just give him make-call   they   are old friend   not

   you naxie bu-biyao-de   ketao   he limao.   suoyi dang Ye
   have those not-necessary courtesy and formality so   when

da-dianhua gei He Jiabing shi, <u>ta</u> *ziran   zhidao* ta   *yuzhe*
make-call give   time he naturally know she meet

sheme kunnan le
some trouble

'Usually, Ye seldom contacted Jiabing. She was busy, and so
was he. Only when she had some matter of urgency, she would
call him. They were old friends, courtesy and formalities were
unnecessary. So when Ye called He Jiabing now, he naturally
knew that she had some problem'.

In this passage, the first few clauses provide background information about
the infrequent contact between the two discourse participants under normal
circumstances, and the last two clauses provide foreground information, the
current telephone call between them. Both participants in this passage are
equally topical in the passage. They are first introduced by proper names,
and then referred to in the subsequent mentions by lexical pronouns. The
transition between background to foreground information is signaled by two
full NPs (proper names), which reinstate both of the referents. Nevertheless,
if one participant is treated more topical than the other, the topical referent
tends to be coded by a lexical pronoun, while the less topical referent is
more often coded by a NP. Consider:

(32) *wen-ge   zhong,* ta *chengwei liu-luo-jietou-de yige*
     Culture-revolution during he become   wander-street   a

     xiao-tou. <u>Ye Zhiqiu</u> *diyici ba* ta *cong paichusuo   ling*
     little-thief (name)   first (OM) him from police-station take

     huilai, ta *shenzhi yaole* <u>ta</u> *yi-kou,* φ *zai* <u>ta</u> *jiali laile yici*
     back   he even   bite her a-bite   at her home make a

     juan-tao. zhe yexu   shi meiyige sang-jia-quan-de jingyan:
     steal-run this maybe is every   lose-home-dog's experience

     jinliang duozhe naxei shen-xiang-ni-de shou, huozhe jiu yao
     try   avoid those reach-toward-you hand or   just bite

     ta yikou.
     it a-bite

     Ye Zhiqiu you yici ba   ta   cong paichusuo
             again once (OM) him from police-station

ling-hui   jia, ...
take-back home

'During the Cultural Revolution, he (Mo Zheng) became a little thief on the street. The first time Ye took him home from the police station, he even bit her, φ ran away with her belongings. This may be the experience of every stray dog: Try to avoid any stretching hand, or bit it instead.
Ye once again took him home from the police station, ...'

The first paragraph starts with the topical character *Mo Zheng* and then introduces another character *Ye*. After that, their interaction is described and both characters are referred to by lexical pronouns (except the topic chain) until the story-line is interrupted by some off-event-line material (a stray dog's experience). When the story line is resumed, the secondary character is referred to by a proper name, but the topical referent is still coded by a lexical pronoun.

Similar patterns are observed when two characters of the same gender are involved in a thematic unit, where potential referential ambiguity exists: NPs are used to refer to one of the characters (normally the less topical one) and lexical pronouns to the other (normally the more topical one) in the unit. For example,

(33)   **Shi Quanqing** juede <u>He Jiabing</u> chun. *ta* he <u>He Jiabing</u>
     (name)   think (name)   stupid he and

    gong-shi   *duo   nian. zheme duo   nian lai,* **ta**
    work-together many year these many year since he

    yan-kanzhe <u>He Jiabing</u> *zaile yige you yige gengtou.* **ta**
    eye-watch   fall   one and one stumble he

    qingchudi kanjian heng-zai <u>He Jiabing</u> *mian-qian-de meiyige*
    clearly   see   lie-at   face-front   every

    zhangai, dan **ta** *conglai bu tixing* <u>He Jiabing</u>. **ta** *babude*
    obstacle but he ever   not warn   he hope

    <u>He Jiabing</u> *shuaide pa-bu-qilai*
             fall   get-not-up

'Shi Quanqing considered He stupid. He had worked with He for many years. During all those years, he had watched He stumble

time and again (politically), he had spotted every obstacle in
He's way, but he had never once alerted He of the danger; he
couldn't wait to see He fall flat and never get up'.

The passage is narrated from the perspective of one of the character
Shi Quanqing. All references to this character are done by lexical pronouns
while the other character is referred to with proper names throughout the
passage. An example of the same pattern can be found in (34).

(34) ***Feng Xiaoxian*** ba   *yanjing   chongxin dai-shang,* φ *dingzhe*
    (name)   (OM) eyeglass again   wear-on   stare

    He Jiabing kanle hen-jiu,   haoxiang He Jiabing yixiazi
    (name)   look   very-long like   suddenly

    chengle dongwu-yuan-li-de xihan dongwu. ta yixia
    become zoo-in   rare   animal he at-once

    xiang-bu-chu gai   zengme huida He Jiabing. ta keyi gei
    think-not-of should how   reply   he may give

    He Jiabing kou ding maozi, dan na   dongxi xianzai bu
                      put a   label   but that thing now   not

    shixinle.
    fashionable

'Feng Xiaoxian put his eye-glasses back on and φ stared at He
for a long time as if He had suddenly turned into some rare
animal in the zoo. He was stuck for a response to He. He could
have pinned a label on He, but nobody took labels seriously
nowadays'.

In general, about 19% (84 out of 443) of lexical pronouns are used for
maintaining more topical referents in a different-gender environment and
about 7% (31 out of 443) in a same-gender environment. Altogether, about
87% of all lexical pronouns are accounted for by our pragmatic principle.

Although the occurrence of lexical pronouns are determined to a large
extent by the pragmatic principle proposed in the study, its occurrence can
sometimes be required by the syntactic structure of a clause (cf. Li and
Thompson 1979). For example, the second NP position in a pivotal construction, the object position in some prepositional phrases, the object posi-

tion after the object marker such as *ba, jiang,* etc. must be filled with an explicit coding form, either a lexical pronoun or a full noun phrase. Nevertheless, syntactically required lexical pronouns only count for about 8% (35 out of 443) of the total pronoun tokens in the 75 pages of the narratives examined in the present study.

5. A formal approach to Chinese zero anaphora

Huang (1984) took an alternative approach to the problem of Chinese zero anaphora. He discusses the distribution and reference of empty pronouns in Chinese with a formal government-binding (GB) analysis. He advocates that the occurrence of zero anaphora in Chinese can be accounted for by syntactic factors based on the grammatical relations and functions. Basically, he argues that: (1) a zero topic can control the occurrence of empty subject and object since Chinese is a discourse-oriented, topic prominent language, and (2) the asymmetry between zero subject and zero object exists in Chinese as does in other languages like English or Spanish, (i.e., Chinese prohibits empty object pronouns). In this section, I argue against the two points made by Huang. On the one hand, the notion of zero topic (though being a discourse notion), syntactically constrained, is too limit to account for the occurrence of zero anaphora in Chinese discourse. On the other hand, the empty subject-object asymmetry, syntactically defined, does not exist in Chinese.

Generally, GB theories recognize four kinds of 'empty categories' (silent categories without phonetic content): NP-trace, WH-trace, PRO and pro (cf. Lasnik and Uriagereka, 1986). English does not have pro, which occurs in languages like Italian and Spanish. Examples of each of the empty categories (EC) are given below, where e represents an EC.

(35)   John was arrested e   (NP-trace)

(36)   Who do you think John saw e   (WH-trace)

(37)   John tried e to win   (PRO)

(38)   e *habla*   *espanol*   (pro)
      speak (3 sg.) Spanish
      ('He/She speaks Spanish')

According to the Binding Theory (Chomsky 1982), an NP-trace is a true anaphor ([+a, −p]) since it is A-bound in its Governing Category (GC), a WH-trace is a variable ([-a, −p]) since it is A-free, PRO is both an anaphor and a pronominal [+a, +p] and it has no GC (and hence ungoverned and caseless), and pro is a true pronominal ([−a, +p]) since it is A-free in its GC. Moreover, each of the ECs must obey one of the two principles:

Empty Category Principle (ECP):
Every trace must be properly governed (either lexical-government or antecedent-government).

Generalized Control Rule (GCR):
Coindex an empty category with the closest nominal element (either NP or Agr).

Chinese zero anaphora, as discussed in the previous sections, can occur in both subject (39 and 40) and object position (41 and 42) in a sentence.

(39) e *kanjian Lisi   le*
      see   (name)
      '(he) saw Lisi'

(40) *Zhangsan shuo* e *kanjian Li   le*
      (name)   say   see   (name)
      'Zhang said that (he) saw Li'

(41) *Zhang kanjian* e *le*
      'Zhang saw (him).

(42) *Zhang shuo ta kanjian* e *le*
            say he see
      'Zhang said that he saw (him)'

(39) resembles very much the Spanish sentence (38) above. However, while the EC in (38) obeys the GCR in that it is coindexed with the closest nominal element (i.e., Agr in the inflection of the verb), there is no such a nominal element to control the EC in (39). The sentence is nevertheless well-formed. Huang (1984) tries to solve the problem by proposing that the EC in sentences like (39) cannot be a genuine pronominal ([−a, +p]) because there is nothing to identify it (for there being no Agr in Chinese). Such an EC is actually a variable ([−a, −p]) bound to a zero topic since Chinese

allows zero topics that are interpreted as discoursally bound to the initial topic of a topic chain (Huang 1984: 555). In other words, (39) can be reanalyzed as (43) as follows:

(43) [e_i TOP] e_i saw Lisi

The zero topic is identified by an NP in a superordinate clause or in the preceding clause. It is in an operator position c-commanding the sentence and coindexing with the zero subject. The sentence is well-formed since the zero subject is a variable Ā-bound by a zero operator. On the other hand, Genuine zero pronominals can also occur in Chinese sentences. For example, the EC in (40) above can be a true pronominal since it can be properly A-bound by *Zhang* (schematized in English in 44a below), the closest nominal element coindexing it (there being no Agr). In addition, it can be a variable bound by a zero topic (44b below). The sentence is therefore ambiguous in Chinese, with the EC referring either to Zhang (as a pronominal) or to a discourse topic distinct from Zhang (as a variable).

(44) a. As a pronominal:
       Zhangsan$_i$ said   [e_i see him le]

      b. As a variable:
       [e_j TOP] Zhangsani said [e_j see him le]

Huang further argues that while a zero subject can be a pronominal, a variable, or both, a zero object in Chinese can only be a variable, not a pronominal. For example, the EC in sentence (41) is analyzed as a variable bound to a zero topic, presented in (45) below.

(45) [e_i TOP] Zhang saw e_i

However, zero object cannot be a pronominal because of the interaction of CGR and Disjoint Reference (Condition B of the Binding Theory). Disjoint Reference (DJR) is given as follows (Huang 1984: 552):

Disjoint Reference (DR):
A pronominal must be free in its governing category.

Now suppose the EC in (45) is a pronominal. Then by GCR it must be coindexed with a nominal element within its own clause, i.e., the subject *Zhang*. Since a zero pronominal is by assumption a pronoun, it is also subject to DJR, which requires it to be free in its GC (disjoint from the clause subject). This leads to a contradiction, and hence the EC in (45) cannot be a pronominal. Similarly, the EC in (42) can only be a variable bound to a zero topic, which is schematized as follows:

(46) [e_i TOP] *Zhang shuo ta kanjian* e_i

It cannot be a pronominal again because of the reduction from the GCR and DJR. Therefore, Huang concludes, zero object in Chinese can never be a pronominal, and in this respect, Chinese, a cool language (with no verb morphology at all), is not different from other medium languages like English (with meager verb morphology), or hot languages like Spanish (with rich verb morphology) in the world (Huang 1984: 557).

Huang's notion of zero topic has developed GB theories to some extent in dealing with zero anaphors in languages like Chinese that do not have verb agreement whatsoever, it nevertheless cannot adequately account for the general distribution of zero anaphora in Chinese discourse. First, it cannot handle the issue of inferences such as the ECs in sentences (17-18) in the Section 4, restated below in (47-48).

(47) Lu Yeming$_i$ took the sack-opening, e_i threw e_i (the sack) onto his shoulder, and carried e_k (the wheat) to the mill to grind.

(48) Huar started to cry. Xiao-chi quickly covered her mouth, he was afraid his parents would hear e (the cry).

As shown by the two passages, the zero anaphors do not refer to any overtly mentioned NPs in the preceding clause, their respective referents (as indicated by the NPs in the parentheses) are simply inferred. Since there is no overt NP-antecedent expressed anywhere in the preceding clause(s), there is nothing for each of the zero anaphors to be identified and coindexed with. The zero anaphors in (47-48) can only be inferred by the hearer based on semantic, pragmatic knowledge and contextual information shared by the speakers of the language. The zero anaphors in sentences like (47-48) cannot therefore be explained on pure syntactic factors.

Second, Huang's notion of zero topic can hardly handle the problem of multiple zero anaphors in a sentence. For example, the second clause in (47) above actually contains both a zero subject and a zero object, as given in (49) below.

(49) e_i threw e_j onto his shoulder

According to Huang, both ECs (a zero subject in the main clause and a zero object) in (49) are variables, which "requires one to assume that a sentence can have multiple topics" (p. 555). Putting aside the technical problems with multiple topicalization, Chinese rarely topicalizes both subject (e_i) and object (e_j) in the same sentence. (50-51) below are not acceptable in Chinese.

*(50) John$_i$, Bill$_j$, e_i see e_j

*(51) John$_i$, Bill$_j$, e_i hit e_j

Huang, however, does give an example (52 below) to show that Chinese can have multiple topics.

(52)   *Zhangsan$_i$, naben shu$_j$, tai hen xihuan* e$_j$
      (name)   that   book   he   very   like
      'Zhangsan, that book, he likes (it) very much'.

Though (52) is a well-formed Chinese sentence, it does not exhibit 'multiple topicalization' as Huang claims. What gets topicalized in (52) is only the object 'that book' which leaves a trace behind; Zhangsan, on the other hand, is left-dislocated which is base-generated and leaves no gap in the sentence. Again, syntactic rules and constraints cannot solve the problem of multiple zero anaphors in a sentence.

     Third, Huang's analysis of the asymmetry between zero subject and object in Chinese does not seem to exist in Chinese. Counter-examples are ample to show that zero objects in Chinese are not always variables as Huang analyzes. The zero objects in the following sentences are not variables since they are coindexed with the matrix subject (also see Xu 1986).

(53)   *ta$_i$ zong yao bieren zhaogu* e$_i$
      he   always   want   someone   take-care
      'He always wants someone to take care of (him)'

(54)   *haizi$_i$ yiwei mama yao zebei* e$_i$ *le*
      child   think   mother   want   blame
      'The child thought the mother would reprimand (him)'

Neither of the zero object in (53-54) is a variable since it is not A-free. Not only is it not a variable, it cannot be identified with any of the four empty categories recognized by GB theories. It is not an anaphor since it is free in its governing category; it is not a PRO since it receives the Objective Case; and it is not a pronominal because of the contradiction deduced from the GCR and DJR.

In summary, the formal analysis proposed by Huang (1984) cannot fully account for the problem of zero anaphora in Chinese discourse. First, zero topic is not adequate enough to cover the general distribution and reference of zero anaphora, second, the asymmetry between empty subject and object is more apparent than real, and third, some of the zero anaphora such as those in (53) and (54) cannot even be described by any of the existing ECs in GB theories.

6. Conclusion

The present study discusses the distribution and reference of zero anaphora in Chinese discourse with quantified text analyses, and illustrates that the occurrence of zero anaphora is not as free as many prior studies have claimed, but constrained, to a large extent, by a discourse-pragmatic principle. The study demonstrates that, first, the zero subject in Chinese discourse appears to be a grammaticalized phenomenon, and second, the employment of Chinese pronominalization in written narratives is mainly a reader-oriented process, by which the writer tries to signal the reader of the thematic coherence or discontinuity of the discourse in order to help the reader build a structural representation congruent with his/her own. The study, taking into consideration pragmatic information and discourse properties, can not only describe the basic patterns of zero anaphora distribution, but also predict, to a large extent, when, where, and why it may not occur in Chinese discourse.

Notes

1. The author is indebted to Talmy Givón and Russ Tomlin for their invaluable comments on earlier drafts of this article. This study was supported in part by SSHRC postdoctoral fellowship No. 756-92-0112.
2. OM = Object Marker.

References

Anderson, A., Garrod S.C. and A.J. Sanford. 1983. "The accessibility of pronominal antecedents as a function of episode shifts in narrative text." *Quarterly Journal of Experimental Psychology* 35A: 427-440.

Ariel, M. 1985. "The discourse functions of given information." *Theoretical Linguistics* 12: 99-113.

Bolinger, D. 1979. "Pronouns in discourse." In *Syntax and Semantics 12: Discourse and Syntax*, T. Givón (ed.), 289-309. New York: Academic Press.

Brown, C. 1983. "Topic continuity in written English." In *Topic continuity in discourse: Quantitative cross-language studies*, T. Givón (ed.), 113-141. Amsterdam: John Benjamins.

Brown, G. and G. Yule. 1983. *Discourse Analysis*. Cambridge: Cambridge University Press.

Chafe, W. 1987. "Cognitive constraints on information flow." In *Coherence and grounding in discourse*, R.S. Tomlin (ed.), 21-51. Amsterdam: John Benjamins.

Chen, P. 1986. Referential Introducing and Tracking in Chinese Narratives. Unpublished PhD thesis, UCLA.

Cheng, R. 1991. *The aged*. Shanghai: Shanghai Art and Literature Press.

Chomsky, N. (1982). Some concepts and consequences of the theory of government and binding. Cambridge: The MIT Press.

Clark, H.H. and E.V. Clark. 1977. *Psychology and Language: An Introduction to Psycholinguistics*. Harcourt Brace Jovanovich Inc.

Denker, H. 1989. *Robert, my son*. Montreal, Quebec: Morrow and Company, Inc.

Du Bois, J.W. 1985. "Competing motivations." In *Iconicity in syntax*, J. Haiman (ed.), 343-365. Amsterdam: John Benjamins.

Gernsbacher, M.A. 1990. *Language comprehension as structure building*. Hillsdale, New Jersey: Lawrence Erlbaum.

Givón, T. 1979. *On understanding grammar*. New York: Academic Press.

Givón, T. 1983. "Topic continuity and word order pragmatics in Ute." In *Topic continuity in discourse: Quantitative cross-language studies*, T. Givón (ed.), 343-363. Amsterdam: John Benjamins.

Givón, T. 1989. *Mind, code and context: Essays in pragmatics*. New Jersey: Erlbaum.

Givón, T. 1992. *English Grammar: A Function-based Introduction*, Vol. I and II. Amsterdam: John Benjamins.

Henderson. 1948. *Handbook of Japanese grammar*. Cambridge: The Riverside Press.

Hinds. 1982. *Ellipsis in Japanese*. Edmonton, Alberta: Linguistics Research, Inc.

Huang, C.J. 1984. "On the distribution and reference of empty pronouns." *Linguistic Inquiry* 15 (4): 531-574.

Karmiloff-Smith, A. 1980. "Psychological processes underlying pronominalization and non-pronominalization in children's connected discourse." *In Papers from the parasession on pronouns and anaphora*, J. Dreiman and A.E. Ojeda (eds.), 231-250. Chicago: Chicago Linguistic Society.

Keenen, E.L. 1976. "Towards a universal definition of 'subject'." In *Subject and Topic*, C.N. Li (ed.), 303-333. New York: Academic Press.

Kuno, S. and E. Kaburaki. 1978. Empathy and syntax. Linguistic Inquiry 8: 627-672

Lasnik, H. and J. Uriagereka. 1986. A course in GB syntax: Lectures on binding and empty categories. Cambridge: The MIT Press.

Li, C.I. 1985. Participant Anaphora in Mandarin Chinese. Unpublished PhD thesis, The University of Florida.

Li, C.N. and S. Thompson. 1979. "Third person pronouns and zero-pronouns in Chinese discourse." In *Discourse and Syntax*, T. Givón (ed.), 311-335. New York: Academic Press.

Li, C.N. and S. Thompson. 1981. *Mandarin Chinese: A functional reference grammar*. Berkeley and Los Angeles: University of California Press.

Luk, K.C. 1977. Interpretation of Coreference Relations in the Use of the Pronoun ta and the PRO-form 0 in Mandarin Chinese. Unpublished PhD Thesis, University of Pennsylvania.

Pu, M.M. 1995. "Anaphoric patterning in English and Mandarin narrative production." *Discourse Processes* 19(2): 279-300.

Pu, M.M. and Y. Wang. 1993. "Syntactic correlates of discourse functions." *Toronto Working Papers of Linguistics*, 509-524. Toronto, Canada.

Schank, R.C. and R.P. Abelson. 1977. *Scripts, plans, goals and understanding*. Hillsdale, New Jersey: Erlbaum.

Sun, C. and T. Givón. 1985. "On the so-called SOV word order in Mandarin Chinese." *Language* 61: 329-351.

Tao, L. 1994. "Topic choice, switch reference and zero anaphora: The on-line construction of grammar." *Proceedings of the Fourth International Symposium on Chinese Languages and Linguistics*. Taiwan: Academia Sinica.

Tomlin, R.S. 1987. "Linguistic reflections of cognitive events." In *Coherence and grounding in discourse*, R.S. Tomlin (ed.), 455-480. Amsterdam: John Benjamins.

Tomlin, R.S. and M.M. Pu. 1991. "The management of reference in Mandarin discourse." *Cognitive Linguistics* 2(1): 65-93.

Tyler, L. and L. Marselen-Wilson. 1982. "The resolution of discourse anaphors: some outline studies." *Text* 2: 263-291.

van Dijk, T. and T. Kintsch. 1983. *Strategies in Discourse Comprehension*. New York: Academic Press.

Wright, and T. Givón. 1987. "The pragmatics of indefinite reference." *Studies in Language* 11(1): 27-71.

Ye, X. 1982. *The Years that Slipped By*. Bejing, China Youth Press.

Xu, L. 1986. "Free Empty Category." *Linguistic Inquiry* 17(1): 75-93.

Zhang, J. 1984. *The Leaden Wings*. Beijing: People's Literature Press.

Dative Shifting and Double Objects in Sahaptin

Noel Rude

Universidad de Sonora

1. Introduction

This paper looks at dative shifting and double object constructions in Sahaptin, an American Indian language of the Pacific Northwest of the United States. Dative shifting and double objects occur in ditransitive clauses, causative constructions, and in complex sentences with nominalized complements. In the latter, complete clause union is involved even though the complement verb remains a separate word. The question asked is whether, in all three construction types, it is possible to specify one object as the direct object. The conclusion, after pitting morphology against accessibility to syntactic processes, is that it is indeed possible.

The first part of the paper examines the coding strategies for grammatical relations in Sahaptin, the dissociation of the direct object from the semantic role of patient, and the relevant behavioral tests for direct objecthood. Though much of the data in this paper is not really representative of texts, it is constructable and interpretable from the basic linguistic resources that are found in texts. And it demonstrates the reality of grammatical relations and their complex interplay in a language in which they are not in any way derivative of constituent order.[1]

2. Transitivity

Transitivity is not determined positionally in Sahaptin, but rather morphologically. It is also necessary to view transitivity in Sahaptin as existing on two levels, a semantic level and a syntactic (or grammatical) level. Sahaptin verbs, for example, have semantic valencies which are intransitive (i.e. *wá* 'be', *wína* 'go', *tíya* 'laugh', etc.), unitransitive (i.e. *tuxʷína* 'shoot', *yík[n]* 'hear', etc.), and ditransitive (e.g. *ní* 'give', *tiyánp* 'take away', etc.). But it is not simply the occurrence of a semantically transitive verb with overt patient NP that determines syntactic transitivity in Sahaptin. It is, rather, morphology which marks a direct object and, as we will see, syntactic transitivity.

2.1. *Morphological features*

2.1.1. *Nomimal case-marking morphology*
Subject NPs have no case marking, either as intransitive subjects (1) or as transitive subjects in active/direct constructions (2). Object NPs are case marked with *-na* (NW *-nan*) (2):

(1) *i-winán-a   iwínš iníit-yaw*
     3NOM-go-PST man   house-ALL
     'The man went to the house' (CR)

(2) *i-q'ínun-a   iwínš iníit-<u>na</u>*
     3NOM-see-PST man   house-OBJ
     'The man saw the house' (CR)

When 3rd person acts upon a Speech Act Participant (i.e. upon a 1st or 2nd person object), the 3rd person subject NP is case marked with *-nɨm* (ex. 3). For want of a better term, I generally label *-nɨm* as "ergative" or "inverse ergative", even though its domain is restricted semantically to only a subset of transitive subjects.

(3) *i-q'ínun-a=aš   iwínš-<u>nɨm</u>*
     3NOM-see-PST=1SG   man-ERG
     'The man saw me' (CR, NW)

In inverse constructions (see §3.4 below), 3rd person transitive NP subjects are case marked associative with *-in* (ex. 5). Ex. 4 contrasts the associative function of *-in*.

(4) *iwínš pa-wiyánawi-ya   isx̣íp-in*
     man 3PL.NOM-arrive-PST younger.brother-ASSOC
     'The man arrived with his younger brother'

(5) *iwínš-na pá-q'inun-a isx̣íp-in*
     man-OBJ INV-see-PST younger.brother-ASSOC
     'The man was seen by his younger brother' (CR)

2.1.2. *Pronominal prefixes*
The verb agrees with 3rd person arguments via a set of pronominal prefixes. The 3rd person nominative prefix *i-* marks subjects in intransitive clauses (6) and in transitive clauses (7). The plural equivalent is *pa-* (8), (9).[2]

(6) *i-wiyánawi-ya*
     3NOM-arrive-PST
     'He arrived'

(7) *i-twánan-a   miyánaš-na*
     3NOM-follow-PST child-OBJ
     'He followed the child'

(8) *pa-wiyánawi-ya*
     3PL.NOM-arrive-PST
     'They arrived'

(9) *pa-twánan-a   miyánaš-na*
     3PL.NOM-follow-PST child-OBJ
     'They followed the child'

The pronominal *á-* (*áw-* before a glottal) codes a 3rd person absolutive argument, i.e. it codes the subject in intransitive clauses and the object in transitive clauses. In the Columbia River and Northeast dialects, however, *á-* codes only possessor subjects in intransitive clauses (10), and 3rd person objects in transitive clause only when the subject is a SAP (11). For the purposes of this paper the relevant use is as an objective pronominal. Note that *á-* has no plural equivalent, coding both singular and plural arguments. The inverse marker *pá-* will be discussed in section 2.2.3. below.

(10) *á̱-wiyanawi-ya pšít*
      3ABS-arrive-PST father
      'His/her/their father arrived'

(11) *á̱-tuuk-šan-a=aš*
      3ABS-see-IMPV-PST=1SG
      'I saw him/her/it/them' (NE)

2.1.3. *Pronominal enclitics*

Speech Act Participants (SAP) are obligatorily coded by 2nd position pronominals when they are actants or core grammatical relations (see Tesnière 1959, Perlmutter 1980), i.e. the grammatical relations of subject and direct object as opposed to oblique case relations. The 1st person pronominal =*naš*, for example, codes an intransitive subject in (12), a transitive subject in (13), and a direct object in (14).

These 2nd position pronominals are markers of the direct object (as in 14), and their absense indicates nonobject status. For example, the lack of =*naš* in (15) shows that the 1st person benefactive is not a direct object.

(12) *wiyánawi-š=naš*
      arrive-PF=1SG
      'I have arrived'

(13) *ɨwínš-na=naš á-q'inu-ša*
      man-OBJ=1SG 3ABS-see-IMPV
      'I see the man' (CR, NW)

(14) *ɨwínš-nɨm=naš i-q'ínu-ša*
      man-ERG=1SG 3NOM-see-IMPV
      'The man sees me' (CR, NW)

(15) *šiʔíx̣ i-wá   in-mí-yay*
      good 3NOM-be 1SG-GEN-BEN
      'It is good for me' (NE)

2.2. Disassociation of direct object from the semantic patient

That the Sahaptin object is a true grammatical object and not simply a patient marking strategy can be seen in the following applicative constructions. Examples (16) and (17) both have semantic allatives and both share the same propositional structure. Example (16) is coded as an intransitive clause with oblique allative NP, whereas example (17) is coded as a transitive clause in which the allative argument is the grammatical object and its semantic case role is marked in the verb by the directive suffix -*áwan*. Though the directive occurs most often in texts with human objects, examples with nonhuman objects, as in (17), are also found.

(16) *iwínš i-winán-a   iníit-yaw*
man   3NOM-go-PST house-ALL
'The man went to the house' (CR)

(17) *iwínš i-winan-awán-a iníit-na*
man   3NOM-go-DIR-PST house-OBJ
'The man went to the house' (CR)

Similarly, an associative argument can be advanced to grammatical object and its associative case role marked in the verb and hence transitivize the verb, as in (19). In the intransitive equivalent (18) the associative argument causes plural subject-verb agreement.

(18) *tílaaki pa-wiyánawi-ya   iwínš-in*
woman 3PL.NOM-arrive-PST man-ASSOC
'The woman arrived with the man' (CR)

(19) *tílaaki i-wiyánawi-twan-a iwínš-na*
woman 3NOM-arrive-ASSOC-PST man-OBJ
'The woman arrived with the man' (CR)

A benefactive object in a transitive clause can be coded as an oblique NP (20) or it can be made the grammatical object (21). In the latter construction, which is more likely in discourse when the benefactive argument is human, the benefactive case role is marked by verbal suffix.

(20) *áw-ani-ya=aš   k'úsi-yay tawtnúk-na*
3ABS-make-PST=1SG horse-BEN medicine-OBJ
'I made the medicine for the horse' (CR)

(21) *áw-ani-yay-a=aš*   *k'úsi-na tawtnúk*
3ABS-make-BEN-PST=1SG horse-OBJ medicine
'I made the horse the medicine' (CR)

3.   Behavior and control criteria for objecthood

We discuss here five grammatical constructions ('processes') that depend on an NP being the direct object. In four of these — reflexive, reciprocal, possessive-reflexive and passive, syntactic de-transitivization is involved. This is not true of the inverse clause, which remains syntactically transitive. All five constructions are equally sensitive to the semantic and/or pragmatic status of the direct object and thus provide tests for its identification.

3.1. *Reflexive*

The reflexive clause is marked by two different verbal prefixes, *piná-* for singular reflexives (22), (24) and *pamá-* for plural (23), (25). It applies when the subject is co-referential with the direct object, but not with an oblique argument (26).

(22) *tílaaki piná-q'inu-ša*
woman SG.REFL-see-IMPV
'The woman sees herself' (CR, NW)

(23) *tílaaki-ma pamá-q'inu-ša*
woman-PL PL.REFL-see-IMPV
'The women see themselves' (CR, NW)

(24) *piná-q'inu-ša=aš*
SG.REFL-see-IMPV=1SG
'I see myself' (CR, NW)

(25) *pamá-q'inu-ša=ataš*
PL.REFL-see-IMPV=1PL.EXC
'We see ourselves' (CR, NW)

(26) *i-wínp-a*   *k'úsi pinmiláyk'ay*
3NOM-get/buy-PST horse 3SG.BEN
'He bought the horse for himself' (CR)

3.2. *Reciprocal*

The reciprocal is marked by the verbal prefix ***pápa-*** (27), (28). Like the reflexive, it is sensitive only to reciprocality between subject and direct object.

(27) *pápa-qaʔan-ša=ataš*
RECIP-respect-IMPV=1PL.EXC
'We (exclusive) respect each other'

(28) *pápa-qaʔan-ša*
RECIP-respect-IMPV
'They respect each other'

3.3. *Antipassive and co-referential possessed objects*

The case marking of nonhuman objects is optional in Sahaptin. The nominal suffix *-na* serves to disambiguate case roles, a function generally redundant when the agent is human and the patient is not. Objective NP case marking also indicates discourse/pragmatic relevance. Constructions in which there is no morphological marker of the object I call the antipassive, e.g. 30. The fully transitive equivalent with direct object case marked is illustrated in (29) below.

(29) *tílaaki   i-nánan-a   k'úsi-na*
woman 3NOM-bring-PST horse-OBJ
'The woman brought the horse'

(30) *tílaaki   i-nánan-a   k'úsi*
woman 3NOM-bring-PST horse
'The woman brought the horse'

The demotion of the object via antipassivization is scalar, as illustrated in (31)-(35) below. Nominal case marking may be stripped while object-verb agreement survives (32). Or both markers may be missing (33). And there may be either pronominal (34) or zero anaphora (35). Most dialects of Sahaptin generally do not permit zero-anaphoric subjects.

(31) *á-nanan-a=aš   k'úsi-na*
3ABS-bring-PST=1SG horse-OBJ
'I brought the horse'

(32) *á-nanan-a=aš*   *k'úsi*
3ABS-bring-PST=1SG horse
'I brought the horse'

(33) *nánan-a=aš*   *k'úsi*
bring-PST=1SG horse
'I brought the horse'

(34) *á-nanan-a=aš*
3ABS-bring-PST=1SG
'I brought it'

(35) *nánan-a=aš*
bring-PST=1SG
'I brought (it)'

When an object is possessed, it is not case marked with -*na* (37). And when the possessor is coreferential with the subject, obligatory antipassivization occurs. That is, the possessed object displays neither nominal case marking nor verbal agreement (37). Since such a construction is ambiguous — with the antipassive which simply demotes an unpossessed patient — an emphatic pronoun is sometimes used to reinforces this meaning (38).

(36) *i-túuk-ata-šan-a*   *k'úsi-na*
3NOM-see-go.for.purpose-IMPV-PST horse-OBJ
'He went to see the horse' (NE)

(37) *i-túuk-ata-šan-a*   *k'úsi*
3NOM-see-go.for.purpose-IMPV-PST horse
'He went to see his own (or the/a) horse' (NE)

(38) *i-túuk-ata-šan-a*   *pinmín k'úsi*
3NOM-see-go.for.purpose-IMPV-PST 3SG.GEN horse
'He went to see his own horse' (NE)

When the possessor of the object is not co-referential with the subject, it is promoted to direct object, and its possessive status is coded in the verb (39).

Since the same suffix, the so-called 'applicative', marks both promoted possessors and promoted benefactive objects, (39) could also mean: 'He went to see the horse for him (him = someone else)'.

(39) *i-túuk-ay-ta-šan-a*   *paaná   k'úsi*
      3NOM-see-GEN-go.for.purpose-IMPV-PST 3SG.OBJ horse
      'He went to see his (someone else's) horse' (NE)

Kinship terms case-marked with the special objective marker *-pa* are
by default co-referentially possessed, as in (40). If the possessor is not coreferential, the same applicative construction as in (39) is used, as in (41).
Here the possessed noun is not case marked since the possessor has been
promoted to direct object.

(40) *i-túuk-ata-šan-a*   *smítway-pa*
      INV-see-go.for.purpose-IMPV-PST spouse-OBJ
      'He went to see his (his own) spouse' (NE)

(41) *i-túuk-ay-ta-šan-a*   *smítway*
      INV-see-GEN-go.for.purpose-IMPV-PST spouse
      'He went to see his (someone else's) spouse' (NE)

3.4. Direct vs. inverse clauses

Third person referent tracking is further accomodated by the contrast
between active/direct (42), (36) and inverse (43) voice constructions. The
inverse in Sahaptin is marked by the verbal prefix *pá-* and the agent NP,
if present, is marked with the associative case, which now acts as the
obviative marker.[3] The patient NP must keep its direct object case marking (*-na*), and a 3/3 transitive valancy is maintained.

In the active/direct, the subject tends to refer to the topic of the preceding main-line clause. In the inverse, on the other hand, it is the object
which most commonly provides such referential continuity. In some narrative texts the inverse is almost as frequent as the active/direct in frequency
(Rude 1994).

(42) *iwínš i-nánan-a*   *tílaaki-na*
      man   3NOM-bring-PST woman-OBJ
      'The man brought the woman'

(43) *iwínš-in*   *pá-nanan-a*   *tílaaki-na*
      man-ASSOC INV-bring-PST woman-OBJ
      'The man brought the woman'
      ('The woman was brought by the man')

This discourse-pragmatic function of the Sahaptin inverse is reminiscent of similar constructions in certain North American languages (Algonquian) in one more respect, that of obligatory "semantic" inversion (Rude 1994).

Obligatory semantic inversion involves the hierarchy of Speech Act Participants (SAP) as given in (44) below. In the Sahaptin active/direct with SAPs, the 1st person acts on 2nd (45). In contrast, the inverse is used when the 2nd person acts on 1st (46). Note that the "semantic" inverse in Sahaptin is marked by the same verbal prefix *pá-* used in the "pragmatic" inversion with two 3rd person arguments (43).

(44)   1st pers. > 2nd pers. > TOP-3rd pers. > not-TOP 3rd pers.

(45)   *q'ínu-ša=maš*
       see-IMPV=1SG/2SG
       'I see you' (CR, NW)

(46)   *pá-q'inu-ša=nam*
       INV-see-IMPV=2SG
       'You see me' (CR, NW)

The inverse marker *pá-*, however, is not used when a 3rd person acts upon a SAP. Instead the grammatical relation of the 3rd person argument is established by verbal agreement — *á-* for object in (47) and *i-* for subject in (48), as well as by nominal case marking — *-na* for the object in (47) vs. the "ergative" *-nɨm* for the obviate subject in (48). Example (48) illustrates the sole function of the NP case marker *-nɨm*.

(47)   *á-q'inu-ša=aš   iwínš-na*
       3NOM-see-IMPV=1SG man-OBJ
       'I see the man' (CR, NW)

(48)   *i-q'ínu-ša=aš   iwínš-nɨm*
       3NOM-see-IMPV=1SG man-ERG
       'The man sees me' (CR, NW)

Note that the prefix *pá-* codes the presence of an individuated object and a singular subject. There are alternate direct-inverse constructions, as in (49) vs. (50) below, which are used in cases when the subject is plural.[4] There is no associative case marking on the plural obviate subject of this inverse (50). The plural marker *-ma* does not co-occur with the associative obviate marker *-in*, nor with the "ergative" obviate marker *-nɨm*.

(49) *awínš-ma pa-q'ínu-ša*   *tílaaki-na*
men-PL   3PL.NOM-see-IMPV woman-OBJ
'The men see the woman' (CR)

(50) *awínš-ma patá-q'inu-ša*   *tílaaki-na*
men-PL   3PL.NOM/3SG.OBJ-see-IMPV woman-OBJ
'The men see the woman or The woman is seen by the men'
(CR)

3.5. *Passive clauses*

Example (51) below illustrates the Sahaptin passive clause, which syntactically closely resembles its English counterpart. The verb is stativized, and tense and subject agreement are marked on the auxiliary 'be'. However, the agent cannot be overtly expressed (in a "by-phrase") in the Sahaptin passive.

(51) *miyánaš sápsik'ʷan-i i-wač-á*
child   teach-PP   3NOM-be-PST
'The child was taught'

Though rather infrequent in discourse — less than 5% of transitive verbs in narrative texts — the Sahaptin passive is readily accepted by speakers in direct elicitation, and can thus provide another test for direct objecthood.

4. Dative shifting and objects of bi-transitive clauses

4.1. *Background*

Bi-transitive clauses often display two objects whose nominal case-marking may be identical. Which of these two objects is the direct object? In this section I attempt to answer this question by applying the various behavior-and-control tests to this construction.

In Sahaptin, when the patient in a bi-transitive clause is a SAP, it is obligatorily the direct object, as in (52) and (53) below. The 2nd-position pronominal clitics *=aš* and *=am* agree with such direct objects in (52) and (53), respectively. In such clauses, the dative object is an indirect object, case-marked by the allative *-yaw* (see (16) above). A human dative in such clauses must also have the genitive suffix preceding the dative. The emphatic object pronouns *ína* 'me' and *imaná* 'you' are optional.[5]

    (52) *pa-ní-ya=aš*   *(ína)*   *miyuux̱-mí-yaw*
          3PL.NOM-give-PST=1SG 1SG.OBJ chief-GEN-ALL
          'They gave me to the chief' (CR, NE)

    (53) *pa-ní-ya=am*   *(imaná) in-mí-yaw*
          3PL.NOM-give-PST=2SG 2SG.OBJ 1SG-GEN-ALL
          'They gave you to me' (CR, NE)

When the patient is 3rd person human, dative shifting is optional. Thus, the patient is direct object in (54) but the dative is the direct object in (55). When this happens the patient loses its erstwhile direct-object case marking.

    (54) *pa-ní-ya*   *tílaaki-na* *miyuux̱-mí-yaw*
          3PL.NOM-give-PST woman-OBJ chief-GEN-ALL
          'They gave the woman to the chief' (CR, NE)

    (55) *pa-ní-ya*   *tílaaki miyúux̱-na*
          3PL.NOM-give-PST woman chief-OBJ
          'They gave the woman to the chief' (CR, NE)

When the 3rd person patient is non-human, dative shifting is obligatory.

    (56) *pa-ní-ya*   *k'úsi miyúux̱-na*
          3PL.NOM-give-PST horse chief-OBJ
          'They gave the horse to the chief' (CR, NE)

Verbs of deprivation are also bi-transitives in Sahaptin. When the patient is human (and a proper context obtains), informants allow sentences such as (57) with a direct-object patient and an oblique-ablative source. This may be compared with (58), where the source has been promoted to direct object.

    (57) *pa-páx̱ʷi-ya*   *miyúux̱-na natitayt-mí-knik*
          3PL.NOM-steal-PST chief-OBJ person-GEN-ABL
          'They stole the chief from the people' (NE)

    (58) *pa-páx̱ʷi-ya*   *miyúux̱-na tílaaki*
          3PL.NOM-steal-PST chief-OBJ woman
          'They stole the woman from the chief' (CR, NE)

As with other bi-transitives, when the patient is a SAP, it is obligatorily the direct object (59). And when the patient is non-human, dative shifting is obligatory (60).

(59) *pa-páx^wi-ya=aš*   *miyuux-mí-knik*
3PL.NOM-steal-PST=1SG chief-GEN-ABL
'They stole me from the chief' (NE)

(60) *pa-páx^wi-ya*   *miyúux-na k'úsi*
3PL.NOM-steal-PST chief-OBJ horse
'They robbed the chief of [his] horse' (NE)

4.2. *The reflexive test*

Since reflexivization in Sahaptin applies only when the subject is coreferential with the direct object, it can serve as a test of direct objecthood. Thus, dative-shifting cannot have occurred when the reflexive involves coreference with the patient in (61). And dative-shifting must have occurred when the reflexive involves coreference with the dative (62).

(61) *piná-ni-ya*   *miyuux-mí-yaw*
SG.REFL-give-PST chief-GEN-ALL
'He gave himself to the chief' (CR, NE)

(62) *piná-ni-ya*   *xaxáyk^w*
SG.REFL-give-PST money
'He gave himself the money'

Note that where dative-shifting did not occur (61), the dative goal is still coded as an indirect object. On the other hand, where dative-shifting did occur (62), the patient is not case marked. In isolation, the only thing in (61) and (62) that distinguishes whether the patient or dative is the coreferent object is the overt presence — with case marking or the lack thereof — of the non-object NP.

Only an indirect object (61) or a demoted patient (62) can occur in a reflexive bi-transitive clause. A case-marked object noun cannot occur, as is evident from the ungrammaticality of (63). This is so because the reflexive is a de-transitivized clause with only one grammatical argument, its subject (64).

(63) *piná-ni-ya   miyúux̣-na
      SG.REFL-give-PST chief-OBJ
      (*'He gave himself to the chief'(CR, NE))

(64) piná-ni-ya   miyúux̣
      SG.REFL-give-PST chief
      'The chief gave himself away' (CR, NE)

In sum then, the reflexive test identifies one of the two objects in the reflexive clause as the direct object, and confirms that dative shifting involves the promotion of the dative and the demotion of the patient from objecthood.

4.3. *The reciprocal test*

The same principles that control reflexivization also apply in reciprocal clauses. When the reciprocal relation involves the subject and patient in a bi-transitive clause, the dative must remain an oblique since shifting cannot have occurred (65). The co-reference can involve the subject and dative only if dative-shifting has occurred. Thus in (66) dative-shifting is obligatory with a non-human patient. As in the reflexive clause, and for the same reasons, a marked object NP cannot appear in a reciprocal clause (67).

(65) pápa-ni-ya=taš   miyuux̣-mí-yaw
      RECIP-give-PST=1PL.EXC chief-GEN-ALL
      'We gave each other to the chief' (CR, NE)

(66) pápa-ni-ya=taš   x̣ax̣áyk^w
      RECIP-give-PST=1PL.EXC money
      'We gave each other money'

(67) *pápa-ni-ya=taš   miyúux̣-na
      RECIP-give-PST=1PL.EXC chief-OBJ
      'We gave each other to the chief'
      'We gave each other the chief' (CR, NE)

Again, the reciprocal test suggests that only one object in the bi-transitive clause bears the grammatical relation of direct object.

4.4. *Coreferentially-possessed object test*

An undemoted patient in a bi-transitive clause is demoted by co-referential possession, and thus loses its object case marking (68). Though a stressed pronoun can emphasize this possession, the absense of case marking on the demoted patient marks it as coreferentially possessed. And when the human dative is promoted to direct object, it is similarly demoted when it is co-referentially possessed (69).

(68)   *i-páx̣ʷi-tux̣n-a*   *(pinmín) miyánaš miyuux̣-mí-knik*
      3NOM-steal-back-PST 3SG.GEN child   chief-GEN-ABL
      'He stole his child back from the chief' (NE)

(69)   *i-ní-ya*   *(pinmín) miyánaš tímaš*
      3NOM-give-PST 3SG.GEN child   book
      'He gave his child a book'

For most kin or relational nouns, however, coreferential possession is expressed by the special object suffix *-pa* (70), (71).

(70)   *i-ní-ya*   *íšta-pa   tímaš*
      3NOM-give-PST child-OBJ book
      'He gave his child a book'

(71)   *i-páx̣ʷi-ya*   *x̣áy-pa   tímaš*
      3NOM-steal-PST friend-OBJ book
      'He stole the book from his friend'

Again, one of the two objects is clearly tagged as the direct object in the bi-transitive clause.

4.5. *The inverse test*

The inverse clause is sensitive to the topicality status of the direct object. Thus in both (72) and (73) below, inversion is triggered because the topic of the preceding clause continues as a direct object. However, in the inverse clause (72), the patient is the direct object and the dative the indirect object. While in the inverse clause (73), the dative has been promoted to direct object.

(72) *ana-kúuk i-wiyánawi-ya   tílaaki*
      REL-then 3NOM-arrive-PST woman
      'When the woman arrived,

      ku   pá-ni-ya   miyuuẋ-mí-yaw
      and INV-give-PST chief-GEN-ALL
      she was given to the chief' (CR, NE)

(73) *ana-kúuk i-wiyánawi-ya   miyúuẋ*
      REL-then 3NOM-arrive-PST chief
      'When the chief arrived,

      ku   pá-ni-ya   tílaaki
      and INV-give-PST woman
      he was given the woman' (CR, NE)

The direct object is again identified unambiguously.

4.6. *The passive test*

Only the direct object of the direct/active can become the subject of the
passive. Thus, when the patient in a passive bi-transitive clause appears as
its subject, the dative must remain the indirect object (74). On the other
hand, when dative-shifting has occurred, as in (75), the dative can now be
further promoted to subject of passive.

(74) *áswan ní-yi   i-wač-á   miyuuẋ-mí-yaw*
      boy   give-PP 3NOM-be-PST chief-GEN-ALL
      'The boy was given to the chief' (CR, NE)

(75) *miyúuẋ ní-yi   i-wač-á   áswan*
      chief give-PP 3NOM-be-PST boy
      'The chief was given the boy' (CR, NE)

All our behavior-and-control criteria thus point to the same conclusion:
The bi-transitive clause in Sahaptin has only one direct object, either the
patient in the non-shifted variant, or the dative in the dative-shifted variant.
Overt morphology notwithstanding, rule-governed syntactic behavior assigns
direct objecthood in an unambiguous fashion.

5. Morphological causatives and clause union

5.1. *Background*

Morphological causativization in Sahaptin involves the verbal prefix *šapá-*.[6] The causativization of transitive verbs results in two potentially-competing direct objects — the causee and the original patient of the complement verb. Dative shifting has an expanded range of application in the causative clause, as compared to the simple bi-transitive clause. For example, when the patient is a SAP, dative-shifting can still occur in causative clauses. Thus, in (76) no dative-shifting has taken place, and consequently the 1st person patient is coded by a 2nd position pronominal. In contrast, in (77) dative-shifting has occurred, and consequently there is no 2nd position pronominal. In examples such as (77), the only way the 1st person can appear is as an object-case-marked personal pronoun.

(76) *iwinš-mí-yaw=naš pa-šapá-wawyan-a*
man-GEN-ALL=1SG 3PL.NOM-CAUS-whip-PST
'They had me whipped by the man'

(77) *iwínš-na patá-šapa-wawyan-a   ína*
man-OBJ 3PL.NOM/SG.OBJ-CAUS-whip-PST 1SG.OBJ
'They had the man whip me' (CR)

When the patient is a 3rd person human, dative-shifting can take place. Thus, compare (78) and (79).

(78) *patá-šapa-wawyan-a   miyánaš-na iwinš-mí-yaw*
3PL.NOM/SG.OBJ-CAUS-whip-PST child-OBJ   man-GEN-ALL
'They had the child whipped by the man' (CR)

(79) *patá-šapa-wawyan-a   miyánaš iwínš-na*
3PL.NOM/SG.OBJ-CAUS-whip-PST child   man-OBJ
'They had the man whip the child' (CR)

One difference between simple bi-transitive clauses and causative clauses is that when dative-shifting has occurred and both objects are human, both objects can be marked by the object suffix *-na*. Thus, compare (55) above, where the patient cannot take the suffix *-na*, with (80) below, where it can and usually does.

(80) *patá-šapa-wawyan-a*   *iwínš-na tílaaki-na*
      3PL.NOM/SG.OBJ-CAUS-whip-PST man-OBJ woman-OBJ
      'They had the man whip the woman' (CR)

(81) *tílaaki-na   patá-šapa-wawyan-a*   *iwínš-na*
      woman-OBJ 3PL.NOM/SG.OBJ-CAUS-whip-PST man-OBJ
      'They had the woman whip the man' (CR)

When double object-marking occurs, the causee and the patient are distinguished by word order — causee before patient. This is true at least in clauses derived from direct elicitation. Such double-marking is the only instance in Sahaptin where I have found word order distinguishing between grammatical relations. Thus, compare (81) above and (82) below.

(82) *iwínš-na patá-šapa-wawyan-a*   *tílaaki-na*
      man-OBJ 3PL.NOM/SG.OBJ-CAUS-whip-PST woman-OBJ
      'They had the man whip the woman' (CR)

However, rather than distinct syntactic arrangement, it is simply a matter of priority of mention.

When the patient is non-human, dative-shifting is obligatory, as in (83). This obligatoriness explains the speaker's reaction to (84). With the unshifted causee, the speaker could only interpret the patient as human.

(83) *iwínš-na patá-šapa-tkʷatan-a*   *núsux*
      man-OBJ 3PL.NOM/SG.OBJ-CAUS-eat-PST salmon
      'They had the man eat the salmon' (CR)

(84) *iwinš-mí-yaw   patá-šapa-tkʷatan-a*
      man-GEN-ALL   3PL.NOM/SG.OBJ-CAUS-eat-PST
      'They had the man "eat a person up"' (CR)

The causative of bi-transitive clauses is unattested in texts. I am thus hesitant to pronounce them valid. Yet native speakers in direct elicitation do accept such clauses, whatever that might mean, and are able to interpret them. Dative-shifting in such complex causatives appears to be governed by hierarchic considerations, i.e. CAUSEE < GOAL < PATIENT. This is illustrated in (85), (86), (87) below.

(85) *iwinš-mí-yaw=naš i-šapá-ni-ya*   *tilaaki-nmí-yaw*
man-GEN-ALL=1SG 3NOM-CAUS-give-PST woman-GEN-ALL
'He had me given to the woman by a man'

(86) *iwinš-mí-yaw=naš i-šapá-ni-ya*   *tílaaki*
man-GEN-ALL=1SG 3NOM-CAUS-give-PST woman
'He had me given the woman by a man'

(87) *iwínš-na=naš i-šapá-ni-ya*   *tílaaki*
man-OBJ=1SG 3NOM-CAUS-give-PST woman
'He had me give the woman to a man'

5.2. *The reflexive test*

When the subject is coreferential with the *patient* object of the complement clause in a causative construction, reflexivization takes place only when the *causee* has not been promoted to direct object. This can be seen in (88) below, where the causee remains an oblique NP. When the causee is promoted to DO, as in (89), the patient may retain its DO case-marking, but now reflexivization can only mark coreference between the subject and the causee:

(88) *tílaaki piná-šapa-qaʔan-šan-a*   *iwinš-mí-yaw*
woman SG.REFL-CAUS-respect-IMPV-PST man-GEN-ALL
'The woman caused herself to be respected by the man'

(89) *tílaaki piná-šapa-qaʔan-šan-a*   *iwínš-(na)*
woman SG.REFL-CAUS-respect-IMPV-PST man-OBJ
'The woman caused herself to respect the man' (CR, NE)

By the reflexive test, then, only one of the objects in the causativized transitive clause — patient in (88), causee in (89) — is the direct object of the merged clause, regardless of surface case-marking.

5.3. *The reciprocal test*

When the reciprocal test is applied to the causative construction, the results fully parallel those of reflexivization, above. Coreference involves the patient of the complement clause when dative-shifting has not applied, as in (90). But if dative-shifting has applied, coreference involves the causee, as in (91):

(90) *pápa-šapa-qaʔan-šan-a   miyuux-mí-yaw*
      RECIP-CAUS-respect-IMPV-PST chief-GEN-ALL
      'They were encouraging each other to be respected by the chief'
      (CR, NE)

(91) *pápa-šapa-qaʔan-šan-a   miyúux-na*
      RECIP-CAUS-respect-IMPV-PST chief-OBJ
      'They were encouraging each other to respect the chief' (CR, NE)

Again, only one of the two objects — patient in (90), causee in (91) — is the direct object of the merged clause.

5.4. *The inverse test*

The topical participant of the preceding clause is coded in the inverse as the direct object. In (92) below, the DO in the inverse clause is the *patient* of the complement of 'cause', and the causee is not promoted to DO. In (93) the causee has been promoted to DO in the inverse clause, while the patient may retain direct-object case marking. Though these examples are pragmatically odd and thus unlikely to occur in natural text, the speakers nonetheless have no trouble interpreting them in isolation.

(92) *ana-kúuk i-wiyánawi-ya   miyúux,*
      REL-then 3NOM-arrive-PST chief
      'When the chief arrived,

      ku pá-šapa-qaʔann-a   aswan-mí-yaw
      and INV-CAUS-respect-PST boy-GEN-ALL
      he was made to be respected by the boy' (NE)

(93) *ana-kúuk i-wiyánawi-ya   áswan,*
      REL-then 3NOM-arrive-PST boy
      'When the boy arrived,

      ku pá-šapa-qaʔann-a   miyúux-(na)
      and INV-CAUS-respect-PST chief-OBJ
      he was made to respect the chief' (NE)

5.5. *Coreference of possessed object*

When the patient of the complement of 'cause' is its direct object and it is possessed by the subject of 'cause', it cannot be case-marked with the DO suffix -*na* (94). When the causee is the direct object of the complement clause and is possessed by the subject of 'cause', it is not case-marked with -*na* (95). In (94), with a possessed patient, the causee is an oblique NP. In (95), the patient may be marked by -*na*. The true direct object in each case undergoes obligatory "stripping" of its DO case-marking.

(94)   *i-šapá-qaʔann-a*   *(pɨnmín) miyánaš miyuux̣-mí-yaw*
     3NOM-CAUS-respect-PST 3SG.GEN child   chief-GEN-ALL
     'He caused his child to be respected by the chief' (NE)

(95)   *i-šapá-qaʔann-a*   *(pɨnmín) miyánaš miyúux̣-(na)*
     3NOM-CAUS-respect-PST 3SG.GEN child   chief-OBJ
     'He caused his child to respect the chief'

5.6. *The passive test*

In the causative clause (96) below, the causee is coded as oblique NP, and in (97) as direct object.

(96)   *šuyapu-nmí-yaw*   *paʔá-šapa-qaʔann-a*   *natítayt-maaman*
     whiteman-GEN-ALL 3PL/3-CAUS-respect-PST person-PL.OBJ
     'They made the whiteman respect the Indians' (NE)

(97)   *šuyápu-na*   *paʔá-šapa-qaʔann-a*   *natítayt-maaman*
     whiteman-OBJ 3PL/3-CAUS-respect-PST person-PL.OBJ
     'They made the whiteman respect the Indians' (NE)

The passive equivalent of (96) is given in (98), the passive of (97) in (99).

(98)   *natítayt-ma pu-uč-á*   *šapá-qaʔann-i*
     person-PL   3PL.NOM-be-PST CAUS-respect-PP

     šuyapu-nmí-yaw
     whiteman-GEN-ALL

     'The Indians were made to be respected by the whiteman' (NE)

(99) *šuyápu*   *i-wač-á*   *šapá-qaʔann-i*   *natítayt-maaman*
whiteman 3NOM-be-PST CAUS-respect-PP person-PL.OBJ
'The whiteman was made to respect the Indians' (NE)

When the patient of the complement clause has been promoted to subject via passivization (98), it loses its nominal case-marking and assumes control of subject-verb agreement. (Here, due to phonological changes, via the 3rd person plural *pu-*). The causee in such cases, if it appears overtly, retains its status as an oblique NP. Note that 'by the whiteman' in (98) refers to the causee, not the causer (passives are obligatorily agentless in Sahaptin). Even though the patient of the complement clause retains its object case-marking in (99), the causee has been promoted to subject. This is evident from the fact that the causee is an unmarked NP and controls verb agreement (*i-*).

6. Object-raising from nominalized complements and dative-shifting

In equi-subjects complements of modality verbs such as 'want', or in equi-subject purpose clauses, what English codes with full lexical verbs are coded in Sahaptin by verbal suffixes. In other words, much like in the case of causatives, full clause-union takes place.

Utterance verbs do appear as lexical verbs, but take only direct-quote complements. The same is most commonly the case with cognition and perception verbs.

Although fairly rare in texts, another complementation pattern is also possible in Sahaptin, that of nominalized non-finite object clauses. In such a pattern, one finds full clause union. When the patient of the nominalized complement clause is raised to direct-object of the merged clause, as in (100) below, its agent is marked with the oblique allative suffix. But the agent of the nominalized complement clause can be promoted to DO, as in (101). This is indicated in this case by the 2nd position pronominal clitic =*aš* on the main verb (note its absence in (100)).

(100) *i-tq'íx-ša*   *in-mí-yaw*   *kíʔlawi-t*   *núsux̣-na*
3NOM-want-IMPV 1SG-GEN-ALL taste-N   salmon-OBJ
'He wants the salmon to be tasted by me' (NE)

(101) *i-tq'íx̣-ša=aš*   *kíʔlawi-t núsux̣*
     3NOM-want-IMPV=1SG taste-N   salmon
     'He wants me to taste the salmon' (NE)

Just as in the causative, the demoted patient may retain its object case-marking. Thus, 'bitterroot' in (102) below may be case-marked with *-na* even though 'woman' has been raised to object of the main clause:

(102) *tílaaki-na*   *pa-wálimsik'ʷa-šan-a*
     woman-OBJ 3PL.NOM-watch-IMPV-PST

     miyímk-t-yaw pyax̣í-(na)
     pound-N-ALL bitterroot-OBJ

     'They are watching the woman pound bitterroot' (NE)

Since in such clause-union constructions two potential objects exist, we apply our behavior-and-control tests to determine which of the two is the direct object.

6.1. The reflexive test

When the reflexive involves coreference of the subject of a main verb and the patient of a nominalized verb, the agent of the nominalized verb must be marked as oblique (103). That agent must be promoted to DO (104) before the coreference in the reflexive can apply to the agent of the nominalized complement.

(103) *piná-tuuk-šan-a=aš*   *iwinš-mí-yaw tux̣ʷína-t-yaw*
     SG.REFL-see-IMPV-PST=1SG man-GEN-ALL shoot-N-ALL
     'I saw myself being shot by the man' (NE)

(104) *piná-tuuk-šan-a=aš*   *tkʷáta-t núsux̣-(na)*
     SG.REFL-see-IMPV-PST=1SG eat-N   salmon-OBJ
     'I saw myself eating salmon' (NE)

6.2. The reciprocal test

The main-verb subject and the patient of the nominalized complement are co-referential in (105), so that the subject of the nominalized clause remains marked as oblique. In (106), on the other hand, the subject of the nominalized complement has been promoted to DO, and now partakes in the reciprocal relation. The patient of the nominalized clause in this case may still retain its object case-marking.

(105) *pápa-tq'ix̣-šan-a   iwinš-mí-yaw túukin*
      RECIP-want-IMPV-PST man-GEN-ALL see.N
      'They wanted each other to be seen by the man' (NE)

(106) *pápa-tq'ix̣-šan-a   núkši-t núsu-(na)*
      RECIP-want-IMPV-PST smell-N salmon-OBJ
      'They wanted each other to smell the salmon' (NE)

6.3. *The inverse test*

In (107) below, the object of the inverse main-clause is the *patient* of the nominalized complement, whose unpromoted agent retains oblique nominal case-marking. In (108), on the other hand, the complement-clause agent has been promoted to direct-object of the merged clause, as is evident from its status as object of the inverse. This does not stop the patient of the nominalized complement from retaining its object case-marking.

(107) *ana-kúuk i-wiyánawi-ya   áswan*
      REL-then 3NOM-arrive-PST boy
      'When the boy arrived,

      ku pá-tuuk-šan-a   wáwya-t wawyaƚa-nmí-yaw
      and INV-see-IMPV-PST whip-N   whipman-GEN-ALL
      he was seen being whipped by the whipman' (NE)

(108) *ana-kúuk i-wiyánawi-ya   wawyaƚá*
      REL-then 3NOM-arrive-PST whipman
      'When the whipman arrived,

      ku pá-tuuk-šan-a   wáwya-t áswan(i-na)
      and INV-see-IMPV-PST whip-N   boy-OBJ
      he was seen to whip the boy' (NE)

6.4. *The coreferent possession test*

In (109) below, the patient of a nominalized complement is possessed by the subject of the main verb. This coreference is marked by the relational possessed-object suffix *-pa*. In such cases, the agent of the nominalized clause verb retains its oblique case-marking. When the agent has been promoted to DO, as in (110), its coreferentiality is marked by *-pa*. The patient in (110) may retain its object case-marking *-na*.

(109) *i-tk' í-šan-a*   *išta-pa wawyała-nmí-yaw wáwya-t-pa*
   3NOM-watch-IMPV-PST son-OBJ whipman-GEN-ALL whip-N-LOC
   'He watched his son being whipped by the whipman' (NE)

(110) *i-tk' í-šan-a*   *x̣áy-pa   núsux̣-(na) tkʷáta-t-yaw*
   3NOM-watch-IMPV-PST friend-OBJ salmon-OBJ eat-N-ALL
   'He watched his friend eat the salmon' (NE)

6.5. *The passive test*

The *agent* of the nominalized complement must be promoted to DO of the merged clause before it can be made subject-of-passive (111) (such promotion that is also demanded by the semantics of the situation here). The 1st person subject of the passive 'be asked', also agent of 'eat' in (111), controls the pronominal clitic =*š* on the main verb and zero agreement on the auxiliary copula. In (112), on the other hand, where the same pronominal clitic and zero agreement is controlled by the *patient* of the nominalized verb, the agent is now marked as an oblique argument of the nominalized clause rather than an argument of the passivized main verb 'be seen'.

(111) *šápni-yi=š wač-á tkʷáta-t-yaw núsux̣*
   ask-PP=1SG be-PST eat-N-ALL   salmon
   'I was asked to eat the salmon'

(112) *q'ínun-i=š wač-á wáwya-t wawyała-nmí-yaw*
   see-PP-1SG be-PST whip-N   whipman-GEN-ALL
   'I was seen being whipped by the whipman' (CR, NW)

7. Concluding remarks

Sahaptin bi-transitive ("double object") clauses may arise from two sources — either as simple clauses with their own semantic patient and dative-recipient; or through clause-union, with both objects initially the patient and agent of a complement clause. Either way, Sahaptin bi-transitive clauses exhibit two distinct case frames for case-marking their objects. In one, schematized in (113) below, the patient is case-marked as object. The other participant, whether dative or agent, is coded as oblique. In the other frame, schematized in (114) below, both arguments may be case-marked as objects, although in the case of the patient such marking is optional.

(113) patient-**OBJ** dative/agent-**OBL**

(114) dative/agent-**OBJ** patient(-**OBJ**)

The second frame (114) may thus involve two nominals marked morphologically as direct object. But regardless of surface case-marking, all our tests, including control of pronominal agreement and all the behavior-and-control tests, clearly point out that there is no ambiguity in the grammatical behavior of the two objects. In the first case-frame (113), the patient is unambiguously the direct object. In the second (114), the dative/agent is the direct object.

The syntactic process usually referred to as "dative shifting" is indeed what can convert the first case-making frame (113) into the second (114). This is thus a promotion to DO process. While word-order is not involved in such promotion, since Sahaptin is a flexible-order language, in all other respects dative shifting in this language is clearly a relation-changing process.

Notes

1. According to Rigsby (1965), the Sahaptin dialects fall into three main clusters, Northwest Sahaptin (which includes Klikitat, Yakima, etc.), Northeast (Walla Walla, Wanapam, Palouse, etc.), and Columbia River (Umatilla, Warm Springs, etc.). All share the same grammatical phenomena described in this paper, most of which is also shared with Nez Perce, a language closely related to Sahaptin (though not mutually intelligible). Sahaptin and Nez Perce together comprise the Sahaptian family of languages. Examples in this paper are all from Sahaptin, and where vocabulary or pronunciation limits them to a specific dialect the dialect is noted. The data in this paper, though much of it consists of sentences which one simply would not encounter in discourse and which another native speaker might reject, was always interpretable as translated, even though it was often only approved after creating an appropriate context. Funding for research was provided in part by grants from Cátedras Patrimonial Nivel II (CONACYT, México, 1994) and the National Science Foundation (BNS-

8919577). Abbreviations are as follows: 1 First person; 2 Second person; 3 Third person; ABL Ablative; ABS Absolutive; ALL Allative; ASSOC Associative; BEN Benefactive; CAUS Causative; CR Columbia River Sahaptin; DIR Directive; DO Direct object; ERG Ergative; EXC Exclusive; GEN Genitive; IMPV Imperfective; INC Inclusive; INV Inverse; N Nominalizer; NE Northeast Sahaptin; NOM Nominative; NW Northwest Sahaptin; OBJ Direct object; PF Present perfect; PL Plural; PP Past participle; PST Past; RECIP Reciprocal; REFL Reflexive; SAP Speech Act Participant; SG Singular.

2. Though there is no grammatical gender in Sahaptin, for simplicity's sake I have generally translated the 3rd person pronominals as 'he' and 'him'. Neither is definiteness overtly coded, but I have generally translated objects (which are as likely indefinite as definite) as definite.

3. It is tempting to consider the inverse *pá-* as a stressed variety of the plural nominative *pa-*. Though the former mediates between SAP as well as between 3rd person arguments (see below), the latter, though currently a 3rd person plural subject pronominal in Sahaptin, was historically also indifferent to person. In Nez Perce the cognate morphemes are /pé-/ which codes only 3/3 transitive action, and /pe-/ which marks subjects plural whatever the person. The nominal prefix *pa-* marks distributive plurals.

4. The CR prefix *patá-* has a NE equivalent *paʔá-*, and in NW Sahaptin its equivalent is marked by the co-occurrence of the 2nd position enclitic *=pat* (a NW 3rd person plural pronominal) and the 3rd person absolutive *á-*.

5. For further discussion of Sahaptin ditransitives, see Rude (1992).

6. Other forms of this causative prefix exist, but *šapá-* is the productive one.

References

Keenan, Edward L. 1976. "Towards a universal definition of 'subject'." In *Subject and Topic*, C.N. Li (ed.), 303-333. New York: Academic Press.

Perlmutter, David M. 1980. *Studies in Relational Grammar 1*. Chicago: University of Chicago Press.

Rigsby, Bruce. 1965. *Linguistic relations in the Southern Plateau*, PhD dissertation, University of Oregon (ms).

Rude, Noel. 1992. "Dative shifting in Sahaptin." *IJAL* 58:316-321.

Rude, Noel. 1994. "Direct, inverse, and passive in Sahaptin." In *Voice and Inversion*, T. Givón (ed.), 101-119, Amsterdam: John Benjamins [Typological Studies in Language 28].

Tesnière, Lucien. 1959. *Éléments de syntaxe structurale*. Paris: Klincksieck.

In the series TYPOLOGICAL STUDIES IN LANGUAGE (TSL) the following titles have been published thus far:

1. HOPPER, Paul J. (ed.): *Tense-Aspect: Between semantics & pragmatics.* 1982.
2. HAIMAN, John & Pamela MUNRO (eds): *Switch Reference and Universal Grammar. Proceedings of a symposium on switch reference and universal grammar, Winnipeg, May 1981.* 1983.
3. GIVÓN, T.: *Topic Continuity in Discourse. A quantitative cross-language study.* 1983.
4. CHISHOLM, William, Louis T. MILIC & John A.C. GREPPIN (eds): *Interrogativity: A colloquium on the grammar, typology and pragmatics of questions in seven diverse languages, Cleveland, Ohio, October 5th 1981-May 3rd 1982.* 1984.
5. RUTHERFORD, William E. (ed.): *Language Universals and Second Language Acquisition.* 1984 (2nd ed. 1987).
6. HAIMAN, John (Ed.): *Iconicity in Syntax. Proceedings of a symposium on iconicity in syntax, Stanford, June 24-26, 1983.* 1985.
7. CRAIG, Colette (ed.): *Noun Classes and Categorization. Proceedings of a symposium on categorization and noun classification, Eugene, Oregon, October 1983.* 1986.
8. SLOBIN, Dan I. & Karl ZIMMER (eds): *Studies in Turkish Linguistics.* 1986.
9. BYBEE, Joan L.: *Morphology. A Study of the Relation between Meaning and Form.* 1985.
10. RANSOM, Evelyn: *Complementation: its Meaning and Forms.* 1986.
11. TOMLIN, Russel S.: *Coherence and Grounding in Discourse. Outcome of a Symposium, Eugene, Oregon, June 1984.* 1987.
12. NEDJALKOV, Vladimir (ed.): *Typology of Resultative Constructions. Translated from the original Russian edition (1983). English translation edited by Bernard Comrie.* 1988.
14. HINDS, John, Shoichi IWASAKI & Senko K. MAYNARD (eds): *Perspectives on Topicalization. The case of Japanese WA.* 1987.
15. AUSTIN, Peter (ed.): *Complex Sentence Constructions in Australian Languages.* 1988.
16. SHIBATANI, Masayoshi (ed.): *Passive and Voice.* 1988.
17. HAMMOND, Michael, Edith A. MORAVCSIK and Jessica WIRTH (eds): *Studies in Syntactic Typology.* 1988.
18. HAIMAN, John & Sandra A. THOMPSON (eds): *Clause Combining in Grammar and Discourse.* 1988.
19. TRAUGOTT, Elizabeth C. and Bernd HEINE (eds): *Approaches to Grammaticalization, 2 volumes (set)* 1991
20. CROFT, William, Suzanne KEMMER and Keith DENNING (eds): *Studies in Typology and Diachrony. Papers presented to Joseph H. Greenberg on his 75th birthday.* 1990.
21. DOWNING, Pamela, Susan D. LIMA and Michael NOONAN (eds): *The Linguistics of Literacy.* 1992.
22. PAYNE, Doris (ed.): *Pragmatics of Word Order Flexibility.* 1992.
23. KEMMER, Suzanne: *The Middle Voice.* 1993.
24. PERKINS, Revere D.: *Deixis, Grammar, and Culture.* 1992.
25. SVOROU, Soteria: *The Grammar of Space.* 1994.
26. LORD, Carol: *Historical Change in Serial Verb Constructions.* 1993.
27. FOX, Barbara and Paul J. Hopper (eds): *Voice: Form and Function.* 1994.

28. GIVÓN, T. (ed.) : *Voice and Inversion*. 1994.
29. KAHREL, Peter and René van den BERG (eds): *Typological Studies in Negation*. 1994.
30. DOWNING, Pamela and Michael NOONAN: *Word Order in Discourse*. 1995.
31. GERNSBACHER, M. A. and T. GIVÓN (eds): *Coherence in Spontaneous Text*. 1995.
32. BYBEE, Joan and Suzanne FLEISCHMAN (eds): *Modality in Grammar and Discourse*. 1995.
33. FOX, Barbara (ed.): *Studies in Anaphora*. 1996.
34. GIVÓN, T. (ed.): *Conversation. Cognitive, communicative and social perspectives*. 1997.
35. GIVÓN, T. (ed.): *Grammatical Relations. A functionalist perspective*. 1997.
36. NEWMAN, John (ed.): *The Linguistics of Giving*. n.y.p.

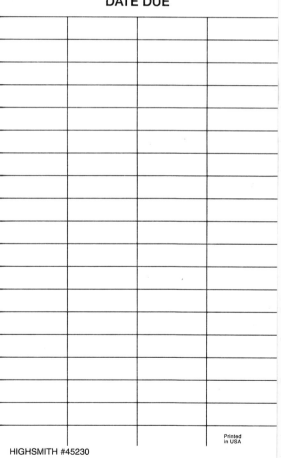

DATE DUE

HIGHSMITH #45230

Printed in USA